The International Education Handbook

Principles and Practices of the Field

The International Education Handbook

Principles and Practices of the Field

Katherine Punteney

NAFSA: Association of International Educators
1307 New York Avenue, NW
8th Floor
Washington, DC 20005-4715

NAFSA is the largest and most comprehensive association of professionals committed to advancing international higher education. Based in the United States, we provide programs, products, services, and a physical and virtual meeting space for the worldwide community of international educators. The association provides leadership to its diverse constituencies through establishing principles of good practice and providing professional development opportunities. NAFSA encourages networking among professionals, convenes conferences and collaborative dialogues, and promotes research and knowledge creation to strengthen and serve the field. We lead the way in advocating for a better world through international education.

Library of Congress Cataloging-in-Publication Data

Names: Punteney, Katherine, 1974– author.
Title: The International Education Handbook: Principles and Practices of the Field / By Katherine Punteney.
Description: Washington, DC: NAFSA: Association of International Educators, [2019]
Identifiers: LCCN 2019015190 (print) | LCCN 2019021976 (ebook) | ISBN 9781942719267 (alk. paper)
Subjects: LCSH: International education. | Education and globalization. | Students, Foreign—Services for.
Classification: LCC LC1090 (ebook) | LCC LC1090 .P86 2019 (print) | DDC 370.116—dc23

Edited by Natalie Ngo, NAFSA
Design and Layout by Kathleen Dyson

Copyright © 2019 by NAFSA: Association of International Educators. No part of this publication may be reproduced, stored in a retrieval system, or transmitted in any form or by any means, electronic, mechanical, photocopying, recording, scanning, or otherwise, except as permitted under Section 107 or 108 of the United States Copyright Act, without the prior written permission of the publisher. Requests to the publisher for permission should be addressed to publications@nafsa.org. Printed in the United States.

BULK PURCHASES
Quantity discounts are available for workshops and staff development.
Call 1.866.538.1927 to order.

First edition, 2019
10 9 8 7 6 5 4 3 2

Contents

Acknowledgments xi

Introduction 1
    The Profession of International Education...................... 2
    Chapter Overview... 5
    Facilitator's Guide.. 6
    Resources 6
    References... 7

1 Trends in International Education............................. 9
    Trend 1: Growth of the Knowledge Economy 9
    Trend 2: Massification of Education 10
    Trend 3: Insufficient Public Funding of Higher Education 11
    Trend 4: Academic Capitalism 13
    Trend 5: Commodification of Education..........................15
    Trend 6: Internationalization of Education.....................16
    Trend 7: Growth in Cross-Border Education 18
    Trend 8: Proliferation of English Language Programs........... 20
    Trend 9: Demand for Quality Assurance in International Education.... 20
    Trend 10: Competition for Global Rankings......................21
    Conclusion.. 23
    References.. 24

2 Global Competence ... 29
- Terminology and Definitions ... 31
- Rationales for Global Competence Education ... 32
- Global Competence Models ... 36
- Core Concepts of Global Competence ... 41
- Assessment of Global Competence ... 43
- Assessment Principles ... 46
- Considerations for Global Competence Education ... 48
- Conclusion ... 51
- Resources ... 52
- References ... 53

3 Internationalization ... 59
- Internationalization of Higher Education ... 60
- Internationalization Activities ... 60
- Internationalization Planning ... 72
- Regional Differences in Approaches to Internationalization ... 80
- Considerations for Internationalization ... 87
- Conclusion ... 89
- Resources ... 90
- References ... 91

4 Education Abroad ... 99
- U.S. Study Abroad ... 99
- Access, Inclusion, and Equity ... 101
- Program Models ... 104
- Program Design Process ... 111
- Roles and Responsibilities of Education Abroad Professionals ... 118
- Professional Organizations and Standards ... 133
- Conclusion ... 135
- Resources ... 135
- References ... 137

5 Experiential Education 147
Experiential Education Theory 147
International Experiential Education 152
Program Types 155
Partnerships 161
Management Roles and Responsibilities 167
Facilitation of Experiential Education 170
Conclusion 178
Resources 179
References 179

6 International Enrollment Management 185
International Students in the United States 186
National Enrollment Management Policies 190
Responsibility for International Enrollment Management 191
International Enrollment Management Strategic Planning 192
International Student Recruitment Methods and Channels 195
Marketing and Brand Management 204
International Student Admissions 205
International Student Retention 211
Considerations for International Enrollment Management 211
Conclusion 213
Resources 214
References 215

7 International Student and Scholar Services 223
Benefits of Hosting International Students and Scholars 224
Adjustments to the United States 225
Acculturation Process 229
Support Services 230
Advising 231
Advising Approaches 234
Supportive Programming 239
Professional Skills and Specialties 245

Considerations for Practitioners 246

   Conclusion. 249

   Resources 249

   References. 250

8 International Schools 255

   History of International Schools 255

   Growth of International Schools 256

   Definitions and Types of International Schools 257

   International Schools in Public Education 259

   International Baccalaureate 259

   Rationales for Adopting the International Baccalaureate Curriculum
   in Public Education. 262

   Internationalization in the United States 264

   Internationalization Strategies. 265

   Teacher Training and Development 278

   Considerations for Practitioners 284

   Future Trends. 286

   Conclusion. 288

   Resources 289

   References. 292

9 Citizen Diplomacy 299

   History of U.S. Citizen Diplomacy...300

   Size of the Sector 303

   Program Models 305

   Citizen Diplomacy Program Examples 308

   Impact of Citizen Diplomacy Programs 311

   Administration of Citizen Diplomacy Programs..................................314

   Assessment of Citizen Diplomacy 316

   Considerations for Practitioners 318

   Conclusion. 319

   Resources 319

   References. 320

10 Related Fields 329
Comparative and International Education 330
Global Mobility 335
Higher Education Administration 339
Intercultural Training 347
International Development and Education 352
Language Program Administration 358
Peacebuilding 363
Student Services 367
Conclusion 371
References 371

Glossary 381
Appendix 401
Index 405

Acknowledgments

Writing a book requires uncountable hours of time alone at the computer, and yet, it is not at all a solo endeavor. I would like to thank the many people who helped to make this project a reality. My colleague Meggan Madden, who first suggested this project, has my gratitude for recognizing both the need for the text and that I might be well suited to writing it.

I'd also like to acknowledge the many students and alumni of the Middlebury Institute of International Studies (MIIS) who served as my research assistants. I thoroughly appreciate the energy and care they gave in spite of the demands of their own studies and lives. They helped me formulate the book proposal, track down sources, comb through reference books and journal articles, edit chapters, and much more. I am beyond grateful for their collaboration: Kylee Arnold, Lennox Atkinson, Harrison Gill, Erin Kelly-Weber, Amanthi Weerasinghe, and Elisa Yanagihashi. Students in MIIS classes read early versions of the chapters and offered feedback, furthering refinement of the text. My fellow faculty at MIIS provided suggestions of resources and feedback in general and in their areas of expertise: Paige Butler, Anne Campbell, Daniel Chatham, Chris McShane, and David Wick. The chapters are stronger for their input, though any confusion or oversights remain mine.

My coauthor of the *Facilitator's Guide to The International Education Handbook: Principles and Practices of the Field*, Jayna Winn, is endlessly knowledgeable, thoughtful, organized, and encouraging. I could not have asked for a better coauthor. Her observations and insights as we wrote the *Facilitator's Guide* helped draw my attention to areas that needed strengthening and clarification in *The International Education Handbook*.

I also want to thank the many friends and family members who offered me encouragement and support throughout the long process of writing.

I am indebted to the team of NAFSA staff who carefully and thoughtfully reviewed chapters, identifying areas for elaboration and clarification and suggesting topics and resources to strengthen the volume. Finally, I am profoundly appreciative of Natalie Ngo, my editor at NAFSA. Without fail, she has been encouraging and responsive to my many questions. She has strengthened each iteration of each chapter with her attention to detail. I am deeply grateful for all of the assistance and support I have received.

Introduction

International education is the profession of designing, managing, and facilitating programs and activities that help participants to appropriately, effectively, and ethically engage in interactions with culturally diverse people and ideas, often across national borders. Based on their belief in the power of education to foster peace and address critical global issues, international educators seek to make a positive impact on society by advancing programs that foster meaningful engagement across cultures.

International education programs strive to help participants develop global competence, which can be defined as "the capacity to examine local, global and intercultural issues; to understand and appreciate the perspectives and world views of others; to engage in open, appropriate, and effective interactions with people from different cultures; and to act for collective well-being and sustainable development" (Asia Society and OECD 2018, 5). Developing global competence in students has become an urgent need at all levels of education. Global competence is considered integral to ensuring economic competitiveness; furthering the ability to solve global issues; cultivating diversity, inclusion, and peace; and promoting engaged citizenship.

Often, international education involves the movement of people across national borders through study abroad programs, international service-learning, international research partnerships, intensive English programs, and more. These educational programs and experiences move students (or participants of any age) out of their comfort zones and into a process of observation, reflection, and experimentation, prompting personal and professional growth. The field seeks to balance student advising and support with the inherent discomfort of crossing cultures to create the optimal conditions for intercultural learning.

Recognizing that a minority of individuals participate in programs involving international travel, the international education profession has expanded to include cross-cultural education efforts "at home." These programs seek to encourage intercultural learning by making educational institutions more international in focus. Some of the approaches taken include integrating international content in the curriculum, teaching world languages, and using technology to connect individuals and classrooms around the world. A strategic planning process referred to as "internationalization" directs the efforts of the educational institutions.

The International Education Handbook: Principles and Practices of the Field identifies the research, trends, challenges, and expectations of good practice that inform the profession of international education. As such, this book serves as a guide for graduate students, new professionals, and those seeking to broaden their understanding of this dynamic field.

The Profession of International Education

International education is a rapidly growing field. Across almost all metrics, there has been a steady increase in participation over the past 2 decades.

- 5 million higher education students studied outside of their home country in 2018, a dramatic increase from 2.1 million students in 2001 (Institute of International Education 2018b).

- More than 1 million international students studied in the United States in 2018, which is more than double the number from 1999 (Institute of International Education 2018a).

- The number of international schools has grown sevenfold over the past 25 years, with more than 7,500 international schools serving almost 4 million students in 2015 (Hallgarten, Tabberer, and McCarthy 2015).

- Almost 90 percent of universities surveyed worldwide reported that internationalization is of high policy importance for the leadership within their universities (Egron-Polak and Hudson 2014).

While international education has existed for centuries, the profession itself is young. In decades past, people usually got into the field by chance, perhaps tasked, as an addendum to their existing job, with "looking after" international students or "taking care of" study abroad programs. These individuals may have been given such responsibilities because of their past travel experience or foreign language skills. However, over the past 30 years or so, the field has professionalized, especially in the United States and other developed countries (Hoffa and DePaul 2010).

With the growth in international education participation, and its importance in institutional strategic plans as well as national government policies, there has been a mounting need for trained professionals to create and administer international education programs. International educators may work in a wide range of sectors including education abroad, international student and scholar services, language programs, citizen diplomacy, and youth education, to name a few. These professionals may have specialized knowledge in such areas as program design, student advising, training and facilitation, curriculum and instruction, marketing and recruitment, admissions, student services, risk management, communications, assessment, and business management. Increasingly, it is being recognized that internationalization requires the efforts of skilled professional international educators to be successful (Hunter 2018; Brandenburg 2016).

International education is no longer an add-on task, but rather the career focus of more than 10,000 specialists in the United States, and many more worldwide. A growing number of international education-related professional associations offer training and networking opportunities, research on the field has become more robust, and standards for ethical practice have been established. Additionally, graduate programs are flourishing and a cadre of new professionals are intentionally choosing a career in international education (Woodman and Punteney 2016; Friedman and Reza 2019).

International Education Professionals

Many international educators have had at least one deeply impactful intercultural experience prior to embarking on the profession. They may have been raised in a bicultural household, lived abroad as a third culture kid, immigrated to a foreign country, or married someone from another culture. They may have studied outside of their home country, worked abroad, or collaborated with individuals from around the world.

One of the resonant themes in the career paths of international educators is, often, the learning and personal growth they have experienced through their intercultural interactions and how passionate they are about facilitating similar opportunities for others (Streitwieser and Ogden 2016). In addition to contributing to the personal and professional growth of program participants, the international education profession brings many benefits to the practitioners themselves. This work offers avenues for:

- Engaging in lifelong intercultural learning;
- Developing a network of contacts and connections around the world;
- Making a difference in the lives of individuals;
- Contributing to global peace and understanding; and
- Pursuing ongoing professional growth and development.

The field is dynamic and constantly adapting to changes in the global environment, adding to the challenges and excitement of a career in international education. The rewards of the field draw many people to the profession. This means that entry-level professional positions in the field are often highly competitive.

Job Marketplace

International education professionals may have educational backgrounds in a variety of disciplines including languages, humanities, social sciences, physical sciences, business, and education. Coming from such a diverse range of personal and academic backgrounds, it is necessary for international education professionals to acquire the necessary knowledge and skills to serve the field. For this reason, NAFSA: Association of International Educators, the world's largest nonprofit association dedicated to international education and exchange, compiled a comprehensive listing of the competencies needed by international education professionals.

The *NAFSA International Education Professional Competencies* (2015) was developed based on multiple rounds of feedback from focus groups, volunteer member-leaders, and invited reviewers and a survey of 2,000 international educators. The resulting guide identifies eight cross-cutting competencies that apply to most, if not all, positions within the international education field. The eight cross-cutting competencies are advocacy, communication with stakeholders across campus and community, financial stewardship, human resources, information technology, intercultural communications, leadership, and strategic planning (NAFSA 2015). Beyond these skill areas, additional competencies are described for professionals working on comprehensive internationalization, education abroad, international enrollment management, and international student and scholar services (NAFSA 2015). Each competency is broken down into component skills based on whether an individual works in a role providing direct service to students/program participants, in management, or in strategy and policy.

The *NAFSA International Education Professional Competencies* can be used by supervisors and mentors as a tool to help create professional development plans for mentees. The *Competencies* can also be used to prompt discussion among groups of practitioners or as a framework for creating professional development trainings. It is recommended that individuals consult the document to identify their current strengths as well as areas in which to seek professional development. The NAFSA Career Print Tool is an online assessment tool, based on the *Competencies*, that allows individuals and teams to identify their competencies and areas for growth. Based on the results, Career Print generates lists of resources specific to the individual or team.

In order to be competitive for hiring, or for career advancement, it is crucial that individuals seek professional development and training through graduate education or the many opportunities offered by professional associations such as NAFSA. Along the same line, this volume can assist individuals entering the international education field or transitioning to new sectors within the field as it offers foundational content, insights, and resources to help professionals build or strengthen their skills sets to better serve their communities.

Chapter Overview

The International Education Handbook: Principles and Practices of the Field is organized into 10 chapters. The first chapter, "Trends in International Education," introduces the broad global context in which international education operates and the factors that are affecting the field. "Global Competence," chapter 2, examines the goals of international education programs, asking crucial questions such as: What is global and intercultural competence? Why is it an important goal of education? And how do we know if students are developing it? The third chapter on "Internationalization" centers on the process of making higher education institutions more international in focus, identifying strategies and tactics that are commonly utilized.

The next six chapters each explore a different professional sector within the international education field: "Education Abroad," "Experiential Education," "International Enrollment Management," "International Student and Scholar Services," "International Schools," and "Citizen Diplomacy." Each chapter introduces the topic; defines key terms, concepts, and challenges; offers a sense of the history and scope of the sector; describes the primary responsibilities of professionals working in the sector; and recommends resources for further study. The final chapter, "Related Fields," provides an overview of a collection of professional specializations that have some overlap with the international education field.

Beyond presenting a specific topic or sector, each of the chapters touches on central themes that have broad applicability across the field. For example, "Trends in International Education" looks at the economic and political forces that are influencing the field. "Global Competence" examines the principles behind assessing learning. "Internationalization" discusses the processes of strategic planning and gaining stakeholder support. "Education Abroad" describes principles of program design and introduces student development theory, while "Experiential Education" offers recommendations for establishing reciprocal community partnerships and facilitating student reflection. "International Enrollment Management" introduces the fundamentals of recruitment, admissions, and retention. "International Student and Scholar Services" considers advising models and cocurricular programming. "International Schools" analyzes the connections between K–12 education and higher education, with an emphasis on teacher training and development. And "Citizen Diplomacy" delves into the role of government in international education. Extremely significant across all sectors, and an essential theme in each chapter, is the importance and challenge of assessment. Issues of diversity and inclusion are also explored throughout the book, as are questions of ethics and equity. These themes are broadly relevant to the field, beyond the specific chapters in which they are introduced, and are essential for rising professionals to recognize and understand.

All texts have their limitations, and this one is no different. While the professionalization of international education is underway around the world, the United States is one of the areas in which the profession is well established. As a result, much of the research and many of the resources noted are produced in the United States, resulting in a disproportionate focus on the U.S. context in the literature of the field. Compounding the bias, the author of this publication is based in the United States. The result is that this volume emphasizes the U.S. context, while striving to include information and resources from other parts of the world as they are available to the author.

The International Education Handbook: Principles and Practices of the Field offers a comprehensive overview of the field of international education, showcasing specializations and highlighting the information and resources most relevant to professionals. It introduces some of the different sectors of the field, examining their history, scope, subsectors, theoretical foundations, and trends. The book can be used by new professionals or those seeking to transition between sectors to develop awareness of the vocabulary, debates, challenges, and resources in the field.

Facilitator's Guide

While relevant to individual readers interested in the field, *The International Education Handbook: Principles and Practices of the Field* may also be used as a graduate textbook or as a resource for professional training programs. To support this purpose, a digital facilitator's guide is available as a complement to this book. Coauthored by Katherine Punteney and Jayna Winn, the *Facilitator's Guide* provides related content for each chapter of this text, including learning outcomes, key terminology and definitions, central concepts, pre-reading questions, discussion questions, and activities with printable materials. The *Facilitator's Guide* reinforces the content of the book through engaging, intentional exercises that resonate with readers. The resource is available as a digital download at www.nafsa.org.

Resources

Below are some additional resources that can support the work and development of international educators.

NAFSA RESOURCES:

- Friedman, Sora H., and Amir Reza. 2019. *Careers in International Education: A Guide for New Professionals.* Washington, DC: NAFSA: Association of International Educators.

- *International Educator* magazine www.nafsa.org/ie

- NAFSA Annual Conference www.nafsa.org/ac
- NAFSA Career Print careerprint.nafsa.org
- *NAFSA International Education Professional Competencies* www.nafsa.org/competencies/
- NAFSA Regions and professional networking groups www.nafsa.org/connect-and-network
- Network.NAFSA online discussion forum network.nafsa.org

ASSOCIATIONS:

- Asia-Pacific Association for International Education (APAIE) www.apaie2019.org/
- Association of International Education Administrators (AIEA) www.aieaworld.org
- Diversity Abroad www.diversitynetwork.org
- European Association for International Education (EAIE) www.eaie.org
- The Forum on Education Abroad www.forumea.org
- NAFSA: Association of International Educators www.nafsa.org

JOURNALS:

- *Frontiers: The Interdisciplinary Journal of Study Abroad* www.frontiersjournal.org
- *International Higher Education* ejournals.bc.edu/ojs/index.php/ihe
- *Journal of International Students* jistudents.org/
- *Journal of Research in International Education* journals.sagepub.com/home/jri
- *Journal of Studies in International Education* journals.sagepub.com/home/jsi

References

Asia Society and OECD. 2018. *Teaching for Global Competence in a Rapidly Changing World*. Asia Society and OECD. https://asiasociety.org/sites/default/files/inline-files/teaching-for-global-competence-in-a-rapidly-changing-world-edu.pdf.

Brandenburg, Uwe. 2016. "The Value of Administrative Staff for Internationalization." *International Higher Education* 85:15–17. https://ejournals.bc.edu/ojs/index.php/ihe/article/view/9239.

Egron-Polak, Eva, and Ross Hudson. 2014. *Internationalization of Higher Education: Growing Expectations, Fundamental Values.* IAU 4th Global Survey. Paris, France: International Association of Universities.

Friedman, Sora H., and Amir Reza. 2019. *Careers in International Education: A Guide for New Professionals.* Washington, DC: NAFSA: Association of International Educators.

Hallgarten, Joe, Ralph Tabberer, and Kenny McCarthy. 2015. *3rd Culture Schools: International Schools as Creative Catalysts for a New Global Education System.* London, United Kingdom: Educational Collaborative for International Schools. https://www.thersa.org/globalassets/pdfs/reports/third-culture-schools-report.pdf.

Hoffa, William W., and Stephen C. DePaul, eds. 2010. *A History of U.S. Study Abroad: 1965–Present.* Carlisle, PA: Frontiers: The Interdisciplinary Journal of Study Abroad and The Forum on Education Abroad.

Hunter, Fiona. 2018. "Training Administrative Staff to Become Key Players in the Internationalization of Higher Education." *International Higher Education* 92:16–17.

Institute of International Education. 2018a. *Open Doors Report on International Educational Exchange.* Institute of International Education. https://www.iie.org/opendoors.

Institute of International Education. 2018b. "Project Atlas 2018 Infographics." Institute of International Education. https://www.iie.org/en/Research-and-Insights/Project-Atlas/Explore-Data/Current-Infographics.

NAFSA: Association of International Educators. 2015. *NAFSA International Education Professional Competencies.* Washington, DC: NAFSA: Association of International Educators. http://www.nafsa.org/competencies.

Streitwieser, Bernhard, and Anthony C. Ogden. 2016. *International Higher Education's Scholar-Practitioners: Bridging Research and Practice.* Oxford, United Kingdom: Symposium Books Ltd.

Woodman, Taylor C., and Katherine N. Punteney. 2016. "Graduate Education in Context: Preparing Scholar-Practitioners as Future International Education Leaders." In *International Higher Education's Scholar-Practitioners: Bridging Research and Practice*, eds. Bernhard Streitwieser and Anthony C. Ogden. Oxford, United Kingdom: Symposium Books Ltd.

Chapter 1

Trends in International Education

Global trends in education are having a profound effect on the field of international education. This chapter provides an overview of 10 trends that are shaping and reshaping international education. The first five trends—the knowledge economy, massification of education, decline in funding, academic capitalism, and commodification of education—are influencing all levels of education at all levels of analysis, including the institutional, local, national, and international. These trends are widely discussed across fields that relate to any aspect of education, such as international development, education policy, higher education administration, student affairs, and curriculum and instruction. The remaining five trends—internationalization, cross-border education, English language program creation, quality assurance in international education, and competition for global rankings—evolve from the pressures of the first five trends. These trends focus more narrowly on shifts affecting international education programs. Together, the 10 trends affect the work of international educators, influencing the economics of the industry, the types of programs available, and the knowledge and skills needed by professionals in the field.

Trend 1: Growth of the Knowledge Economy

In a knowledge economy, information (rather than natural resources) is the primary input for producing value. While all societies process raw materials and manufacture goods, in a knowledge economy, most economic growth is the result of using expertise, data, and analysis to create and improve products and services. Technology supports the knowledge economy by increasing human capacity to gather, organize, and communicate information.

As the knowledge economy grows, so too does the importance of quality education at every level, especially higher education. The quality of education is important to both individuals' abilities to prosper in the workforce and a country's ability to maintain economic growth. Research universities, in particular, play a central role in the knowledge economy; they train skilled workers, conduct research, communicate scientific findings, and develop networks of experts to share information (Altbach 2013a).

Economists and policymakers generally agree that there is a connection between a strong system of higher education and a country's economic competitiveness (Jain 2015; Lim 2015; Altbach 2013a). As countries' economies become more prosperous, they typically shift toward a knowledge economy approach, which is driven by the efforts of university graduates with advanced knowledge and expertise. Advanced knowledge workers make further economic growth possible and, in turn, increase the need for skilled workers. Improving higher education and growing the knowledge economy is a virtuous cycle—a pattern in which the cycle reinforces itself with positive outcomes (Jain 2015; Lim 2015).

Trend 2: Massification of Education

Historically, education, particularly at the higher levels, served the elite segments of society. In recent years, however, education is increasingly serving students from all backgrounds. This is known as the "massification of education," or the shift toward education serving the masses. This emphasis on creating educational opportunities for people of all socioeconomic, ethnic, and religious backgrounds, as well as ensuring gender equality in education, has been a key priority of governmental and institutional initiatives in many countries over the past 20 years.

One hundred and sixty-four countries adopted the United Nations Educational, Scientific and Cultural Organization (UNESCO)'s Education for All framework, which comprised six goals to be reached between 2000 and 2015. Those six goals (UNESCO 2015) included:

1. Expanding early childhood care and education;
2. Ensuring that all children are enrolled in free primary education;
3. Ensuring life skills learning for youth and adults;
4. Achieving a 50 percent improvement in levels of adult literacy;
5. Achieving gender equality in education; and
6. Improving the quality of education.

Some progress was made toward the Education for All goals; for example, the number of primary school-aged children attending school around the world increased from 84 percent in 1999 to 93 percent by 2015 (UNESCO 2015). The United Nations's Sustainable Development Goals build on this work with a plan for 2016–2030 that includes the objective that all girls and boys receive free, quality primary and secondary education (United Nations 2015).

As more children enroll in and complete primary education, the result is increased enrollment in secondary education. Likewise, as more students complete secondary education, there is greater student demand for (and enrollment in) higher education (British Council 2017; Jacob and Gokbel 2017). The pressures of the knowledge economy incentivize students to enroll in universities. The power of the knowledge economy also drives governments and institutions to develop policies and programs to enroll more students in higher education in order to graduate students with advanced expertise who will contribute to the economy. As an outcome of this demand from students and the policy motivation of governments, higher education enrollment is expanding dramatically (Knight 2008).

The United States established the first mass higher education system in the 1920s, followed by Europe in the 1960s and parts of Asia in the 1970s; these areas now enroll more than 60 percent of their university-aged students (Altbach 2013b). In all world regions, higher education enrollment has been increasing rapidly as a result of massification, with more than 170 million students enrolled and over 18,000 universities operating worldwide (Altbach 2014). Between 1995 and 2011, the percentage of university-aged students worldwide who were enrolled in higher education increased from 15 to 30 percent (Marginson 2015).

Among the benefits of this massification, educational access in some countries has been expanded to previously excluded groups including women, students from low socioeconomic backgrounds, racial and ethnic minorities, and religious minorities (Altbach 2013b). However, as the demand for higher education has increased, some governments have not had the financial resources to be able to serve all students qualified for higher education (Jacob and Gokbel 2017; Knight 2008). For individual students with the financial means, or where the government is able to provide scholarships, study in another country can be a partial solution.

Trend 3: Insufficient Public Funding of Higher Education

Throughout most of the 1900s, it was widely believed that education had broad benefits for society (Altbach 2013b); education was believed to be the foundation for a country's economic prosperity, scientific progress, public health, and civil society, among many other societal advances. The corresponding belief was that, because of its importance to society, education should be provided by the government and supported through taxes. This principle propels the education initiatives described above that seek to ensure free primary and secondary education for all students worldwide. However, beliefs about who should pay for higher education, and how much they should pay, are shifting (Daviet 2016; Hensley, Galilee-Belfer, and Lee 2013; Johnstone 2011; Schleicher 2019).

In many developing countries, the massification of secondary education is resulting in a sharp increase in the demand for higher education (Altbach 2013b). Likewise, governmental development policies are encouraging the pursuit of higher education for students from underrepresented groups. However, these countries typically do not have the higher education infrastructure to enroll all eligible students, nor do they have the financial resources to dramatically expand the infrastructure. Public health, physical infrastructure, environmental restoration, and other needs often compete for limited government resources (Johnstone 2011).

One way in which the tension between the demand for and the shortage of resources has been accommodated is through the increasing differentiation of systems of higher education. When governments cannot afford to offer all students access to the most advanced technologies, top faculty, extensive libraries, and other supports, governments may maintain levels of quality at the top universities while letting lower status institutions decline somewhat in quality. In this way, higher education systems may become stratified, offering tiers of service (Altbach 2013b). There may also be a limited number of seats in public universities; therefore, the students who do not gain admission to the government-funded public universities may opt to pay to attend private universities (if they can afford it) or not enroll in higher education at all.

The insufficiency of funding for public higher education, and the shift toward the idea that higher education should be privately funded, is not limited to developing countries. Even in wealthier countries, such as the United States, there has been a sharp decline in public funding for higher education. With many governments now providing less than full funding for the majority of students enrolled in higher education, universities have been forced to either cut costs or increase revenue from other sources. Cost-cutting tactics may include hiring fewer full-time faculty members while hiring more adjunct (part-time) instructors. These adjunct instructors are typically paid much lower wages and may not receive full benefits. Forced to teach at multiple institutions to earn a living wage, these adjunct instructors are often less available to advise students, serve on committees, and engage as part of the campus community (Edmonds 2015; Hurlburt and McGarrah 2016; Rhoades and Slaughter 2004). Other forms of cost-cutting measures might include not offering areas of study that are less profitable for the university, deferring maintenance on facilities, not updating technology, etc. (Johnstone 2011).

Given the challenge of cutting expenses, many universities are aggressively seeking alternative forms of revenue. One source of revenue is the students themselves. As public funding provides less support, students are being asked to contribute a higher percentage of the cost of their education through tuition payments (Hensley, Galilee-Belfer, and Lee 2013; Jacob and Gokbel 2017; Johnstone 2011). Higher education is increasingly considered to be a private investment, rather than a public benefit (Hensley, Galilee-Belfer, and Lee 2013).

Asking individuals to fund part, or all, of their education has prompted discussion among educators, raising the question of the extent to which the government is responsible for educating citizens to meet the needs of the future workforce. Johnstone (2011) asks: How much does education spending benefit the individual students, and how much does it benefit society? Should this influence the cost-sharing relationship between the government and individual students? Should the students pay tuition proportionate to their benefit? Should different areas of study charge differently because some create more individual benefit and some create more societal benefit? How can access and equity be ensured? What support structures, such as national loan programs, should be in place to ensure access?

The ways in which these questions are being answered vary widely across the globe. An analysis of Organisation for Economic Co-operation and Development (OECD) countries identifies four approaches (Schleicher 2019):

1. Students are charged low or no tuition, and high levels of government funding support higher education.

2. Students are charged moderate tuition, with some financial aid support provided by the government.

3. Students are charged high tuition fees, with extensive financial aid infrastructures in place.

4. Students are charged high tuition fees, with modest financial aid infrastructures in place.

The United States is identified as part of the third group in the OECD analysis. In many U.S. institutions, differential tuition, or varied tuition costs for different majors, is already the norm (Nelson, Wolniak, and George 2017). Worldwide, students and families are contributing, on average, 5 to 40 percent of the costs of higher education, depending on their location (Johnstone 2011).

Trend 4: Academic Capitalism

Bolstered by the desire of universities to diversify their revenue sources, academic capitalism has flourished in recent decades. Rhoades and Slaughter (2004, 37) were early leaders in bringing attention to this phenomena, defined as "the involvement of colleges and faculty in market-like behaviors." Attributing the growth of academic capitalism to the growth of the knowledge economy and declining public funding for education, Rhoades and Slaughter (2004) observe that there has been a fundamental change in the relationship between universities, governments, and the private sector, and that policies have been intentionally created to support this change. Writing about the United States, Rhoades and Slaughter (2004) provide some examples of ways in which the change is manifested, with institutions now:

- Adopting corporate-like, top-down styles of management;

- Using graduate assistants and part-time faculty to teach classes because they are paid less;

- Lowering academic standards to admit more students;

- Designing courses based on what would attract more students, rather than based on a pedagogical foundation;

- Placing less emphasis on serving underrepresented populations;

- Creating programs for working professionals because they have the capacity to pay more for their education;

- Shifting copyright of professors' work to the university for institutional profit; and

- Profiting from research (with licenses, patents, etc.) instead of sharing it for public benefit.

Universities are also outsourcing some of the work that might have traditionally been supported by university faculty and staff such as dining services, housing, and even admissions and some student support services (Choudaha 2017).

A significant portion of academic research is now sponsored by nonuniversity sources, including companies and corporations (Altbach 2013a; British Council 2017). There is an increasing blurring of the division between public and private—public institutions receive private funding, and most private institutions receive some public funding. There is also some blurring caused by nonprofit universities engaging substantially in for-profit enterprises. (Knight 2008; Somers et al. 2018). An example includes an institution supporting research that has commercial profit potential because of the ability to patent and sell a discovery, but the same institution providing less or no funding for research that could benefit society but does not have a profit mechanism. Another example is putting resources into developing executive and online education, rather than investing in programs for local underserved communities, because the profit margin is higher for programs that serve people who are already employed and have available funding (Somers et al. 2018). There is a risk that as government funding continues to decrease, education providers will offer only those programs that are most profitable (Knight 2008).

At the heart of these observations is the idea that higher education institutions now make most of their decisions based on financial considerations, which may be informed by corporate practices. This change comes at the expense of traditional ways of work that were driven primarily by the faculty, pedagogical considerations, commitment to underrepresented groups in society, and concern for the advancement of society (Hensley, Galilee-Belfer, and Lee 2013; Rhoades and Slaughter 2004; Somers et al. 2018).

Trend 5: Commodification of Education

Commodities are goods that can be bought and sold. Many critics argue that neoliberal ideologies often dominate in global politics and finance, and that neoliberal ideals may result in education being treated like a commodity, rather than a public service. Neoliberalism values the idea of free market capitalism and believes that free, unfettered competition—without government subsidy or policy interference—results in the best outcomes for consumers and for the economy (Monbiot 2016). When applied to education, the belief is that unrestrained competition among education providers will increase the quality of educational offerings that consumers can choose among. At the primary and secondary education levels, policies that support the rights of students to attend the school of their choice as well as promote market-driven schools (e.g., magnet schools), school-based management, and the decentralization of educational systems are the direct result of these ideologies (Doherty et al. 2012; Resnik 2012). In higher education, these neoliberal beliefs have put pressure on governments to decrease financial aid and spending on university education, while increasingly expecting individuals to self-fund their education (Hensley, Galilee-Belfer, and Lee 2013).

Neoliberal policies are apparent in the General Agreement on Trade in Services (GATS), a treaty of the World Trade Organization (WTO). Taking effect in 1995 and still in use today, GATS created a set of rules for the 160+ member countries of the WTO, covering international trade in services (as opposed to trade in goods, which were covered in a previous treaty) (Knight 2008; WTO n.d.). GATS aims to increase free trade in services by removing barriers to trade and ensuring transparency of trade regulations (Deschamps and Lee 2015; Knight 2008). Education is specifically named as a service sector covered by GATS, within which five subsectors are identified: primary education, secondary education, higher education, adult education, and other education (Knight 2008). "Other education" is not clearly defined; it is unclear whether language testing services, student recruitment services, quality assessment services, etc., are covered in this subcategory (Knight 2008).

GATS permits countries to determine the degree to which they will allow individual sectors to be opened to international competition. So, countries are not required to open up trade in education. However, if they do open some sectors, they must allow all WTO member countries the same access and they cannot discriminate between domestic and international providers. Also, any country can request that another country open up trade in a particular area, and governments then negotiate for these changes.

Education is one of the service sectors that has been the least opened up, though GATS does expect countries to eliminate additional trade barriers in each round of negotiations

(Knight 2008). Countries can also file complaints, and the WTO may require the elimination of particular barriers to trade. For example, U.S. complaints led to the removal of regulations in Turkey and Italy that dictated that foreign education providers could only instruct noncitizens. A U.S. complaint also led to the elimination of the regulation in China that all foreign education providers must partner with Chinese universities (Deschamps and Lee 2015).

GATS identifies four principal modes of service, all of which have implications for international education. Knight (2008) offers examples of each:

1. "Cross-border supply" refers to services (not people) that cross borders. An example of this is online education, which may be produced in one country and received by students in another country.

2. "Consumption abroad" refers to people moving to the country of the supplier of the service. An example is study abroad, where students (the consumers) go to another country to enroll in courses.

3. "Commercial presence" refers to establishing a commercial facility in another country in order to provide a service. International branch campuses of universities are an example (discussed in detail below).

4. "Presence of natural persons" refers to people temporarily traveling to another country to provide a service. Examples include visiting professors (the service providers) who go to another country to teach a course.

Many people argue that education was commodified when it was included in GATS (Knight 2009). In other words, rather than considering education to be a public service rightfully provided (and controlled and protected) by governments, the GATS treaty adopted neoliberal policies of promoting the involvement of private companies in education and encouraging competition among education providers. The argument in favor of this shift is that increased competition will increase the overall quality of the education provided. Opponents argue that this policy steers education away from a focus on serving society, particularly, underserved populations, and instead promotes a focus on profit making (Knight 2009). Further, opponents argue that wealthy countries and companies are positioned by GATS to be able to exploit less wealthy countries.

Trend 6: Internationalization of Education

In order to prepare graduates for success in the global knowledge economy—and in recognition that global issues such as environmental degradation, terrorism, health epidemics, human rights, armed conflict, and population growth are not challenges contained within national borders—many institutions are focusing on internationalization (Knight 2008). While the term "internationalization" means many things to many people, the definition most commonly cited in the international education literature is "the process of integrating an international, intercultural, or global dimension into the purpose, functions or delivery of post-secondary education" (Knight 2004, 11).

Common components of institutional internationalization plans include increasing the international focus of the curriculum, emphasizing foreign language study, promoting study abroad, recruiting international students, developing joint degrees and other collaborative partnerships, engaging in international research and scholarship, and hiring diverse faculty with international experience (Deschamps and Lee 2015; Egron-Polak and Hudson 2014; Knight 2009). On the institutional level, while rationales for internationalization based on solving global problems and serving the needs of graduates remain relevant, they now exist concurrently with motivations focused on financial sustainability and economic competitiveness. Institutions have come to view internationalization as a revenue generator, through the direct provision of education in exchange for tuition payments, and indirectly through the increased boost in reputation that institutions receive for their international activity (Deschamps and Lee 2015; Rumbley, Altbach, and Reisberg 2012; Shah and Nair 2011; Wadhwa 2016).

Internationalization is evident on the national level as well and is often supported by national policies (British Council 2017). Ziguras and McBurnie (2015) suggest that three motivations affect many governments' internationalization policies. First, many governments share a commitment to free trade, which leads them to support the inclusion of the education sector in GATS and other treaties, believing that it will increase the quality of education and international education. Second, governments seek to avoid brain drain, increased inequity, and the exploitation of students, which may lead some governments to try to regulate international trade in education within their borders. Third, governments believe they have the right and responsibility to regulate the movement of people in and out of national borders to control the potential effects on the economy and society.

Whichever one of these three beliefs (or combination of beliefs) government leaders value the most can often influence their policy decisions. In some instances, decisions may result in policies that eliminate trade barriers in education. In other cases, governments may set policies that lead to the development and funding of programs to develop the national workforce through education programs, including those emphasizing global knowledge and language skills. Through lawmaking, policy statements, promotion, data collection and monitoring, and/or the creation of international education initiatives, governments can help or hinder national and institutional internationalization efforts.

Trend 7: Growth in Cross-Border Education

Internationalization efforts are sometimes divided into two categories: internationalization at home (IaH) and cross-border education. Internationalization at home refers to activities taking place on U.S. university campuses, such as adding international content to the curriculum and organizing campus and community events to promote intercultural understanding. In contrast, cross-border education refers to the initiatives that move people and/or programs across national borders (Knight 2013, 2014). The terms "transnational education" and "borderless education" are sometimes used to refer to cross-border education (Rumbley, Altbach, and Reisberg 2012). With a few exceptions, developed countries are usually the providers of cross-border education, while developing countries are the receivers, creating some concern about the unequal distribution of benefits (Youssef 2014).

The movement of people across borders for education-related purposes is known as "academic mobility." As of 2018, more than 5 million higher education students were studying outside of their home country (Institute of International Education 2018). This number has been growing rapidly over the last few decades; for comparison, in 2001, there were only 2.1 million students studying internationally (Institute of International Education 2018). In fact, it is projected that there will be 8 million students studying internationally by 2025 (ICEF Monitor 2017).

The countries receiving the largest number of international students are the United States, the United Kingdom, China, Australia, and France. The top sending region, by far, is East Asia and the Pacific (Institute of International Education 2017). The recruitment of international students has increasingly become a part of institutions' internationalization plans. While acknowledging the talent and diverse perspectives that international students can bring to a university campus, another significant driver for the push to recruit international students is often financial, with international students seen as a viable source of revenue (Altbach and de Wit 2018; British Council 2017; Jacob and Gokbel 2017).

The movement of people across borders for education is one of the primary areas of focus in the international education field. In addition to *people* crossing borders, international education *programs* are now crossing borders. Since the early 2000s, universities worldwide have been setting up collaborative degree offerings with foreign university partners. These offerings include joint, double, and dual degrees. By aligning their curricula, partner universities are able to offer their students one or two degrees earned by taking courses in both countries (see chapter 3 for more information on collaborative degrees). The primary institutional motivations for offering these degrees are to broaden educational offerings, strengthen research collaborations, advance internationalization, and raise international prestige (Obst and Kuder 2011; West 2015). Although data on cross-border programs are not collected systematically

(Knight 2008), surveys of higher education institutions show that at least 85 percent of responding institutions offer collaborative degrees (Obst and Kuder 2009, 2011).

Another example of cross-border education is the establishment of international branch campuses. In this case, it is not simply *programs* crossing borders, but the *providers* themselves. When establishing an international branch campus, a university sets up a campus in another country, not just as a short-term study abroad site, but as a site offering full degrees. The motivation for the university may be expanding its international reputation, creating a new revenue source, and/or creating more opportunities for collaboration between students and faculty on the home campus and those in the host country. Host country governments may offer U.S. universities enticements such as tax relief, land, facilities, and other inducements with the goal of expanding the educational offerings available to their citizens and improving their societies and economies with a well-educated workforce.

The Cross-Border Education Research Team (2017) has compiled a list of 247 international branch campuses. The primary exporters of international branch campuses are universities in Western countries, particularly the United States, the United Kingdom, France, Russia, and Australia, while the largest importer (host) countries are in Asia and the Middle East, primarily China, the United Arab Emirates, Singapore, Malaysia, and Qatar (Cross-Border Education Research Team 2017).

Beyond international branch campuses, there are other forms of provider mobility such as online or distance learning. This kind of cross-border education can increase access to high-quality education for students who might not have had such access before. The type of providers getting involved in the delivery of education is also changing. In addition to nonprofit public and private universities, there are now media companies, multinational corporations, corporate universities, professional associations, and others delivering cross-border education programs (Knight 2008).

Developing transnational education programs is not easy, and many initiatives have floundered (Rumbley, Altbach, and Reisberg 2012; West 2015). Faculty and administrators at partnering institutions must forge mutually beneficial relationships and negotiate beliefs and expectations about learning and teaching. Partner universities must shepherd new programs through the curriculum approval processes at both institutions, meeting all requirements. At the same time, the legal issues, taxes, labor regulations, and other policy issues in both countries must be addressed. Success in cross-border education requires a commitment of time and money to work across cultures and systems (Rumbley, Altbach, and Reisberg 2012; West 2015). Cross-border education has the potential to offer innovative education programs that help students to develop global competence, increasing the global collective ability to overcome cultural divides and enabling the world to solve the most challenging problems.

Trend 8: Proliferation of English Language Programs

English is the predominant language of science and higher education. More than half of all international students study in English-speaking countries, and English is the world's most studied second language (Altbach 2013b). In Europe, there has been a 50-fold increase in the number of bachelor's degree programs taught in English over the last decade (Sandstrom 2019). The products of international partnerships, such as joint-degree programs and international branch campuses, are typically administered in English, and the faculty involved are often expected to be proficient in English (Altbach 2013a).

The governments of many non-English-speaking countries believe that improving their citizens' competence in English often has a positive effect on their gross domestic product (GDP), so they develop education policies to promote the study of English, though they may struggle with shortages of trained primary and secondary school teachers who are fluent in English. In these countries, there may also be a number of higher education faculty members with expertise in their subject area, but not enough language ability to teach or write in English (British Council 2017). For students, English language proficiency may be a requirement for university admission, even in non-English-speaking countries (Altbach 2013a).

Globally, there is a push to offer higher education programs taught in English. This aims to both improve the capacity of local graduates and attract international students (Altbach 2013a; British Council 2017). The emphasis on the English language has given providers of cross-border education from English-speaking countries an advantage, although many non-English-speaking countries are now offering programs in English as well (Deschamps and Lee 2015). Altbach (2002) argues that the combination of multinational corporations and elite universities owning most new technologies, Western countries dominating global science, and the dominance of the English language creates a system that favors English-speaking countries. This advantage may be weakening, though, as English language proficiency is growing globally, and more and more countries are offering education programs taught in English to both international and domestic students.

Trend 9: Demand for Quality Assurance in International Education

Across higher education, there is a growing demand for proof of outcomes. Universities are being asked by accreditation agencies to demonstrate what students have learned, how the education affects graduate employment, how research spending contributes to tangible outcomes for society, etc. (Jacob and Gokbel 2017; Stensaker and Harvey 2010). This broad trend is increasingly being applied to internationalization initiatives. International education professionals are expected to collect hard data, analyze the data, and communicate the findings in order to demonstrate the benefits of international education programs (Hudzik 2011).

In many countries around the world, national governments oversee quality assurance by offering accreditation to the institutions that the governments have reviewed and consider to be delivering quality education. (The United States is a notable exception, where national and state governments have some oversight, but accreditation is provided by nonprofit regional accreditation organizations.) Because national accreditation systems are established to oversee public and private educational institutions headquartered and delivered within the country, cross-border education programs being imported and exported out of the country may have little oversight (Knight 2008). It is often unclear which governments can or should provide oversight of cross-border education initiatives.

While many cross-border education programs are of high quality, Altbach (2013b, 30) observes that with the increasing commodification of education, "bottom-feeders entered the market, as usually happens when financial gain becomes the central motivator," creating a need for greater quality control. Indeed, there has been an increase in the number of low-quality education providers, as well as degree mills (selling degrees) and bogus accreditation agencies (selling low-quality providers meaningless accreditations in order to fool consumers) (Knight 2013; Youssef 2014).

Developing countries may be at risk from the lack of quality assurance processes in cross-border education. Seeking to expand the capacity of their educational systems to facilitate economic growth, many of these countries have opened their economies to import education programs. This phenomenon heightens the importance of having well-developed accreditation and quality assurance mechanisms to ensure that education programs are legitimate and produce robust educational outcomes for students (Rumbley, Altbach, and Reisberg 2012).

Trend 10: Competition for Global Rankings

In the competitive environment in which higher education currently operates, with students able to choose from a wide variety of international options for their education, global rankings are gaining in importance. Students are increasingly using published rankings to evaluate the quality of prospective institutions. Universities, in turn, are competing for high rankings in order to attract students and establish their reputations as world-class universities (Abdullah, Aziz, and Ibrahim 2017; Holbrook and Caruson 2017; Lim 2015; O'Connell and Saunders 2013). At the national policy level, governments are taking interest in these rankings. In some cases, rankings are used to set targets for national education strategies, and in other cases, rankings are used to evaluate the success of educational reforms (Lim 2015; O'Connell and Saunders 2013).

The oldest global ranking system, established in 2003, is the Academic Ranking of World Universities (ARWU), sometimes referred to as the "Shanghai Rankings" for the research center at Shanghai Jiao Tong University where the ranking system was developed. Soon after, *Times Higher Education* (*THE*) launched its ranking system in 2004. The QS World University Rankings then launched in 2010 (Holbrook and Caruson 2017; Marginson 2010). While these three are the most well-known global rankings, other rankings include Center for World University Rankings, CWTS Leiden Ranking, Global Research Benchmarking System, Scimago Institutions Ranking, Thomas Reuters, U-Multirank, uniRank, Webometrics Ranking of World Universities, and Youth Incorporated Magazine (Holbrook and Caruson 2017).

Each ranking system uses a different formula for assessing university quality. ARWU prioritizes strong publications in the sciences and measures per capita research performance by the number of articles published. ARWU also looks at prestigious prizes won by alumni and employees (Holbrook and Caruson 2017). *THE* uses a broader formula than ARWU, including data on teaching, research, knowledge transfer, international outlook, and international reputation to identify the world's top 200 international universities. Forty percent of the score is based on reputational surveys submitted by peer universities (Holbrook and Caruson 2017). QS split from *THE* and established its own ranking system based on academic reputation, employer reputation, faculty-student ratio, percentage of international faculty and students, and faculty research citations (Holbrook and Caruson 2017). Critics argue that some of the data that are used as proxies for desired qualities in these various ranking systems are not actually measuring what they are meant to (Lim 2015; O'Connell and Saunders 2013).

Because one of the rationales for internationalization is related to maintaining global competitiveness—particularly through scientific and technological achievement—some scholars argue that most of these higher education rankings emphasize research output with little regard for the quality of teaching (Altbach 2013b; Marginson 2010). The rankings can encourage and prioritize developing research capacity; however, establishing a research university with all of the latest scientific facilities is an expensive undertaking, and it can be particularly daunting for developing countries (Altbach 2013a; Somers et al. 2018). With such weight placed on research, which is primarily measured by the number of citations that articles receive, the ranking systems seem to privilege English-speaking countries and more developed countries. English has become the dominant language of education and, therefore, in order to receive a wide readership and more citations, academics may be compelled to publish in English (Altbach 2013b; Marginson 2010). Not only is this easier for scholars in English-speaking countries, Altbach (2013b) points out that because many of the leading English-language journals are not interested in local matters, the local needs of non-English-speaking countries may be ignored or minimized in the top research publications.

There is a concern that competition for rankings pushes all institutions toward the research university model, without regard for the institution type or mission (Marginson 2010; O'Connell and Saunders 2013; Somers et al. 2018). Altbach (2013b) suggests that ranking systems could be improved if they separated rankings by category based on institution type. He also argues that rankings presume a "nonexistent zero-sum game," forcing universities into competition with each other (Altbach 2013b, 82). The ARWU rewards the most well-established universities by measuring research performance over the past century, while the QS measures research citations for the past 5 years (Jons and Hoyler 2013). Lim (2015) points out that the rankings reinforce the power of the most high-status institutions, with institutions that have the most resources and best reputations attracting the best students and scholars, thus being the most well placed to continue to do well in the rankings.

Conclusion

This chapter gave an overview of 10 trends shaping education today. Five of the trends—growth of the knowledge economy, massification of education, the decline in public funding for higher education, academic capitalism, and the commodification of education—affect primary, secondary, and higher education systems around the world. These five trends are relevant to economics, trade, international development, teacher education, and educational administration, among other fields. The remaining five trends—internationalization of education, growth in cross-border education, proliferation of English language programs, the demand for quality assurance in international education, and competition for global ranking—are more specific to the field of international education. These five trends often interact with each other, frequently reinforcing one another.

The trends presented in this chapter shape the context in which international education administrators and practitioners design and operate programs. While these trends may have the capacity to improve access to education and the quality of educational offerings, many critics warn of the risk of exacerbating existing inequities if education focuses more on money than on public service and quality assurance. The trends influence the types of programs that are established, the finances of international education organizations, the education policies of governments, and the knowledge and skills needed by international education professionals.

The remainder of the book focuses specifically on the field of international education. Chapter 2 explores the concept of global competence—what it is and how practitioners can assess whether or not their organization is successful in developing students' global competence. Chapter 3 focuses on internationalization, or the process of making education more international in focus. Chapter 4 examines study abroad programs, while chapter 5 delves into international programs focused on experiential education. Chapter 6 covers the processes involved in bringing international students to the United States to study, while chapter 7 highlights the advising and support services offered to international students and scholars living in the United States. Chapter 8 discusses the spread of international schools. Chapter 9 introduces programs that support professionals and individual citizens in forging meaningful connections across cultures. Chapter 10 provides an overview of additional fields related to international education. Together, these chapters consider the work of international education professionals across a wide variety of specializations, offering a guide to the profession.

References

Abdullah, Doria, Mohd Ismail Abd Aziz, and Abdul Latiff Mohd Ibrahim. 2017. "The Stories They Tell: Understanding International Student Mobility Through Higher Education Policy." *Journal of Studies in International Education* 21, 5:450–466. https://doi.org/10.1177/1028315317720766.

Altbach, Philip G. 2002. "Perspectives on International Higher Education." *Change: The Magazine of Higher Learning* 34, 3:29–31. https://doi.org/10.1080/00091380209601852.

Altbach, Philip G. 2013a. "Advancing the National and Global Knowledge Economy: The Role of Research Universities in Developing Countries." *Studies in Higher Education* 38, 3:316–330. https://doi.org/10.1080/03075079.2013.773222.

Altbach, Philip G. 2013b. *The International Imperative in Higher Education*. Rotterdam, The Netherlands: Sense Publishers.

Altbach, Philip G. 2014. "The Emergence of a Field: Research and Training in Higher Education." *Studies in Higher Education* 39, 8:1306–1320. https://doi.org/10.1080/03075079.2014.949541.

Altbach, Philip G., and Hans de Wit. 2018. "Are We Facing a Fundamental Challenge to Higher Education Internationalization?" *International Higher Education* 93:2–4.

British Council. 2017. "10 Trends: Transformative Changes in Higher Education." British Council.

Choudaha, Rahul. 2017. *Landscape of Third-Party Pathway Partnerships in the United States*. Washington, DC: NAFSA: Association of International Educators.

Cross-Border Education Research Team. 2017. "C-BERT Branch Campus Listing." Albany, NY: Cross-Border Education Research Team. http://cbert.org/resources-data/branch-campus/.

Daviet, Barbara. 2016. "Revisiting the Principle of Education as a Public Good." Education Research and Foresight Working Papers. Paris, France: UNESCO.

Deschamps, Eric, and Jenny J. Lee. 2015. "Internationalization as Mergers and Acquisitions: Senior International Officers' Entrepreneurial Strategies and Activities in Public Universities." *Journal of Studies in International Education* 19, 2:122–139. https://doi.org/10.1177/1028315314538284.

Doherty, Catherine, Allan Luke, Paul Shield, and Candice Hincksman. 2012. "Choosing Your Niche: The Social Ecology of the International Baccalaureate Diploma in Australia." *International Studies in Sociology of Education* 22, 4:311–332. https://doi.org/10.1080/09620214.2012.745346.

Edmonds, Dan. 2015. "More than Half of College Faculty Are Adjuncts: Should You Care?" *Forbes*. May 28, 2015. https://www.forbes.com/sites/noodleeducation/2015/05/28/more-than-half-of-college-faculty-are-adjuncts-should-you-care/.

Egron-Polak, Eva, and Ross Hudson. 2014. *Internationalization of Higher Education: Growing Expectations, Fundamental Values*. IAU 4th Global Survey. Paris, France: International Association of Universities.

Hensley, Brad, Mika Galilee-Belfer, and Jenny J. Lee. 2013. "What Is the Greater Good? The Discourse on Public and Private Roles of Higher Education in the New Economy." *Journal of Higher Education Policy and Management* 35, 5:553–567. https://doi.org/10.1080/1360080X.2013.825416.

Holbrook, Karen A., and Kiki Caruson. 2017. *Globalizing University Research: Innovation, Collaboration and Competition*. New York, NY: Institute of International Education.

Hudzik, John K. 2011. *Comprehensive Internationalization: From Concept to Action*. Washington, DC: NAFSA: Association of International Educators.

Hurlburt, Steven, and Michael McGarrah. 2016. *The Shifting Academic Workforce: Where Are the Contingent Faculty?* New York, NY: TIAA Institute.

ICEF Monitor. 2017. "OECD Charts a Slowing of International Mobility Growth." ICEF Monitor. September 20, 2017. http://monitor.icef.com/2017/09/oecd-charts-slowing-international-mobility-growth/.

Institute of International Education. 2017. "Project Atlas Infographics 2017." Institute of International Education. https://www.iie.org/en/Research-and-Insights/Project-Atlas/Explore-Data.

Institute of International Education. 2018. "Project Atlas 2018 Infographics." Institute of International Education. https://www.iie.org/en/Research-and-Insights/Project-Atlas/Explore-Data/Current-Infographics.

Jacob, W. James, and Veysel Gokbel. 2017. "Global Higher Education Learning Outcomes and Financial Trends: Comparative and Innovative Approaches." *International Journal of Educational Development* 58:5–17. https://doi.org/10.1016/j.ijedudev.2017.03.001.

Jain, Chaya R. 2015. "The Knowledge Economy and the Transformational Dynamics of Education in Asia's Emergent Economic Growth." In *Asia: The Next Higher Education Superpower?*, eds. Rajika Bhandari and Alessia Lefebure. New York, NY: Institute of International Education.

Johnstone, D. Bruce. 2011. "The Funding of Universities in the Twenty-First Century." In *Leadership for World-Class Universities: Challenges for Developing Countries*, ed. Philip G. Altbach. New York, NY: Routledge.

Jons, Heike, and Michael Hoyler. 2013. "Global Geographies of Higher Education: The Perspective of World University Rankings." *Geoforum* 46:45–59.

Knight, Jane. 2004. "Internationalization Remodeled: Definition, Approaches, and Rationales." *Journal of Studies in International Education* 8, 1:5–31. https://doi.org/10.1177/1028315303260832.

Knight, Jane. 2008. *Higher Education in Turmoil: The Changing World of Internationalization*. Taipei, Taiwan: Sense Publishers.

Knight, Jane. 2009. "New Developments and Unintended Consequences: Whither Thou Goest, Internationalization?" In *Higher Education on the Move: New Developments in Global Mobility*, eds. Rajika Bhandari and Shepherd Laughlin. New York, NY: Institute of International Education.

Knight, Jane. 2013. "The Changing Landscape of Higher Education Internationalisation – For Better or Worse?" *Perspectives: Policy and Practice in Higher Education* 17, 3:84–90. https://doi.org/10.1080/13603108.2012.753957.

Knight, Jane. 2014. "Three Generations of Crossborder Higher Education: New Development, Issues, and Challenges." In *Internationalisation of Higher Education and Global Mobility*, ed. Bernhard Streitwieser. Oxford, United Kingdom: Symposium Books.

Lim, M. 2015. "Global University Rankings: Determining the Distance between Asia and 'Superpower Status' in Higher Education." In *Asia: The Next Higher Education Superpower?*, eds. Rajika Bhandari and Alessia Lefebure. New York, NY: Institute of International Education.

Marginson, Simon. 2010. "Global Comparisons and the University Knowledge Economy." In *Higher Education, Policy, and the Global Competition Phenomena*, eds. Laura M. Portnoi, Val D. Rust, and Sylvia S. Bagley. New York, NY: Palgrave Macmillan.

Marginson, Simon. 2015. "Systemic Challenges to Education Quality and Global Competitiveness." In *Asia: The Next Higher Education Superpower?*, eds. Rajika Bhandari and Alessia Lefebure. New York, NY: Institute of International Education.

Monbiot, George. 2016. "Neoliberalism – The Ideology at the Root of All Our Problems." *The Guardian.* April 15, 2016. http://www.theguardian.com/books/2016/apr/15/neoliberalism-ideology-problem-george-monbiot.

Nelson, Glen R., Gregory C. Wolniak, and Casey E. George. 2017. "Study Snapshot: Unmasking College Costs: Challenges in the Era of Differential Tuition Practices." Presented at the American Educational Research Association 2017 Annual Meeting. http://www.aera.net/Newsroom/News-Releases-and-Statements/Study-Snapshot-Unmasking-College-Costs-Challenges-in-the-Era-of-Differential-Tuition-Practices.

Obst, Daniel, and Matthias Kuder, eds. 2009. *Joint and Double Degree Programs: An Emerging Model for Transatlantic Exchange*. New York, NY: Institute of International Education.

Obst, Daniel, and Matthias Kuder. 2011. *Joint and Double Degree Programs in the Transatlantic Context: A Survey Report*. New York, NY: Institute of International Education and Freie Universität Berlin.

O'Connell, Catherine, and Murray Saunders. 2013. "Mediating the Use of Global University Rankings: Perspectives from Education Facilitators in an International Context." *Journal of Studies in International Education* 17, 4:354–376. https://doi.org/10.1177/1028315312453743.

Resnik, Julia. 2012. "The Denationalization of Education and the Expansion of the International Baccalaureate." *Comparative Education Review* 56, 2:248–269. https://doi.org/10.1086/661770.

Rhoades, Gary, and Sheila Slaughter. 2004. "Academic Capitalism in the New Economy: Challenges and Choices." *American Academic* 1, 1:37–59.

Rumbley, Laura E., Philip G. Altbach, and Liz Reisberg. 2012. "Internationalization Within the Higher Education Context." In *The SAGE Handbook of International Higher Education*, eds. Darla K. Deardorff, Hans de Wit, John Heyl, and Tony Adams. Thousand Oaks, CA: Sage Publications.

Sandstrom, Anna-Malin. 2019. "English-Taught Bachelor's Programs in Europe." *International Higher Education* 96:12–13.

Schleicher, Andreas. 2019. "Financing the Future." *International Educator* XXVIII, 1:16–23.

Shah, Mahsood, and Chenicheri Sid Nair. 2011. "International Higher Education in Australia: Unplanned Future." *Perspectives: Policy and Practice in Higher Education* 15, 4:129–131. https://doi.org/10.1080/13603108.2011.597888.

Somers, Patricia, Cory Davis, Jessica Fry, Lisa Jasinski, and Elida Lee. 2018. "Academic Capitalism and the Entrepreneurial University: Some Perspectives from the Americas." *Roteiro* 43, 1:21–41. https://doi.org/10.18593/r.v43i1.13088.

Stensaker, Bjorn, and Lee Harvey, eds. 2010. *Accountability in Higher Education: Global Perspectives on Trust and Power*. New York, NY: Routledge.

UNESCO. 2015. *Education for All 2000–2015: Achievements and Challenges*. Paris, France: UNESCO.

United Nations. 2015. *Transforming Our World: The 2030 Agenda for Sustainable Development*. United Nations. https://doi.org/10.1891/9780826190123.ap02.

Wadhwa, Rashim. 2016. "New Phase of Internationalization of Higher Education and Institutional Change." *Higher Education for the Future* 3, 2:227–246. https://doi.org/10.1177/2347631116650548.

West, Charlotte. 2015. "Degrees Without Borders." *International Educator* XXIV, 4:20–32. https://www.nafsa.org/professional-resources/publications/international-educator-july-august-2015.

World Trade Organization. n.d. "WTO: Members and Observers." World Trade Organization. Accessed January 19, 2018. https://www.wto.org/english/thewto_e/whatis_e/tif_e/org6_e.htm.

Youssef, Leïla. 2014. "Globalisation and Higher Education: From Within-Border to Cross-Border." *Open Learning: The Journal of Open, Distance and e-Learning* 29, 2:100–115. https://doi.org/10.1080/02680513.2014.932686.

Ziguras, Christopher, and Grant McBurnie. 2015. *Governing Cross-Border Higher Education*. New York, NY: Routledge.

Chapter 2

Global Competence

Many governments around the world are making students' development of global competence a goal in their education policies. These governments argue that global competence is a necessity for both individual learners and for society; it drives innovation and prosperity, enhances career opportunities for graduates, promotes intercultural understanding, and increases world peace. An educational focus on the global "has the capacity to help students find their commitments, advocate for their position, and develop compassion and convictions within and beyond their immediate world" (Kahn and Agnew 2017, 58). Thus, developing the global competence of students is a foundational objective of international education.

Harris (2014) observes that youth and young adults today are more global than ever. Each year, there are 5 million students studying outside of their home country for higher education (Institute of International Education 2018). In a vastly different form of mobility, more than half of all displaced persons are children (Harris 2014). This movement of people has resulted in more people in this generation than past generations holding hybrid and transnational identities and cosmopolitan beliefs and practices. Harris (2014) argues that this upcoming generation has the capacity to embrace multiple identities and communities as long as their social and economic needs are met. However, she warns that if those essential needs are not met, these individuals may be drawn into defensive and protectionist identity politics (Harris 2014). Global competence should not be a benefit only to select students, such as those who study abroad, but should be developed in all students so that they can function in an increasingly globalized world, regardless of whether they ultimately settle in their home community or elsewhere (Gregersen-Hermans 2017).

Green (2012, 1) acknowledges the degree to which global thinking represents a mindset or an orientation to life, suggesting that while national citizenship is an "accident of birth," global citizenship "is a choice and a way of thinking." In keeping with the broader trend toward assessment and demonstrable outcomes in education, there has been a strong demand for evidence-based strategies for internationalization, and for internationalization to focus on outcomes. This has resulted in a drive to understand how to develop and measure global competence and related constructs (Deardorff 2015; Gregersen-Hermans 2017).

In order to better promote global competence among students, researchers and practitioners should examine the literature of both the primary/secondary and higher education levels. These bodies of scholarship should be synthesized because: (a) increasing numbers of high school graduates are entering higher education, making it essentially one continuous education process; (b) the global forces influencing both levels of education are similar; and (c) due to flexible learning opportunities such as distance and lifelong learning initiatives, the barriers between formal schooling and higher education are lower than ever (Yemini 2014). Despite this logic, much of the literature of the field focuses on either higher education or kindergarten through 12th grade (K–12) education.

This chapter introduces the idea of global competence at all education levels, discussing terminology and definitions, rationales for global competence education, theoretical models, core concepts across models, assessments of global competence, and areas to consider for practitioners. The remaining chapters of this book explore in greater depth how global competence is developed within each sector of the international education field.

Global Competence in the United States

In the United States, the concept of global competence can be traced back to Title VI of the National Defense Education Act of 1958, which funded foreign language studies and areas studies, and the Fulbright-Hays Act of 1961, which created the Fulbright Program to support international study, research, and teaching (Schwarzer and Bridglall 2015). In the 1960s and 1970s, antiwar movements, civil rights movements, and the environmental movement called for greater international and cross-cultural understanding, collaboration, and peace. This bolstered the call for global education (Standish 2014). At the same time, others responded by calling for the United States to focus more attention at home and give less attention, and fewer resources, to international affairs (Hoffa 2007).

In the late 1980s and early 1990s, the end of the cold war and uncertainty about the global political future added further pressure on the U.S. educational system to increase emphasis on international and intercultural content (Standish 2014). The 1990s and 2000s were characterized by advances in technology and communication that facilitated more international and intercultural connections than ever before. By 2012, the U.S. Department of Education launched its first ever international strategy. This strategy emphasizes the need for a world-class education for all students, the development of global competencies in all students, international benchmarking for quality control, and the need for educational diplomacy partnerships (U.S. Department of Education 2012).

The global emphasis, across all forms of education, on ensuring quality by conducting measurable assessment of student learning is evident in the U.S.

(continued on next page)

Global Competence in the United States (continued)

international education field. A survey performed by the Association of American Colleges & Universities found that 89 percent of the member institutions measure their students' knowledge of global cultures, 79 percent of the institutions measure their students' intercultural skills, and 79 percent measure their students' knowledge of U.S. diversity (Lucas and Blair 2017). The Forum on Education Abroad's 2012 State of the Field Survey found that 45 percent of education abroad programs assess students' intercultural competence (Lucas and Blair 2017). It is now normal for primary, secondary, and higher education institutions to consider the development of global competence to be an essential component of their educational goals.

However, arguing for the importance of global competence is much easier than ensuring its development in students. Much of the existing data available on U.S. youths' proficiencies indicate a deficit in students' global knowledge. Surveys conducted by Asia Society, National Geographic, and the National Assessment of Educational Progress show that fewer than one in three U.S. students is proficient in geography, with 25 percent of college-bound students unable to name the ocean between California and Asia, 37 percent unable to find China on a map, and 80 percent unaware that India is the world's largest democracy (Stewart 2012). According to the data, U.S. students from low-income and minoritized backgrounds are often found to particularly lag behind their peers in other countries in terms of their knowledge of geography, languages, and world cultures (National Education Association 2010). These data and the desire to ensure that all students develop global competence are compelling motivations for many international educators.

Terminology and Definitions

In addition to the term "global competence," many related and overlapping terms are used in the international education field. Some of the terms in use include cosmopolitanism, cultural competence, cultural humility, democratic education, education for international understanding, global citizenship, global citizenship education, global education, global learning, global mindedness, global-ready graduate, global understanding, human rights education, ideal global graduate, intercultural competence, intercultural education, international education, multiculturalism, multicultural education, peace education, transnational citizenship, and world studies (Goren and Yemini 2017; Hayden and Thompson 2008; Lilley, Barker, and Harris 2015; Marshall 2011; Murray-Garcia and Tervalon 2017; Oxley and Morris 2013; United Nations Educational, Scientific and Cultural Organization 2015).

In addition to the abundance of terms in use related to global competence, there is debate about the actual definitions of each of the terms. The competing definitions leave scholars arguing about which term is preferable, the conceptual distinctions between the terms, and which of the competing definitions are superior. Here are three sample definitions:

- The Organisation for Economic Co-operation and Development (OECD) defines global competence as "the capacity to examine local, global, and intercultural issues; to understand and appreciate the perspectives and world views of others; to engage in open, appropriate, and effective interactions with people from different cultures; and to act for collective well-being and sustainable development" (Asia Society and OECD 2018, 5).

- Oxfam (n.d.) defines a global citizen as "someone who is aware of and understands the wider world – and their place in it. They take an active role in their community, and work with others to make our planet more equal, fair, and sustainable."

- A survey of leading scholars identified this as the best definition of intercultural competence: "the ability to communicate effectively and appropriately in intercultural situations based on one's intercultural knowledge, skills, and attitudes" (Deardorff 2006).

In interviews with higher education experts, Lilley, Barker, and Harris (2017) found that while the scholars preferred to use a variety of different terms, the underlying constructs are similar. This chapter accepts their assertion that agreeing on the exact terms used is less important than moving forward with an understanding of how to develop global competence (or whatever other term is preferred) in students. For this reason, this chapter utilizes the term "global competence," one of the more widely used terms, while synthesizing scholarship on global competence, global citizenship, and intercultural competence, among other dimensions.

Rationales for Global Competence Education

Global competence has become an important focus for all levels of education. Five rationales that are commonly argued by proponents for inclusion of a global competence curriculum include competitiveness, solutions to global problems, multiculturalism, citizenship and governance, and academic benefits. The rationales contend that both individuals and societies benefit from global competence education. In calls to action, multiple rationales are often listed together to make the case for prioritizing internationalization and global learning.

Competitiveness

Perhaps the most frequently cited rationale for global competence education emphasizes the rapid rate of change in the world and the need for individuals, institutions, and nations to have the competence to deal with future developments. This reasoning is often reinforced by the accelerating advances in technology, communication, and trade, and it also plays on the (possibly justified) fear of being left behind.

When focused on the individual level, the issue of competitiveness is tied to employability. The National Education Association (NEA) (2010) argues that graduates need to be able to think critically and must develop a thorough understanding of the economic, social, and technological changes taking place in the world. Stewart (2012) reiterates this focus on the global knowledge economy, noting that children entering school today will be in the workforce until 2070 and, thus, must be prepared to adapt to changing conditions of technology and economics. Stewart (2012) specifically emphasizes these outcomes of a global education:

- Scientific and technological literacy;
- Ability to think critically about sustainable economies and scarce resources;
- Global knowledge and skills as core competence; and
- Innovation, creativity, and knowledge of how to learn.

Suarez-Orozco and Qin-Hilliard (2004, 3) likewise highlight the need for competitiveness to keep up with the changes in the global knowledge economy, noting that "globalization means that the lives of children growing up today will be shaped in no small measure by global processes in economy, society, and culture. Educational systems tied to the formation of nation-state citizens and consumers bonded to local systems to the neglect of larger global forces are likely to become obsolete, while those that proactively engage globalization's new challenges are more likely to thrive." Globally competent citizens who have the knowledge, skills, and innovative spirit to navigate through future trends help to elevate individuals and nations on the global stage.

Solutions to Global Problems

While the previous rationale emphasized competition, another rationale in support of global education emphasizes cooperation. This rationale is based on the premise that global issues such as poverty, epidemics, war, and environmental degradation are fundamentally global issues and the solutions to such issues are dependent on the work and collaborations of globally competent individuals. The OECD states that helping students to develop global competence is necessary to achieve the United Nations's Sustainable Development Goals (see chapter 10). The 2030 Agenda for Sustainable Development declares that developing generations of students "who care about global issues and engage in tackling social, political, economic, and environmental challenges" will help to achieve human rights, gender equality, and peace, among other goals (OECD 2018, 5).

Likewise, a 2013 International Association of Universities survey that examined internationalization efforts at 1,336 higher education institutions in 131 countries found that students' increased international awareness and engagement with global issues was the most frequently cited anticipated benefit of internationalization (Egron-Polak and Hudson 2014). These arguments stress the need to cross disciplinary boundaries and build interconnected networks to solve some of the world's more intractable problems.

Multiculturalism: Diversity, Tolerance, and Peace

A third line of reasoning for emphasizing global competence in educational systems is that nations are becoming increasingly multicultural and, in order for peace to prevail, all people need to learn to get along with those of cultural backgrounds different from their own. Emphasis is placed on the exploration of identities of self and others. For many scholars, critical inquiry into issues of power, injustice, and inequity is also essential (Aktas et al. 2017; Andreotti 2006).

Students seek to understand a world that is largely characterized by division, conflict, inequity, and poverty. Schools and universities can provide a space to explore these complex issues, helping students to develop their global competence in order to be able to function more effectively and collaboratively in multicultural settings (Hayden 2006; OECD 2016; Oxfam n.d.). Leeman (2003) offers a list of objectives that students who live in multicultural societies need to work toward:

- Develop knowledge about ethnic-cultural diversity;
- Develop a multiple perspective outlook;
- Develop knowledge about inequity and skills to tackle inequality;
- Develop values and skills aimed at safeguarding ethnic-cultural diversity, personal autonomy, and communality in school and society; and
- Develop values and skills necessary for living democratically in a multiethnic context.

These goals underscore the importance of understanding and tolerance, with a focus on the study of identity and intercultural communication. There is evidence that global learning can support overall efforts for domestic, as well as international, diversity and inclusion by helping students "view the world through the perspective of others, critically understand diversity, challenge stereotypes, confront prejudice, recognize their own identities and biases, and ultimately negotiate relationships that lead to action" (Kahn and Agnew 2017, 56). According to this rationale, globally competent students should learn theories and models of identity development, intergroup interactions, and intercultural communication.

Many scholars also call attention to the importance of critical inquiry. They recommend that students analyze the historical, political, economic, and social structures that create power and inequity (Kahn and Agnew 2017). Failure to incorporate discussions of power differences can reinforce stereotypes and inequities. To avoid this outcome, global competence education must guide learners to analyze and critique their own and others' assumptions about "how we came to think/be/feel/act the way we do and the implications of our systems of belief in local/global terms in relation to power, social relationships and the distribution of labour and resources" (Andreotti 2006, 49). Once students are aware of their own position in society, as well as their power relationships with others, they can begin to build authentic connections and move toward peacebuilding.

Citizenship and Governance

Another commonly used rationale for the importance of global competence education is that graduates will need to be engaged professionally and personally as informed global citizens who can work to make the world a better place. Oxfam (n.d.) contends that a global citizen is someone who:

- Is aware of the wider world and has a sense of his or her own roles as a world citizen;
- Respects and values diversity;
- Has an understanding of how the world works;
- Is passionately committed to social justice;
- Participates in the community at a range of levels from the local to the global;
- Works with others to make the world a more equitable and sustainable place; and
- Takes responsibility for his or her actions.

This rationale spotlights the responsibilities of citizenship and the development of graduates who will be engaged personally and professionally in the governance of their societies. It argues that an informed citizenry is best able to govern, particularly in democratic societies.

Academic Benefits

One argument that is less frequently employed is that global learning has academic and cognitive benefits. In other words, developing global competence will help students to learn better in other arenas. The National Education Association (2010) proclaims that students who study a foreign language often have enhanced cognitive development, higher-order thinking, and increased creativity. NEA (2010) further asserts that foreign language learning can improve skills in reading, writing, mathematics, and other subjects, and these students often exhibit stronger performances on the SAT and ACT tests. The American Council on the Teaching of Foreign Languages (ACTFL) has also compiled research demonstrating the benefits of language learning. ACTFL finds that bilingualism often relates to stronger memory skills, metalinguistic skills, problem-solving ability, and verbal and spatial abilities (ACTFL n.d.). For example, the Seattle, Washington, public school district has opened multiple schools focused on global learning and has seen that students in those schools often outperform their peers at other district schools in subject tests for math, science, reading, and writing (Vega and Terada 2013).

Beyond language learning, Cushman (2013) argues that global learning outcomes correlate with the goals of a liberal arts education. The Association of American Colleges & Universities

(2009, 2014) recognized the importance of global competence for critical thinking by releasing a Global Learning VALUE Rubric and an Intercultural Knowledge and Competence VALUE Rubric to help institutions assess student learning. Some of the skills cultivated through a liberal arts education, which are improved through the development of global competence, include the ability to communicate, reason, problem-solve, and work well with others (Schejbal and Irvine 2009).

Other rationales in support of global competence education are also used. These may be particular to the priorities, needs, and interests of different people, institutions, and countries. Just as there are diverse motivating factors, there are several ways to approach and develop global learning.

Global Competence Models

Even though the rationales for global competence education can vary, the true challenge felt by all lies in understanding how it is developed and how student learning in this area can be assessed. Theoretical models provide insights into the components of global competence and the processes of developing global competence. While many scholars have proposed global competence models, four of the most prominent are described in this section.

Developmental Model of Intercultural Sensitivity

Bennett's (1986) Developmental Model of Intercultural Sensitivity (DMIS) has been influential in guiding international educators' understanding of their work. This model, shown in figure 1, demonstrates the ways in which individuals perceive difference, and it suggests that there are six developmental stages that individuals *may* progress through over their lifetime—starting from denial and moving to integration. The majority of people will not reach the final stage, and they may stop developing somewhere along the continuum. The DMIS model refers to not only interactions with people of other nationalities, but to all encounters with people who are perceived to be from a different group (e.g., gender, religion, ethnicity, etc.) than oneself.

FIGURE 1 Developmental Model of Intercultural Sensitivity

ETHNOCENTRISM			ETHNORELATIVISM		
Denial	Defense	Minimization	Acceptance	Adaptation	Integration

Direction of Intercultural Sensitivity Development

Source: Bennett (1986).

The first three stages of the DMIS model are considered to be ethnocentric, meaning that people see the world through their own cultural lens. The latter three stages of the model are ethnorelative, meaning that people are able to interpret the world through multiple cultural lenses. In the latter three stages, people recognize behaviors, values, and interactions to be profoundly shaped by cultural influences and processes. Bennett (1986) argues that there is a particular developmental strategy or, put another way, something that needs to be learned in order for an individual to move from one stage to the next. Figure 1 illustrates the DMIS model, while table 1 offers simplified descriptions of each stage and the correlating learning task.

TABLE 1 — **Developmental Model of Intercultural Sensitivity: Stages and Learning Goals**

Stage	Description	Learning Goals and Strategy to Reach Next Stage
DENIAL	Individual has had limited contact with difference and lives in a largely homogenous community. Has little awareness of difference.	**Goal:** Simple recognition of difference. **Strategy:** Create more awareness of categories of cultural difference. For example, a cultural awareness event such as "Mexico Night," where traditional Mexican music, food, dance, and costumes are shared. Travelogues, history lectures, etc., may also serve this purpose. Avoid deep discussions for now.
DEFENSE	Individual wants to defend own worldview as right and natural and, therefore, engages in negative stereotyping, attributing undesirable characteristics to every member of culturally distinct groups. Assumes own culture is most evolved. May be "tolerant" of other cultures, considering them to be in the process of developing to be like one's own.	**Goal:** Find the commonality of all cultures, with particular focus on "good" aspects. **Strategy:** Guide discussions to what is good about own culture and what is good about other cultures. Emphasize the commonality of all cultures.
MINIMIZATION	Individual attempts to bury differences by focusing on cultural similarities. Cultural differences are no longer negatively evaluated, but they are trivialized. Assumes that there are universal rules or principles that guide life.	**Goal:** Acknowledge that culture is relative, rather than absolute. **Strategy:** Use simulations, personal narratives, and other means to emphasize differences in how a behavior can be interpreted. Bring in representatives of other cultures (who must be at the acceptance stage or beyond) to speak with small groups.
ACCEPTANCE	Individual perceives difference as necessary and desirable. Judgment is suspended. Accepts that language and communication vary, and that people see the world in profoundly different ways. Begins to focus on cultural difference as a process and people as cocreators of their realities.	**Goal:** Recognize values differences as part of a process. **Strategy:** Emphasize practical application of understanding differences in behaviors and values. Focus on using understanding for intercultural communication success.
ADAPTATION	Individual demonstrates empathy and is able to see events as if through another person's eyes. Able to shift between two or more cultural worldviews, known as "biculturalism" or "multiculturalism."	**Goal:** Regard self-identity as a dynamic process involving choice at every level. **Strategy:** Provide opportunities for interaction with people from other cultures. This might be structured as conversation partners or interviews of people from other cultures.
INTEGRATION	Individual applies ethnorelativism to self-identity, able to see self in various cultural ways. Judgment returns, not to designate good or bad, but to evaluate appropriateness of phenomena in relation to particular cultural contexts.	**Goal:** Construct an ethical system to guide choices. This is difficult because topics can be viewed from many perspectives. **Strategy:** Introduce ethics frameworks to be used as tools in constructing a personal ethic.

Source: Bennett (1986).

Intercultural Communicative Competence

Byram (1997) developed the Intercultural Communicative Competence model, which builds on language education theories. His model describes the traits of a person who is able to communicate effectively and appropriately in a language other than his or her native language. Byram (1997) conceptualized this individual as having both foreign language skills and intercultural skills. The foreign language skills are made up of linguistic competence (grammar, syntax, and vocabulary to construct sentences), sociolinguistic competence (appropriate use of language for the setting), and discourse competence (how sentences are put together to make conversations, persuasive arguments, informative reports, etc.). These language skills complement five intercultural traits: skill of interpreting and relating, knowledge of self and others and the corresponding cultural groups, attitudes of relativism and valuing culturally different others, skill of discovery and interaction, and political education and critical cultural awareness. Figure 2 illustrates the Intercultural Communicative Competence model.

FIGURE 2 Intercultural Communicative Competence Model

Source: Adapted from Byram (1997).

Process Model of Intercultural Competence

Another well-known model is Deardorff's (2006) Process Model of Intercultural Competence. Based on multiround surveys with experts in the intercultural field, Deardorff solicited input on the definition of intercultural competence, the process of developing intercultural competence, and ways of assessing intercultural competence. Drafts based on initial survey results were shared with the experts for feedback, and findings were further refined in a total of three rounds of review (Deardorff 2006). Based on the findings, Deardorff designed a visual representation of the process of developing intercultural competence, shown in figure 3.

The Process Model of Intercultural Competence begins with individuals who have a positive attitude toward intercultural people and topics; they respect and value other cultures, are open and withholding of judgment, and are curious to discover while also tolerant of ambiguity (Deardorff 2006). With these attitudes, individuals often seek knowledge such as cultural self-awareness, deep cultural knowledge, and sociolinguistic awareness. These individuals may also seek to strengthen their skills, including the ability to listen, observe, evaluate, analyze, interpret, and relate.

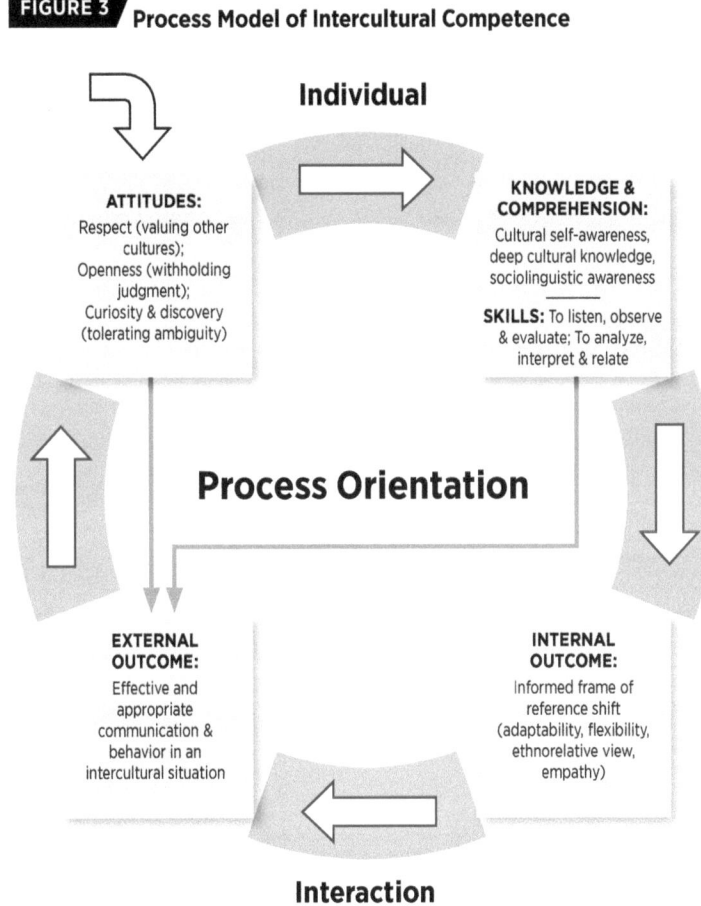

FIGURE 3 Process Model of Intercultural Competence

Source: Deardorff (2006). Reprinted with Permission of SAGE Publications, Inc.

This combination of attitudes, knowledge, and skills can result in an internal frame of reference shift within the individuals. They may begin to demonstrate greater adaptability, flexibility, ethnorelativism, and empathy (Deardorff 2006). The internal shift may lead to externally visible outcomes, for example, effective and appropriate communication and behaviors in intercultural situations. Growth continues as individuals repeatedly travel through this learning cycle. Deardorff (2006) notes that the appropriate attitudes, knowledge, and skills are sometimes enough on their own to bring about effective and appropriate external behaviors. However, she argues that the positive change in the external outcomes will be even stronger when individuals have gone through the internal shift (Deardorff 2006).

Educating for Global Competence

Another leading model of global competence, presented in a publication titled *Educating for Global Competence: Preparing Our Youth to Engage the World*, was developed collaboratively by the Asia Society and the Council of Chief State School Officers (see Boix Mansilla and Jackson 2011). The model offers a holistic set of four learning outcomes (see figure 4) that can be applied to any age level or subject or interdisciplinary study. The model postulates that globally competent students are generally able to:

- Investigate the world beyond their immediate environment, framing significant problems and conducting well-crafted and age-appropriate research.

- Recognize perspectives (others' and their own), articulating and explaining such perspectives thoughtfully and respectfully.

- Communicate ideas effectively with diverse audiences, bridging geographic, linguistic, ideological, and cultural barriers.

- Take action to improve conditions, viewing themselves as players in the world and participating reflectively.

FIGURE 4. Educating for Global Competence Model

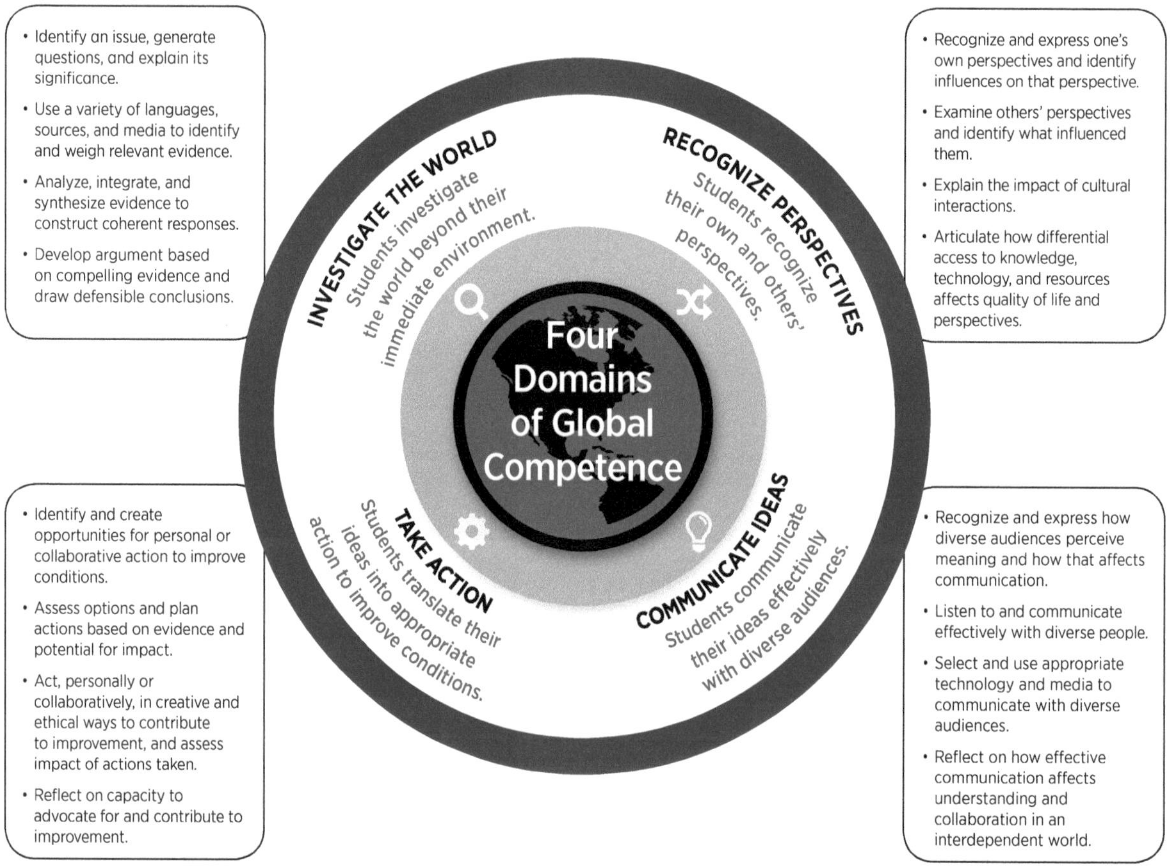

- Identify an issue, generate questions, and explain its significance.
- Use a variety of languages, sources, and media to identify and weigh relevant evidence.
- Analyze, integrate, and synthesize evidence to construct coherent responses.
- Develop argument based on compelling evidence and draw defensible conclusions.

INVESTIGATE THE WORLD — Students investigate the world beyond their immediate environment.

- Recognize and express one's own perspectives and identify influences on that perspective.
- Examine others' perspectives and identify what influenced them.
- Explain the impact of cultural interactions.
- Articulate how differential access to knowledge, technology, and resources affects quality of life and perspectives.

RECOGNIZE PERSPECTIVES — Students recognize their own and others' perspectives.

Four Domains of Global Competence

- Identify and create opportunities for personal or collaborative action to improve conditions.
- Assess options and plan actions based on evidence and potential for impact.
- Act, personally or collaboratively, in creative and ethical ways to contribute to improvement, and assess impact of actions taken.
- Reflect on capacity to advocate for and contribute to improvement.

TAKE ACTION — Students translate their ideas into appropriate action to improve conditions.

COMMUNICATE IDEAS — Students communicate their ideas effectively with diverse audiences.

- Recognize and express how diverse audiences perceive meaning and how that affects communication.
- Listen to and communicate effectively with diverse people.
- Select and use appropriate technology and media to communicate with diverse audiences.
- Reflect on how effective communication affects understanding and collaboration in an interdependent world.

Source: Boix Mansilla and Jackson (2011). © Asia Society. Reprinted with permission from Asia Society.

The nine-chapter *Educating for Global Competence: Preparing Our Youth to Engage the World* publication offers detailed insights into application of the model, including a chapter on each of the four learning outcomes (Boix Mansilla and Jackson 2011). With an emphasis on primary and secondary education, each chapter offers sample activities and resources for teachers. Additional chapters address schoolwide approaches and public policy recommendations. The appendix demonstrates how these four learning outcomes can be applied to science, math, art, language, world languages, and social studies.

Core Concepts of Global Competence

As the models depicted above demonstrate—and as Lilley, Barker, and Harris (2017) found in their survey of experts' use of key terminology—whether the term "global competence," "global citizenship," "intercultural competence," or another is used, the constructs behind the terms have some underlying similarities. While the constructs are not identical, they are interrelated. In a review of the literature on these overlapping areas, including the four models presented in this chapter, several core ideas emerge:

Global competence is relevant to everyone. It is widely asserted that all people should have the opportunity to develop global competence. Further, it is argued that even though many people will live and work in their home community (as opposed to living in another country), there is always a need for global competence because the local and global are inescapably intertwined (Boix Mansilla and Jackson 2011; Green 2012; Harris 2014).

Global competence requires the development of knowledge, skills, and attitudes. There is broad agreement in the literature that the development of global competence requires students to develop their knowledge, skills, and attitudes. Knowledge should include an understanding of local, national, and global systems; an understanding of the interdependence of local and global concerns; and an understanding of the underlying power dynamics (United Nations Educational, Scientific and Cultural Organization 2015). Knowledge may also include insight into global issues (e.g., environmental sustainability, human rights, etc.), intercultural communications, and the role that social and political institutions play in society (OECD 2016).

Beyond knowledge, individuals must learn and practice intercultural skills to be able to navigate across cultures, analyze cultural dynamics, reflect critically on themselves, and engage with the community (Kahn and Agnew 2017). Students need "a meta-level ability to recognize and analyze (cross-cultural) patterns and relationships" that they can apply in diverse cultural settings (Punteney 2016, 140). Key intercultural skills may include foreign language skills, communication skills, the ability to reason with information, the ability to examine a topic from multiple perspectives, and conflict resolution skills (OECD 2016).

To use their knowledge and skills effectively, individuals must develop attitudes of curiosity, humility, respect for others, commitment to collaboration, and more (Asia Society and OECD 2018; Deardorff 2006; Murray-Garcia and Tervalon 2017; Piacentini 2017; Punteney 2016; United Nations Educational, Scientific and Cultural Organization 2015). Fantini's (2009) research has identified eight attitudes exhibited by those who are interculturally competent: empathy, openness, patience, curiosity, flexibility, suspended judgment, tolerance for ambiguity, and humor (Arasaratnam-Smith 2017; Fantini 2009). Emphasizing empathy and cultural sensitivity, Goren and Yemini (2017) suggest that humanistic values underlie the attitudinal component of global competence. Kahn and Agnew (2017, 54) concur, suggesting that it is important for students to "go beyond an academic analysis…to [understanding] what it means to be human in a particular time and place."

Global competence embraces the intersectionality of identity. There is general consensus in the field that the reference to cultures within all of the constructs can comprise many types of cultures, including "ethnic and national cultures, and also religious, linguistic, gender, socio-economic, regional, and organizational cultures," among others (Punteney 2016, 139). Each individual belongs to multiple cultures and groups concurrently. Individuals' various identities and group memberships hold more or less salience in their sense of self at a particular point in time, depending on the context. People identify with not just one identity, but with multiple identities simultaneously. This is known as the "intersectionality of identity" (OECD 2016; Punteney 2016, 2017; Wijeyesinghe 2012).

Global competence involves a sense of self-awareness. Scholars across the literature concur that having global competence means being aware of one's own biases and perceptions, as well as one's impact on the world and other individuals. This is explicit in Oxfam's definition of a "global citizen" above and widely discussed in research and practice. In Deardorff's (2006) study, self-awareness of one's own culture was one of the three elements most commonly cited as essential, along with awareness/knowledge of other cultures and intercultural experience.

Global competence promotes effective and appropriate responses. Not only does global competence help individuals achieve their aims in an intercultural interaction (effectiveness), the literature acknowledges that global competence is demonstrated by achieving aims in a way that others consider appropriate (Arasaratnam-Smith 2017; Deardorff 2006; Murray-Garcia and Tervalon 2017). Effectiveness and appropriateness are essential for global competence and cross-cultural relationship building. This is made explicit in both the intercultural competence and global competence definitions shared earlier in this chapter.

Global competence directs ethical and social responsibility. Many recent definitions of global competence, such as those cited from OECD and Oxfam, have incorporated the idea that an individual with global competence has both the inclination and responsibility to contribute to global society in positive ways. Some authors argue that issues of power and inequity must be understood and must guide actions for true global competence (Andreotti, Biesta, and Ahenakew 2015; Green 2012; Killick 2018; Lucas and Blair 2017; Mannion et al. 2011; Paracka and Pynn 2017; Punteney 2017; United Nations Educational, Scientific and Cultural Organization 2015).

Global competence is a lifelong learning process. Another core idea that is endorsed throughout the literature is that the development of global competence is a lifelong process. It is not something that can happen in a single course, or even over multiple years of study. It is not as simple as having it or not having it. In fact, given the multiplicity of cultures that exist and the ways in which they are always evolving, global competence is something that can never be fully achieved. Instead, it is a lifelong developmental process with both gains and losses in learning (Arasaratnam-Smith 2017; Blair 2017; Deardorff 2015; Harris 2014; Lucas and Blair 2017; Murray-Garcia and Tervalon 2017).

Assessment of Global Competence

As discussed in chapter 1, "Trends in International Education," there is an increasing emphasis on assessment, and international educators are being asked to "prove" the impact of their programs. This requires measuring and documenting students' learning outcomes. On a pragmatic level, this documentation is needed for both accreditation purposes and to advocate for funding (Hudzik 2015). Pedagogically, the assessment of learning can improve the quality of learning and the quality of teaching by informing both the student and the instructor of the progress made by the student (Deardorff 2017). Additionally, looking at the assessments for a group of students offers insights into the effectiveness of particular pedagogies and learning activities, helping to shape future iterations of courses or identify promising practices that can be applied in other settings.

Assessments of Student Learning and Programs

In the quest to develop students' global competence, two types of assessment are important: (a) assessment of student learning, and (b) program assessment. Assessment of student learning determines the extent of what individual students have learned and provides feedback to individual students (and their instructors) on their learning progress and areas that need improvement. It is important to reiterate here that global competence is a lifelong learning process. Thus, the assessment of student learning does not result in a "yes" or "no" answer about whether or not the student is globally competent; instead, the degree of competence in particular areas is assessed. This type of assessment helps the individual student and the instructor guide the student's studies in the most needed directions. Deardorff (2017) argues that students should not be passive recipients of the assessment results but, rather, they should be actively engaged, along with the instructor, in conducting the assessment in order to maximize their learning.

In contrast to the assessment of student learning, program assessment determines the extent to which the program has achieved its intended outcomes. At its simplest level, program assessment may simply be looking at the assessment of learning of a whole cohort of students. For example, an elementary school teacher may teach students the names of countries in Latin America and assess individual learning with a map quiz. When the instructor looks at each individual student's quiz and gives feedback to help the student identify areas of success and areas for continued learning, that is considered to be assessment of student learning. Conversely, when the teacher looks at all of the students' quizzes collectively and determines whether the teaching methodologies used were effective and whether the class as a whole is ready to go on to the next topic, that is program assessment. It tells the teacher to what extent the goals of the curriculum module were met.

Of course, program assessment can go beyond the sum total of students' individual learning. For example, if that map lesson was part of an after-school program with the goal of encouraging more low-income youths to develop global competence, then assessment of the after-school program could go beyond measuring students' map-labeling abilities and could measure those students' attitudes toward other cultures, the number of past participants taking language courses in high school, and perhaps even track the college majors they study a decade or more later.

Process of Assessment

To assess the extent to which an institution is helping its graduates develop global competence, an assessment team should be formed. The team should include broad representation from across the organization, including faculty, staff, assessment experts, and institutional researchers (Green 2013). Students may also be included. Organizing inclusive campuswide discussions of the assessment of global competence will encourage more community members to actively engage not only in the assessment efforts, but in advancing and supporting new efforts to develop global competence (Green 2013). A quality assessment effort must be multidimensional, multiperspective, ongoing, integrated into the program, aligned at all levels, and intentional (Deardorff 2006; Fantini 2009).

The process of assessment must begin by articulating the student learning outcomes that the program (or institution) hopes to achieve. Chapter 4, "Education Abroad," describes the process of developing measurable student learning outcomes (whether for study abroad or any other type of program). Outcomes should be realistic and perceptible and, to the degree possible, aligned with the larger institutional mission. A survey conducted by the International Association of Universities in 2013 found that 57 percent of universities have established, or are establishing, global learning outcomes that they will be able to assess (Egron-Polak and Hudson 2014). In the United States, 64 percent of institutions have articulated global learning outcomes for some or all students (Helms and Brajkovic 2017).

After establishing the desired outcomes, student learning must be measured before, during, and after the learning is expected to take place. These assessments may be formative or summative. Formative assessments are conducted partway through the learning process to see what progress has been made and to allow time for modification of the learning process; examples include journaling and projects due throughout the course. Summative assessment takes place at the end of, or after, a course or program and usually makes a judgment about whether the student has learned enough to satisfactorily complete the module, course, or program; examples include

Global Competence Assessment Tools

Fantini (2009) identifies more than 40 existing tools for measuring intercultural and global competence. Some of the most commonly used tools are listed below.

TABLE 2 Measurement Tools for Intercultural and Global Competence

AAC&U VALUE Rubrics	The Association of American Colleges & Universities (AAC&U) has 16 rubrics to assess undergraduate learning, including one on *global learning* and one on *intercultural knowledge and competence*. www.aacu.org/value-rubrics
ACTFL Proficiency Scale and Guidelines	The American Council on the Teaching of Foreign Languages (ACTFL) rubrics help to assess an individual's *foreign language competence* in listening, speaking, reading, and writing. The ACTFL Oral Proficiency Interview (OPI) is often used by trained examiners to test students' speaking and listening abilities. www.actfl.org/publications/guidelines-and-manuals
Beliefs, Events, and Values Inventory (BEVI)	BEVI assesses an individual's *degree of openness to transformative international education experiences*, based on an equilintegration theory that explains how beliefs, values, and worldviews are established and revised. thebevi.com
Cross-Cultural Adaptability Inventory (CCAI)	The CCAI survey tool measures an individual's *potential for cross-cultural adaptability*, based on the idea that there are common feelings, experiences, and perceptions among those who are adapting to other cultures. ccaiassess.com
Global Perspectives Inventory (GPI)	The GPI self-report survey focuses questions on three areas of intercultural learning: cognitive, interpersonal, and intrapersonal. The GPI measures the degree to which the individual has a *global perspective*. www.gpi.hs.iastate.edu
Intercultural Conflict Style Inventory (ICS)	The ICS survey, available in multiple languages, assesses an individual's approach to *communicating, resolving conflicts, and solving problems*. The ICS concentrates on the degree to which communication is direct or indirect and emotionally restrained or expressive. icsinventory.com
Intercultural Development Inventory (IDI)	The IDI survey measures groups' and individuals' *intercultural competence* along a developmental spectrum based on the Developmental Model of Intercultural Sensitivity. The IDI is facilitated by trained administrators and available in multiple languages. Extensive statistical testing for reliability and validity has been conducted. idiinventory.com

final exams and cumulative papers. Summative assessment can also help to determine if the overall program was effective in meeting its goals. Other assessments may be used in addition to the course assignments, such as surveys or tests of language proficiency. Whatever form they take, it is essential that the assessments align with the learning outcomes. If they do not, the assessments will be useless for determining what learning, if any, was accomplished.

While organizations can use their own instruments to assess their students' global competence, it can often be more efficient to use an existing tool. Many of the established tools, typically surveys, have the advantage of having gone through years of refinement as well as statistical validation of the assessments. Well-established survey instruments can allow for comparative analysis of program effectiveness with the large data set of past responses already gathered (Lucas and Blair 2017). International educators should consider the following questions when evaluating assessment tools (Deardorff 2006; Fantini 2009):

- Does the tool measure the thing you are trying to measure?
- Does use of the tool improve your overall assessment plan?
- Does the tool have a theoretical foundation?
- Does the tool have a cultural bias, limiting its effective use to one ethnic or national group?
- Is the tool appropriate for the age/developmental level of the students?
- Do you have the resources to use the tool (i.e., financial resources and time to gain access to the tool, train assessors, conduct the assessment, analyze the results, and use the results to inform the program and teaching)?

Professional associations such as NAFSA: Association of International Educators and The Forum on Education Abroad, as well as numerous accreditation agencies, offer useful guidelines for the assessment process (Lucas and Blair 2017).

Assessment Principles

A review of the literature on the assessment of global competence (and related topics) identifies some common principles that should guide the assessment process.

Assessment should be organization specific. There is no single best way to conduct assessment. Instead, each institutional assessment team must find its own way of approaching assessment, based on factors such as size, control, mission, priorities, available resources, and other elements (Green 2013). Each organization must decide which concepts (i.e., global competence, intercultural competence, etc.) it is using and select the definitions that will be used, so that the organization's efforts are focused and the stakeholders are working in alignment (Deardorff 2017). Failure to define the concepts in advance may result in the assessment team not being able to clearly define evidence of learning, which, in turn, makes it difficult to choose the assessment tools that are the best fit (Gregersen-Hermans 2017).

Assessment design should be an iterative process. The assessment plan should be developed at the same time as the program design and should measure the learning outcomes identified in the program design. This is an iterative process in that the assessment plan will need multiple revisions. It is necessary to go back and forth between working on the program design and the assessment plan because further thinking on each helps to refine the other. As each round of assessment is completed, the assessment plan and process are refined based on what was effective and what was not.

Assessment should be cyclical. Collecting data is a waste of time and resources if the data are not analyzed or if the conclusions are not used to refine the curriculum and teaching methods (Deardorff 2017). As curricular or program changes are made based on assessment evidence, new or repeated assessments will need to be undertaken to determine the effectiveness of those changes. It is an ongoing cycle of continuous improvement (Green 2013). For the cyclical process of design and assessment, the conclusions should result in refinement of the program; and with ongoing cycles of assessment, the conclusions can determine the extent to which the changes supported or hindered achievement of the desired program learning outcomes. The insights gained from both levels of assessment should be shared by the assessment team across the institution and, depending on the scope, in the literature. Lucas and Blair (2017) encourage international educators to publish their assessment results to help advance the field.

Assessment should be focused. As discussed earlier in the chapter, global competence is a complex topic with many facets. Assessing each element is unreasonable in terms of the time and resources it would take. Thus, the assessment team should focus on two to three priority areas for assessment (Green 2013; Lucas and Blair 2017). These priority areas should be directly related to the program's (or institution's) student learning outcomes (Deardorff 2017; Lucas and Blair 2017).

There are limits to self-reporting assessments. Surveys asking students to rate their own learning or growth are commonly used in international education. In particular, pre- and post-surveys are often used at the beginning and end of the program, asking students to report on their knowledge, skills, and attitudes. Changes in a student's responses from pre to post are considered as evidence of learning. Unfortunately, people are notoriously poor at self-assessing, leading to questions about the validity and potential biases of this assessment method (Deardorff 2017; Lucas and Blair 2017). The pre-post model also does not allow for any formative assessment, which means that students do not have the opportunity to use the feedback to improve their learning.

Assessment methods should be triangulated. An important way to ensure the validity of the assessment is to use multiple tools and to measure multiple types of evidence. This helps to make sure that the conclusions of the assessment are robust and representative of what is being measured. Ideally, the assessment should include elements that are both direct and indirect, formative and summative; it should focus on individual students and focus on the program as a whole; and it should examine particular moments in time as well as change over time (Deardorff 2017; Lucas and Blair 2017). The tools used for assessment must be a fit for what the team is trying to measure (Deardorff 2017).

PISA Assessment of Global Competence

The Programme for International Student Assessment (PISA) is an international exam that tests the skills and knowledge of 15-year-olds worldwide. The test is conducted every 3 years, with more than a half million students in over 70 countries taking the exam. Students have been assessed in science, mathematics, reading, collaborative problem-solving, and financial literacy. The data are used by national educational systems to shape and strengthen their educational offerings (OECD 2018; Piacentini 2017).

For the 2018 test, PISA added an assessment of global competence. It is an unusual approach to assessment because it is comparative, while also emphasizing attitudes and values. The assessment of global competence has two components: (a) a cognitive test, and (b) a series of questionnaires completed by students, principals, teachers, and parents. For the one-hour cognitive test, students work on several short scenarios. Students are evaluated on their ability to reason with information, analyze conflicting perspectives and views, understand differences in communication, and evaluate actions and consequences. Students should be able to demonstrate that they recognize stereotypical and inappropriate communication.

The questionnaires focus on self-reported knowledge, skills, and attitudes. Students are asked about their level of familiarity with global issues, language skills, interest in other cultures, opportunities in school to learn about other cultures, etc. Parent and teacher questionnaires ask about beliefs regarding curriculum, school policies, and diversity and inclusion at their child's school (Piacentini 2017, 509).

It is hoped that the PISA results will provide national-level insights into education policies, teaching methods, and teacher training. Additionally, individual schools will be able to get feedback on how they can improve their approaches to the teaching of global competence (Piacentini 2017).

Considerations for Global Competence Education

According to the literature on global competence education, there are several areas that international education professionals should be aware of as they consider their conceptualization of global competence.

Relativism and Activism

International educators strive to teach students to appreciate cultures other than their own, recognizing that differences are culturally relevant. That is, the values and practices of another culture should not be evaluated as "right" or "wrong" or "better" or "worse" than what the students are used to in their own cultures. Instead, students are encouraged to recognize that cultural values and practices emerge from the specific history, climate, politics, and other contextual factors of the other culture. In other words, the other culture's way of doing things is not wrong, it is simply rooted in a context that the students do not understand yet. International educators should push students to explore their emotional reactions to the unfamiliar and to broaden their perspectives by seeking to understand other cultural perspectives.

As highlighted by the Developmental Model of Intercultural Sensitivity (see figure 1 and table 1), cultural relativism is a fundamental outlook for those individuals whose global competence is well developed. Yet, many scholars argue that it is not sufficient on its own. They point out that, taken too far, nothing is deemed unacceptable (OECD 2016). They question what a student should do when encountering human rights violations, for example. Should the student merely conclude that these violations are not wrong because it is another culture? Or should the student decry the offense as universally unacceptable? Or something in between? Lucas and Blair (2017) suggest that educators must constantly monitor the balance between appreciating, tolerating, and criticizing other cultures. They insist that educators must help students grapple with the dilemma of identifying when something is simply different, when it is actually bad, and when it is complicated. Punteney (2016, 143) adds, "students will need to wrestle with their consciences, making decisions about when to accept differences as culturally relative and neither good nor bad, when to draw moral lines, and how to work for social change within the inequities of society."

While many international education programs appropriately put great emphasis on teaching cultural relativism, scholars are also increasingly arguing that taking action is a fundamental social responsibility and an intrinsic part of global competence. The notion of action is included in many of the definitions and models introduced earlier in the chapter. Many scholars profess that globally competent individuals have not only the knowledge and skills to act, but also the commitment (attitude) to making a positive impact globally. Accordingly, globally competent students are often expected to be engaged in social activism of some sort.

Despite this theoretical commitment to social change, there is disagreement about whether schools and universities are the place to teach such values (Lilley, Barker, and Harris 2014). Educators and educational organizations are often reluctant to be seen as imposing values on students, leaving the activism element of global competence often underdeveloped in the curriculum. One solution is to develop a curriculum that asks students to explore and clarify their own values, while trying not to influence what those values entail (Lilley, Barker, and Harris 2015).

Western Bias

Many scholars point out that the concept of global competence appears to reflect a Western bias. Kahn and Agnew (2017, 53) maintain that concepts such as global competence are rooted in "specific historical and sociopolitical moments" and that they, therefore, are a product of the context in which they are developed, rather than conceptualizations shared globally across diverse cultures. Furthermore, Arasaratnam-Smith (2017) observes that most of the research on the subject is conducted in the West, conducted in English, and conducted in societies where technology is abundant, shaping how people think about the topic.

Also reflecting a Western bias, the focus on "competence" emphasizes individual skills prioritized by results-oriented individualistic cultures, while downplaying emphasis on relationship building and group harmony, which are dominant values of more collectivist (group-oriented) cultures (Arasaratnam-Smith 2017; Mannion et al. 2011; OECD 2016; Punteney 2016). Goren and Yemini (2017) have found that local cultures often adapt the imported concepts of intercultural competence, global competence, global citizenship, etc., to fit their local contexts. Goren and Yemini (2017) warn that in many countries, curricular efforts aimed at developing graduates' global competence may focus almost exclusively on students learning the English language.

Assessment Challenges

Another key consideration is that many international educators have limited training in assessment methodology (Deardorff 2017). Even those who do have the training often find that they have so many other demands on their time that it is difficult to prioritize assessment. Given the limitations of time and training, assessment efforts sometimes lack clarity of thought and purpose. To overcome this, assessment teams must determine whether they are focused on assessing individual student learning or the program as a whole (Deardorff 2017). Teams must identify the definitions and theoretical models with which they are working and the specific aspects of global competence they are seeking to assess. They must be certain that the data they are collecting actually represent the concepts they are trying to assess and that the methods of analysis are sound (Deardorff 2017). Finally, the assessment findings must result in tangible actions to improve student learning. To the extent that there is a lack of clarity around the assessment purposes and procedures, the findings will likely be muddled or misleading.

Need for More Substantive Efforts

A final consideration regarding global competence education is that efforts may be based more in rhetoric than reality. While global competence and its related terms are increasingly discussed in education, they are sometimes utilized in practice without in-depth explorations of the concepts (Goren and Yemini 2017). Aktas et al. (2017) analyzed the global citizenship programs at 24 universities. The programs ranged in scope, with some offering courses, some offering certificates, and some offering bachelor's degrees. The programs ranged in length from 1 semester to 4 years. Aktas et al. (2017) found that:

- 25 percent of the programs required international travel;
- 29 percent of the programs required foreign language study, though usually at superficial levels;
- 71 percent of the programs focused on both local and global engagement, with service-learning as the most common form of engagement; and
- Program learning outcomes focused on self-reflection (75 percent), social responsibility (67 percent), employability (58 percent), leadership (38 percent), problem-solving (33 percent), and entrepreneurship (8 percent).

Finding some of the programs' required amounts of engagement to be modest, Aktas et al. (2017) concluded that there is a risk that some programs are too limited, in length or depth, to be transformative. The abstract nature of global competence can often make it difficult to create effective curricula (Harris 2014). Without an investment of resources, in both time and money, it is likely that there will be a lot of talk without action. Thoughtful and rigorous program design and assessment are needed to support the development of globally competent graduates.

Conclusion

International educators have an obligation to ensure that their students are developing global competence. While there is ongoing debate about the terms and definitions to use, scholars have established several theoretical models to identify core concepts for the development of global competence and ways to measure and assess student learning. Clearly articulating what students should learn, and measuring their learning, allows educators to improve their curricula as well as advocate for the importance of their programs. International educators can use assessment data to demonstrate how incorporating global learning into any and all levels of education is likely to ensure that students are educationally prepared for the job market, citizens are able to be informed and engaged in governance, peace and understanding prosper in diverse societies, complex global challenges can be addressed, and nations remain economically competitive.

Chapter 3, "Internationalization," builds on the discussion of global competence by examining how global competence education is approached within universities under larger institutional internationalization strategies. From chapter 4 onward, the book explores the ways in which global competence is developed within the practice of particular sectors of the international education field.

Resources

READINGS:

- Boix Mansilla, Veronica, and Anthony Jackson. 2011. *Educating for Global Competence: Preparing Our Youth to Engage the World.* New York, NY: Asia Society and Council of Chief State School Officers. https://asiasociety.org/files/book-globalcompetence.pdf.

- Deardorff, Darla K. 2015. *Demystifying Outcomes Assessment for International Educators: A Practical Approach.* Sterling, VA: Stylus Publishing.

- Deardorff, Darla K., and Lily A. Arasaratnam-Smith, eds. 2017. *Intercultural Competence in Higher Education: International Approaches, Assessment and Application.* London, United Kingdom: Routledge.

- Green, Madeleine F. 2013. *Improving and Assessing Global Learning.* Washington, DC: NAFSA: Association of International Educators.

- Lucas, James M., and Scott G. Blair. 2017. "Learning Outcomes and Assessment." In *Learning Across Cultures: Locally and Globally, Third Edition*, eds. Barbara Kappler Mikk and Inge Ellen Steglitz. Washington, DC: NAFSA: Association of International Educators and Stylus Publishing.

- Organisation for Economic Co-operation and Development (OECD). 2018. *Preparing Our Youth for an Inclusive and Sustainable World: The OECD PISA Global Competence Framework.* Paris, France: Organisation for Economic Co-operation and Development. https://www.oecd.org/education/Global-competency-for-an-inclusive-world.pdf.

- United Nations Educational, Scientific and Cultural Organization (UNESCO). 2015. *Global Citizenship Education: Topics and Learning Outcomes.* Paris, France: United Nations Educational, Scientific and Cultural Organization. http://unesdoc.unesco.org/images/0023/002329/232993e.pdf.

References

Aktas, Fatih, Kate Pitts, Jessica C. Richards, and Iveta Silova. 2017. "Institutionalizing Global Citizenship: A Critical Analysis of Higher Education Programs and Curricula." *Journal of Studies in International Education* 21, 1:65–80. https://doi.org/10.1177/1028315316669815.

American Council on the Teaching of Foreign Languages (ACTFL). n.d. "What the Research Shows." Alexandria, VA: American Council on the Teaching of Foreign Languages. https://www.actfl.org/advocacy/what-the-research-shows.

Andreotti, Vanessa. 2006. "Soft Versus Critical Global Citizenship Education." *Policy & Practice: A Development Education Review* 3:40–51.

Andreotti, Vanessa, Gert Biesta, and Cash Ahenakew. 2015. "Between the Nation and the Globe: Education for Global Mindedness in Finland." *Globalisation, Societies and Education* 13, 2:246–259. https://doi.org/10.1080/14767724.2014.934073.

Arasaratnam-Smith, Lily A. 2017. "Intercultural Competence: An Overview." In *Intercultural Competence in Higher Education: International Approaches, Assessment and Application*, eds. Darla K. Deardorff and Lily A. Arasaratnam-Smith. London, United Kingdom: Routledge.

Asia Society and OECD. 2018. *Teaching for Global Competence in a Rapidly Changing World*. Asia Society and OECD. https://asiasociety.org/education/teaching-global-competence-rapidly-changing-world.

Association of American Colleges & Universities (AAC&U). 2009. "Intercultural Knowledge and Competence VALUE Rubric." Washington, DC: Association of American Colleges & Universities. https://www.aacu.org/value/rubrics/intercultural-knowledge.

Association of American Colleges & Universities (AAC&U). 2014. "Global Learning VALUE Rubric." Washington, DC: Association of American Colleges & Universities. https://www.aacu.org/value/rubrics/global.

Bennett, Milton J. 1986. "A Developmental Approach to Training for Intercultural Sensitivity." *International Journal of Intercultural Relations*, Special Issue: Theories and Methods in Cross-Cultural Orientation 10, 2:179–196. https://doi.org/10.1016/0147-1767(86)90005-2.

Blair, Scott G. 2017. "Mapping Intercultural Competence: Aligning Goals, Outcomes, Evidence, Rubrics, and Assessment." In *Intercultural Competence in Higher Education: International Approaches, Assessment and Application*, eds. Darla K. Deardorff and Lily A. Arasaratnam-Smith. London, United Kingdom: Routledge.

Boix Mansilla, Veronica, and Anthony Jackson. 2011. *Educating for Global Competence: Preparing Our Youth to Engage the World*. New York, NY: Asia Society and Council of Chief State School Officers. https://asiasociety.org/files/book-globalcompetence.pdf.

Byram, Michael. 1997. *Teaching and Assessing Intercultural Communicative Competence*. Philadelphia, PA: Multilingual Matters.

Cushman, Jenifer. 2013. "Juniata College: Assessing Global Learning: Lessons from the Field." In *Improving and Assessing Global Learning*, by Madeleine F. Green. Washington, DC: NAFSA: Association of International Educators.

Deardorff, Darla K. 2006. "Identification and Assessment of Intercultural Competence as a Student Outcome of Internationalization." *Journal of Studies in International Education* 10, 3:241–266. https://doi.org/10.1177/1028315306287002.

Deardorff, Darla K. 2015. *Demystifying Outcomes Assessment for International Educators: A Practical Approach*. Sterling, VA: Stylus Publishing.

Deardorff, Darla K. 2017. "The Big Picture of Intercultural Competence Assessment." In *Intercultural Competence in Higher Education: International Approaches, Assessment and Application*, eds. Darla K. Deardorff and Lily A. Arasaratnam-Smith. London, United Kingdom: Routledge.

Egron-Polak, Eva, and Ross Hudson. 2014. *Internationalization of Higher Education: Growing Expectations, Fundamental Values*. IAU 4th Global Survey. Paris, France: International Association of Universities.

Fantini, Alvino. 2009. "Assessing Intercultural Competence: Issues and Tools." In *The SAGE Handbook of Intercultural Competence*, ed. Darla K. Deardorff. Thousand Oaks, CA: Sage Publications.

Goren, Heela, and Miri Yemini. 2017. "Global Citizenship Education Redefined – A Systematic Review of Empirical Studies on Global Citizenship Education." *International Journal of Educational Research* 82 Supplement C:170–183. https://doi.org/10.1016/j.ijer.2017.02.004.

Green, Madeleine F. 2012. "Global Citizenship: What Are We Talking about and Why Does It Matter?" *Trends & Insights*. Washington, DC: NAFSA: Association for International Educators.

Green, Madeleine F. 2013. *Improving and Assessing Global Learning*. Washington, DC: NAFSA: Association of International Educators.

Gregersen-Hermans, Jeanine. 2017. "Intercultural Competence Development in Higher Education." In *Intercultural Competence in Higher Education: International Approaches, Assessment and Application*, eds. Darla K. Deardorff and Lily A. Arasaratnam-Smith. London, United Kingdom: Routledge.

Harris, Anita. 2014. "Generation G, Global Connectedness & Global Responsibility." International Education Association of Australia. https://www.ieaa.org.au/documents/item/292.

Hayden, Mary. 2006. *Introduction to International Education: International Schools and Their Communities*. London, United Kingdom: Sage Publications.

Hayden, Mary, and Jeff Thompson. 2008. *International Schools: Growth and Influence*. Paris, France: UNESCO: International Schools: Growth and Influence. http://unesdoc.unesco.org/images/0018/001803/180396e.pdf.

Helms, Robin Matross, and Lucia Brajkovic. 2017. *Mapping Internationalization on U.S. Campuses: 2017 Edition*. Washington, DC: American Council on Education. https://www.acenet.edu/news-room/Documents/Mapping-Internationalization-2017.pdf.

Hoffa, William W. 2007. *A History of U.S. Study Abroad: Beginnings to 1965*. Carlisle, PA: Frontiers: The Interdisciplinary Journal of Study Abroad and The Forum on Education Abroad.

Hudzik, John K., ed. 2015. *Comprehensive Internationalization: Institutional Pathways to Success*. London, United Kingdom: Routledge.

Institute of International Education. 2018. "Project Atlas 2018 Infographics." Institute of International Education. https://www.iie.org/en/Research-and-Insights/Project-Atlas/Explore-Data/Current-Infographics.

Kahn, Hilary E., and Melanie Agnew. 2017. "Global Learning Through Difference: Considerations for Teaching, Learning, and the Internationalization of Higher Education." *Journal of Studies in International Education* 21, 1:52–64. https://doi.org/10.1177/1028315315622022.

Killick, David. 2018. *Developing Intercultural Practice*. New York, NY: Routledge.

Leeman, Y. A. M. 2003. "School Leadership for Intercultural Education." *Intercultural Education* 14, 1:31–45. https://doi.org/10.1080/1467598032000044638.

Lilley, Kathleen, Michelle Barker, and Neil Harris. 2014. "Exploring the Process of Global Citizen Learning and the Student Mind-Set." *Journal of Studies in International Education* 19, 3:225–245. https://doi.org/10.1177/1028315314547822.

Lilley, Kathleen, Michelle Barker, and Neil Harris. 2015. "Educating Global Citizens: A Good 'Idea' or an Organisational Practice?" *Higher Education Research & Development* 34, 5:957–971. https://doi.org/10.1080/07294360.2015.1011089.

Lilley, Kathleen, Michelle Barker, and Neil Harris. 2017. "The Global Citizen Conceptualized: Accommodating Ambiguity." *Journal of Studies in International Education* 21, 1:6–21. https://doi.org/10.1177/1028315316637354.

Lucas, James M., and Scott G. Blair. 2017. "Learning Outcomes and Assessment." In *Learning Across Cultures: Locally and Globally, Third Edition*, eds. Barbara Kappler Mikk and Inge Ellen Steglitz. Washington, DC: NAFSA: Association of International Educators and Stylus Publishing.

Mannion, Greg, Gert Biesta, Mark Priestley, and Hamish Ross. 2011. "The Global Dimension in Education and Education for Global Citizenship: Genealogy and Critique." *Globalisation, Societies and Education* 9, 3–4:443–456. https://doi.org/10.1080/14767724.2011.605327.

Marshall, Harriet. 2011. "Instrumentalism, Ideals and Imaginaries: Theorising the Contested Space of Global Citizenship Education in Schools." *Globalisation, Societies and Education* 9, 3–4:411–426. https://doi.org/10.1080/14767724.2011.605325.

Murray-Garcia, Jann, and Melanie Tervalon. 2017. "Rethinking Intercultural Competence: Cultural Humility in Internationalising Higher Education." In *Intercultural Competence in Higher Education: International Approaches, Assessment and Application*, eds. Darla K. Deardorff and Lily A. Arasaratnam-Smith. London, United Kingdom: Routledge.

National Education Association (NEA). 2010. "Global Competence Is a 21st Century Imperative." Washington, DC: National Education Association.

Organisation for Economic Co-operation and Development (OECD). 2016. *Global Competency for an Inclusive World*. Paris, France: Organisation for Economic Co-operation and Development.

Organisation for Economic Co-operation and Development (OECD). 2018. *Preparing Our Youth for an Inclusive and Sustainable World: The OECD PISA Global Competence Framework*. Paris, France: Organisation for Economic Co-operation and Development. https://www.oecd.org/education/Global-competency-for-an-inclusive-world.pdf.

Oxfam. n.d. "What Is Global Citizenship?" Oxford, United Kingdom: Oxfam. https://www.oxfam.org.uk/education/who-we-are/what-is-global-citizenship.

Oxley, Laura, and Paul Morris. 2013. "Global Citizenship: A Typology for Distinguishing its Multiple Conceptions." *British Journal of Educational Studies* 61, 3:301–325. https://doi.org/10.1080/00071005.2013.798393.

Paracka, Daniel J., and Lily A. Pynn. 2017. "Towards Transformative Reciprocity: Mapping the Intersectionality of Intercultural Competence." In *Intercultural Competence in Higher Education: International Approaches, Assessment and Application*, eds. Darla K. Deardorff and Lily A. Arasaratnam-Smith. London, United Kingdom: Routledge.

Piacentini, Mario. 2017. "Developing an International Assessment of Global Competence." *Childhood Education* 93, 6:507–510. https://doi.org/10.1080/00094056.2017.1398564.

Punteney, Katherine. 2016. "Deliberations on the Development of an Intercultural Competence Curriculum." *Intercultural Education* 27, 2:137–50. https://doi.org/10.1080/14675986.2016.1145457.

Punteney, Katherine. 2017. "Social Psychology in Intercultural Contexts." In *Learning Across Cultures: Locally and Globally, Third Edition*, eds. Barbara Kappler Mikk and Inge Ellen Steglitz. Washington, DC: NAFSA: Association of International Educators and Stylus Publishing.

Schejbal, David, and George Irvine. 2009. "Global Competencies, Liberal Studies, and the Needs of Employers." *Continuing Higher Education Review* 70:125–142.

Schwarzer, David, and Beatrice L. Bridglall, eds. 2015. *Promoting Global Competence and Social Justice in Teacher Education: Successes and Challenges Within Local and International Contexts*. Lanham, MD: Lexington Books.

Standish, Alex. 2014. "What Is Global Education and Where Is It Taking Us?" *The Curriculum Journal* 25, 2:166–186. https://doi.org/10.1080/09585176.2013.870081.

Stewart, Vivien. 2012. *A World-Class Education: Learning from International Models of Excellence and Innovation*. Alexandria, VA: ASCD.

Suarez-Orozco, Marcelo, and Desiree B. Qin-Hilliard, eds. 2004. *Globalization: Culture and Education in the New Millennium*. Berkeley, CA: University of California Press.

United Nations Educational, Scientific and Cultural Organization (UNESCO). 2015. *Global Citizenship Education: Topics and Learning Objectives*. Paris, France: United

Nations Educational, Scientific and Cultural Organization. http://unesdoc.unesco.org/images/0023/002329/232993e.pdf.

U.S. Department of Education. 2012. "Succeeding Globally through International Education and Engagement: U.S. Department of Education International Strategy 2012–2016." Washington, DC: U.S. Department of Education.

Vega, Vanessa, and Youki Terada. 2013. "Research Supports Global Curriculum." Edutopia. January 29, 2013. https://www.edutopia.org/stw-global-competence-research.

Wijeyesinghe, Charmaine L. 2012. "The Intersectional Model of Multiracial Identity." In *New Perspectives on Racial Identity Development: Integrating Emerging Frameworks, Second Edition*, eds. Charmaine L. Wijeyesinghe and Bailey W. Jackson. New York, NY: New York University Press.

Yemini, Miri. 2014. "Internationalisation Discourse: What Remains to Be Said?" *Perspectives: Policy and Practice in Higher Education* 18, 2:66–71. https://doi.org/10.1080/13603108.2014.888019.

Chapter 3

Internationalization

Internationalization is the process of making education more international in focus. As Meda and Monnapula-Mapesela (2016, 284) point out, "internationalization is not an end in itself, but a means to an end." While definitions of internationalization are often debated and dissected (Hudzik 2015; Knight 2004, 2012), one of the definitions most commonly adopted is "the process of integrating an international, intercultural or global dimension into the purpose, functions or delivery of post-secondary education" (Knight 2004, 11). Hudzik (2018) similarly emphasizes that internationalization pervades the work of the university. He defines comprehensive internationalization as "a commitment and action to infuse international, global, and comparative content and perspective throughout the teaching, research, and services missions of higher education" (Hudzik 2018, 6). Both definitions emphasize that internationalization is a strategic, intentional process with outcomes related to global competence. Knight (2004, 2012) adds that internationalization is happening in a broad range of education-related organizations, including nonprofits, governments, and public and private universities.

While Knight's and Hudzik's definitions focus on higher education, it is important to acknowledge that internationalization of primary and secondary education is also underway. Yemini's (2014) analysis of K–12 and higher education internationalization literature concludes that internationalization at both levels is nearly identical in process and strategy. Chapter 8 of this book, "International Schools," explores internationalization of K–12 schools, while this chapter focuses primarily on higher education.

This chapter introduces some of the most common internationalization activities, including internationalization of the curriculum, internationalization of research, academic mobility, strategic partnerships, and faculty development. Then, it presents an internationalization strategic planning process, as well as the organizational and contextual factors that help to promote successful outcomes. Differences in internationalization approaches across world regions are considered, followed by a discussion of considerations for international educators engaging in internationalization.

Internationalization of Higher Education

Worldwide, as many as 87 percent of higher education institutions include within their mission statements a reference to internationalization, and 78 percent of institutions report that internationalization has been increasing in importance within their institutions, according to a 2010 survey conducted by the International Association of Universities (IAU) (Egron-Polak and Hudson 2010). A 2013 survey, also led by IAU, examined internationalization efforts at 1,336 higher education institutions in 131 countries and found that 75 percent of institutions had or were preparing an internationalization policy, and 61 percent had a dedicated budget for internationalization (Egron-Polak and Hudson 2014).

A survey by the American Council on Education (ACE) (2012) found that 51 percent of U.S. colleges and universities reference "internationalization" or "international education" in their mission statements. And according to a 2016 ACE survey of 1,164 U.S. higher education institutions, 72 percent of institutions reported that internationalization has accelerated in recent years; additionally, 30 percent of institutions reported high or very high internationalization levels, while only 11 percent of institutions reported low levels (Helms and Brajkovic 2017).

Internationalization Activities

While internationalization refers to the process, rather than the activities themselves, familiarity with some of the activities commonly enacted as part of an internationalization strategy can aid in understanding the process. Internationalization activities are sometimes loosely divided into two categories: internationalization at home (IaH) and cross-border internationalization. Internationalization at home includes all activities that take place on the home campus (e.g., offering courses with an international focus, internationally themed events, etc.). Cross-border internationalization refers to those programs in which people physically cross national boundaries (e.g., recruiting international students, scholars going overseas to conduct research, etc.). If intentionally structured and effectively facilitated, all of these activities, both at home and abroad, have the potential to develop students' intercultural skills and global competence.

Activities that many universities undertake include internationalizing the curriculum, sending students abroad, recruiting international students, hosting visiting scholars, supporting faculty international research, and establishing partnerships with international universities. Other activities that some universities may employ include establishing overseas sites, engaging with local communities, undertaking international development projects, and using technology for classroom-to-classroom connections and other forms of international engagement (Hudzik 2015). Student services, according to Knight's and Hudzik's definitions, should also be internationalized, but this is less frequently addressed in the internationalization literature (Punteney 2012).

Whatever activities an institution adopts, the effort must be holistic and involve most, if not all, parts of the university for the outcomes to be transformative for students (Meda and Monnapula-Mapesela 2016). It is particularly important for the senior leaders on campus to be committed to internationalization and to provide direction and resources to support the effort. The following sections examine specific activities that universities most commonly engage in as part of their efforts.

Internationalization of the Curriculum

Internationalization of the curriculum is one of the most impactful changes that a university can make to develop the global competence of its graduates. The 2016 ACE survey found that 56 percent of institutions were working on internationalizing the undergraduate curriculum, and 49 percent of institutions said that they require that undergraduates take at least one general education course with a global focus (Helms and Brajkovic 2017), however:

- Only 30 percent of institutions provide funding for the internationalization of courses.

- Only 34 percent of institutions have articulated global student learning outcomes for all students.

- Only 17 percent of institutions require that all undergraduates take foreign language courses.

Making the curriculum more international in scope can happen at the course, department, and/or institution level. Course-level changes can be enacted by the individual instructor by adding content on international issues and offering perspectives from authors or guest speakers from other parts of the world. Department-level changes focus on revamping the requirements for academic majors and the range of courses being offered to make sure that all graduates are able to understand their major in a global context. Institution-level changes update general education or graduation requirements, ensuring that students have substantial engagement with internationalized courses as part of their education. Institutional-level changes require commitment from both faculty and administrators (Uraneck 2002; Leask 2015; Hudzik 2015).

The process of internationalizing a course or a degree program involves evaluating the current curriculum, imagining what is possible, identifying areas for improvement, developing plans and priorities, taking action, and evaluating the results (Leask 2015). Betty Leask's "Questionnaire on Internationalization of the Curriculum" is a tool often used to guide structured reflection (see Leask [2015] for two versions of the questionnaire). Technology can also be extremely useful for internationalizing the curriculum because of the easy access to authentic, current international materials, as well as the opportunity to connect individuals, classrooms, and faculty without the financial and logistical burdens of physical travel (Ward 2016). For example, in working with the State University of New York (SUNY) Collaborative Online International Learning (COIL) center, the American Council on Education launched the Internationalization Through Technology Awards Program. This program spotlights exemplar programs in order to inspire others to use technology to enhance curriculum internationalization (Ward 2016).

It is important to acknowledge that it is more than the course materials and content that need to be internationalized; curriculum internationalization also includes reflecting on and improving teaching and learning practices (Clifford and Montgomery 2015; Green and Mertova 2016; Korhonen and Weil 2015). This may include acknowledging one's own biases, finding ways to be more inclusive of international students and others, using student-centered pedagogies, putting social justice and equity firmly within the curriculum, and more (Clifford and Montgomery 2015; Green and Mertova 2016).

Internationalization of Language Education

Foreign language education deserves particular consideration during the process of internationalization. Foreign language proficiency is essential for facilitating meaningful intercultural interactions. Yet, despite the increasing emphasis on internationalization, the Modern Language Association of America reports that U.S. enrollments in foreign languages at the higher education level declined 9.2 percent between fall 2013 and fall 2016 (Looney and Lusin 2018). The same study found that only 7.5 percent of U.S. college and university students were enrolled in foreign language courses in fall 2016, when the study was conducted, matching a low point dating back to 1980 (Looney and Lusin 2018). In fact, only 17 percent of U.S. institutions have a foreign language requirement for all of their undergraduates, while 29 percent of institutions have foreign language requirements for some students, presumably those with explicitly internationally focused majors (Helms and Brajkovic 2017). The majority of institutions requiring foreign language study for all undergraduates are bachelor's degree-focused institutions, rather than community colleges or universities with large graduate programs.

In countries where English is not the dominant language, a key focus of internationalization is often on developing graduates' skills in English so that they can engage more fully in global communications. This emphasis on the development of English skills is believed to be not only a personal benefit to the students, but also a factor in the successful economic and political engagement of the nation. For example, the *Professionals in International Education* (*PIE*) News website reports that Switzerland benefits from a 9 percent boost to its economy on the basis of its multilingual workforce (Civinini 2018). For this reason, the promotion of English language study is often a central policy strategy within government-prompted internationalization initiatives and may even result in entire programs being offered in English.

Internationalization of Research

Among higher education organizations' primary contributions to society are their research outputs, which often lead to increased understanding of global phenomena as well as new inventions and solutions to problems (Hudzik 2011; Caruson 2018). Holbrook and Caruson (2017) argue that universities and governments often have overlapping goals related to research, including:

- Preparing scientists and engineers;

- Cultivating an entrepreneurial culture;

- Creating an environment conducive to innovation and strong intellectual property protection; and

- Prioritizing sustainability initiatives that contribute to society.

There is a long history of international scientific collaboration, during the course of which researchers have engaged with international colleagues through conferences, academic and professional associations, international journals, joint publications, and research partnerships (Holbrook and Caruson 2017; Caruson 2018). In the United States, it has been the federal government's policy since the 1940s to support research and development in order to foster economic competitiveness. In addition to providing government funding for research at agencies such as the National Science Foundation and the National Institutes of Health, the U.S. government has established a system in which basic research done at universities can be disseminated freely so that applied research and innovation can follow. In this way, higher education, government, and industry are all connected through research (Jain 2015).

While the United States, Japan, and Europe dominated global research output through the 1970s, many emerging economies have grown in research productivity since that time, especially China, India, Russia, and South Korea. In the early 1970s, 73 percent of research publications were written by authors in Canada, France, Germany, Italy, Japan, the United Kingdom, and the United States, the largest and most industrialized economies in the world; now, only around 50 percent of research publications come from these seven countries (Adams, Pendlebury, and Stembridge 2013). The trend toward greater international diversity in the production of research continues, with some of the increase prompted by growing government research funding in those countries (Adams, Pendlebury, and Stembridge 2013).

Research Partnerships

The strongest and most sustainable international research partnerships typically come from faculty connections with foreign colleagues that develop organically from the researchers' academic interests (Holbrook and Caruson 2017; Laughlin 2008). Types of international research collaborations can be varied and may include individual partnerships between faculty, scholars, and postdocs; student research abroad; university-to-university partnerships; government collaborations; alliances; faculty and student exchanges; research on international topics and global issues; and research conducted by people with international perspectives (Holbrook and Caruson 2017).

While many universities express an interest in international research collaboration, and even actively seek it out by advertising for research partners or promoting their international research in the *Chronicle of Higher Education* or other media outlets, few institutions have an intentional strategy to grow or manage their international research (Holbrook and Caruson 2017). International research can be supported by a university research support services office that identifies and distributes funding opportunities, profiles the research interests of faculty, monitors and evaluates the university's international work, and facilitates interdisciplinary partnerships. Universities may create resources and publications on how to get international projects started and offer advising on tax, purchasing, legal, and human resource compliance to ensure successful international work (Holbrook and Caruson 2017). An advisory board can be useful to provide both internal and external oversight, set priorities and directions, and help figure out which projects should be approved (Holbrook and Caruson 2017).

The University of Waterloo in Waterloo, Ontario, Canada, offers the following recommendations for internationalizing research (Holbrook and Caruson 2017):

- Develop a record-keeping system to track international research projects.
- Ensure that promotion and tenure reviews reward international engagement.
- Establish seed funding to support new international projects.
- Include international initiatives among fundraising goals.
- Establish a target for overhead funds generated to help support international initiatives.
- Establish guidelines to distribute overhead funds and international student tuition to those who lead international initiatives.
- Promote the university's strengths in major journals and research publications.
- Host international conferences at the university to showcase the research.

Political tensions can often impede research, as can government policies and regulations. Beyond the political and legal contexts, cultural and logistical matters can be challenging to manage. A 2014 survey of young scientists revealed some of the challenges for international research collaboration (Holbrook and Caruson 2017):

- Need for coordinated policies regarding resources, funding, and data;
- Inefficiencies and ambiguous or lengthy time frames in research;
- Limited funding for collaboration;
- Regulatory mandates;
- Inadequate human subjects protection policies in some countries;
- Data sharing responsibility;
- Safeguarding intellectual property;
- Managing technical "secrets";
- Fear of being "scooped";
- Overemphasis on competition;
- Prioritizing short-term gain over long-term relationship building;
- Language barriers;
- Inflexible cultural norms;
- Racial- and gender-related power inequities;
- Political, social, and economic conditions that may be risky; and
- National security.

Barrett, Crossley, and Fon (2014) point out that research partnerships are often financially supported by government funders in developed countries, even if the partnership involves researchers in both developed and developing countries. This can result in power inequities, with the developed countries dominating the lead researcher positions, imposing their cultural ways of work, and controlling the research agenda.

Academic Mobility

One of the most visible internationalization activities is academic mobility. This term refers to the movement of students and scholars (i.e., professors, researchers, postdocs, etc.) across national borders for purposes related to academic study, teaching, and research. Academic mobility is tracked by Project Atlas, which is funded by the U.S. Department of State Bureau of Educational and Cultural Affairs and managed by the Institute of International Education (IIE), in partnership with higher education data collection agencies from around the world.

Project Atlas, using data from United Nations Educational, Scientific and Cultural Organization (UNESCO), reports that in 2018, more than 5 million higher education students were studying outside of their home country for a year or longer (IIE 2018b). Regionally, Western Europe generally receives the most international students, while East Asia and the Pacific sends the most students. By nation, the United States receives the largest number of international students, with 22 percent of the total, followed by the United Kingdom (10 percent), China (10 percent), Australia (7 percent), Canada (7 percent), France (7 percent), Russia (6 percent), and Germany (5 percent) (IIE 2018b).

Push and Pull Factors

The reasons why international students are attracted to studying in the host countries are often referred to as "pull factors." These commonly include the perceived prestige of the host university, rankings of the host university, effective marketing, specialized study opportunities, the opportunity to be more competitive in the job market after graduation, the opportunity to learn a language or explore a culture, a connection to a particular country through diaspora linkages, home country support, and affordability or funding opportunities (Macready and Tucker 2011).

The reasons why international students find their home country's educational opportunities insufficient are referred to as "push factors." Common push factors include a perception that educational offerings in the home country are lower quality, the higher education system may not have the capacity to meet the enrollment demands (a shortage of "seats"), the home country's political or societal climate, and a desire to study a subject or specialization that is not available in the home country (Macready and Tucker 2011; Wächter 2014).

"Anti-push factors" are those barriers that make it difficult for students to leave their home country for travel, even if that is their goal. These anti-push factors may include the lack of financial means, safety concerns, family objections or obligations, the lack of foreign language ability, and difficulty in obtaining a visa for the host country or exit permission from the home country (Macready and Tucker 2011).

Data on Academic Mobility

There are some challenges in gathering data on academic mobility. Most notably, data are gathered and reported by national governments, however, definitions of "international student" and "international scholar" do vary. Some countries include in their tallies all people who are foreign born or who hold another citizenship. This means that immigrants with no intention of returning home are included in the tallies (Macready and Tucker 2011; Wächter 2014). The

Project Atlas data attempt to capture only those people who are temporarily in another country for academic purposes (though they may later change to immigrant status); however, the data are not always available in that format (Macready and Tucker 2011).

Another challenge of the data is that countries have different definitions and qualifications for who counts as an international student. Many countries count and report students enrolled to earn degrees abroad (Macready and Tucker 2011; Wächter 2014). The data reported may or may not include some students who go abroad for shorter periods, for example, an academic year, a semester, or even a few weeks, and return to continue their education at their home university after the international experience. This shorter model of mobility is popular in some countries, such as the United States, where more than 330,000 students study abroad and then return to their home institution each year (IIE 2018a). In contrast, fewer U.S. students complete their entire degree programs abroad. A 2013 examination of the data from 14 countries that are popular destinations for U.S. study abroad students found that only 46,500 U.S. students were enrolled in degree-length programs in those countries (Belyavina, Li, and Bhandari 2013).

Wächter (2014) distinguishes between short- and long-term experiences, using the term "degree mobility" to refer to students studying outside their home country for an entire degree, and the term "credit mobility" to refer to students studying abroad for a shorter period of time and then transferring the academic credit back to their home institution. The factors prompting these two types of mobility are quite different. Degree mobility is usually undertaken by students from countries with inadequate higher education systems in terms of either quality or capacity, creating a push effect. Wächter further characterizes this mobility as "vertical," that is, students go from countries with too few or too weak higher education institutions to those countries with perceived better options. By contrast, Wächter characterizes credit mobility as primarily "horizontal" in that the goal is not to move to a better university, but rather to move to one that is different or contrasting in terms of language, culture, teaching styles, etc. In credit mobility, students are pulled in to the opportunities offered at the host university, while assuming that the institutions are of relatively equal quality.

Project Atlas data show key changes in academic mobility flows over time. Notably, the number of higher education students studying outside of their home country has more than doubled from 2.1 million in 2001 to 5.0 million in 2018 (IIE 2018b). Another key shift is in where students are going. The United States, although still the leading destination for international students and increasing in the absolute number of international students, has been declining in dominance, hosting 28 percent of all international students in 2001 and only 22 percent in 2018 (IIE 2018b). Meanwhile, other countries are increasing in market share, including China, which was not even among the top eight receiving countries in 2001, but as of 2018 is the third largest host, receiving 10 percent of all international students in higher education (IIE 2018b).

In terms of the mobility of international faculty and researchers, comprehensive international data are not compiled. However, the Institute of International Education reports that 134,379 international scholars were engaged in temporary research or teaching activities in the United States during the 2016–17 academic year (IIE 2018a).

In addition to sending their students abroad and recruiting international students, some universities are now offering educational programs outside of their national borders with the explicit goal of serving international students. This is what was described in chapter 1 as "program mobility." The American Council on Education examined the frequency of these initiatives among U.S. doctoral-level institutions (Helms and Brajkovic 2017):

FACE-TO-FACE FORMAT:

- 19 percent offer full degree programs.
- 8 percent offer nondegree programs.
- 24 percent offer individual courses.

ONLINE OR DISTANCE LEARNING FORMAT:

- 22 percent offer full degree programs.
- 13 percent offer nondegree programs.
- 29 percent offer individual courses.

COMBINATION OF IN-PERSON AND ONLINE FORMATS:

- 17 percent offer full degree programs.
- 8 percent offer nondegree programs.
- 22 percent offer individual courses.

These programs can enhance the sponsoring university's international reputation, as well as create a new source of revenue for the institution. For the enrolled international students, this can be an avenue to access quality education without leaving their home country.

Strategic Partnerships

Strategic partnerships have the potential to contribute greatly to internationalization in a variety of areas and activities including curriculum, research, and academic mobility. Partnerships between two universities may be established for student and faculty exchange, joint research projects, classroom-to-classroom connections, and more (Gatewood Forthcoming). This section explores two additional types of partnerships: double and joint degrees and branch campuses.

Double and Joint Degrees

Joint degrees, in which students earn one degree awarded jointly by two partner institutions, and double degrees, in which students earn a degree from each of the two partner institutions, are becoming increasingly common. The 2016 survey by the American Council on Education found that among the higher education institutions surveyed, 24 percent of doctoral-level institutions (see Carnegie Classifications table in chapter 10) offer joint degrees and 10 percent are working on establishing them (Helms and Brajkovic 2017). The study also found that 58 percent of doctoral-level institutions offer double degrees and 13 percent are working on establishing them (Helms and Brajkovic 2017). By contrast, only 2 percent of U.S. community colleges offer joint degrees and 4 percent offer double degrees (Helms and Brajkovic 2017). Many of the joint- and double-degrees programs have been launched since 2001, with aims to prepare graduates for the global workforce, internationalize the curriculum, attract prospective students (see chapter 6), add to institutions' prestige, and help contribute to nations' competitiveness in business, science, and technology (Delisle 2009; Obst, Kuder, and Banks 2011).

Branch Campuses

Some institutions have established branch campuses, often through a cooperative agreement with a foreign government. When establishing an international branch campus, a university sets up a campus in another country, not just as a short-term study abroad site, but as a site offering full degrees. For the home institution, the goals for establishing such a campus may include developing new revenue sources, providing study abroad opportunities for students from the home institution, and increasing the institution's international prestige.

For the host country government, the motivation to engage in the partnership may be to expand and improve its higher education system, and to do so, government leaders may be willing to invest significantly by offering land, buildings, tax incentives, and other benefits (Witte 2010; Redden 2015). Host country students often enroll in branch campuses because they are attracted to the prospect of earning a prestigious foreign degree without having to leave their family and home country. If students from both the home country and host country (and potentially, students from other countries as well) are enrolled in the branch campus, it can allow students from different countries to meet each other for true cross-cultural learning (Marginson 2016).

The Cross-Border Education Research Team (2017) has identified 247 branch campuses around the world, with 22 more in the planning stages and 42 branch campuses that have closed. The Middle East is one of the regions that has been most welcoming of branch campuses. United Arab Emirates (UAE) and Qatar are both host to several branch campuses. These campuses are sometimes built in close proximity to each other in order to share services and create a reputation for educational excellence. Examples include Qatar's Education City and Dubai's Knowledge Village (Witte 2010; Vardhan 2015; Andersen 2015; Redden 2015).

An examination of 103 private higher education institutions on the Arabian Peninsula found that 70 either had partnerships with an international university or were branch campuses of international universities (Vardhan 2015). In recent years, some of the interest has been shifting to Asia, and it appears that branch campuses will continue to proliferate (Redden 2015).

One of the challenges of branch campuses is that the resources, teaching styles, teaching quality, and courses may be substantially different from the home university, which may lead to questions of whether the branch campus is of equal quality to the esteemed home campus (Altbach 2013). Also, branch campuses are typically established by top administrators at the home university, often without faculty input, which can result in protests on the home campus that the institutional mission is not being served, that the appropriate role of faculty in setting the institution's direction is not being respected, or that resources are being directed away from the home institution (Altbach 2013).

Partnerships, whether for joint degrees, branch campuses, or any other type, are very labor-intensive and, thus, challenging to establish and maintain. Partnerships can be further complicated by language barriers, cultural differences, cultural approaches to education and communication, the need to design a program to work within the potentially contradictory rules and regulations of two educational systems, and the dynamics of working with and appeasing two bureaucracies. A great deal of time and energy needs to be invested in relationship building and in communication and logistics. Partnerships are often most successful when building on smaller, already established partnerships—for example, adding a joint-degree program where there is already a successful faculty research collaboration—because some of that required commitment, patience, and trust have been formed on both sides (Obst and Kuder 2011; West 2015).

Faculty Development

Internationalization can be integrated into faculty development processes, including hiring faculty with international expertise and developing that acumen in existing faculty. Funding needs to be provided to allow faculty to conduct international research, teach abroad, attend international conferences, internationalize their courses, and launch international initiatives that support institutional goals. Potential benefits of investing in the development of faculty members' global competence include (Punteney and Wei 2018):

- Faculty can create courses that are internationalized.

- Faculty can lead study abroad programs.

- Faculty can better support international students in their classrooms.

- Faculty can make meaningful contributions to solving global challenges through research and collaboration.

- Faculty are more likely to develop international partnerships that the institution can build on for curriculum and research initiatives.

Beyond hiring faculty with international experience and providing funds to support faculty professional development, the international work that faculty undertake must also be valued and rewarded in tenure and promotion reviews. Despite its importance, when the American Council on Education surveyed U.S. higher education institutions and asked whether they have guidelines that place international work and experience into the consideration process during promotion and tenure deliberations, the study found that only 4 percent of institutions have these guidelines for all faculty, and 6 percent have these guidelines for faculty in some departments (Helms and Brajkovic 2017).

With promotion and tenure systems putting such intense pressure on faculty to publish research, and no explicit institutional statement of support for international work, faculty members usually have little incentive to invest their limited time in the time-consuming work of internationalizing their courses, developing international partnerships, or other internationalization activities (Brewer 2015; Williams and Lee 2015; Pysarchik 2015). The American Council on Education's report *Internationalizing the Tenure Code: Policies to Promote a Globally Focused Faculty* offers the following advice for institutions that want to demonstrate the value of internationalization through their promotion and tenure codes (Helms 2015):

- Ensure that comprehensive internationalization is embedded in the culture and operations of an institution before internationalizing the promotion and tenure code.

- Align promotion and tenure criteria with institutional internationalization goals.

- Examine the "lived reality" of the tenure process—to what extent are the policies in the written codes given weight by the promotion and tenure review committees when it comes down to making the actual decisions?

- Engage all campus stakeholders throughout the process of making changes to the promotion and tenure code.

- Be careful about listing criteria with "and" versus "or." The former makes internationalization efforts required rather than optional, but the latter may be more realistic about how much can be achieved.

- Add internationally focused criteria to faculty position announcements.

- Provide funding for the international activities that faculty are expected to do to earn promotions and tenure.

- Identify and dismantle barriers to faculty pursuing international activities.

- Make it easy for faculty to showcase their internationalization-related work by offering examples of activities that are valued for promotions and tenure, while also allowing faculty to identify other types of activities they are doing that contribute toward the institution's internationalization goals.

Investing in faculty development and incentivizing and rewarding international engagement are both essential to the overall success of internationalization at an institution. As one of the main drivers of internationalization, securing faculty input and support can help propel institutional efforts.

Internationalization Planning

Internationalization, if done effectively, is a strategic process. It is more than a collection of independent activities; instead, it is an intentional and thoughtful planning process that results in articulated goals and a coherent plan to achieve those goals. The component efforts are aligned, and resources are allocated to meet the goals. The results are regularly monitored and discussed, leading to revision of the plan, refined initiatives, and increasingly productive efforts. Like all strategic planning processes, internationalization is cyclical, following a format of reflection, planning, action, accountability, and assessment. More and more institutions are trying to formalize this process by developing internationalization policies, supportive infrastructures, and methods of assessing progress (Egron-Polak and Hudson 2014).

To support institutions' internationalization planning efforts, NAFSA: Association of International Educators offers many resources and publications focused on developing institutional strategy, internationalizing the curriculum, and assessing internationalization. The American Council on Education offers the ACE Internationalization Laboratory, which provides guidance for U.S. institutions working on internationalization. Each institution forms a leadership team for comprehensive internationalization and works through ACE's guided process of evaluation and planning (ACE 2018).

American Councils for International Education (known as "American Councils") (2015) has developed a useful internationalization planning guide (see figure 1) that leads institutions through a seven-stage process:

1. Introduce the planning process on campus.
2. Evaluate the current level of internationalization efforts.
3. Perform a gap analysis.
4. Develop a plan.
5. Implement the plan.

6. Measure the results.
7. Revisit, refine, and recommit.

Getting Started with the Internationalization Plan

An institution embarking on internationalization planning may have a modest level of international engagement already underway, or it may have robust international programs and curricula already in place. The initial call for internationalization may emerge from faculty, international education professionals, or upper administration. Those advocates may promote the value of recruiting international students and participating in education abroad, curriculum reform, international development initiatives, and cross-border research (Hudzik 2011).

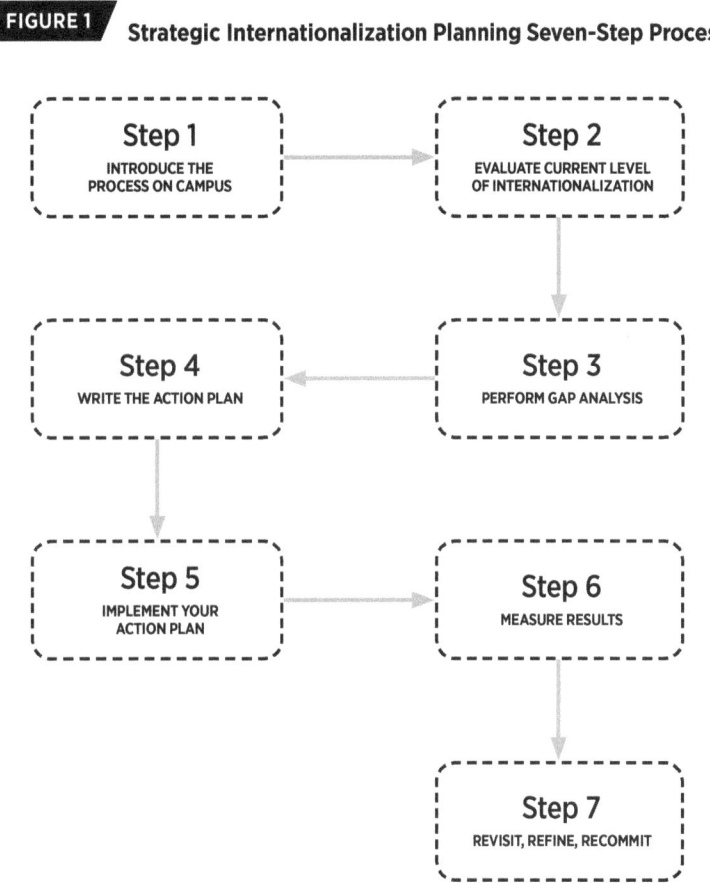

FIGURE 1 Strategic Internationalization Planning Seven-Step Process

Source: American Councils for International Education (2015).

Whatever the impetus, to be robust, the internationalization initiative must expand beyond the specialization of the original proponents in order to be fundamentally incorporated into and across the work of all parts of the institution. Internationalization is only sustainable and able to have a large impact if it is adopted throughout the organization. This includes, but is not limited to, topics related to students, faculty, curriculum, research, governance, and engagement (Gao 2015). Hudzik (2018, 2011, 2015) refers to this organization-wide integration as "comprehensive internationalization."

Getting started with internationalization requires two key tasks: (1) gathering data, and (2) identifying allies. These tasks correlate to steps 1 and 2 in the American Councils model (see figure 1). Data gathering entails compiling a list of all existing international ventures within the institution, such as data on education abroad participation, international student enrollments, foreign language course enrollments, courses that are global or international in focus, memoranda of understanding (MOUs) or other partnerships with international organizations, faculty conducting international research or leading international projects, and faculty participation in international conferences. As much data as possible should be gathered, including potentially less readily available data on faculty and staff with international heritages or experiences; institutional connections within local immigrant communities; student, staff, and faculty speakers of foreign languages; courses in which students use technology to engage with people across borders, etc.

Existing institutional and departmental strategic or operational plans should also be examined to see if there are international initiatives already underway. Wherever available, data on the outcomes of all of these programs should be collected; these outcomes may include career outcomes, grant revenue, community outcomes, graduation rates, and other measures of impact.

In the process of this data collection, people will emerge from within and around the organization as proponents of internationalization, or at least potential proponents. Assembling a list of names and contact information of allies is invaluable as the internationalization process moves forward.

Equipped with data on the history and current status of campus international activities, a Strengths, Weaknesses, Opportunities, Threats (SWOT) analysis should be performed to start the process of internationalization. This is step 3 in the American Councils model (see figure 1). In this SWOT process, the gathered data are evaluated, discussed, and debated in order to answer the following questions:

- What are the institution's strengths as it relates to internationalization?
- What are the institution's weaknesses as it relates to internationalization?
- What external opportunities for internationalization exist?
- What external threats might hinder internationalization?

The questions regarding opportunities and threats take into consideration conditions beyond the institution, including shifts in public opinion, government policies and funding, population demographics, market trends, regulations, etc. While the SWOT analysis can be carried out by the institutional leadership team, it may be more effective and more energizing if an event is held in which faculty, staff, and students—particularly those who have already been identified as potential allies—are invited and encouraged to share their thoughts and reactions. Through facilitated small group conversations, ideas and input can be gathered from a wide range of perspectives, and priorities can begin to be distilled for follow-up by the leadership team.

Crafting the Internationalization Plan

Building on the input gained from the data gathering and SWOT analysis, the next step in the internationalization process is drafting a written plan. This is represented by step 4 in the American Councils model (see figure 1). The written plan must be fully aligned with the organization's mission, vision, and ethos. This plan must explicitly state the institution's rationales for internationalization and the expected benefits. It must articulate clear goals that the institution wishes to reach, specific tasks to be undertaken, which individuals or departments are responsible for each initiative, performance indicators, and a clear timeline for each task. Whenever possible, there should be more than one performance indicator per goal in order to provide a well-rounded understanding of whether the goal has been met (Brandenburg et al. 2009).

Hudzik (2011) identifies strategic questions that each institution should ask after the data have been gathered and used in the process of developing an internationalization plan that is uniquely suited to the institution:

- How well is comprehensive internationalization linked to the institutional mission?
- What are the intellectual drivers and motivations for comprehensive internationalization?
- Who are the clients of comprehensive internationalization?
- What is the scope and strength of institutional commitment to comprehensive internationalization?
- Is there a commitment to allocating resources strategically?
- How programmatically encompassing will comprehensive internationalization be?
- Which academic disciplines and professions will be engaged?
- Which countries and regions will be prioritized?
- How will leadership and support be organized (centralized versus decentralized coordination) for comprehensive internationalization?
- Will key stakeholders (faculty, academic governance committees, support units such as records/financial aid/student services, accreditation bodies, government authorities, etc.) be supportive?
- Who will be responsible and assessed for contributions to comprehensive internationalization?
- What will be the roles of the senior international officer and the international offices on campus?

The divisions between data analysis, reflection, and the crafting of the plan are a bit blurred. It is normal for organizations to move back and forth between data analysis and goal-setting as they work through the internationalization process.

Since most institutions have an institution-wide strategic plan already, it may make sense to organize an internationalization plan under the headings for the overall institutional strategic plan. In that way, it can be made explicit how internationalization contributes to the institutional goals (Hudzik 2011). Hudzik (2011) recommends setting audacious goals that cover the entirety of the topic at hand; for example, setting a goal that *all* students take at least three courses on global issues or that *all* faculty present their research at international conferences. This helps the organization to push itself to achieve larger, more inclusive goals.

Collaboration with Stakeholders

Having support from stakeholders all across campus is essential to the internationalization process. Faculty are, of course, crucial partners in this process. They develop the curricular requirements, choose content for their courses, support and encourage students, and give input on who to hire or promote within departments. As allies in internationalization efforts, they can have a transformative impact.

All of the student services divisions are also key players in supporting students and facilitating activities. The financial aid office can help make it possible for students to study, intern, or research abroad by allowing their financial aid to be used. The records office is needed to process students' credits from joint degrees and study abroad and to award international studies recognitions at the time of graduation. The writing center can offer tutelage to international students studying in a second language. The career center may be asked to provide advising on students' international job searches.

Other departments on campus have a role in internationalization, too. The facilities department may be willing to hang international flags or create multilingual signage to make the campus more welcoming. Food services could offer halal or kosher meals. Information technology departments can enable international classroom-to-classroom connections, international collaborative research, and distance learning. The grants management office will need to work with foreign currencies to manage international projects. The communications office is needed for designing print and digital materials to articulate the value of internationalization. And the advancement office can approach donors about supporting internationalization initiatives. Ultimately, every department on campus can contribute to internationalization in different ways.

However, despite best efforts from faculty and administrators, there may be resistance from some stakeholders on campus for varied reasons. Some may view internationalization as an inconvenience, an interference with their academic freedom, a competitor for resources, or even something harmful (Hudzik 2011). Many people may prefer to keep things as they are, without internationalizing their work. Others may seek to minimize the importance of internationalization by arguing that their discipline is inherently universal (such as math or engineering, for example) and, therefore, their departments are already internationalized. Some may feel that they are too busy to add any projects to their workload.

(continued on next page)

Collaboration with Stakeholders (continued)

Building support and overcoming resistance requires investing time and energy into relationship building. It is worthwhile for international education professionals to meet with individuals and groups across campus as often as possible to discuss the benefits of internationalization. Faculty and staff may have ideas for initiatives or ways that they can contribute to internationalization. If they have concerns, acknowledge those concerns and address them if possible.

Once stakeholders are on board, it is essential to establish policies that promote or necessitate internationalization. If internationalization is part of the institution's strategic plan, it is reasonable for campus leaders to direct departments to identify ways in which they will each contribute. Human resources policies can support the hiring of international faculty and staff through a willingness to process visa sponsorship paperwork. Faculty evaluation policies can explicitly reward international activities in the hiring and promotion processes. Through intentional building of relationships and the codification of internationalization priorities through policy, it is possible to build stakeholder support that advances the internationalization plan.

Implementing the Internationalization Plan

The implementation of the internationalization plan is step 5 in the American Councils model (see figure 1). Throughout the process of implementation, campus leaders must continuously build support and momentum for the plan. This means that leaders must regularly make the case for the importance of internationalization to all stakeholder groups. If internationalization is not seen as integral to the institution as a whole, the internationalization effort will stagnate (Hudzik 2011). One lesson learned from watching countless institutions working to internationalize is that clear and consistent direction from top administrators is critical for success (Hudzik 2011).

The administration's level of commitment to internationalization directly correlates to the degree to which resources (human and financial) are allocated to the achievement of the plan's goals. Besides ensuring that there are enough personnel and funds to implement the specific items named in the plan, administrators should also fund pilot and demonstration projects that allow students, faculty, and staff to pioneer efforts that may spark new initiatives or provide a model for others in the campus community (Hudzik 2011).

Faculty Engagement

It would be impossible to internationalize an institution without the support and involvement of faculty members because of the important role they play in academic governance (Hudzik 2011). Faculty members determine their own course content with relative autonomy, and they elect representatives to comprise the institution's curriculum committee, which oversees the creation or modification of major, general education, and graduation requirements. Additionally, faculty members are the most effective advocates to encourage students to participate in education abroad, and their support can help promote the academic success of international students in the

Structure of a Sample Internationalization Plan

In the process of structuring an internationalization plan, it can be helpful to have a summary document outlining the rationales, goals, and primary strategies of the plan and then a more specific operational chart that lists the details. Table 1 offers an excerpt of an operational plan, with categories and specific goals listed under broader institutional goals.

It is crucial that the plan holds individuals and departments across the institution accountable for their contributions to internationalization. For this reason, it may be best to ask each unit to identify its own goals. At the very least, each unit must confirm that the performance indicators and timelines listed are achievable.

TABLE 1 Sample of Internationalization Operational Plan

INSTITUTIONAL STRATEGIC GOAL: ENHANCE STUDENT LEARNING				
Internationalization Plan: Curriculum				
Goal	Person(s) Responsible	Performance Indicator	Due	Status
1 Increase offerings and enrollments in entry-level courses with an international focus	Course Instructor	Increase enrollment in International Forum course by 10 percent per year	Fall 2022	In progress
	Dean of Humanities	Creation of International Films course	Spring 2019	Completed
2 Expand foreign language offerings and enrollments	Dean of Humanities; Foreign Languages Department Chair	Increase number of languages being taught to 16	Fall 2024	Not started
		Increase number of foreign language majors and minors by 3 percent	Fall 2020	In progress
		Increase number of students enrolled in foreign language courses by 5 percent	Fall 2020	Exceeded
Internationalization Plan: Education Abroad				
3 Increase diversity of majors participating in study abroad	Director of Education Abroad	Require that all majors have a study abroad component that is 8 weeks or longer, each year	Fall 2020	Ongoing
		Develop performing arts study abroad program	Fall 2021	In progress
		Partner with three more providers for international service-learning programs	Spring 2022	In progress
INSTITUTIONAL STRATEGIC GOAL: STRATEGICALLY MANAGE RESOURCES				
Internationalization Plan: Advancement				
4 Develop and implement advancement plan to support internationalization efforts	Vice President for Advancement	Plan campaign	Fall 2019	Completed
		Approach donors and prospective donors	Summer 2020	In progress
		Achieve annual campaign targets	2022–2027	Ongoing

classroom. Further, the strongest international partnerships usually evolve from faculty contacts at international institutions. In these and many other ways, faculty engagement is pivotal to the success of internationalization, and leaders are advised to cultivate faculty allies and recruit faculty members into leadership roles within the internationalization initiative.

Institutional Policies

Effective internationalization requires that the international goals be incorporated into the policies of the institution, including those that apply to the recruitment, hiring, contract renewal, promotion, and tenure of faculty (Hudzik 2011). At the simplest level, international experience, language ability, international collaborations, and efforts to internationalize teaching and research should be rewarded through these processes. Faculty and administrators can ensure that this happens by establishing explicit criteria for each faculty review process that encourage or require this international knowledge and engagement.

On a more practical level, policies must support the institutional message that internationalization is important. For example, job announcements should be advertised internationally, diverse candidates should be encouraged to apply, the human resources department should be prepared for the additional expense and time of processing employment paperwork for a foreign employee's visa and work authorization, etc.

Policies large and small across the institution should be examined and, if needed, rewritten to support rather than hinder internationalization. This includes policies related to the languages in which the website is published, orientation programs, campus housing, dining hall menus, tuition payments, fundraising, alumni relations, and countless other areas.

Assessing the Internationalization Plan

As the internationalization plan is being implemented, with support being provided in both words and actions, it is necessary to monitor the progress toward the internationalization goals and regularly report to stakeholders on the plan's progress (Hudzik 2011). This is step 6 of the American Councils model (see figure 1).

Assessment of internationalization requires that institutions have clear and measurable goals developed as part of the plan (Hudzik 2011). Once the goals are in place, the measurement of outputs and outcomes is achievable. Outputs are the "deliverable targets measured most often through numbers (e.g., number of international students, number of study-abroad programs, percentage of students studying abroad, number of students studying foreign languages, number of foreign-born faculty" (Deardorff 2015, 57). Outcomes are defined as the "changes that occur in learners and in programs (could be short-, medium-, and long-term outcomes), usually focused on changes in skills, knowledge, attitudes, and behavior (e.g., language ability, intercultural competence development, civic engagement, adaptability, emotional resilience, global knowledge, communication skills, critical thinking skills)" (Deardorff 2015, 57).

Appropriate performance indicators should be meaningful, objective, grounded in research, intelligible, consistent over time, cost-effective to measure, linked to policy, and able to allow for international comparison (Gao 2015). During the creation of the internationalization plan and identification of performance indicators, thought should have been given to how (and by whom) the data would be collected, stored, and organized. With that preliminary thinking already done, this stage of the internationalization process is the time to collect and analyze the data.

One common mistake made by institutions is gathering data only on outputs, without consideration for outcomes (Deardorff 2015; Hudzik 2015). Achievement of the outcomes is the very reason for internationalization, so assessment must capture these data to provide meaningful information on success in achieving the overall purposes of internationalizing. As higher education becomes ever more focused on accountability, international educators are increasingly required to demonstrate the accomplishment of both outputs and outcomes using hard data (Hudzik 2011). Failure to conduct assessment not only misses the opportunity to strengthen the internationalization effort, but it also jeopardizes future support and resources.

Revising the Internationalization Plan

The assessment process should survey the current status of institutional internationalization, record changes over time, highlight the strengths and weaknesses of the internationalization process, and inform administrators and stakeholders as they make decisions on policies and practices (Gao 2015). Such data and insights are used to then revise the internationalization plan as needed; this is step 7 of the American Councils model (see figure 1). The internationalization plan should be updated on a regular basis, perhaps once a year, adjusting goals, targets, and timelines to reflect the new understandings that emerge from the assessment.

Achievement of goals should be recognized and rewarded, and failure to achieve goals should be addressed with revised planning and, if needed, corrective action from management. Through the ongoing, iterative cycle of assessment, revision of the plan, adapted implementation, and assessment again, the goal is to increase the effectiveness of the internationalization process and move toward achieving the internationalization purposes.

Regional Differences in Approaches to Internationalization

Thus far, this chapter has focused on higher education internationalization with an emphasis on the U.S. context. But the strategic significance placed on internationalization is evident at universities around the world. Despite the common interest in internationalization, there are regional and national differences in the motivations and perceived risks, governmental approaches to internationalization policies, and the internationalization activities that receive the most emphasis.

Much of the data in this section come from the International Association of Universities (IAU), which conducts a survey of universities around the world every 4 years, measuring the status, motivations, activities, and processes of internationalization. In the most recent iteration of the survey, 6,879 institutions were invited to participate and 1,336 universities responded (Egron-Polak and Hudson 2014). Table 2 summarizes some of the highlights of this survey, while the following sections provide additional detail. IAU publishes the data according to world region, with the acknowledgment that the survey results are generalizations and that there is great diversity within individual regions.

Africa

Internationalization in Africa is predominately focused on strengthening research production and knowledge production capacity, according to the IAU survey. While strengthening research was the most frequently cited anticipated benefit of internationalization listed in Africa, it was not among the top three anticipated benefits for any other world regions (Egron-Polak and Hudson 2014, 2010). This is most likely because Africa produces only around 1 percent (mostly in the fields of medicine and agriculture) of the world's overall research output, while other world regions have more expansive and established research capabilities (Jowi 2010). Brain drain is common in sub-Saharan Africa (International Monetary Fund 2016). Brain drain, the movement of students, recent graduates, and academics away from less developed countries to more developed countries, only exacerbates the challenges of developing research capacity (Jowi 2010; International Monetary Fund 2016).

When asked about the internationalization activities their universities employ, the IAU survey respondents identified international research collaborations as the most important activity, which aligns with the emphasis on strengthening research capacity as a goal of internationalization (Egron-Polak and Hudson 2014). Outgoing faculty and staff mobility was ranked as the second most important activity, and international development and capacity building was ranked third. Within the IAU survey, Africa was the only world region to include international development and capacity building among the top three internationalization activity priorities (Egron-Polak and Hudson 2014).

When asked about the potential risks of internationalization, African institutions, as in most other regions, cited concern that only the students with financial resources will be able to access international education opportunities. In the survey, respondents identified brain drain, unequal sharing of internationalization benefits, and the dominance of Western ways of knowing as risks to the institutions and/or society (Egron-Polak and Hudson 2014). However, efforts are being undertaken to develop regional quality assurance programs in order to counter the challenges with the recognition of qualifications (Jowi 2010).

As in all the regions, African universities cited the lack of funding as the most significant obstacle to internationalization. Additional obstacles named by African institutions included difficulties with the recognition of qualifications and programs, insufficient exposure to international opportunities, visa restrictions, and the lack of national policy priorities in favor of internationalization (Egron-Polak and Hudson 2014). Only the African region named the lack of a national policy as one of the top three external obstacles to internationalization (Egron-Polak and Hudson 2014).

Asia-Pacific

The Asia-Pacific region is large and diverse. It is the region of the world that sends out the most students to study in another country, and the third largest region (after Western Europe and North America) in terms of the number of international students it receives (IIE 2018b). China is notable as the nation that sends out the most students annually, and the third largest national receiver of international students, hosting more than 400,000 international students annually (IIE 2018b). Australia is the world's fourth largest receiver of international students, with more than 300,000, making up 23.8 percent of Australia's total higher education enrollment (IIE 2018b). Academic mobility, both recruiting international students and sending students abroad, is one of the primary internationalization activities in the Asia-Pacific region (Huang 2015; Wu 2010; Yemini and Sagie 2016).

More than half of Asian institutions have internationalization policies, with the most highly ranked anticipated benefit being an increase in students' international awareness (Egron-Polak and Hudson 2014). For the IAU survey, when asked how internationalization might be a risk to the institution, the most frequently cited responses were that opportunities might be limited to students with financial resources, it might foster excessive competition among higher education institutions, and it might be pursued only for reasons of prestige (Egron-Polak and Hudson 2014). When the Asian institutions were asked how internationalization might be a risk to society, the top concerns were the commodification of education and foreign degree mills and/or low-quality providers (Egron-Polak and Hudson 2014).

In the Asia-Pacific region, cited obstacles to higher education internationalization include a lack of internal funding, limited public funding, insufficient exposure to international opportunities, and difficulties related to the recognition of qualifications and programs (Egron-Polak and Hudson 2014). One particular challenge faced in Asia that other regions may see less of is that governments sometimes censor free speech, limiting the ability of academics to engage in societal critique. This can lead to other challenges in international collaborations when the partners have differing expectations of their roles within society (Marginson 2016).

Europe

European Union policies help propel internationalization in Europe. Particular programs such as the Comenius Programme and the Erasmus Programme promote student academic mobility at the K–12 and higher education levels, respectively, while the Erasmus Mundus Joint Master Degree program supports the establishment of joint degrees (Macready and Tucker 2011; Woodfield 2010). European Union policy initiatives such as the Bologna Process, Lisbon Strategy, Europe 2020 Strategy, and others have been instrumental in shaping and reforming higher education in the region. The Bologna Process implemented structural reforms to bring European higher education institutions into alignment to allow for and encourage greater academic mobility. The Lisbon Strategy and the 2020 Strategy aim to reinforce the European knowledge economy, including strengthening higher education and research. These two initiatives resulted in the creation of a European Research Area and funding for international research partnerships (Woodfield 2010).

In the IAU survey of institutions, European institutions were among the most likely to report that they had internationalization policies, and Europe was the only region to report that regional policies were one of the top external drivers of internationalization (Egron-Polak and Hudson 2014). More than in any other region, institutions in Europe confirmed that their internationalization policies included regional prioritization, with the priority being activities focused within Europe (Egron-Polak and Hudson 2014).

Outgoing student mobility was cited by European institutions as the most important internationalization activity they undertake, and when asked about internationalization at home activities, they identified the provision of scholarships for outbound mobility as most important (Egron-Polak and Hudson 2014). Among the European region respondents to the IAU survey, 6 percent confirmed that they have specific internationally focused learning outcomes identified for their students (Egron-Polak and Hudson 2014).

The potential for improved quality of teaching and learning was the most highly ranked anticipated benefit reported by European institutions. Like other regions, commodification and commercialization of education was rated as the highest risk of internationalization. Notably, Europe is the only region that did not list among the top three concerns the risk that international opportunities would be available only to students with financial resources (Egron-Polak and Hudson 2014). Lack of internal funding and lack of public funding were listed as obstacles to internationalization, as well as language barriers and the limited experience of faculty and staff (Egron-Polak and Hudson 2014). In summary, Europe employs a regional approach to both education and internationalization that emphasizes mobility as well as international partnerships.

Latin America and the Caribbean

In Latin America and the Caribbean, one of the primary motivations to internationalize higher education is to contribute to economic development by taking advantage of international opportunities and developing knowledge and skills among students and faculty (Burges 2014). In the IAU survey, compared with other world regions, fewer Latin American and Caribbean institutions cited that internationalization is a priority or that they have internationalization policies. However, most reported that internationalization is gaining importance in the region (Gacel-Ávila 2010).

The region has relatively low participation rates in both inbound and outbound academic mobility (Gacel-Ávila 2010; IIE 2018b). The most highly ranked anticipated benefit of internationalization is the increased networking opportunities it provides for faculty and researchers (Egron-Polak and Hudson 2014). When asked about their most important internationalization activity, the Latin American and Caribbean respondents most frequently selected outgoing student mobility. When asked about internationalization at home, they most often chose foreign language learning as their priority (Egron-Polak and Hudson 2014).

With regard to the risks of internationalization, institutions in Latin America and the Caribbean identified unequal sharing of internationalization benefits as the top risk. They also expressed concern that international partnerships would be pursued only for reasons of prestige (Egron-Polak and Hudson 2014). Lack of internal funding and limited public funding were the most common reported obstacles to internationalization, followed by the limited experience of faculty and staff members and the language barrier (Egron-Polak and Hudson 2014).

In the IAU survey, when asked about their values in terms of engaging in international partnerships, all world regions identified achievement of academic goals as most important. However, institutions in Latin America and the Caribbean cited shared benefits, respect, and fairness in international partnerships as second most important, while all other regions chose local and global social responsibility as second most important (Egron-Polak and Hudson 2014). Acknowledging the low rates of academic mobility, institutions within Latin America and the Caribbean have focused internationalization efforts on the establishment of international partnerships to provide opportunities for students, faculty, and staff.

Middle East

Institutions of higher education in the Middle East (with some exceptions) are closely aligned with their national governments and may be restricted in terms of choices about their international partners, language of instruction, and enrollment of international students. Much of the decisionmaking is done on the national level, and governments in the region are active in developing internationalization strategies. For example, Saudi Arabia is adopting English as the language of instruction and moving to a U.S.-style system of semesters and credit hours. The region hosts a particularly high number of branch campuses, and Qatar and the United Arab Emirates are establishing education hubs, physical spaces in which groups of universities (often branch campuses) are located close together and both domestic and international students are enrolled (Cross-Border Education Research Team 2017; Vardhan 2015; Witte 2010).

In the IAU survey, the Middle East had the smallest proportion of respondents, only 13 percent, that said internationalization is part of their overall institutional strategy (Egron-Polak and Hudson 2014). The desire to improve national and international rankings was selected as the most significant driver of internationalization, and improved quality of teaching and learning was the most highly ranked anticipated benefit (Egron-Polak and Hudson 2014). An analysis of the website text of 167 higher education institutions in the region found that

Regional Differences in Approaches to Internationalization

The International Association of Universities (IAU) conducts a survey of higher education institutions around the globe in order to identify progress toward internationalization. One of the benefits of this study is that it highlights differences among world regions. IAU's 4th Global Survey reports on the responses from 1,336 universities (Egron-Polak and Hudson 2014). While acknowledging that there is diversity within regions, table 2 identifies some of the areas in which regional responses were different from the global aggregate responses.

TABLE 2 Regional Differences in Approaches to Internationalization

Africa	▪ Goal of internationalization: Strengthening research production and knowledge production capacity ▪ Important internationalization activity: International research partnerships ▪ Risks of internationalization: Brain drain, unequal sharing of internationalization benefits, and dominance of Western ways of knowing
Asia-Pacific	▪ Important internationalization activities: Academic mobility and international research collaborations ▪ Benefit of internationalization: Increasing students' international awareness ▪ Risks of internationalization: Fostering excessive competition and pursing internationalization only for reasons of prestige
Europe	▪ Region in which institutions were most likely to report that they have internationalization policies ▪ Important internationalization activity: Outbound student mobility ▪ External policy drivers: European Union policies and regional (European) prioritization
Latin America and the Caribbean	▪ Benefit of internationalization: Increasing networking opportunities for faculty and researchers ▪ Important internationalization at home activity: Foreign language learning ▪ Important values with regard to internationalization: Shared benefits, respect, and fairness in international partnerships
Middle East	▪ Significant driver of internationalization: Improving rankings ▪ Region that had the smallest proportion of institutions that reported that internationalization is part of their overall institutional strategy ▪ Risks of internationalization: Brain drain and loss of cultural identity
North America (Canada and the United States)	▪ Internationalization activities: Recruiting fee-paying international undergraduates (among top three activities) ▪ Important internationalization at home activity: Offering courses with an international theme ▪ Obstacle to internationalization: Lack of public funding

Source: Data from Egron-Polak and Hudson (2014).

stated rationales for internationalization frequently included the growing population, growing economy, and desire for international status (Vardhan 2015).

The risk most frequently identified by institutions in the Middle East is that international opportunities will be limited to students with financial resources (Egron-Polak and Hudson 2014). Brain drain and loss of cultural identity were also listed as important risks. The Middle East is the only region that did not name the commodification and commercialization of education as one of the top three risks (Egron-Polak and Hudson 2014).

Like other regions, lack of internal funding and limited public funding were named as the most common obstacles (Egron-Polak and Hudson 2014). Visa restrictions imposed on international students, researchers, and academics was considered the next major external obstacle, and insufficient exposure to international opportunities was selected as the next most important internal obstacle (Egron-Polak and Hudson 2014).

All world regions other than the Middle East described academic goals as the most central institutional value as it relates to internationalization; while institutions in the Middle East most frequently cited principles of scientific integrity and research ethics as most important (Egron-Polak and Hudson 2014). When institutions in the Middle East were asked to identify their most important internationalization activities, international research collaboration was named most important, outgoing faculty or staff mobility was second most important, and international marketing and promotion was third (Egron-Polak and Hudson 2014). The Middle East was the only region to include marketing and promotion among the top three activities. Among the respondents, 35 percent of institutions in the Middle East confirmed that they have identified specific internationally focused learning outcomes for students (Egron-Polak and Hudson 2014). Common threads throughout the responses from the region include an emphasis on improving research and mobility, the desire to develop in ways that are consistent with the culture of the region, and the strong role that government plays in educational decisionmaking.

North America

The IAU survey classifies Mexico as part of Latin America and the Caribbean, so this subsection refers only to Canada and the United States. Universities in these two countries have relatively high degrees of autonomy—although the national governments are engaged in the promotion of internationalization. The Canadian government has been actively encouraging inbound student mobility by creating welcoming visa policies, promoting and funding study in Canada, and creating authorizations for students to work during and after their studies (Macready and Tucker 2011).

The U.S. government also promotes internationalization in several key ways, such as recruiting international students through the Department of State's EducationUSA network of advising offices around the world and by sponsoring citizen diplomacy programs such as the Fulbright Program, International Visitor Leadership Program, Humphrey Fellowships,

Boren Fellowships, and many others. More than 55,000 participants travel overseas through Department of State-funded exchanges each year (Bureau of Educational and Cultural Affairs 2018). The Department of State recently created the Office of U.S. Study Abroad within the Bureau of Educational and Cultural Affairs. Additionally, there are at least 30 U.S. state-based consortia to recruit international students (Kacenga 2019).

In the IAU survey, North American respondents ranked students' international awareness as the most important benefit of internationalization (Egron-Polak and Hudson 2014). Notably, while all other regions cited national and global rankings as a primary driver of internationalization, it was not among the top three drivers selected by North American institutions. The most important internationalization activity was outgoing student mobility (Egron-Polak and Hudson 2014). North America was the only region to list recruiting fee-paying international undergraduates as one of its top three internationalization activities. When institutions were asked about internationalization at home, offering courses with an international theme was selected as most important (Egron-Polak and Hudson 2014). Among the respondents, 48 percent of the institutions said that they have identified specific internationally focused learning outcomes for their students, the highest percentage among all the world regions (Egron-Polak and Hudson 2014).

Commodification and commercialization of education was ranked as the highest risk that could occur with internationalization (Egron-Polak and Hudson 2014). Also listed as a top risk was too much focus on the recruitment of international fee-paying undergraduates, something that was not a top risk for any other region. Lack of funding was cited as the most common internal obstacle, followed by curricula that are too rigorous and inflexible (Egron-Polak and Hudson 2014). Limited public funding was named the most common external obstacle, followed by visa restrictions for students, researchers, and academics (Egron-Polak and Hudson 2014). Overall, North America benefits from a reputation for strong higher education programs, a large share of the world's academic mobility, the fact that many international institutions seek North American partners, and relative institutional autonomy.

Considerations for Internationalization

The literature provides several caveats and considerations for practitioners around the world engaged in internationalization, ranging from debates over terminology to arguments about best practices to questions of equity, ethics, and social justice. One concern is that the term "internationalization" may be inaccurately interchanged with the concept of "globalization" (Bedenlier and Zawacki-Richter 2015; Hudzik 2015; Knight 2004). Another critique is that the term "internationalization" is becoming a catchall phrase to cover all things international and, in that process, is losing its true meaning.

All too often, the concept of internationalization is focused on the collection of international activities undertaken, rather than on the strategic process of making an institution more international (de Haan 2014; Knight 2011). Knight's (2011) "Five Myths about Internationalization" (below) summarizes some of the ways she has observed that the concept of internationalization is misunderstood. International educators are advised to define the terms they are using and articulate their understanding of the process and benefits of internationalization to ensure alignment across campus.

Five Myths about Internationalization

In her well-known article on the "Five Myths about Internationalization," Knight (2011) identifies and addresses five false beliefs about internationalization. Those arguments are summarized here:

MYTH 1 **Foreign students are internationalization agents.**

It must not be assumed that simply having international students enrolled at an institution means that the domestic students are getting an internationalized education. Instead, many domestic students choose to never engage with the international students unless required.

MYTH 2 **International reputation is a proxy for quality.**

It is not necessarily true that having an internationalized university or high global rankings means that students are getting a high-quality education.

MYTH 3 **International institutional agreements equate to internationalization.**

It is not true that a greater number of international partnerships means that a university is more internationalized. Partnerships require large investments of time and energy to do them well, so a smaller number of robust and thriving partnerships may serve students and the institutions better than a large number of undernurtured partnerships.

MYTH 4 **International accreditation equates to internationalization.**

It is incorrect to assume that holding many accreditations from international agencies signifies a better institution. There are many accrediting agencies of varying quality, and what they measure might not be aligned with what an institution prioritizes.

MYTH 5 **Global branding is the goal of internationalization.**

Internationalization should not be confused with a global marketing campaign—these are separate activities. Recognition and international visibility may be by-products of internationalization, but they should not be the end goals. The goal must be to incorporate an international or intercultural dimension into the teaching, research, and service work of the organization.

Beyond debating the terminology and processes of internationalization, many educators are apprehensive about potential negative societal outcomes. Equity of access to international education is a significant issue in the United States and internationally. As the IAU survey indicates, the worry that students without financial resources will not have access to international opportunities is found across all world regions (Egron-Polak and Hudson 2014). There is additional concern that particular groups will be discriminated against and participation in programs will be intentionally or unintentionally limited by nationality, religion, language, gender, sexuality, or other factors (McLellan 2011; Knight 2014). International educators must take care to ensure that they engage a diverse group of students and stakeholders in internationalization activities and planning.

There is also some apprehension that with the commercialization of education and the growth in internationalization and cross-border education, certain nations will benefit from internationalization, while others will lose. The loss may be because of brain drain, because Western ways of thinking may prevail, or because particular nations will likely dominate global education rankings. An overarching concern is that providers of international education will be mostly from developed countries, while the consumers of the education will be mostly from less developed countries, sending the flow of talent and money in the direction of developed countries (Barrett, Crossley, and Fon 2014; Clifford and Montgomery 2015; Knight 2014; Marginson 2010; Mertova 2014; Ziguras and McBurnie 2015). International educators should work to ensure reciprocity and equitable sharing of benefits as they develop internationalization programs and partnerships, a topic that will be explored in chapter 5.

Conclusion

Internationalization is an influential force shaping the education received by students at all levels, as well as the directions of research and the production and distribution of knowledge. As a process, internationalization offers institutions a strategy and cyclical process for incorporating international or intercultural dimensions into all aspects of their work. However, strategic planning for internationalization is often muddled by the lack of a common definition, with the term meaning different things to different people.

Across world regions, approaches to internationalization vary based on the political and economic contexts, as well as the structure of the national educational systems and the role of government in education. There are common concerns about the commodification of education and a fear that internationalization may exacerbate global and local inequities. While there are challenges, there is a shared promise that internationalization has the potential to develop students' global competence, mitigate global problems, build international understanding, and create a more peaceful and just world.

Resources

READINGS:

- Hudzik, John K. 2011. *Comprehensive Internationalization: From Concept to Action.* Washington, DC: NAFSA: Association of International Educators.

- Hudzik, John K., ed. 2015. *Comprehensive Internationalization: Institutional Pathways to Success.* New York, NY: Routledge.

- Hudzik, John K. 2017. *Comprehensive and Strategic Internationalization: Lessons Learned and Future Prospects.* Washington, DC: NAFSA: Association of International Educators.

- Knight, Jane. 2004. "Internationalization Remodeled: Definition, Approaches, and Rationales." *Journal of Studies in International Education* 8, 1:5–31.

- Leask, Betty. 2015. *Internationalizing the Curriculum.* New York, NY: Routledge.

DATA REPORTS:

- American Council on Education *Mapping Internationalization on U.S. Campuses* www.acenet.edu/news-room/Pages/Mapping-Internationalization-on-U-S-Campuses.aspx

- Institute of International Education *Open Doors* www.iie.org/opendoors

- International Association of Universities (IAU) Global Survey www.iau-aiu.net/Global-survey-on-Internationalization

- Organisation for Economic Co-operation and Development Education GPS gpseducation.oecd.org/

- Project Atlas www.iie.org/Research-and-Insights/Project-Atlas

- UNESCO Education Statistics uis.unesco.org/

WORKBOOKS/GUIDES:

- American Council on Education Toolkit www.acenet.edu/news-room/Pages/Internationalization-Toolkit.aspx

INTERNATIONALIZATION AWARDS:

- Institute of International Education Heiskell Awards www.iie.org/en/Research-and-Insights/Best-Practices-Resource/Award-Winners

- NAFSA: Association of International Educators Senator Paul Simon Award for Campus Internationalization www.nafsa.org/simonaward

References

Adams, Jonathan, David Pendlebury, and Bob Stembridge. 2013. *Building BRICKS: Exploring the Global Research and Innovation Impact of Brazil, Russia, India, China, and South Korea.* Philadelphia, PA: Thomson Reuters.

Altbach, Philip G. 2013. *The International Imperative in Higher Education.* Rotterdam: The Netherlands: Sense Publishers.

American Council on Education (ACE). 2012. *Mapping Internationalization on U.S. Campuses: 2012 Edition.* Washington, DC: American Council on Education. https://www.acenet.edu/news-room/Documents/Mapping-Internationalizationon-US-Campuses-2012-full.pdf.

American Council on Education (ACE). 2018. "ACE Internationalization Laboratory." ACE Internationalization Laboratory. Washington, DC: American Council on Education. https://www.acenet.edu/news-room/Pages/ACE-Internationalization-Laboratory.aspx.

American Councils for International Education. 2015. *Access Knowledge. Access the World. Internationalization Planning Guide.* Washington, DC: American Councils for International Education.

Andersen, Nick. 2015. "In Qatar's Education City, U.S. Colleges Are Building and Academic Oasis." *Washington Post.* December 6, 2015. https://www.washingtonpost.com/local/education/in-qatars-education-city-us-colleges-are-building-an-academic-oasis/2015/12/06/6b538702-8e01-11e5-ae1f-af46b7df8483_story.html?utm_term=.726c32daa7d3.

Barrett, Angeline M., Michael Crossley, and Titanji Peter Fon. 2014. "North-South Research Partnerships in Higher Education: Perspectives from South and North." In *Internationalisation of Higher Education and Global Mobility*, ed. Bernhard Streitwieser. Oxford, United Kingdom: Symposium Books.

Bedenlier, Svenja, and Olaf Zawacki-Richter. 2015. "Internationalization of Higher Education and the Impacts on Academic Faculty Members." *Research in Comparative and International Education* 10, 2:185–201. https://doi.org/10.1177/1745499915571707.

Belyavina, Raisa, Jing Li, and Rajika Bhandari. 2013. *New Frontiers: US Students Pursuing Degrees Abroad.* Washington, DC: Institute of International Education.

Brandenburg, Uwe, Harald Ermel, Gero Federkeil, Stephen Fuchs, Martin Groos, and Andrea Menn. 2009. "How to Measure the Internationality and Internationalisation of Higher Education Institutions: Indicators and Key Figures." In *Measuring Success in the Internationalisation of Higher Education*, ed. Hans de Wit. Amsterdam, The Netherlands: European Association for International Education.

Brewer, Elizabeth. 2015. "Beloit College: Internationalization in the American Midwest." In *Comprehensive Internationalization: Institutional Pathways to Success*, ed. John K. Hudzik. New York, NY: Routledge.

Bureau of Educational and Cultural Affairs. 2018. "Facts and Figures." Washington, DC: Department of State Bureau of Educational and Cultural Affairs. https://eca.state.gov/impact/facts-and-figures.

Burges, Sean W. 2014. "Australia-Latin America Education Relations." In *Australia and Latin America: Challenges and Opportunities in the New Millennium*, eds. Barry Carr and John Minns. Canberra, Australia: Australian National University Press.

Caruson, Kiki. 2018. *International Research Partnerships*. Washington, DC: NAFSA: Association of International Educators.

Civinini, Claudia. 2018. "UK: Gap Widening in Foreign Language Learning." *PIE News*. June 27, 2018. https://thepienews.com/news/gap-foreign-language-learning/.

Clifford, Valerie, and Catherine Montgomery. 2015. "Transformative Learning Through Internationalization of the Curriculum in Higher Education." *Journal of Transformative Education* 13, 1:46–64. https://doi.org/10.1177/1541344614560909.

Cross-Border Education Research Team. 2017. "C-BERT Branch Campus Listing." Albany, NY: Cross-Border Education Research Team. http://cbert.org/resources-data/branch-campus/.

Deardorff, Darla K. 2015. *Demystifying Outcomes Assessment for International Educators: A Practical Approach*. Sterling, VA: Stylus Publishing.

de Haan, Haijing (Helen). 2014. "Internationalization: Interpretations Among Dutch Practitioners." *Journal of Studies in International Education* 18, 3:241–260. https://doi.org/10.1177/1028315313496571.

Delisle, Pascal. 2009. "Rationales and Strategies Behind Double Degrees: A Transatlantic Approach." In *Joint and Double Degree Programs: An Emerging Model for Transatlantic Exchange*, eds. Daniel Obst and Matthias Kuder. New York, NY: Institute of International Education.

Egron-Polak, Eva, and Ross Hudson. 2010. *Internationalization of Higher Education: Global Trends, Regional Perspectives*. IAU 3rd Global Survey. Paris, France: International Association of Universities.

Egron-Polak, Eva, and Ross Hudson. 2014. *Internationalization of Higher Education: Growing Expectations, Fundamental Values*. IAU 4th Global Survey. Paris, France: International Association of Universities.

Gacel-Ávila, Jocelyne. 2010. "Latin America and the Caribbean." In *Internationalization of Higher Education: Global Trends, Regional Perspectives*, eds. Eva Egron-Polak and Ross Hudson. Paris, France: International Association of Universities.

Gao, Yuan. 2015. "Toward a Set of Internationally Applicable Indicators for Measuring University Internationalization Performance." *Journal of Studies in International Education* 19, 2:182–200. https://doi.org/10.1177/1028315314559030.

Gatewood, Jane, ed. Forthcoming. *NAFSA's Guide to International Partnerships: Developing Sustainable Academic Collaborations*. Washington, DC: NAFSA: Association of International Educators.

Green, Wendy, and Patricie Mertova. 2016. "Transformalists and Transactionists: Towards a More Comprehensive Understanding of Academics Engagement with 'Internationalisation of the Curriculum.'" *Research in Comparative and International Education* 11, 3:229–246. https://doi.org/10.1177/1745499916662372.

Helms, Robin Matross. 2015. *Internationalizing the Tenure Code: Policies to Promote a Globally Focused Faculty*. Washington, DC: American Council on Education. https://www.acenet.edu/news-room/Documents/Internationalizing-the-Tenure-Code-Policies-to-Promote-a-Globally-Focused-Faculty.pdf.

Helms, Robin Matross, and Lucia Brajkovic. 2017. *Mapping Internationalization on U.S. Campuses: 2017 Edition*. Washington, DC: American Council on Education. https://www.acenet.edu/news-room/Documents/Mapping-Internationalization-2017.pdf.

Holbrook, Karen A., and Kiki Caruson. 2017. *Globalizing University Research: Innovation, Collaboration and Competition*. New York, NY: Institute of International Education.

Huang, Futao. 2015. "The Internationalization of Japan's Academy Across Research and Non-Research Universities." *Journal of Studies in International Education* 19, 4:379–393. https://doi.org/10.1177/1028315315574102.

Hudzik, John K. 2011. *Comprehensive Internationalization: From Concept to Action*. Washington, DC: NAFSA: Association of International Educators.

Hudzik, John K., ed. 2015. *Comprehensive Internationalization: Institutional Pathways to Success*. London, United Kingdom: Routledge.

Hudzik, John K. 2018. *Comprehensive and Strategic Internationalization: Lessons Learned and Prospects*. Washington, DC: NAFSA: Association of International Educators.

Institute of International Education (IIE). 2018a. *Open Doors Report on International Educational Exchange*. New York, NY: Institute of International Education. https://www.iie.org/opendoors.

Institute of International Education (IIE). 2018b. "Project Atlas 2018 Infographics." Institute of International Education. https://www.iie.org/en/Research-and-Insights/Project-Atlas/Explore-Data/Current-Infographics.

International Monetary Fund. 2016. *World Economic Outlook: October 2016*. Washington, DC: International Monetary Fund.

Jain, C. R. 2015. "The Knowledge Economy and the Transformational Dynamics of Education in Asia's Emergent Economic Growth." In *Asia: The Next Higher Education Superpower?*, eds. Rajika Bhandari and Alessa Lefebure. New York, NY: Institute of International Education.

Jowi, James Otieno. 2010. "Africa." In *Internationalization of Higher Education: Global Trends, Regional Perspectives*, eds. Eva Egron-Polak and Ross Hudson. Paris, France: International Association of Universities.

Kacenga, George. 2019. "On the Rise: State Consortia." *International Educator* XXVIII, 1:40–43.

Knight, Jane. 2004. "Internationalization Remodeled: Definition, Approaches, and Rationales." *Journal of Studies in International Education* 8, 1:5–31. https://doi.org/10.1177/1028315303260832.

Knight, Jane. 2011. "Five Myths about Internationalization." *International Higher Education* 62. https://doi.org/10.6017/ihe.2011.62.8532.

Knight, Jane. 2012. "Concepts, Rationales, and Interpretive Frameworks in the Internationalization of Higher Education." In *The SAGE Handbook of International Higher Education*, eds. Darla K. Deardorff, Hans de Wit, John Heyl, and Tony Adams. Thousand Oaks, CA: Sage Publications.

Knight, Jane. 2014. "Three Generations of Crossborder Higher Education: New Development, Issues, and Challenges." In *Internationalisation of Higher Education and Global Mobility*, ed. Bernhard Streitwieser. Oxford, United Kingdom: Symposium Books.

Korhonen, Vesa, and Markus Weil. 2015. "The Internationalisation of Higher Education: Perspectives on Self-Conceptions in Teaching." *Journal of Research in International Education* 14, 3:198–212. https://doi.org/10.1177/1475240915615447.

Laughlin, Shepherd. 2008. "Trends and Models of Academic Exchange between China and the U.S." In *U.S.-China Educational Exchange: Perspectives on a Growing Partnership*, ed. Shepherd Laughlin. New York, NY: Institute of International Education.

Leask, Betty. 2015. *Internationalizing the Curriculum*. London, United Kingdom: Routledge.

Looney, Dennis, and Natalia Lusin. 2018. "Enrollments in Languages Other than English in United States Institutions of Higher Education, Summer 2016 and Fall 2016: Preliminary Report." New York, NY: Modern Language Association. https://www.mla.org/content/download/83540/2197676/2016-Enrollments-Short-Report.pdf.

Macready, Caroline, and Clive Tucker. 2011. *Who Goes Where and Why? An Overview and Analysis of Global Educational Mobility*. Washington, DC: Institute of International Education. https://www.iie.org:443/en/Research-and-Insights/Publications/Who-Goes-Where-and-Why.

Marginson, Simon. 2010. "Global Comparisons and the University Knowledge Economy." In *Higher Education, Policy, and the Global Competition Phenomena*, eds. Laura M. Portnoi, Val D. Rust, and Sylvia S. Bagley. New York, NY: Palgrave Macmillan.

Marginson, Simon. 2016. *The Dream Is Over: The Crisis of Clark Kerr's California Idea of Higher Education*. Oakland, CA: University of California Press.

McLellan, Carlton E. 2011. "International Education Travel and Youth of Color: College Is Too Late!" *Education and Urban Society* 43, 2:244–265. https://doi.org/10.1177/0013124510379874.

Meda, Lawrence, and Mabokang Monnapula-Mapesela. 2016. "Going Wide, Not Wild: Varying Conceptualizations of Internationalization at a University of Technology in South Africa." *Journal of Studies in International Education* 20, 3:282–294. https://doi.org/10.1177/1028315316637340.

Mertova, Patricie. 2014. "Academic Perspectives on Internationalisation in Three Countries." *Research in Comparative and International Education* 9, 2:137–148. https://doi.org/10.2304/rcie.2014.9.2.137.

Obst, Daniel, and Matthias Kuder. 2011. *Joint and Double Degree Programs in the Transatlantic Context: A Survey Report*. New York, NY: Institute of International Education.

Obst, Daniel, Matthias Kuder, and Clare Banks. 2011. *Joint and Double Degree Programs in the Global Context: Report on an International Survey*. New York, NY: Institute of International Education.

Punteney, Katherine. 2012. "International Careers: The Gap Between Student Interest and Knowledge." *Journal of Studies in International Education* 16, 4:390–407.

Punteney, Katherine, and Yilin Wei. 2018. "Dynamics of Internationalization in U.S. and Chinese Higher Education." In *The Rise of China-U.S. International Cooperation in Higher Education: Views from the Field*, eds. Christopher J. Johnstone and Li Li Ji. Leiden, The Netherlands: Brill Sense.

Pysarchik, Dawn Thorndike. 2015. "Michigan State University: Origins and Evolution of an Institution Toward a Global Frame." In *Comprehensive Internationalization: Institutional Pathways to Success*, ed. John K. Hudzik. New York, NY: Routledge.

Redden, Elizabeth. 2015. "The Branch Campus Boom(s)." *Inside Higher Ed*. March 16, 2015. https://www.insidehighered.com/news/2015/03/16/international-branch-campus-phenomenon-just-fad.

Uraneck, Madeline. 2002. *Planning Curriculum in International Education*. Madison, WI: Wisconsin Department of Public Instruction.

Vardhan, Julie. 2015. "Internationalization and the Changing Paradigm of Higher Education in the GCC Countries." *SAGE Open* 5, 2. https://doi.org/10.1177/2158244015580377.

Wächter, Bernd. 2014. "Recent Trends in Student Mobility in Europe." In *Internationalisation of Higher Education and Global Mobility*, ed. Bernhard Streitwieser. Oxford, United Kingdom: Symposium Books.

Ward, Heather. 2016. *Internationalization in Action: Special Edition. Connecting Classrooms: Using Online Technology to Deliver Global Learning*. Washington, DC: American Council on Education. https://www.acenet.edu/news-room/Documents/Connecting-Classrooms-Using-Online-Technology-to-Deliver-Global-Learning.pdf.

West, Charlotte. 2015. "Degrees Without Borders." *International Educator* XXIV, 4:20–32.

Williams, Rhiannon D., and Amy Lee, eds. 2015. *Internationalizing Higher Education: Critical Collaborations Across the Curriculum*. Rotterdam, The Netherlands: Sense Publishers.

Witte, Spencer. 2010. "Different Emirates, Different Models: Creating Global Institutions in the Gulf States." In *Innovation Through Education: Building the Knowledge Economy in the Middle East*, eds. Daniel Obst and Daniel Kirk. New York, NY: Institute of International Education.

Woodfield, Steve. 2010. "Europe." In *Internationalization of Higher Education: Global Trends, Regional Perspectives*, eds. Eva Egron-Polak and Ross Hudson. Paris, France: International Association of Universities.

Wu, Thomas. 2010. "Asia and Pacific." In *Internationalization of Higher Education: Global Trends, Regional Perspectives*, eds. Eva Egron-Polak and Ross Hudson. Paris, France: International Association of Universities.

Yemini, Miri. 2014. "Internationalisation Discourse: What Remains to Be Said?" *Perspectives: Policy and Practice in Higher Education* 18, 2:66–71. https://doi.org/10.1080/13603108.2014.888019.

Yemini, Miri, and Netta Sagie. 2016. "Research on Internationalisation in Higher Education - Exploratory Analysis." *Perspectives: Policy and Practice in Higher Education* 20, 2–3:90–98. https://doi.org/10.1080/13603108.2015.1062057.

Ziguras, Christopher, and Grant McBurnie. 2015. *Governing Cross-Border Higher Education*. New York, NY: Routledge.

Chapter 4

Education Abroad

"Education abroad" is the term used to describe educational programs that move people across national borders. This includes study abroad programs, in which students travel internationally and take academic courses for credit, and many other educational programs such as work abroad, intern abroad, volunteer abroad, research abroad, and international service-learning. Many international educators work for organizations that offer more than one type of opportunity. For that reason, increasingly, professionals in the field refer to themselves as "education abroad advisers," rather than "study abroad advisers," to reflect the full scope of their work and expertise. This chapter focuses specifically on study abroad, and chapter 5, "Experiential Education," explores additional types of education abroad programs.

While there is great diversity in study abroad program types and scopes, what all programs have in common is that they center around learning. And the learning opportunities provided through study abroad are different from those offered at the home university (Rodman and Merrill 2010). Study abroad programs exist for the purpose of student learning, and the importance of curricular planning and assessment of that learning cannot be overemphasized.

U.S. Study Abroad

In contrast to international trends in which students typically go abroad to earn a full degree, in the United States, it is more common for students to go abroad for a portion of their degree program, such as for a summer or semester, and transfer credits back to their U.S. university. An annual publication from the Institute of International Education (IIE), called *Open Doors*, reports on students enrolled at U.S. colleges and universities who study abroad. The self-reported data are gathered through a survey sent to all U.S. colleges and universities. Not all colleges and universities respond to the survey each year, and *Open Doors* captures only the numbers of students, destinations, etc., and does not address qualitative questions about why students study abroad or what they gain from the experience. Despite the limitations, *Open Doors* comprises the most comprehensive data available on U.S. students studying abroad.

Open Doors reports that in the 2016–17 academic year, 332,727 U.S. students studied abroad (IIE 2018). The top five destinations were the United Kingdom (12.0 percent), Italy (10.6 percent), Spain (9.4 percent), France (4.9 percent), and Germany (3.8 percent) (IIE 2018). As is apparent, Western European destinations attract the most U.S. students, a destination pattern that has been consistent since the *Open Doors* report first began tracking study abroad in 1985. There has, however, been a gradual increase in student interest in non-European destinations. China is the sixth most popular destination, hosting 3.6 percent of all U.S. study abroad students in 2016–17 (IIE 2018). During the same year, short-term programs for the summer or 8 weeks or less were most common, with 64.6 percent of the total participants; one semester or one or two quarter programs enrolled 33.1 percent of the participants; and academic or calendar year programs enrolled 2.3 percent of the participants (IIE 2018). Although the number of U.S. students studying abroad continues to increase, only 1.8 percent of all U.S. undergraduates studied abroad in 2016–17, and only 16 percent of those who earned bachelor's degrees in 2016–17 had studied abroad (IIE 2018).

History of Study Abroad

William Hoffa's (2007) book, *A History of U.S. Study Abroad: Beginnings to 1965*, offers insights into the antecedents of study abroad and the historical and political forces that have shaped today's programs. Below are a few examples that are described in the book.

The tradition of wandering scholars dates back to ancient India and Greece, and probably earlier. Long before libraries existed, wisdom was passed on orally. The University of Takshasila offered curriculum in Persian and Greek to traveling scholars during a period believed to span from 600 BC to AD 250 (Hoffa 2007). It attracted many scholars from outside of India, including Alexander the Great. Unlike universities today, these were not places that focused on generating new knowledge, but places where accepted wisdom was passed from generation to generation.

The University of Nalanda in Northern India was founded in AD 450 and lasted about 7 centuries, attracting scholars from China (Hoffa 2007). It was a center for study by Buddhist monks who memorized sacred texts, studying under the guidance of masters. From the fourth through the ninth centuries, scholars at the Persian University of Jundishapur brought together ideas of medicine, philosophy, and literature from Jewish, Christian, Hindu, and Persian traditions (Hoffa 2007). From the later Middle Ages to well past the Renaissance, scholars would move from library to library, mentor to mentor, and university to university with few diplomatic barriers because national boundaries were not yet defined and guarded.

The term "Grand Tour" was introduced in Richard Lessels's (1670) book *Voyage to Italy* and grew

(continued on next page)

History of Study Abroad (continued)

in popularity in the seventeenth and eighteenth centuries. These Grand Tours were not adopted by wandering scholars, but young men from elite families traveling to other countries pursuing social, diplomatic, familial, and pragmatic goals. The young men typically traveled for 2 to 4 years and often came back more knowledgeable, worldly, and ready to undertake their family responsibilities. The Grand Tour was the foundation of tourism, combining enjoyment and enlightenment.

In the United States, study abroad began to take shape in the 1920s. World War I had just ended and there was a national sense that the United States was now positioned as a world leader. Internationalists believed that a more active U.S. presence overseas would help prevent future wars. Former soldiers, diplomats, and others remembered not just the fighting, but the more positive experiences they enjoyed overseas, engaging with people and learning new things. AFS-USA, a youth exchange program, started during the war as an ambulance service. After the war, "the spirit of fellowship among volunteers and their shared revulsion at the ravages of war were so strong that AFS turned its energies and resources to funding students from France and the United States to study in each other's countries" (Hoffa 2007, 63).

The current model of university study abroad (taking classes abroad and applying the credits toward a degree at the home institution) started in the United States in the 1920s. Pedagogically, the study abroad concept was based on a realization by some U.S. colleges and universities that exposure to the world should be part of a well-rounded undergraduate education. Three program structures appeared during this period: junior year abroad, faculty-led study tours, and summer study on a particular theme or discipline. Early programs were to Europe, especially France, and continued until World War II interrupted them. Following WWII, there was another wave of support for study abroad, with the goals of fostering peace and intercultural understanding.

Access, Inclusion, and Equity

A closer look at IIE's *Open Doors* data on study abroad for the 2016–17 academic year suggests that some demographic groups are participating at lower rates than others. Among the students who studied abroad, 67.3 percent of the participants were female and 32.7 percent were male (IIE 2018). By comparison, of the students enrolled in U.S. degree-granting institutions in 2016, 56.5 percent were female and 43.5 percent were male (Snyder, de Brey, and Dillow 2018, table 303.10). The data reveal that female students are studying abroad at higher rates than male students, even taking into account that more female students are enrolled in higher education.

Race and Ethnicity

The *Open Doors* data show trends in participation levels among racial and ethnic groups. Table 1 displays data on the race and ethnicity of students studying abroad in 2016–17, shown in comparison with national data on the enrollment of undergraduate students in U.S. higher education. As the data show, white and Asian students are overrepresented in study abroad in comparison with national higher education enrollments, and all other racial/ethnic groups are underrepresented in study abroad.

TABLE 1. Percentage of Students Studying Abroad and in Higher Education, by Race and Ethnicity

	Students Studying Abroad in 2016–17*	U.S. Undergraduate Students Enrolled in U.S. Higher Education Institutions in 2016*
White	70.8%	55.7%
Hispanic or Latino(a)	10.2%	19.4%
Asian, Native Hawaiian, or Other Pacific Islander	8.2%	6.7%**
Black or African American	6.1%	13.6%
Multiracial	4.3%	3.7%
American Indian or Alaska Native	0.4%	1.0%

Sources: Institute of International Education (2018); Snyder, de Brey, and Dillow (2018).
*International students are not included in these statistics. U.S. higher education data are from table 306.50 of Snyder, de Brey, and Dillow (2018).
**In this data set, Native Hawaiians are not listed separately.

Research focusing on why students of color are underrepresented in study abroad point to several barriers, including rigid academic program structures, length of study, and lack of family support (Lu et al. 2015). Students may also face financial barriers, or the perception of financial barriers, discouraging them from studying abroad (Tolan and McCullers 2018). Moreover, studies show that students of color often receive less information about study abroad opportunities and are less likely to have role models who support study abroad (Lu et al. 2015). Of course, not all individuals have the same experience, and not all cultural groups have the same experience.

In a study of Latinx students who had not studied abroad, McClure et al. (2010) found that the majority of the students they interviewed had previous international travel experience. The students had been interested in study abroad but chose not to participate; they recognized the value of study abroad for their careers but found the program offerings fairly Eurocentric. Instead, the students reported that they hoped to go abroad in the future in another context, such as in the summer or after graduation (McClure et al. 2010). Most of these Latinx students expressed interest in visiting Spanish-speaking countries in Latin America or Spain. When McClure et al. (2010) explored these students' barriers to participating in study abroad, they found three common reasons. First, students were closely connected to their family and found the idea of a semester away from family to be intimidating. Second, students were concerned about the financial burden that participation would put on their family. Third, students expressed concern that studying abroad would jeopardize their ability to complete their degrees on time.

Finances and Logistics

Beyond gender and ethnicity, other groups are underrepresented in study abroad programs as well. Study abroad is generally less feasible for low-income students. Even with financial aid being applied to study abroad tuition, commuting students would have to pay for housing abroad and working students would need to give up their jobs (Hoffa and DePaul 2010). Students may have family financial obligations, such as providing care for parents, children, or other relatives (Hoffa and DePaul 2010).

Some students feel that they cannot participate in study abroad programs for logistical reasons rooted in the curriculum structure. For example, students studying in the science, technology, engineering, and mathematics (STEM) fields often have to take more credits than students in the humanities, and they tend to have more prerequisite courses, making it harder for them to spend time away from campus. Athletes may also face logistical difficulties because of training expectations, game schedules, and scholarships tied to their participation on sports teams. Many of these logistical challenges may be within the control of, and can be resolved by, the university. Study abroad professionals can work with faculty to develop programs to specifically fit the needs and schedules of these students.

Although real and perceived barriers do exist, students are usually advised that they can study abroad in any major as long as they plan ahead and think carefully about their general education and major course requirements (DeWinter and Rumbley 2010). While not a fully equitable solution to providing access, some of the short-term faculty-led programs available can make participation more feasible for underrepresented students, such as students with families, students with restrictive curricula, athletes, working students, graduate students, and professional school students, because the time away from campus is shorter and focused (Chieffo and Spaeth 2017; Rodman and Merrill 2010). Shorter-term programs typically have more diverse participation (Ogden 2017).

Education Abroad Advocates

Hoffa and DePaul (2010) argue that study abroad will not reach its full potential until there is greater diversity of study abroad destinations and more representative participation in programs. Institutions can work toward equitable access and inclusion in education abroad by cultivating a network of education abroad advocates with whom underrepresented students can relate. These may be student peers who have already studied abroad or staff in offices that serve underrepresented groups on campus. Institutions can engage these allies to help recruit and advise prospective students (Meadows 2014; Brux and Fry 2010).

Faculty can also serve a very important role in encouraging students to take their education abroad. Many students would not have participated in study abroad if they had not been encouraged to do so by a faculty member (Lu et al. 2015). For example, in a study of African

American students who chose to study abroad, the encouragement of a respected African American faculty member prompted many students to consider study abroad, including those who had not considered it before (Lu et al. 2015). Faculty and institutional leaders can take several steps to encourage and promote access to study abroad opportunities. For example, they can ensure that resources are available to support students with specific needs, such as students with disabilities and lesbian, gay, bisexual, transgender, and queer (LGBTQ) students (Malveaux 2016).

Staff across all departments should be expected to promote access and inclusion, including encouraging students of diverse backgrounds to study abroad (Butler, Madden, and Smith 2018). Staff members in academic and career advising offices can help to motivate students and provide reassurances by showing them which courses can be taken each semester to allow for participation in study abroad (Brux and Fry 2010; Thebodo 2014). Additionally, in working closely with the marketing and communications departments on campus, faculty and staff can prominently communicate the personal and professional benefits of study abroad to further attract students (Bandyopadhyay and Bandyopadhyay 2015). The reach of education abroad offices is expanded and supported by deep connections with other student affairs offices on campus (Butler, Madden, and Smith 2018). With advocates and allies across campus, institutions can develop and implement study abroad programs that address the needs, challenges, and interests of larger, more diverse pools of students.

Program Models

There is tremendous variation among study abroad programs in terms of length, language requirements, teaching styles, amounts of structured time, accommodations, and level of community engagement. During the design process, faculty and staff must determine whether the program will be general versus specialized, limited to students from one institution or open to many, offer course choices or have a prescribed curriculum, focus on experiential learning or traditional classroom learning, etc. (McCallon and Holmes 2010; Rodman and Merrill 2010; Thebodo 2014). There is no one best model. The program design choices depend on the students, institution, host culture, trends in higher education, and learning goals, among many other factors (Rodman and Merrill 2010). Three common program models are presented in this section, though it must be noted that many programs do not neatly fit a single model and instead combine elements of two or more models in hybrid formats.

Direct Enrollment

The term "direct enrollment" refers to a program in which the entity that is managing the study abroad program is an organization other than the student's home university. In practice, the term has several related uses within the field of international education. The term direct enrollment may be used to describe a student who applies for admission to a foreign university, gains admittance, and studies there for a full degree program (also referred to as "degree mobility" in chapter 3). Direct enrollment may also be used to refer to U.S. students studying abroad on programs run by provider organizations, which are nonprofit and for-profit organizations that manage education abroad programs. In this case, direct enrollment describes a student enrolling in a provider's study abroad program, with limited facilitation by the student's home university. A third use of the term is describing any education abroad program in which students take courses from host country universities, joining classes primary populated by host country students. All of these scenarios have their own set of benefits and challenges.

When direct enrollment results in the student taking classes with local students at the host university, it is often considered to be a very "authentic" form of study abroad because the student is directly and deeply immersed in the host culture. The student is interacting closely with instructors and peers and experiencing the educational system as it is in the country, rather than experiencing something that has been adapted to the expectation of U.S. students (Butler 2017). The student is held to the same academic expectations as the local students and has access to the same support services.

While the potential benefits of direct enrollment are apparent, there are also some challenges. One key challenge for direct enrollment students is the language of instruction (also known as the "medium of instruction") (Chisholm and Berry 2002). In many cases, students studying abroad are not fluent in the local language and do not have the language skills to complete advanced academic work in a second language. Engle and Engle (2012, 288) argue that the linguistic challenge of direct enrollment "is often too unrealistically high to be pedagogically sound." There are also some cultural differences to be considered, including the expectations surrounding student-professor interactions, classroom conduct, assignments, grading, and assumed background knowledge (Engle and Engle 2012).

Education Abroad Program Providers

Education abroad program providers are nonprofit and for-profit organizations that specialize in running education abroad programs. They are key players in the international education field, facilitating international learning opportunities for large numbers of students and expanding the capacity of higher education institutions to offer a diverse range of education abroad programs. Providers may offer programs aimed at youths, university-aged participants, and/or working professionals. Provider organizations operate in two primary modes: (a) designing customized programs for specific institutions, and (b) developing their own programs to serve students from multiple institutions.

One way that program providers work directly with colleges and universities is arranging customized programs. These are often faculty-led programs in which the faculty member is responsible for the curriculum and teaching and the provider is responsible for the program logistics. Many program design choices, such as identifying the

(continued on next page)

Education Abroad Program Providers (continued)

most pertinent field excursions, directly link the curriculum with the logistics, so the faculty member and provider work closely on many aspects of the customized program design. Some providers also arrange study tours. These may be short spring break trips, or programs for groups such as traveling student athletes or student musicians who are participating in performances and exhibitions, paired with the opportunity for the students to learn about the countries and cultures visited.

Providers may also decide to design their own education abroad programs in countries and focus areas that they think will appeal to students and connect to the educational goals of higher education institutions. The providers enroll students from multiple universities in short-term, semester, or yearlong programs. They may work with partner universities to market these programs and to get the programs preapproved for credit transfers to the students' home institution.

In the case of individual students enrolling directly with a program provider, a student works with a provider organization throughout the study abroad process. The provider may offer its own academic courses, assist students in enrolling in local university courses, or present a combination of these two modes of study. The provider is usually able to deliver cultural advising and may coordinate extracurricular programs. The provider guides the student through the admission process, predeparture preparation and orientation, visas, travel, housing, course enrollment, etc. The provider may have on-site staff at the study abroad location to support the student, especially during an emergency.

Enrollment with a provider organization can be very helpful to students who are inexperienced with international travel, want more structure and support, or are not proficient in the language of the host country. While direct enrollment through a provider organization does not foster quite as much independence as direct enrollment with a university, it can be just as beneficial. In fact, research shows that students enrolled in courses that are geared toward their needs as study abroad students may sometimes experience more intercultural learning than students in direct enrollment programs (Engle and Engle 2012).

Because provider programs are not managed by the home university, there are some special considerations. Common issues include the complexity of credit transfer, the difficulty of applying financial aid to provider programs, and the lack of home institution quality control (Butler 2017). While working with a provider may increase the cost of the program, providers can offer knowledge about local laws and regulations, connect with networks of host country contacts, provide professional support in crises, utilize their business infrastructure to make payments in the host country in local currency, and take on some of the liability, among other benefits (Butler 2017). Provider-managed programs are one of the least resource-intensive models from the home institution's point of view and are a popular and valuable study abroad program option for many students (Butler 2017).

Exchange Programs

In bilateral exchange programs, students from two universities "trade places" and take courses at the other school. Exchange programs are jointly managed by the two partner universities. These reciprocal exchanges typically last a semester or a year. The exchange may be set up by a particular department for its students only, or the program may be available to students from across the whole institution (Sanderson 2014). Exchanges may also be multilateral, meaning that multiple institutions participate. In this case, each institution sends the same number of exchange students out each year as it receives onto its campus, but the institutions and countries it is sending students to may not be the same ones from which it is receiving students (Thebodo 2014).

The exchange model has many advantages. Generally, exchange students pay their usual tuition costs to their home university, and no money is exchanged between the institutions (Thebodo 2014). Thus, the students are able to use their financial aid toward their tuition expenses, and the institutions do not lose that tuition revenue (as in the case of direct enrollment at a foreign university). Additionally, exchange programs can be built from existing faculty or staff contacts, require limited financial resources to establish, and can diversify the student bodies of the partnering institutions (Butler 2017; Sanderson 2014).

But the exchange model also comes with several challenges. From the students' perspective, they may face similar challenges in terms of foreign language ability and differences in academic norms that were described earlier in connection to direct enrollment. On the administrative level, the biggest challenge is maintaining the exchange balance between the two partnering institutions. This model is built on the premise of exchanging the same number of students from each institution, so that neither institution loses financially in terms of student tuition and fees. Unfortunately, it is rarely the case that the level of interest among students in each country is the same. Study abroad professionals, thus, must work carefully with partners to monitor the exchange balance year after year and ensure that, through recruitment efforts and program admissions decisions, the numbers remain equal (Butler 2017; Sanderson 2014).

Another challenge is that establishing an exchange agreement takes significant time and energy; it can often take 6 months or more to find appropriate institutional partners and come to an agreement that works for all parties involved (Sanderson 2014). The academic calendars and course curricula between the two institutions must have some alignment, and both partners must agree to the level of student services that will be provided to support the exchange students (Butler 2017). Once the agreement is signed, the relationship must be nurtured and supported with adequate resources. Many exchange agreements that are established are never implemented or fizzle out over time due to a lack of resources, interest, or clear desired outcomes (DeWinter and Rumbley 2010).

Faculty-Led Programs

A faculty-led program is one in which a faculty member from the home institution travels abroad with a group of students and teaches one or more courses in her or his area of expertise. Though the model is sometimes used for semester and yearlong programs, faculty-led programs are one of the most common models for short-term study abroad programs (Butler 2017). Many programs are as short as a week or two, during spring break or a January term, for instance.

Faculty-led programs are managed by the home university or, in some cases, the home university in partnership with a provider organization. Some may be intentionally designed to complement, or be imbedded into, a course happening on campus during the regular academic term. While some educators argue that these short-term programs blur the line between study abroad and educational tourism, others say they open the door for students with families, limited budgets, curricular constraints, and no prior international experience (DeWinter and Rumbley 2010).

Because faculty-led programs are partially or fully organized by the home institution, there is greater assurance that the programs meet institutional expectations of quality and follow institutional policies. In other words, there is strong home institution control (Sanderson 2014). Institutions also benefit from the faculty members' involvement because they may bring back new knowledge, perspectives, and teaching strategies that can contribute to increased internationalization of the home campus (McCallon and Holmes 2010).

Some of the challenges of this model are that students have to assume the program and travel costs, minimum enrollment numbers must be met for viability, and the institution has greater liability (Butler 2017). There may also be some considerations with respect to faculty training and development. While the faculty members who lead programs abroad typically have international travel experience and are experts in the curricular content, they may not have training in the field of international education or experience in shepherding a group of students. A faculty member who is used to interacting with students primarily in the classroom may find that the relationship with students becomes much more intimate and complex as they travel together. In addition to handling the travel logistics, faculty members may find themselves managing group dynamics, advising students on their intercultural adjustment, supporting students in medical and mental health emergencies, addressing disciplinary issues, and responding to many other areas in which they may not have experience (McCallon and Holmes 2010; Sanderson 2014).

Most faculty-led programs are initiated by faculty members, and many universities require that faculty members develop detailed program proposals. A committee, typically managed by the education abroad office and including faculty members, often decides which programs will be offered based on an assessment of the soundness of the program proposal. Committee members consider the feasibility of the proposed learning outcomes; the curriculum; the program's relation to institutional priorities; the faculty member's capacity to manage the program; the details and reasonableness of the budget, emergency plans, and other proposal elements; and the likelihood that the program will attract enough students to be able to run (McCallon and Holmes 2010; Sanderson 2014). The logistics (e.g., application process, predeparture orientation, accommodations, classroom space, transportation, excursions, etc.) can be organized by the faculty member, by a staff member in the education abroad office (sometimes the faculty-led program coordinator), or by the two working together (McCallon and Holmes 2010). Alternatively, many universities contract with education abroad providers. In the case of faculty-led programs, the provider will arrange the logistics of the program, leaving the faculty member to focus more on preparing the course curriculum.

Education Abroad Program Characteristics

Education abroad programs vary greatly in their design. Table 2 displays some of the terms commonly used in the field to describe the characteristics of education abroad programs. A single program may be described by several of these characteristics. For additional terms, see the extensive glossary available on The Forum on Education Abroad's website (forumea.org/resources/glossary).

TABLE 2 Common Terms Used to Describe Education Abroad Programs

Consortium	A consortium program is one in which multiple institutions collaborate to offer the study abroad program. By combining resources and student populations, the institutions can offer a broader range of program options and run programs that might have had enrollments that were too low to run otherwise. A lead institution often manages the logistics (Butler 2017).
Embedded	An embedded program is part of a regular on-campus course, such as a spring break study abroad program as part of a semester-long course (Butler 2017).
Island	An island program is one in which students from the home country are grouped together for coursework and/or housing abroad. A mostly self-contained program, it can be designed to meet the needs and expectations of the students and home institution. This type of program is becoming less common, and the term has a negative connotation in the field because this type of program, by its design, limits interactions with the local people (Thebodo 2014; Sanderson 2014).
DIY	DIY is a term borrowed from the home improvement world that means "do it yourself." In the context of study abroad, it refers to university faculty and staff arranging the logistics of a study abroad program themselves rather than contracting with a provider. It is a very time- and energy-intensive way to create a program, but it does allow for control over all the details (McCallon and Holmes 2010).
Provider	A provider is a nonprofit or for-profit organization that runs education abroad programs. Staffed by international education specialists, providers typically offer professional expertise, global networks, and well-developed crisis management plans. Usually running a selection of programs, they attract students from many institutions, thereby expanding the range of offerings that institutions can promote. Providers must charge fees to cover their operating expenses, potentially increasing the cost of the programs.
Customized	Customized study abroad programs are designed and operated by a provider organization specifically for one institution or group, enrolling only that group of students in the program. Customized programs harness the benefits of a provider, while allowing for the specific requirements of the institution to be met. There are, of course, added costs because of the added work the provider is doing to create the program (Thebodo 2014; Sanderson 2014).
Immersion	Immersion is a broad term used to refer to any program that requires student engagement with the host culture and people. Common immersion practices include direct enrollment courses and homestays. Metaphorically, immersion is the act of surrounding the students with the culture in the same way they would be surrounded by water if thrown in the swimming pool. There is often an assumption in the field of international education that when the study abroad experience is immersive, cultural learning will be robust and effortless (Passarelli and Kolb 2012).

(continued on next page)

Education Abroad Program Characteristics (continued)

Language Immersion	Language immersion programs attempt to immerse the students not only in the culture, but also in the local language. This is often done through language pledges in which students agree to speak only the local language during their program. Courses are taught entirely in the local language. Direct enrollment, homestays, and other program elements may also be used to increase the opportunities for students to practice their language skills (Engle and Engle 2012; Passarelli and Kolb 2012).
Stationary	A stationary program is based in a single location for its duration. It may include short day trips to other destinations, but most of the time is spent in one city or town (McCallon and Holmes 2010).
Multistop	In a multistop program, students spend significant time in two or more locations. These traveling programs are well suited to comparisons of regions and examinations of global issues, but, by their nature, may lead to less time for deep engagement with each culture (Hoffa 2007; McCallon and Holmes 2010; DeWinter and Rumbley 2010).
Freshman/ First-Year Program	A growing number of study abroad programs are being offered to first-year university students. These programs can be educationally impactful and help incoming students form bonds with each other and the university. In addition to the curricular considerations, these programs can serve a very pragmatic need for institutions by decreasing the demand for first-year student housing (DeWinter and Rumbley 2010).
Field Study	Field study programs offer hands-on experience to students in a particular discipline, for example, giving archaeology students the opportunity to participate in an archaeological dig in another country. The programs can provide students with career benefits and real-world research skills. These programs may offer more basic accommodations than some other programs (McCallon and Holmes 2010).
Independent Study	In a program with an independent study component, students work on individual research projects that complement their other studies. The project may be a capstone project for their study abroad program (McCallon and Holmes 2010).
Experiential Learning	Experiential learning is based on Kolb's (1984) theory of experiential learning. It involves four stages: concrete experience, reflective observation, abstract conceptualization, and active experimentation. Field study, independent study, service-learning, and other educational approaches may be forms of experiential learning if they involve the cyclical stages of doing, reflecting, thinking, and hypothesizing.
Study Tour	A study tour is often a short multistop program that focuses on a particular theme. It has some resemblance to tourism in that it may not allow for significant immersion (Thebodo 2014).
Internship	Increasingly, study abroad programs have included an internship component. Students may undertake an internship after completing their coursework, or they may do a part-time internship concurrently with their studies. Adding an internship to a study abroad program allows the students to experience not only the academic culture, but also the workplace culture in the host country.
Service- Learning	Service-learning programs bring the act of community service together with the learning element of an intentionally designed curriculum. It may be added to a study abroad program for credit, or as an extracurricular activity, and exposes students to an additional host country context beyond the academic setting (McCallon and Holmes 2010).

Chapter 5, "Experiential Education," covers many of the benefits, challenges, and considerations of these programs in greater depth.

Program Design Process

There is no single "best" study abroad program model, and no program characteristic is inherently superior to any other program characteristic. Decisions made by the program planners during the program design process must fit the context (i.e., faculty and student interest, available resources, existing programs, applicable regulations, etc.) as well as the institutional values. In the past, study abroad programs may have been designed without careful articulation of the intended learning outcomes or a plan for assessment; however, this is rapidly shifting. Current thinking is that curriculum/program design and assessment are intrinsically linked and cannot be separated.

In recognition of the bond between design and assessment, the starting point for designing any educational program or curriculum is determining the measurable learning outcomes that students should have attained by the end of the program. The second step is to identify the evidence that will demonstrate that the learning outcomes have been achieved. Third, program planners should select the teaching methodologies and learning activities for the program that will best enable the students to reach the designed outcomes. The fourth step in the design process is to gather the resources needed to facilitate the learning activities identified and verify their availability. The resources used, learning activities, teaching methods, evidence of learning, and outcomes must all align. Even the program logistical choices should be guided by the desired learning outcomes.

Program design is an iterative process, meaning that it takes many drafts and revisions to develop a curriculum or program plan with this level of alignment. Known as "backward design" because it starts with the outcomes assessment and moves toward the design, this process is an effective way to approach any learning endeavor, including the development of global competence (Deardorff 2015; Gregersen-Hermans 2017; Lucas and Blair 2017; Wyatt Knowlton and Phillips 2013). The backward design process can be applied at any scope: a single lesson, course, program, degree, or even a national curriculum. It can be used to develop international education programs in any sector of the field. In this chapter, the backward design process is described in relation to the development of study abroad programs.

Step 1: Determining Learning Outcomes

One major goal of study abroad programs is to develop students' global competence, which is their ability to interact effectively, appropriately, and ethically with people of cultural backgrounds different from their own. There are likely additional curricular goals specific to the program focus (such as learning archaeology skills or developing a sophisticated understanding of global health practices). The first step in the program design process is establishing the program learning outcomes specific to that program. Many institutions choose to look at global competence models for ideas and then develop their own set of desired learning outcomes. On the other hand, already established models of global learning outcomes have typically already undergone multiple rounds of refinement and feedback from experts, so they may have the advantage of being ready for institutional use with little or no revision.

The Organisation for Economic Co-operation and Development (OECD 2016, 1) states that "global competence includes the acquisition of in-depth knowledge and understanding of global and intercultural issues; the ability to learn from and live with people from diverse backgrounds; and the attitudes and values necessary to interact respectfully with others." When establishing learning outcomes for a curriculum or program, program planners should consult the literature on global competence and incorporate the knowledge, skills, and attitudinal goals that best fit the context (see chapter 2, "Global Competence," for useful resources). It may be more effective when developing learning outcomes to phrase them as, "By the time students complete this lesson/course/program/degree, they will be able to…" This sentence structure can work with knowledge, skill, and attitudinal learning outcomes.

Step 2: Identifying Evidence of Learning

As the learning outcomes are being established, consider the ways in which evidence of students' learning can be observed. A useful resource is Bloom's taxonomy, which is a hierarchical model of cognitive processes from remembering and understanding at the least complex levels to evaluating and creating at the most advanced levels. Bloom's taxonomy can assist with selecting appropriate, measurable action verbs to be used in writing the learning outcomes. For example, it is more effective to say: "Students will be able to *explain* the causes of deforestation using examples from at least three continents" rather than "Students will *know* the causes of deforestation on at least three continents." The instructor can ask students to explain something in a class presentation, by making a video, by writing a research paper, or by writing an exam answer. What students *know,* however, is invisible. As illustrated in this example, outcomes must be behaviorally visible in order to assess the learning (Blair 2017).

Writing measurable outcomes for attitudinal learning can be difficult. Lilley, Barker, and Harris (2014, 241) identify some observable traits that reflect attitudes important to developing global competence:

- Shows courage by going on a mobility experience;
- Engages and works with different "others";
- Uses moral and ethical reasoning in problem-solving;
- Questions assumptions;
- Articulates other perspectives and possibilities;

- Recognizes common humanity and environmental sustainability; and

- Shows patience with those speaking in a foreign language.

Each of these behaviors has the advantage of being concrete enough that educators can observe whether the student is demonstrating them within classroom and program activities.

With careful thought and multiple rounds of revision, a set of learning outcomes can be established as a program is being designed. In a study abroad context, some of the outcomes may be focused on the development of global competence, while other outcomes are focused on the course theme. The program design process must be explicit in outlining the ways in which the learning outcomes will be demonstrated by the students, so that the program instructors can observe and confirm that the learning has happened, and they can also offer feedback and advice to deepen students' learning.

Step 3: Selecting Learning Activities and Teaching Methodologies

In study abroad, both formal and nonformal education typically play a role in the development of global competence (Asia Society 2009; Kahn and Agnew 2017). "Formal education" refers to the formal national systems of schooling, including classes offered for credit in higher education. "Nonformal education" refers to educational programs with structured curricula that happen outside of the formal school system, such as extracurricular programs. "Informal learning," by contrast, refers to life lessons such as learning what to expect when crossing an international border by doing so several times and noting the patterns. Informal learning is learning that is unplanned. So, while there is no doubt that informal learning happens in study abroad, informal learning is, by definition, not part of the study abroad planning process.

Continuing to work through the backward design process, once program planners and/or instructors decide what evidence they expect to see students demonstrate, they can then choose the learning activities and teaching methodologies that will help the students acquire the needed knowledge, skills, and attitudes. The literature on global competence offers some direction on the selection of learning activities and the most impactful teaching and learning methodologies for study abroad programs.

Student Motivations

It is important to engage students by offering learning opportunities that tap into their intrinsic motivations. Student interest can be harnessed by having students choose the projects, making the experiences authentic, ensuring that the projects have global significance, and providing opportunities to exhibit their work to a real audience or use their work for a real-life purpose (Asia Society and OECD 2018). Typically, students want their educational experiences to help them to build networks, gain professional experience, and develop personally. But they also want to have fun.

Research on youth attitudes shows that personal choice, responsibility, and autonomy all appeal to youth as much, or more than, messages about social responsibility (Harris 2014). Adult learning theory emphasizes that adults should be involved in directing their own learning, and that learning should be connected to their past life experiences (Merriam and Bierema 2014). In designing study abroad programs, planners and instructors should (a) make sure that the course activities and assignments draw on the participants' skills and motivations and connect to their personal biographies, and (b) ensure the quality of the students' contact with culturally different others (Gregersen-Hermans 2017).

Range of Possible Activities

In study abroad, decisions about program structure, curriculum, learning activities, and extracurricular programming are highly intertwined. Learning can happen in classes (formal education), in extracurricular programs (nonformal education), at campus and community events, and in many other venues (informal learning). Correspondingly, instructional approaches can take a wide range of shapes, including structured debates, organized discussions, current event dialogues, games and simulations, project-based learning, and service-learning (Asia Society and OECD 2018). In the event that students engage in experiential activities, instructors should be explicit about the intentions of the exercise so that it does not set a precedent that activities outside the classroom are just for fun/tourism (Swart and Spaeth 2017).

Self-Reflection

Global learning must start with self-reflection and self-awareness. More specifically, people need to recognize how the cultures to which they belong have shaped their perceptions and biases. Through self-critique and reflection on one's own biases, learning grows (Murray-Garcia and Tervalon 2017). Learners must "recognize that their own understanding of the world is inevitably partial" (OECD 2016, 1), and that others' perspectives are equally valid. As students recognize their own culture, bringing the unconscious to the conscious level, mindfulness and intentionality help students to recognize their preconceptions and biases (Paracka and Pynn 2017). This process of self-reflection should be structured into the program to happen before, during, and after the study abroad experience (Killick 2018). This might be achieved through journaling, discussion, art projects, and many other activities that create a time and mechanism for reflection (see chapter 5 for a discussion on facilitating reflection).

Examination of Difference

Once students are more aware of their identities and cultural biases, they can begin to explore the similarities and differences between people, between places, and between cultures from a more nonjudgmental perspective. According to Kahn and Agnew (2017, 53), "Global learning demands that students and educators understand the *universal* through the *particular* and the *particular* through the *universal*. Global learning requires the integration of multiple, and often diverse and conflicting, perspectives, across both macro and micro contexts. In global learning, difference is as much a primary component as is similarity. This is why…the feature of *difference* may ironically be one of the few 'non-negotiable universals of global learning.'" Study abroad program instructors must take care that examinations of differences do not result in stereotyping by ensuring that all learning activities bring out the complexities of culture and identity (Punteney 2017). When students have role models who have sophisticated understandings of cultural differences, it encourages them to adopt a similar appreciation (Lilley, Barker, and Harris 2017). Coteaching with two instructors from different disciplines or backgrounds allows students to observe respectful debates and differing perspectives (Kahn and Agnew 2017).

Interactions with Diverse Others

Evidence suggests that simple exposure to, and superficial interaction with, people of different cultures is not enough to facilitate deep learning (Engle and Engle 2012; Gregersen-Hermans 2017; Kahn and Agnew 2017; Vande Berg, Paige, and Lou 2012). This is particularly pertinent to study abroad program design because it emphasizes that mere contact with people from another culture does not ensure learning. Therefore, homestays, direct enrollment, and cultural activities are not automatically guaranteed to increase students' intercultural learning. Instead, meaningful discussion and interactions must be facilitated that move conversations beyond the superficial.

Students need structured opportunities for meaningful interaction with local people in ways that reduce the boundaries between the students and the locals. Conversation partners, games, sports, and volunteer work are some possible activities that allow for sustained contact over time and are interactive, if designed with forethought and planning. In addition to student peers and host families, program planners may find potential partners in think tanks, government agencies, nongovernmental organizations, media, museums, art exhibits, local leaders, religious organizations, and nonprofit organizations (Swart and Spaeth 2017).

As another pathway for engagement, rather than having students spend time online using the same home country media platforms to which they are accustomed, programs may assign students to use local social media outlets. Students can publish, share, and discuss content online in forums that are based in the host country and populated by host country individuals to increase the frequency and depth of their engagement with locals (Canny 2014; Engle and Engle 2012). Students need opportunities to interact with people with perspectives different from their own, and program instructors can provide them with the structures to prompt their reflections on those differing perspectives (Swart and Spaeth 2017; Teague 2014).

Collaboration with Diverse Others

Going beyond conversations with others, genuine collaboration with people from differing cultural backgrounds is a very effective learning activity. Instructors can help students to engage deeply and meaningfully across cultures by incorporating collaborative projects in their courses (Kahn and Agnew 2017; Lindsay and Davis 2012; Tavangar 2017). For learning to occur from this intercultural contact, the interactions between students from different cultures must be significant and structured, and the power and status between groups must be perceived as equal (Gregersen-Hermans 2017; Soria and Troisi 2014).

It is essential that time for students to build these friendships is structured into the project; relationship building must include socializing and getting to know each other, beyond the scope of the project task (Gregersen-Hermans 2017). Deep levels of collaboration are generally more difficult to coordinate in short-term programs of only a few weeks and therefore require very intentional design for this type of interaction. Students must be pushed a bit beyond their comfort zone to prompt learning; even moderate levels of discomfort prompt learning (Kahn and Agnew 2017; Lilley, Barker, and Harris 2017).

Step 4: Securing Resources Needed

As is evident, study abroad programs require a substantial investment of time and energy in the program design stage. Institutions must commit to internationalization, making it a key priority for their faculty and staff, otherwise personnel are unlikely to use their limited time to develop international education programs (including study abroad) thoughtfully and effectively (Green 2013; Gregersen-Hermans 2017). Gathering allies, as described in chapter 3, "Internationalization," is a key task of international educators in securing this institutional support. Institutions must also be willing to finance the operations of study abroad programs once they are designed, or the design process will have been a waste of effort. The careful management of budgets is essential in order to make the most effective use of limited resources.

To summarize, study abroad professionals can utilize a backward design process to identify the learning outcomes for their programs, the evidence that will demonstrate student achievement of the learning outcomes, and the learning activities that will help students to develop the desired competencies. It is important to consider how the activities can engage students' intrinsic motivations, intertwine curricular and extracurricular initiatives, and prompt student reflection to achieve those desired learning outcomes.

Study Abroad Outcomes

Many studies show that students who study abroad earn higher grades and are more likely to graduate than those students who do not. However, it is difficult to know if the students who studied abroad were already doing well academically and were already on track to graduate, or if the study abroad program gave them an advantage. After all, good grades are sometimes a screening criterion for study abroad program participation, and any student who can navigate the study abroad application and predeparture process can probably comfortably navigate the bureaucratic hurdles to graduation.

Research on study abroad has tended to focus on small-scale and qualitative studies of individual programs or institutions. These studies can offer a depth of understanding on that particular program but are not intended to be generalizable. Scholars have found that it is challenging to conduct large-scale quantitative studies for several reasons: (a) study abroad programs tend to be small in terms of the number of students in each program; (b) the setting and program design can vary so much that it is difficult to compare data between programs; and (c) participants are not randomly selected to participate in study abroad, making it difficult to find a comparable control group. Despite these challenges, there have been a few large-scale studies; three are profiled below.

The GLOSSARI Project

The GLOSSARI project was an assessment effort of the University System of Georgia study abroad programs. The initial study gathered data from approximately 250 students who studied abroad (Sutton and Rubin 2004). One thing that makes this study unusual is that the researchers also surveyed approximately 250 students who did not study abroad (Sutton and Rubin 2004). One potential limitation of the study is that the study abroad group included fewer men and fewer minority students than the non-study abroad group.

Even when the researchers used statistical methods to account for differences in GPA between the two groups of students, the study found that students returned from study abroad had significantly better functional knowledge (ability to handle daily life abroad), knowledge of world geography, knowledge of cultural relativism (recognizing that cultures should not be viewed though the perspective of another culture), and knowledge of global interdependence (Sutton and Rubin 2004).

The Georgetown Consortium Project

The Georgetown Consortium Project examined the characteristics of study abroad programs that led to the greatest gains in foreign language proficiency and intercultural competence. Approximately 1,000 students studying on 61 study abroad programs from multiple home universities participated in the study, along with a small control group of 138 students (Vande Berg, Connor-Linton, and Paige 2009). Students were tested before and after their study abroad programs. Vande Berg, Connor-Linton, and Paige (2009) found that the following factors resulted in students having greater gains in intercultural competence:

- Studying abroad (compared with not studying abroad);
- Being female;
- Having studied foreign language in high school or college;
- Having not lived abroad previously;
- Studying abroad for a semester (compared with shorter and longer* programs);

(continued on next page)

---

*Those who studied abroad for more than a semester seemed to plateau in their intercultural competence.

Study Abroad Outcomes (continued)

- Taking one or more content courses in a foreign language;
- Taking classes with other U.S. students or in a mixed group of U.S., host culture, and international students;
- Meeting with an on-site mentor;
- Living with U.S. or local students (as opposed to living with international students or host families);
- Spending more (51–75 percent) time with the host family (as opposed to spending less);
- Spending moderate (26–50 percent) amount of time with host nationals (as opposed to more or less time); and
- Spending the least amount of time with U.S. people.

Vande Berg, Connor-Linton, and Paige (2009) found that the following factors resulted in students having greater gains in foreign language oral proficiency:

- Studying abroad (compared with not studying abroad);
- Being female;
- Participating in longer programs; and
- Taking content courses taught in the target language.

From the analysis, the Georgetown Consortium Project concluded that students must be given free time to explore and interact with their environment. If all of their needs are met (with too little challenge), they will learn less. At the same time, if students lack language instruction, cultural mentoring, and structured reflection opportunities (too little support), they will not learn as much either. The most impactful program designs offer an intentional balance of challenge and support.

Global Careers

Mohajeri Norris and Gillespie (2009) surveyed 3,723 Institute for International Education of Students (IES) participants who had studied abroad between 1950 and 1999. The researchers asked IES alumni questions about how study abroad had affected their career trajectories. Sixty-two percent of the respondents said study abroad had ignited interest in a career direction that they pursued, 65 percent said it improved their ability to use a foreign language at work, 49 percent said it offered an internship that shaped their career choices, and 77 percent said it helped them to acquire skills that influenced their career path (Mohajeri Norris and Gillespie 2009).

While the scope and frequency of large-scale studies on study abroad outcomes are still not at the desired levels, there has been more of a concerted push for institutions to collect data on students' learning and share it in the literature of the field. These data can be used to advocate for more institutional resources, promote the benefits to government officials and policymakers, and elevate nations' reputations on the global stage.

Roles and Responsibilities of Education Abroad Professionals

Within the university organization, education abroad offices may be situated in the division of student affairs or academic affairs. The current trend is for education abroad offices to be part of academic affairs, which is considered the more powerful of the two situations (DeWinter and Rumbley 2010; Pelton 2017). In some cases, study abroad operations are highly centralized, with one office serving the entire university. In other cases, separate divisions of the university may have their own study abroad offices and programs. In a decentralized model, for example, the continuing education office might handle the program marketing, enrollment, registration, and logistics, while the academic department develops the curriculum and the study abroad office is responsible for health and safety and predeparture orientation. Short-term faculty-led programs, in particular, may be run in this more decentralized manner (Pelton 2017). While institutional policies may or may not require that all study abroad programs be developed in collaboration with the study abroad office, increasingly, institutions are requiring some level of oversight from the study abroad office or a campuswide advisory committee for risk management purposes. The movement toward centralization is meant to limit institutional liability, strengthen academic integrity, ensure careful selection of participants, and standardize processes (Pelton 2017).

Professional Positions

The "education abroad adviser" at a college or university is one of the most common positions in the education abroad sector. Based at the home university, these advisers provide support to students leading up to departure, during their time abroad, and after their return to campus. In the shorthand jargon of the field, advisers may say that they work on the "outbound" side of international education; in comparison, "inbound" usually refers to international students coming to the home university. In terms of responsibilities, education abroad advisers typically recruit students; advise students on program selection and application; design and run orientation programs; ensure that registration, financial aid, and credit transfer processes are smooth; support overseas program staff; respond to crises; support students through the process of reentry back into the home culture; and perform many other duties.

While the adviser role is one of the most well-known job positions in education abroad, there are many other contexts in which international education professionals work. For example, some people work "on site," receiving participants in the host country. Often, a student services coordinator will be in the host country engaged in welcoming students, assisting with housing arrangements, arranging excursions and extracurricular activities, and providing advising support for logistical, academic, and cultural adjustment. An on-site director will typically focus on the curriculum, instruction, budget, staff management, crisis prevention and response, and the assessment of learning.

Education abroad professionals can also choose to work for program providers that specialize in offering programs to youths and adults. Provider staff recruit participants from different universities and interact with international educators at many universities. They may also seek to attract nonstudent participants such as professionals or retirees. Some education abroad professionals work primarily in recruitment and admissions, while others focus on program design and development and may have little direct contact with students. Some provider staff members are overseas with students. The diversity of professional roles and workplace settings reflects the range of organizations, programs, locations, and participants engaged in education abroad.

Professional Competencies

Following a survey of 2,000 international educators, and multiple rounds of review with focus groups, NAFSA: Association of International Educators (2015) developed the *NAFSA International Education Professional Competencies*, a detailed list of cross-cutting competencies that international educators must have to be successful in any sector. Those competencies include advocacy, communication with stakeholders, financial stewardship, human resources, information technology, intercultural communications, leadership, and strategic planning (NAFSA 2015). An additional set of competencies is outlined specifically for professionals in education abroad: contributing to comprehensive internationalization, developing and implementing programs, funding and financing, office administration, risk assessment and crisis management, student advising, and student health and safety (NAFSA 2015). This section of the chapter focuses on the management aspects of work in education abroad and incorporates many of these cross-cutting and specific competency areas.

Advocacy

Whatever the structure of the office, education abroad professionals work closely with stakeholders across the campus. Many departments and groups are close collaborators, including students, parents, faculty, academic advisers, registrar, financial aid, student judicial affairs, legal counsel, learning technology staff, career services, counseling, alumni relations, donors, athletics, institutional research, international student organizations, and more (Canny 2014; Sevigny 2014). In order to build support for study abroad, international educators must find allies among these stakeholder groups who will work to address the needs of students and advocate for the importance of education abroad among campus priorities (Tuma 2017).

Partner and Stakeholder Relationships

Education abroad professionals often manage a variety of partnerships with entities beyond the campus, including foreign institutions, exchange program partnerships, and education abroad program providers. To begin, staff members evaluate potential partners and engage in discussion about mutual goals. If the desires are congruent, they will draft a memorandum of understanding (which does not bind institutions to labor or financial contributions) and then sign and implement the partnership agreements (which are legally binding). The agreements must be monitored, the exchange balances tracked (if applicable), the relationships cultivated, and any issues addressed. Challenges that may emerge from partnerships include cultural differences, differing communication styles, and insufficient funding, to name a few (Gorlewski 2014). Because partnerships must be nurtured in order to remain productive, institutions typically find it more valuable and sustainable to have a smaller number of robust partnerships rather than trying to manage a large array of ineffective partnerships.

Program Development

A major area of responsibility for education abroad professionals is program development and, in turn, student learning. As detailed earlier in this chapter, the process of developing a program must be centered around the program learning outcomes. Alongside discussion of the curriculum, teaching and learning methodologies, and assessment of learning, there are numerous logistical matters for education abroad advisers to consider in program development. These include the academic calendar, number of course credits, admissions criteria, faculty workload and salary, program size, staffing, faculty guests/family participation, amount of free time in the schedule, accommodations, academic facilities (e.g., library access), etc. (Pelton 2017; Swart and Spaeth 2017).

In the case of faculty-led programs, the design process usually starts with a faculty member proposing an idea for a course (Swart and Spaeth 2017). The education abroad office may have a person designated as the faculty-led program coordinator to assist the faculty member in developing a program proposal. It is strategic to offer programs that meet home campus requirements for specific majors or general education in order to attract students (Swart and Spaeth 2017). The faculty member will need to develop a syllabus that makes the most of the international location, incorporating excursions, guest lectures, field work, etc. Structured opportunities for interactions with locals are essential, but the program itinerary should not be fully scheduled. Students need some free time to develop independence, confidence, and intercultural skills. Some programs offer blocks of free time, such as the weekends, to allow time for independent student travel and growth (Swart and Spaeth 2017).

Beyond the syllabus and itinerary, a faculty-led program proposal document likely addresses the curricular rationale for the program, target audience, competing courses/programs, description of the destination, on-site resources, budget, health/safety/risk management, and more (Pelton 2017). The education abroad office, or an oversight committee facilitated by the education abroad office, reviews the proposal and makes the determination about whether the program can run. Usually, there are two levels of review: academic and logistical. When considering the academics, the committee members look at the likelihood of the learning outcomes being achieved, the academic rigor of the program, and the nature of integration with the host culture. Regarding logistics, the committee members consider the experience of the faculty leader, the program cost, the attractiveness of the program for students, whether or not there are competing programs, the student selection criteria, plans in case of low enrollment, the feasibility and comprehensiveness of the budget and logistical plans, what student support services are available, and whether the risk prevention plans are adequate (Pelton 2017).

Marketing and Recruitment

Education abroad relies on successful marketing to attract students to programs. Education abroad professionals can work closely with marketers, or the campus marketing and communications unit, to develop the website and videos, utilize social media, and create brochures and other print materials to promote programs and opportunities (Shipley 2014). Following the lead of the education abroad staff, the marketing team members may research the interests of prospective students, compare current programs to competitor programs, identify the programs' strengths, and, ultimately, develop and implement strategic marketing plans that spark student interest. In a university setting, the marketing responsibilities may reside with one person or they may be shared across programs. Education abroad program providers usually have multiple staff working in marketing.

Education abroad professionals are also actively engaged in recruitment, talking with individuals or groups of students about the benefits of study abroad, the program options, logistics (such as financing), and the application process. Within universities, education abroad advisers, or the students whom they have trained, take on the recruitment role. They give classroom presentations, host booths at events, and hold information sessions to reach out to prospective students (Shipley 2014). Education abroad program providers often send recruiters to study abroad fairs and to visit university campuses.

International educators engaged in recruitment must spend time getting to know individual students in order to help them identify the programs that are the best fit for their goals, such as finding which programs best align with their major requirements, professional goals, and language abilities (Meadows 2014). Recruiters must also address any reservations the students may have about studying abroad, including concerns about finances, safety, and the political and social climate (Meadows 2014).

Admissions

At a university, education abroad advisers and/or faculty may make the decisions about whether or not to accept students into a program. In cases where the university has approved programs run by education abroad program providers, advisers may guide students through the application process and counsel students on whether or not they are likely to meet a provider's admissions requirements. Large program providers often employ highly specialized personnel who focus on program admission.

The program application process may involve the submission of transcripts, an essay or statement of purpose, and/or an interview (Adams and Reinig 2014). Education abroad management software, such as Terra Dotta, Horizons, Via TRM, Study Abroad Manager, Abroadster, EduAgent CRM, and Abroad Office may be used to manage the application process, as well as many other processes for admitted students.

Some study abroad programs are in high demand and are highly selective, while other programs are likely to accept all students who meet the minimum requirements. DeWinter and Rumbley (2010, 104) observe that "some colleges have demanded a high grade point average for admission to study abroad programs, and where appropriate, auditions and portfolios; others have argued that if students are in good standing on the home campus, they should be allowed to study abroad. In short, for some institutions, study abroad is regarded as a privilege, for others it is considered a student's right." Education abroad advisers should be well versed in the qualifications of the different programs offered by their institution or know where to direct students with additional questions and information.

Student Advising

Advising individual students is a primary responsibility of many international educators. Advising generally focuses on three primary themes: student learning, student development, and preparedness for education abroad (Thebodo 2014). In education abroad, advisers must know about the curriculum requirements, program options, institutional policies, government regulations, higher education systems around the world, and cultural norms. Advisers need to understand student development, advising techniques and strategies, and resources for advising (Thebodo 2014). (See chapter 7 for a discussion of advising models.)

Advisers should learn about student development theories and how they apply to education abroad. Some of the most well-known psychosocial theories are presented by Erik Erikson, James Marcia, Ruthellen Josselson, and Arthur Chickering. Moreover, scholars like William Perry, Lawrence Kohlberg, and Carol Gillian focus on students' moral development. Advisers should also be familiar with theories of racial, ethnic, general, sexual, national, and spiritual development. Essential theories of learning include David Kolb's (1984) Experiential Learning Cycle, Nancy Schlossberg's (1981) Transition Theory, and Jack Mezirow's (1978) Transformational Learning Theory (Patton et al. 2016; Thebodo 2014). (For more on student development theories, see table 3.)

Finally, advisers should be knowledgeable about the institution's varied curriculum so that they can guide students toward programs that will best satisfy their academic goals and credit requirements. Increasingly, institutions are moving toward a model of advising by major, rather than advising by destination, thus emphasizing the learning goals rather than the locale. Education abroad advisers may be tempted to open up conversations with students by asking where they want to go, but it is more important to find out students' learning goals. For this reason, an adviser might first ask students why they want to study abroad and what they want to study. Discussing goals and expectations with students, and how study abroad fits with their academic plan, can then lead to discussions on the programs that best suit their goals, interests, and needs (Thebodo 2014).

Student Development Theories

Strange and King (2011) suggest that a skilled education professional understands theories of student development, connects their theoretical understanding to research, uses practices generally endorsed by peers, evaluates the outcomes of their practice, and articulates a clear set of values. Strange and King consider these competencies to be cyclically linked—meaning that they cannot exist without theoretical knowledge. Some of the theories that educators should be familiar with are listed in table 3.

TABLE 3. Student Development Theories Relevant to Advising

Critical Race Theory	Critical race theory examines the interactions between race, racism, and power. The history and settings of human interactions are examined and equity of law, economics, politics, ethics, and more are questioned (Delgado and Stefancic 2017).
Emerging Adulthood	Arnett (2000) identified a developmental period focusing on ages 18 to 25 that is characterized by frequent change and exploration in the areas of housing, love, education, work, and worldview. He argues that this phase only exists in those cultures that allow young people of this age range a degree of relative independence.
Feminist Theory	Feminist theories look at the intersections between gender, race, socioeconomic class, and other identities, and how these intersectional identities are reflected in power and control in interpersonal interactions and in society. Recent feminist theories have emphasized the role of affect, or emotion, in these interactions (Disch and Hawkesworth 2016).
Gender Identity Development	From the 1960s through the 1990s, Josselson explored the development of women's sense of identity and concluded that there are four pathways to developing a sense of self related to whether or not the woman has been through an identity crisis and whether the woman has developed a resolved sense of self (Evans et al. 2009). More recent theories of gender identity development also examine male and nonbinary gender identities.
Intersectionality of Identity	There are theories that focus on the intersectionality of identity, examining how each individual's identities, including nationality, race, ethnicity, gender, socioeconomic class, religion, and more, intersect. A key theme is that identity is always changing, and the elements of identity that are most salient change over time and are based on context (Wijeyesinghe 2012).
Racial Identity Development	There are many models of racial identity development, including those for African Americans, Asian Americans, Latinx Americans, Native Americans, and white Americans. Common themes include the findings that there are many possible healthy identities, that identities may shift over time, and that identities may shift based on the specific situation a person is in (Evans et al. 2009). Biracial identity development is also increasingly being explored (Renn 2008).
Self-Authorship	Magolda (2001) defines self-authorship as the ability to define one's own identity, beliefs, and social relations. Reaching self-authorship requires a phase of being dissatisfied with one's own life and then clarifying one's own beliefs and choices and standing up for them. This is done by trusting the internal voice, building a personal philosophy, and integrating internal and external worlds.

(continued on next page)

Student Development Theories (continued)

Seven Vectors	Chickering's seven vectors describe seven areas of personal development that are common among university-aged students. These areas include developing competence, managing emotions, moving through autonomy toward interdependence, developing mature interpersonal relationships, establishing identity, developing purpose, and developing integrity (Evans et al. 2009).
Stages of Psychosocial Development	Erikson's model describes eight stages of life based on approximate age. For each stage, he identifies a core tension, or area of personal growth. Those aged 13 to 21, for example, are focused on developing a sense of one's own identity (Evans et al. 2009).
Student Engagement and Student Success	Kuh's research on student engagement and student success emphasizes that students will be most successful if they are held to high standards, introduced to the resources available for support, and engaged with cocurricular programs. Students benefit from living on campus and participating in high-impact practices such as internships, service-learning, study abroad, and research with a faculty member (Kuh 2011; National Survey of Student Engagement 2018).
Student Involvement	Astin's (1999) theory states that the more physical time and emotional and mental energy that students put into being involved in their education, the greater their learning. The theory suggests that student time is a resource and that institutional policies can positively or negatively affect how students spend their limited time.
Transition Theory	Schlossberg (1995) points out that any life transition (e.g., changes in employment status, living situation, educational program, etc.), whether anticipated or not, causes stress and challenges. She identified factors that influence an individual's ability to cope: the specifics of the situation, personality and demographic traits, social supports, and coping strategies.

There are many more theories related to student development than those introduced here. Additional theories that educators may want to study include Phinney's Theory of Racial and Ethnic Identity Development, Kohlberg's Theory of Moral Development, Super's Theory of Career Development, Perry's Theory of Cognitive Development, Park's Theory of Faith Development, Hettler's Model of Wellness, Astin's Theory of Student Involvement, Sanford's Challenge and Support Theory, Tinto's Theory of Student Departure/Retention, and Pascarella's Model for Assessing Student Change (Long 2012). As educators learn about each of these theories, they must be careful to remain alert to the limitations of each theory. Many of the theories were developed based on studies of a particular population of students and, therefore, it cannot be automatically assumed that each theory will apply to all students of every background. It also cannot be assumed that every individual's experience will fit every theory since social science theories, by their very nature, generalize complex topics.

Orientation

Education abroad advisers organize and lead orientation programs held before study abroad programs begin. These "predeparture orientations" may be held in person, online, or both, and may range from a single three-hour session to a series of sessions over the course of several months. Orientation is often accompanied by predeparture information packets and online materials. "On-site orientation" is commonly led by in-country education abroad staff at the beginning of the program and can last a few hours to days in the host country. Most study abroad programs offer both predeparture and on-site orientations. There is also a trend toward "ongoing orientation," which recognizes that students (a) may be overwhelmed at the beginning of the program and have limited ability to absorb information, and (b) may have somewhat different needs in the first few days of the program than they do in the weeks that follow. Ongoing orientation may be structured as optional or required sessions throughout the first weeks or months of the program.

Orientation, like advising, should focus on student learning, student development, and preparedness for the study abroad program. Regarding student learning, the goal of orientation should be helping students learn a framework for their experiences that generates interest, shows them how to acknowledge and process their perceptions, and stimulates critical thinking. The framework should direct students away from making assumptions and should instead inspire curiosity and tolerance (Canny 2014). Intercultural training resources, such as the University of the Pacific's "What's Up with Culture?" modules, can assist with promoting this type of learning (Bathurst and La Brack 2012).

An important aspect of orientation is providing students with opportunities to build cognitive skills, expand intellectual analysis, and prompt personal reflection. Activities related to student development should guide students to reflect on their own identities. These activities might include writing, discussion, art projects, and role-play exercises, among many possibilities. Education abroad advisers should facilitate exercises that allow students to consider their strengths and identify plans for growth. It is beneficial to have ongoing orientation to help students process their experiences. A key message is that they will likely face cultural and linguistic challenges and they should not expect everything to be like it is at home (Buffington 2014). Students should use those encountered differences to learn more about themselves and their place in the world.

The aspects of orientation, both predeparture and on site, that focus on preparedness typically include information on the schedule, facilities, program rules, cultural etiquette, and health and safety. Students may find it difficult to absorb extensive information on these topics (and during on-site orientation, likely have the added challenge of feeling jet-lagged). It is often most effective to have small group sessions, and younger staff or local students sharing their personal experiences about safety, drugs/alcohol, etc. (Buffington 2014).

While a robust orientation focused on the three areas of student learning, student development, and preparedness is recommended, it is the unfortunate reality that study abroad orientations are commonly short and focused heavily on preparedness, at the expense of student learning and development. Instead of this more shallow approach, orientation should be treated like an academic course, breaking down highly specific material into learning outcomes organized in a sequence (Canny 2014). In fact, there is a growing trend toward offering actual orientation courses prior to and during the program: "That such courses are sometimes given academic credit by a growing number of institutions suggests the seriousness with which some colleges and universities are taking the study abroad experience as an academic element within the curricular mainstream" (DeWinter and Rumbley 2010, 97). These orientation courses should utilize high-impact practices that demand that students invest substantive time and energy in purposeful tasks, engage with faculty and peers over time, increase the likelihood of contact with diverse others, and receive feedback to see how their learning applies in multiple contexts (Canny 2014).

Housing

The decisions that education abroad advisers make with regard to housing arrangements during the design of a study abroad program can significantly impact both student learning and student satisfaction. Coordinating housing arrangements can often be a time-consuming process for education abroad professionals. Study abroad programs may arrange housing for students, or they may provide resources for students to find their own housing. Housing options include homestays, residence halls, apartments, hotels, fieldwork sites, hostels, and campgrounds (McCallon and Holmes 2010).

Homestays are considered by many to be an ideal setting for students' language acquisition and cultural immersion. It is believed that students in homestays are more exposed to the real way of life in the host country and can practice a foreign language regularly (Buffington 2014). However, homestays can also prove to be the greatest challenge of all the accommodations if the student and family are not a good match. Using a homestay model requires a thorough vetting process of host families and an orientation and ongoing support for students to have a good experience. Advisers should work with students and host families to set expectations, addressing levels of treatment, privacy, attention, security, and compensation (which is typical for homestay programs) (McCallon and Holmes 2010).

Like homestays, residence halls allow for interactions with locals; however they may also lead to feelings of loneliness as students struggle to enter the social scene and break into existing cliques. Shared apartments with local students may work well for providing meaningful and frequent interactions with local people (Buffington 2014).

Living with fellow students from the home country is also a possibility and has the advantage of providing an opportunity for students to vent and process their experiences, which may be useful in a program with intensive cultural and language immersion in other parts of the program (e.g., courses, extracurricular activities, etc.) (Buffington 2014).

Group Dynamics and Personal Advising

On-site education abroad staff, including the faculty director who is responsible for the curriculum as well as the overall program, must support the students individually as well as manage group dynamics. Both areas of advising tend to be more complex than on the home campus due to the intensity of the study abroad experience. If the faculty director is used to teaching only on the home campus, this responsibility can be a new experience. The on-site instructors and staff are responsible for arranging for psychological counseling and emotional support as needed, as well as providing advising to individuals. Instructors and staff are also the ones who must deal with issues related to discipline, drugs, and alcohol. They must respond to complaints and mediate between individuals in conflict.

Students usually need some level of support as they adapt to a new culture and an unfamiliar academic environment. While these adjustment issues affect individuals differently and are often addressed accordingly, issues affecting one student can quickly cause tension in the whole group. All instructors and staff need to be alert to these group dynamics and be prepared to intervene appropriately (Buffington 2014; McCallon and Holmes 2010; Peifer and Meyer-Lee 2017).

Reentry

Returning to the home country can be disorienting for some students, in part, because they do not expect to have to adapt when they return home. Yet, students often find that they have changed in ways they did not initially realize. Once home, they may find that they have new interests and new perspectives. They may feel out of touch with family and friends or find that family and friends have a limited interest in hearing their stories from abroad. Reentry orientation, led by education abroad advisers, can address some of these challenges and can also increase student learning.

Reentry orientation can be conducted abroad before students return, or at home after return (Kindred 2014). Education abroad advisers around the United States have collaborated to organize city- and state-wide reentry conferences that enable students to explore the impacts of their study abroad experience. At these conferences, students consider how they can continue their intercultural learning with graduate school and intercultural career options. They also practice articulating their learning outcomes and acquired skill sets so that they can explain the value of their study abroad experiences on their résumé and in interviews.

While reentry orientation often comprises sessions of only a few hours, there is the potential for the orientation to be conducted as a course or other longer-term program that continues and deepens student learning from their experience abroad. For example, at the University of the Pacific, students take an academic course prior to study abroad and another course after study abroad. Reflection assignments are part of the reentry course, which not only help students to cement their learning but also provide data for program assessment purposes (Bathurst and La Brack 2012). Engaging returned students in advising (with appropriate trainings) other students who will be going abroad can be of mutual benefit—it allows the returned students to continue to reflect on the significance of their experience, motivates prospective study abroad students, and serves to support understaffed study abroad offices (Kindred 2014).

Data Collection

As discussed in chapter 2 of this book, international educators are increasingly being asked to provide evidence of student learning to justify the expense of operating their programs. They are also being held accountable for the choices they make in spending limited funds. Ogden (2014) lays out key questions about education abroad that each institution needs to address with data:

- What are the college- or department-specific priorities for education abroad?
- Is the portfolio of education abroad programs being offered responsive to the institutional demographic?
- Which populations are underrepresented, and how can greater inclusion be fostered?
- How does financial need impact education abroad enrollment?
- What role does education abroad have in student recruitment and admissions?
- Does education abroad participation impact retention (remaining enrolled in university)? How so?

Educators are likely to be expected to compile sophisticated enrollment reports, develop multiyear projections, and produce detailed, data-supported strategic plans (Ogden 2014). Thus, data collection and analysis have become key tasks of education abroad professionals for use in advocacy, benchmarking, strategic planning, grant writing, and program assessment. University databases (e.g., Peoplesoft, Banner, etc.) must be coded to indicate which students participated in education abroad programs, or it will be impossible to run any statistical analysis within institutions (Ogden 2014).

The daily demands of running an education abroad program can make it hard to find time to collect and analyze data, and many international educators do not have the training and expertise. As a result, this is one of the most in-demand skills in the international education field. Many education abroad offices develop relationships with the institutional research offices for assistance with data collection and interpretation.

Funding and Financing

Education abroad professionals are responsible for developing a budget and managing the finances of their study abroad programs. To do so, they often work closely with staff in the institutional finance office and student financial aid office. In practice, there are a wide variety of financial models used. For students participating in summer, semester, or yearlong programs organized by the university or an education abroad program provider, the most common financial structure involves having students pay the home university tuition regardless of the actual cost of their program or having students pay the varied rates set for each program. In the case of exchange programs, it is most common for each participating student to pay the home university tuition (Cressey and Stubbs 2010). When institutions choose to have all students pay the home tuition, the result is that the programs that are cheaper to run ultimately subsidize the programs that are more expensive to operate.

Some universities charge program costs based on the actual costs of operating the program, as is the case with most faculty-led programs. This may feel more equitable, but it may also limit access to expensive programs to those students who have greater financial resources. Faculty-led programs often operate with the expectation of being financially self-sufficient and with the program price based on the actual program expenses (Henke 2014).

Some institutions strategically set program prices to generate funds that they can give back in the form of scholarships, thus expanding access to more students. Some institutions charge a study abroad fee to help support the operating expenses of the study abroad office (Henke 2014). Given the range of funding models discussed here, students may pay very different prices for their education abroad experience. This is both because education abroad program providers charge differently and because sending institutions charge students according to different models (Cressey and Stubbs 2010). Students who enroll directly in a foreign institution may pay the same tuition rate as local students, or they may pay an international student rate.

Beyond establishing program prices, directors of education abroad offices are also engaged in managing their organizational expenses. These may include salaries, facilities, utilities, translation services, office equipment, office supplies, insurance, retainers for legal and accounting professionals, site visit expenses, marketing expenses, and staff development (Cressey and Stubbs 2010). Host country inflation and currency fluctuation must also be planned for, and additional funds may need to be set aside for emergencies and large, unpredicted expenses (Cressey and Stubbs 2010).

Education abroad directors need to learn how budgets are developed at their institution, ascertain which budget items are encumbered (reserved for specific purposes), and track and predict spending (Henke 2014). Institutional decisions around budgets and finances are often political ones.

While the 1992 Higher Education Act eliminated some barriers to using federal financial aid for study abroad, and most universities allow federal and institutional financial aid to be used, some individuals or institutions may worry about loss of revenue to the home campus and create policies that make it harder for students to participate in study abroad (Cressey and Stubbs 2010). In university settings, international educators need to show the impact of their work and the value of study abroad for both students and the institution in order to advocate for sufficient funding to run their department and programs.

Risk Prevention and Crisis Management

Education abroad professionals are committed to the health and safety of students abroad, out of concern for students' well-being and to avoid institutional liability. Time and attention must be given to both risk prevention and the development of effective crisis management plans. Failure to do so can potentially result in harm to students and lawsuits brought against the institution or staff. Learning goals cannot be achieved when conditions of health and safety are ignored. And legal liability arises if reasonable, prudent care was owed to the injured party and the duty was breached by the individual or organization that owed that care (Malveaux 2016).

Despite the prevalence of large-scale political and security issues in the news, Malveaux (2016) argues that, in fact, the largest risks during study abroad are medical injury or illness, sexual assault, and supervisory neglect. There are many reports of student drinking, drug use, and risky behaviors abroad (Buffington 2014; Passarelli and Kolb 2012) that may result in injury, death, or arrest. Some students on study abroad programs may struggle with mental health issues including depression, anxiety, bipolar disorder, eating disorders, and attention-deficit/hyperactivity disorder (ADHD). The physical, mental, and emotional transitions involved in the study abroad experience can be stressful, which can affect mood and behavior. The adjustment process can exacerbate conditions that may have been well managed by the student at home (Lindeman 2016, White 2014). This is especially true if proper medication is not brought overseas with a supply to last the duration of the program. Other risks that could occur while abroad include medical emergencies, conflict between students or staff, crime, violence, discrimination, transportation accidents, environmental disasters, fires, kidnapping, terrorism, political instability, etc. (Rhodes 2014). The majority of legal cases involving study abroad programs are settled out of court, resulting in underreporting of the number of legal cases that arise from study abroad (Malveaux 2016).

For each program, there must be cultural awareness and knowledge of foreign laws, a thoughtful participant selection process, consultation with the institution's legal counsel, well-written waivers and codes of conduct, clear communication of risk, orientation, emergency response and communication plans, and an adequate number of qualified staff to support students (Malveaux 2016). It is recommended that after program admissions notifications are sent, a participant medical history is collected from each student and used by staff as an advising tool. Working with the students, advisers should develop health contingency plans before departure. Areas to address in advising about health issues include overseas resources that can be accessed (e.g., counseling, medications, medical care, etc.), accommodations, emergency responses, sharing information with program providers, permission to contact parents, etc. To comply with U.S. laws, it is important to consult with legal counsel on this process (White 2014). International educators must know their legal responsibilities, as well as the limits of their expertise, and turn to professionals such as counselors and legal counsel in case of a crisis. Based on U.S. law, universities are expected to use reasonable care in the design and management of their programs, inform students of risk, and appropriately manage the trust and money that students have invested into the educational programs (Friend 2017).

In terms of liability, it is always better to overreact to a risk than underreact to a risk (Malveaux 2016). A key first step is to try to make sure all students read the waivers and safety information. This is not only about liability, it is also about protecting the students and holding them accountable for their actions (Malveaux 2016; Rhodes 2014). Good risk prevention practices include discussing relevant information in predeparture orientation, training faculty leaders, ensuring that foreign partners follow policies and practices acceptable to the home institution, using reputable travel companies, seeking resources and training from international education organizations and conferences, and following good practices identified by professional associations (Malveaux 2016; Rhodes 2014). Institutions must have adequate insurance and emergency assistance coverage, and advisers should be knowledgeable about those policies (Rhodes 2014). Most institutions put together a risk/crisis management team that, in addition to international educators, likely includes staff from the campus police, counseling center, government relations office, health center, legal counsel, public relations, and student affairs unit (Rhodes 2014).

Specializations Within Education Abroad

Education abroad job titles vary significantly from institution to institution. A survey conducted by The Forum on Education Abroad (2008) of 309 of its members found that among the respondents, there were 146 different job titles, often for similar job portfolios. Education abroad professionals may have one or more of these job roles:

- Admissions officer;
- Adviser;
- Community outreach coordinator;
- Exchange program coordinator;
- Faculty-led program coordinator;
- Instructor;
- International internship adviser;
- Marketing and social media coordinator;
- Partnership administrator;
- Program developer;
- Program director;
- Program manager;
- Recruiter;
- Risk management administrator; or
- Student services coordinator.

Regardless of position title, it is a safe generalization to say that in a large organization, positions are typically highly specialized, and an individual may focus most or all of his or her time on one of these roles. In a smaller organization, one person may be responsible for many of these areas.

Professional Organizations and Standards

Given the range and complexity of the work of education abroad professionals, professional associations play an essential role in establishing standards for the field and providing training, resources, and professional networks. This section introduces resources available from NAFSA and other international education associations.

Diversity Abroad

Diversity Abroad is an organization committed to ensuring that students from all backgrounds have access to, and take advantage of, international education opportunities. The website (www.diversityabroad.com), which is aimed at students, provides information and advice for students considering education abroad. Diversity Abroad organizes the Diversity Abroad Network (diversitynetwork.org), a consortium of educational institutions, government agencies, nonprofit organizations, and for-profit organizations committed to diversity and inclusion in education abroad. The Diversity Abroad Network website is intended for international educators and includes publications, resources, training opportunities, and information on the Diversity Abroad annual conference.

The Forum on Education Abroad

The Forum on Education Abroad is a nonprofit group of member universities and organizations focused on developing and implementing standards of good practice for the education abroad field. The Forum (2015) has published nine *Standards of Good Practice for Education Abroad* and offers training in each area:

- Standard 1: Mission and Goals
- Standard 2: Student Learning and Development
- Standard 3: Academic Framework
- Standard 4: Student Selection, Preparation, and Advising
- Standard 5: Student Code of Conduct and Disciplinary Measures
- Standard 6: Policies and Procedures
- Standard 7: Organizational and Program Resources
- Standard 8: Health, Safety, Security, and Risk Management
- Standard 9: Ethics

The standards are available on The Forum's website (forumea.org), along with two guides titled *Leading Short-Term Education Abroad Programs* (2017) and the *Code of Ethics for Education Abroad* (2011). Professionals who complete all of the training modules and a culminating project can earn a professional certification in education abroad and may add The Forum's "Certified Professional" mark to their résumé and other materials.

Organizations can have their programs reviewed by trained experts from The Forum's Quality Improvement Program (QUIP), and if the programs substantially meet the standards, the organizations can use The Forum's "Recognized for Meeting Standards" logo on their website and materials.

The Forum on Education Abroad has an annual conference each spring that provides opportunities for professional development and networking. The Forum also hosts a European conference every 2 years. In addition, The Forum conducts studies of the key issues and trends in the field and publishes study findings on education abroad professionals' workloads, salaries, and job descriptions. The organization produces books and resources, runs webinars, and hosts professional development events.

NAFSA: Association of International Educators

The Education Abroad Knowledge Community is one of the largest of NAFSA's five Knowledge Communities. In addition to attending and contributing many NAFSA annual and regional conference sessions, this group organizes webinars and trainings on a wide range of topics including advising, program development, diversity and inclusion, international internships, crisis management, and education abroad office management. NAFSA publications focused on education abroad issues include *NAFSA's Guide to Education Abroad for Advisers and Administrators* (2014), *Crisis Management for Education Abroad* (2017), and *The Guide to Successful Short-Term Programs Abroad* (2017).

Network.NAFSA (network.nafsa.org) offers an extensive online collection of resources on advising, program management, visas, faculty-led programs, financing education abroad, health and safety, marketing and recruitment, orientation and programming, and diversity and inclusion. NAFSA members may join more than 3,000 professionals on the Education Abroad Knowledge Community Network listserv/discussion board at network.nafsa.org. NAFSA's annual conference draws up to 10,000 international education professionals from around the world for networking, professional development sessions, lectures, and other discussions.

Other Organizations

Many other organizations offer professional training and resources to education abroad professionals. For example, several study abroad organizations organize their own annual conferences, such as the Council on International Educational Exchange (CIEE), IES Abroad, and the Institute for Study Abroad (IFSA Butler). Another annual conference, the Workshop on Intercultural Skills Enhancement (WISE), focuses on intercultural skills development in study abroad. The Asia-Pacific Association for International Education (APAIE) and the European Association for International Education (EAIE) also convene major annual conferences in the field, as do other region-specific organizations with an emphasis on study abroad. The Institute of International Education (IIE) and the Association of International

Education Administrators (AIEA) hold conferences for international education leaders with many sessions related to education abroad. All of these organizations also produce timely practitioner resources.

Conclusion

The number of U.S. students studying abroad, especially in shorter programs, has been growing for decades (IIE 2018) and will likely maintain an upward trajectory as internationalization continues to gain importance as a priority in higher education. Yet, when compared with U.S. higher education enrollments, it is still a small percentage of students who participate in study abroad. The dramatic discrepancy raises questions and requires international educators to work to expand their reach.

At the same time, education abroad professionals continue to face many demands on their time and energy. The management of education abroad programs and offices is complex and labor-intensive. Furthermore, international education practitioners are increasingly expected to conduct robust assessments of their programs to document the evidence of student learning. Overall, the field is becoming more professionalized, more grounded in research, and less accepting of academic shortcomings (Hoffa and DePaul 2010). Program design is becoming more thoughtful and rigorous as the field becomes increasingly engaged in the assessment of learning.

Resources

READINGS:

- Barclay Hamir, Heather, and Nick Gozik, eds. 2018. *Promoting Inclusion in Education Abroad*. Sterling, VA: Stylus Publishing and NAFSA: Association of International Educators.

- Chieffo, Lisa, and Catherine Spaeth, eds. 2017. *The Guide to Successful Short-Term Programs Abroad, Third Edition*. Washington, DC: NAFSA: Association of International Educators.

- The Forum on Education Abroad. 2011. *Code of Ethics for Education Abroad, 2nd ed*. Carlisle, PA: The Forum on Education Abroad. https://forumea.org/resources/standards-of-good-practice/code-of-ethics/.

- The Forum on Education Abroad. 2017. *Leading Short-Term Education Abroad Programs: Know the Standards*. Carlisle, PA: The Forum on Education Abroad. https://forumea.org/wp-content/uploads/2017/03/ST_Program-Leaders_8.5x11_P1.pdf.

- Hernandez, Magnolia, Margaret Wiedenhoeft, and David Wick, eds. 2014. *NAFSA's Guide to Education Abroad for Advisers and Administrators, Fourth Edition.* Washington, DC: NAFSA: Association of International Educators.

- Lindeman, Barbara, ed. 2017. *Addressing Mental Health Issues Affecting Education Abroad Participants.* Washington, DC: NAFSA: Association of International Educators.

- Martin, Patricia C., ed. 2017. *Crisis Management for Education Abroad.* Washington, DC: NAFSA: Association of International Educators and University Risk Management and Insurance Association, Inc.

- McCallon, Melanie, and Bill Holmes. 2010. *Faculty-Led 360: Guide to Successful Study Abroad.* Charleston, IL: Agapy LLC.

- Vande Berg, Michael, R. Michael Paige, and Kris Hemming Lou, eds. 2012. *Student Learning Abroad: What Our Students Are Learning, What They're Not, and What We Can Do About It.* Sterling, VA: Stylus Publishing.

- Wyatt Knowlton, Lisa, and Cynthia C. Phillips. 2013. *The Logic Model Guidebook: Better Strategies for Great Results, 2nd ed.* Thousand Oaks, CA: Sage Publications.

ORGANIZATIONS:

- Diversity Abroad www.diversitynetwork.org

- The Forum on Education Abroad

    - *Code of Ethics for Education Abroad* forumea.org/resources/standards-of-good-practice/code-of-ethics/

    - *Leading Short-Term Education Abroad Programs* forumea.org/resources/standards-of-good-practice/leading-short-term-education-abroad-programs/

    - *Standards of Good Practice for Education Abroad* forumea.org/resources/standards-of-good-practice/

- Mobility International USA www.miusa.org/

- NAFSA: Association of International Educators www.nafsa.org

    - Education Abroad Knowledge Community www.nafsa.org/eakc

    - Education Abroad Resources www.nafsa.org/ea

- SECUSS-L (education abroad listserv) listserv.buffalo.edu/cgi-bin/wa?A0=SECUSS-L

OTHER:

- California State University-Dominguez Hills Center for Global Education Safety Abroad First – Educational Travel Information (SAFETI) clearinghouse globaled.us/safeti/index.asp

- Council for the Advancement of Standards in Higher Education *Education Abroad Programs Standards Self-Assessment Guide* www.cas.edu/store_product.asp?prodid=57

- *Frontiers: The Interdisciplinary Journal of Study Abroad* frontiersjournal.org/

References

Adams, Rebecca, and Mandy Reinig. 2014. "Student Application, Selection, and Acceptance." In *NAFSA's Guide to Education Abroad for Advisers and Administrators, Fourth Edition*, eds. Magnolia Hernandez, Margaret Wiedenhoeft, and David Wick. Washington, DC: NAFSA: Association of International Educators.

Arnett, Jeffrey Jensen. 2000. "Emerging Adulthood: A Theory of Development from the Late Teens Through the Twenties." *American Psychologist* 55, 5:469–480.

Asia Society. 2009. *Expanding Horizons: Building Global Literacy in Afterschool Programs*. Washington, DC: Asia Society. http://asiasociety.org/files/Expanding%20Horizons%20guidebook.pdf.

Asia Society and OECD. 2018. *Teaching for Global Competence in a Rapidly Changing World*. Asia Society and OECD. https://asiasociety.org/education/teaching-global-competence-rapidly-changing-world.

Astin, Alexander W. 1999. "Student Involvement: A Developmental Theory for Higher Education." *Journal of College Student Development* 25, 4:297–308.

Bandyopadhyay, Soumava, and Kakoli Bandyopadhyay. 2015. "Factors Influencing Student Participation in College Study Abroad Programs." *Journal of International Education Research* 11, 2:87–94. https://doi.org/10.19030/jier.v11i2.9189.

Bathurst, Laura, and Bruce La Brack. 2012. "Shifting the Focus of Intercultural Learning: Intervening Prior to and After Student Experiences Abroad." In *Student Learning Abroad: What Our Students Are Learning, What They're Not, and What We Can Do About It*, eds. Michael Vande Berg, R. Michael Paige, and Kris Hemming Lou. Sterling, VA: Stylus Publishing.

Blair, Scott G. 2017. "Mapping Intercultural Competence: Aligning Goals, Outcomes, Evidence, Rubrics, and Assessment." In *Intercultural Competence in Higher Education: International Approaches, Assessment and Application*, eds. Darla K. Deardorff and Lily A. Arasaratnam-Smith. London, United Kingdom: Routledge.

Brux, Jacqueline Murray, and Blake Fry. 2010. "Multicultural Students in Study Abroad: Their Interests, Their Issues, and Their Constraints." *Journal of Studies in International Education* 14, 5:508–527. https://doi.org/10.1177/1028315309342486.

Buffington, Heidi. 2014. "The Experience of Students On Site." In *NAFSA's Guide to Education Abroad for Advisers and Administrators, Fourth Edition*, eds. Magnolia Hernandez, Margaret Wiedenhoeft, and David Wick. Washington, DC: NAFSA: Association of International Educators.

Butler, Paige E. 2017. "Program Models." In *The Guide to Successful Short-Term Programs Abroad, Third Edition*, eds. Lisa Chieffo and Catherine Spaeth. Washington, DC: NAFSA: Association of International Educators.

Butler, Paige E., Meggan Madden, and Nickie Smith. 2018. "Undocumented Student Participation in Education Abroad: An Institutional Analysis." *Frontiers: The Interdisciplinary Journal of Study Abroad* 30, 2:1–31.

Canny, Eric A. 2014. "Preparation and Orientation." In *NAFSA's Guide to Education Abroad for Advisers and Administrators, Fourth Edition*, eds. Magnolia Hernandez, Margaret Wiedenhoeft, and David Wick. Washington, DC: NAFSA: Association of International Educators.

Chieffo, Lisa, and Catherine Spaeth, eds. 2017. *The Guide to Successful Short-Term Programs Abroad, Third Edition*. Washington, DC: NAFSA: Association of International Educators.

Chisholm, Linda A., and Howard A. Berry. 2002. *Understanding the Education - and Through It the Culture - in Education Abroad*. New York, NY: International Partnership for Service-Learning.

Cressey, William, and Nancy Stubbs. 2010. "The Economics of Study Abroad." In *A History of U.S. Study Abroad: 1965–Present*, eds. William W. Hoffa and Stephen C. DePaul. Carlisle, PA: Frontiers: The Interdisciplinary Journal of Study Abroad and The Forum on Education Abroad.

Deardorff, Darla K. 2015. *Demystifying Outcomes Assessment for International Educators: A Practical Approach*. Sterling, VA: Stylus Publishing.

Delgado, Richard, and Jean Stefancic. 2017. *Critical Race Theory: An Introduction, Third Edition.* New York, NY: New York University Press.

DeWinter, Urbain J., and Laura E. Rumbley. 2010. "The Diversification of Education Abroad Across the Curriculum." In *A History of U.S. Study Abroad: 1965–Present*, eds. William W. Hoffa and Stephen C. DePaul. Carlisle, PA: Frontiers: The Interdisciplinary Journal of Study Abroad and The Forum on Education Abroad.

Disch, Lisa, and Mary Hawkesworth, eds. 2016. *The Oxford Handbook of Feminist Theory.* New York, NY: Oxford University Press.

Engle, Lilli, and John Engle. 2012. "Beyond Immersion: The American University Center of Provence Experiment in Holistic Intervention." In *Student Learning Abroad: What Our Students Are Learning, What They're Not, and What We Can Do About It*, eds. Michael Vande Berg, R. Michael Paige, and Kris Hemming Lou. Sterling, VA: Stylus Publishing.

Evans, Nancy J., Deanna S. Forney, Florence M. Guido, Lori D. Patton, and Kristen A. Renn. 2009. *Student Development in College: Theory, Research, and Practice, Second Edition.* San Francisco, CA: Jossey-Bass.

The Forum on Education Abroad. 2008. "The Forum Pathways to the Profession Survey 2008: Report and Results." Carlisle, PA: The Forum on Education Abroad.

The Forum on Education Abroad. 2015. *Standards of Good Practice for Education Abroad*, 5th ed. Carlisle, PA: The Forum on Education Abroad.

Friend, Julie Anne. 2017. "Mitigating Organizational Liability: A Review of U.S. Case Law and Regulations." In *Crisis Management for Education Abroad*, ed. Patricia C. Martin. Washington, DC: NAFSA: Association of International Educators and University Risk Management and Insurance Association, Inc.

Gorlewski, Emily. 2014. "Partnerships and Advocacy." In *NAFSA's Guide to Education Abroad for Advisers and Administrators, Fourth Edition*, eds. Magnolia Hernandez, Margaret Wiedenhoeft, and David Wick. Washington, DC: NAFSA: Association of International Educators.

Green, Madeleine F. 2013. *Improving and Assessing Global Learning.* Washington, DC: NAFSA: Association of International Educators.

Gregersen-Hermans, Jeanine. 2017. "Intercultural Competence Development in Higher Education." In *Intercultural Competence in Higher Education: International Approaches,*

Assessment and Application, eds. Darla K. Deardorff and Lily A. Arasaratnam-Smith. London, United Kingdom: Routledge.

Harris, Anita. 2014. "Generation G, Global Connectedness & Global Responsibility." International Education Association of Australia. https://www.ieaa.org.au/documents/item/292.

Henke, Corrine. 2014. "Managing an Education Abroad Budget." In *NAFSA's Guide to Education Abroad for Advisers and Administrators*, Fourth Edition, eds. Magnolia Hernandez, Margaret Wiedenhoeft, and David Wick. Washington, DC: NAFSA: Association of International Educators.

Hoffa, William W. 2007. *A History of U.S. Study Abroad: Beginnings to 1965*. Carlisle, PA: Frontiers: The Interdisciplinary Journal of Study Abroad and The Forum on Education Abroad.

Hoffa, William W., and Stephen C. DePaul, eds. 2010. *A History of U.S. Study Abroad: 1965–Present*. Carlisle, PA: Frontiers: The Interdisciplinary Journal of Study Abroad and The Forum on Education Abroad.

Institute of International Education (IIE). 2018. *Open Doors Report on International Educational Exchange*. Institute of International Education. https://www.iie.org/opendoors.

Kahn, Hilary E., and Melanie Agnew. 2017. "Global Learning Through Difference: Considerations for Teaching, Learning, and the Internationalization of Higher Education." *Journal of Studies in International Education* 21, 1:52–64. https://doi.org/10.1177/1028315315622022.

Killick, David. 2018. *Developing Intercultural Practice*. New York, NY: Routledge.

Kindred, Chelsea. 2014. "Post Study Abroad." In *NAFSA's Guide to Education Abroad for Advisers and Administrators*, Fourth Edition, eds. Magnolia Hernandez, Margaret Wiedenhoeft, and David Wick. Washington, DC: NAFSA: Association of International Educators.

Kolb, David A. 1984. *Experiential Learning: Experience as the Source of Learning and Development*. Upper Saddle River, NJ: Prentice Hall.

Kuh, George D. 2011. "Student Success." In *Student Services: A Handbook for the Profession*, eds. John H. Schuh, Susan R. Jones, and Shaun R Harper. San Francisco, CA: Jossey-Bass.

Lilley, Kathleen, Michelle Barker, and Neil Harris. 2014. "Exploring the Process of Global Citizen Learning and the Student Mind-Set." *Journal of Studies in International*

Education 19, 3:225–245. Published electronically September 11, 2014. https://doi.org/10.1177/1028315314547822.

Lilley, Kathleen, Michelle Barker, and Neil Harris. 2017. "The Global Citizen Conceptualized: Accommodating Ambiguity." *Journal of Studies in International Education* 21, 1:6–21. https://doi.org/10.1177/1028315316637354.

Lindeman, Barbara, ed. 2016. *Addressing Mental Health Issues Affecting Education Abroad Participants.* Washington, DC: NAFSA: Association of International Educators

Lindsay, Julie, and Vicki A. Davis. 2012. *Flattening Classrooms, Engaging Minds: Move to Global Collaboration One Step at a Time*. Boston, MA: Pearson.

Long, Dallas. 2012. "Theories and Models of Student Development." In *Environments for Student Growth and Development: Librarians and Student Affairs in Collaboration*, eds. Lisa Janicke Hinchliffe and Melissa Autumn Wong. Chicago, IL: Association of College and Research Libraries.

Lu, Charles, Richard Reddick, Dallawrence Dean, and Veronica Pecero. 2015. "Coloring Up Study Abroad: Exploring Black Students' Decision to Study in China." *Journal of Student Affairs Research and Practice* 52, 4:440–451. https://doi.org/10.1080/19496591.2015.1050032.

Lucas, James M., and Scott G. Blair. 2017. "Learning Outcomes and Assessment." In *Learning Across Cultures: Locally and Globally, Third Edition*, eds. Barbara Kappler Mikk and Inge Ellen Steglitz. Washington, DC: NAFSA: Association of International Educators and Stylus Publishing.

Magolda, Marcia B. Baxter. 2001. *Making Their Own Way: Narratives for Transforming Higher Education to Promote Self-Development.* Sterling, VA: Stylus Publishing.

Malveaux, Gregory F. 2016. *Look Before Leaping: Risks, Liabilities, and Repair of Study Abroad in Higher Education.* Lanham, MD: Rowman and Littlefield.

McCallon, Melanie, and Bill Holmes. 2010. *Faculty-Led 360: Guide to Successful Study Abroad.* Charleston, IL: Agapy LLC.

McClure, Kevin R., Katalin Szelenyi, Elizabeth Niehaus, Aeriel A. Anderson, and Jeffrey Reed. 2010. "'We Just Don't Have the Possibility Yet': U.S. Latina/o Narratives on Study Abroad." *Journal of Student Affairs Research and Practice* 47, 3:363–382. https://doi.org/10.2202/1949-6605.6056.

Meadows, Mary. 2014. "Marketing for Education Abroad Advisers." In *NAFSA's Guide to Education Abroad for Advisers and Administrators*, Fourth Edition, eds. Magnolia Hernandez, Margaret Wiedenhoeft, and David Wick. Washington, DC: NAFSA: Association of International Educators.

Merriam, Sharan B., and Laura L. Bierema. 2014. *Adult Learning: Linking Theory and Practice*. San Francisco, CA: Jossey-Bass.

Mohajeri Norris, Emily, and Joan Gillespie. 2009. "How Study Abroad Shapes Global Careers: Evidence From the United States." *Journal of Studies in International Education* 13, 3:382–397. https://doi.org/10.1177/1028315308319740.

Murray-Garcia, Jann, and Melanie Tervalon. 2017. "Rethinking Intercultural Competence: Cultural Humility in Internationalising Higher Education." In *Intercultural Competence in Higher Education: International Approaches, Assessment and Application*, eds. Darla K. Deardorff and Lily A. Arasaratnam-Smith. London, United Kingdom: Routledge.

NAFSA: Association of International Educators. 2015. *NAFSA International Education Professional Competencies*. Washington, DC: NAFSA: Association of International Educators.

National Survey of Student Engagement. 2018. "High-Impact Practices." Bloomington, IN: Indiana University Center for Postsecondary Research. http://nsse.indiana.edu/html/high_impact_practices.cfm.

Ogden, Anthony C. 2014. "Effective Utilization of Institutional Data for Strategic Education Abroad Planning and Campus Advocacy." In *NAFSA's Guide to Education Abroad for Advisers and Administrators, Fourth Edition*, eds. Magnolia Hernandez, Margaret Wiedenhoeft, and David Wick. Washington, DC: NAFSA: Association of International Educators.

Ogden, Anthony C. 2017. "What Do We Know: A Review of Literature on Short-Term Program Abroad." In *The Guide to Successful Short-Term Programs Abroad, Third Edition*, eds. Lisa Chieffo and Catherine Spaeth. Washington, DC: NAFSA: Association of International Educators.

Organisation for Economic Co-operation and Development (OECD). 2016. "Global Competency for an Inclusive World." Paris, France: Organisation for Economic Co-operation and Development.

Paracka, Daniel J., and Lily A. Pynn. 2017. "Towards Transformative Reciprocity: Mapping the Intersectionality of Intercultural Competence." In *Intercultural Competence in Higher*

Education: International Approaches, Assessment and Application, eds. Darla K. Deardorff and Lily A. Arasaratnam-Smith. London, United Kingdom: Routledge.

Passarelli, Angela M., and David A. Kolb. 2012. "Using Experiential Learning Theory to Promote Student Learning and Development in Programs of Education Abroad." In *Student Learning Abroad: What Our Students Are Learning, What They're Not, and What We Can Do About It*, eds. Michael Vande Berg, R. Michael Paige, and Kris Hemming Lou. Sterling, VA: Stylus Publishing.

Patton, Lori D., Kristen A. Renn, Florence M. Guido, and Stephen John Quaye. 2016. *Student Development in College: Theory, Research, and Practice, Third Edition*. San Francisco, CA: Jossey-Bass.

Peifer, Janelle, and Elaine Meyer-Lee. 2017. "Program Design for Intercultural Development." In *The Guide to Successful Short-Term Programs Abroad, Third Edition*, eds. Lisa Chieffo and Catherine Spaeth. Washington, DC: NAFSA: Association of International Educators.

Pelton, Woody. 2017. "Administrative Processes." In *The Guide to Successful Short-Term Programs Abroad, Third Edition*, eds. Lisa Chieffo and Catherine Spaeth. Washington, DC: NAFSA: Association of International Educators.

Punteney, Katherine. 2017. "Social Psychology in Intercultural Contexts." In *Learning Across Cultures: Locally and Globally, Third Edition*, eds. Barbara Kappler Mikk and Inge Ellen Steglitz. Washington, DC: NAFSA: Association of International Educators and Stylus Publishing.

Renn, Kristen A. 2008. "Research on Biracial and Multiracial Identity Development: Overview and Synthesis." *New Directions for Student Services* 2008, 123:13–21. https://doi.org/10.1002/ss.282.

Rhodes, Gary. 2014. "Risk Management Planning for Education Abroad: Issues, Challenges, and Resources." In *NAFSA's Guide to Education Abroad for Advisers and Administrators, Fourth Edition*, eds. Magnolia Hernandez, Margaret Wiedenhoeft, and David Wick. Washington, DC: NAFSA: Association of International Educators.

Rodman, Richard, and Martha Merrill. 2010. "Unlocking Study Abroad Potential: Design Models, Methods and Masters." In *A History of U.S. Study Abroad: 1965–Present*, eds. William W. Hoffa and Stephen C. DePaul. Carlisle, PA: Frontiers: The Interdisciplinary Journal of Study Abroad and The Forum on Education Abroad.

Sanderson, Jason. 2014. "Education Abroad Models." In *NAFSA's Guide to Education Abroad for Advisers and Administrators, Fourth Edition*, eds. Magnolia Hernandez, Margaret

Wiedenhoeft, and David Wick. Washington, DC: NAFSA: Association of International Educators.

Schlossberg, Nancy K. 1995. *Counseling Adults in Transition: Linking Practice with Theory*. New York, NY: Springer Publishing Company.

Sevigny, Joe. 2014. "Education Abroad Applications: Balancing Data Collection and Student Preparation." In *NAFSA's Guide to Education Abroad for Advisers and Administrators, Fourth Edition*, eds. Magnolia Hernandez, Margaret Wiedenhoeft, and David Wick. Washington, DC: NAFSA: Association of International Educators.

Shipley, David. 2014. "Marketing and Promotion." In *NAFSA's Guide to Education Abroad for Advisers and Administrators, Fourth Edition*, eds. Magnolia Hernandez, Margaret Wiedenhoeft, and David Wick. Washington, DC: NAFSA: Association of International Educators.

Snyder, Thomas D., Cristobal de Brey, and Sally A. Dillow. 2018. *Digest of Education Statistics, 2016*. Washington, DC: National Center for Education Statistics, Institute of Education Sciences, U.S. Department of Education.

Soria, Krista M., and Jordan Troisi. 2014. "Internationalization at Home Alternatives to Study Abroad: Implications for Students' Development of Global, International, and Intercultural Competencies." *Journal of Studies in International Education* 18, 3:261–280.

Strange, C. Carney, and Patricia M. King. 2011. "The Professional Practice of Student Development." In *College Student Development Theory, Second Edition*, ed. Maureen E. Wilson. New York, NY: Pearson Learning Solutions.

Sutton, Richard C., and Donald L. Rubin. 2004. "The GLOSSARI Project: Initial Findings from a System-Wide Research Initiative on Study Abroad Learning Outcomes." *Frontiers: The Interdisciplinary Journal of Study Abroad* 10:68–82.

Swart, William J., and Catherine Spaeth. 2017. "Designing the Academic Course: Principles and Practicalities." In *The Guide to Successful Short-Term Programs Abroad, Third Edition*, eds. Lisa Chieffo and Catherine Spaeth. Washington, DC: NAFSA: Association of International Educators.

Tavangar, Homa Sabet. 2017. "Unlocking the Secret of Global Education." *Childhood Education* 93, 6:457–463. https://doi.org/10.1080/00094056.2017.1398546.

Teague, Thomas. 2014. "While Abroad." In *NAFSA's Guide to Education Abroad for Advisers and Administrators, Fourth Edition*, eds. Magnolia Hernandez, Margaret Wiedenhoeft, and David Wick. Washington, DC: NAFSA: Association of International Educators.

Thebodo, Stacey Woody. 2014. "Education Abroad Advising." In *NAFSA's Guide to Education Abroad for Advisers and Administrators, Fourth Edition*, eds. Magnolia Hernandez, Margaret Wiedenhoeft, and David Wick. Washington, DC: NAFSA: Association of International Educators.

Tolan, Michelle, and Margaret McCullers. 2018. "First-Generation College Students and Study Abroad: Examining the Participation Gap and Successful Strategies for Promoting Access." In *Promoting Inclusion in Education Abroad*, eds. Heather Barclay Hamir and Nick Gozik. Sterling, VA: Stylus Publishing and NAFSA: Association of International Educators.

Tuma, Kathy. 2017. "Building Institutional Support." In *The Guide to Successful Short-Term Programs Abroad, Third Edition*, eds. Lisa Chieffo and Catherine Spaeth. Washington, DC: NAFSA: Association of International Educators.

Vande Berg, Michael, Jeffrey Connor-Linton, and R. Michael Paige. 2009. "The Georgetown Consortium Project: Interventions for Student Learning Abroad." *Frontiers: The Interdisciplinary Journal of Study Abroad* 18:1–75.

Vande Berg, Michael, R. Michael Paige, and Kris Hemming Lou, eds. 2012. *Student Learning Abroad: What Our Students Are Learning, What They're Not, and What We Can Do About It*. Sterling, VA: Stylus Publishing.

White, Jennifer. 2014. "Physical and Mental Health of Students." In *NAFSA's Guide to Education Abroad for Advisers and Administrators, Fourth Edition*, eds. Magnolia Hernandez, Margaret Wiedenhoeft, and David Wick. Washington, DC: NAFSA: Association of International Educators.

Wijeyesinghe, Charmaine L. 2012. "The Intersectional Model of Multiracial Identity." In *New Perspectives on Racial Identity Development, Second Edition*, eds. Charmaine L. Wijeyesinghe and Bailey W. Jackson III. New York, NY: New York University Press.

Wyatt Knowlton, Lisa, and Cynthia C. Phillips. 2013. *The Logic Model Guidebook: Better Strategies for Great Results, 2nd ed*. Thousand Oaks, CA: Sage Publications.

Chapter 5

Experiential Education

In the previous chapter, study abroad was introduced as, arguably, the most well-known type of education abroad program. This chapter explores other types of education abroad programs, including international internships, work abroad, teach abroad, research abroad, international service-learning, and global health programs. Many of these programs, particularly internships, service-learning, and international research programs, are frequently designed based on the principles of experiential education, prioritizing learning that takes place outside of a conventional classroom setting.

Experiential education is both an educational philosophy and an educational method in which a real-life experience serves as the foundation for structured reflection, which in turn results in student learning (Association for Experiential Education n.d.). International experiential education programs usually involve partnerships between higher education institutions or education abroad program providers (nonprofit and for-profit organizations that manage education abroad programs for students and adults) that send program participants abroad and the international corporations, nonprofit agencies, government agencies, community groups, or other entities that host the participants. This chapter introduces the philosophy and practice of experiential education, as well as considerations for the management and facilitation of these programs and partnerships.

Experiential Education Theory

John Dewey (1859–1952) is considered to be a founding theorist on experiential education. Dewey was interested in the relationship between society and the education of individual students. In addition to promoting hands-on learning, Dewey argued that education should be structured in such a way that students increase their capacity for social service. He maintained that when students work on solving societal problems and then reflect on the meaning of the solutions within society, learning happens (Jacoby 2018; Kolb and Kolb 2017; Seaman and

Gingo 2011). In addition to Dewey, many educators, psychologists, sociologists, and others have been influential in shaping approaches to experiential education. Important influencers include Paulo Freire, William Kilpatrick, Kurt Lewin, Maria Montessori, Mary Parker Follett, Johann Heinrich Pestalozzi, Jean Piaget, Nevitt Sanford, Rudolph Steiner, and Lev Vygotsky (Kolb and Kolb 2017; Roberts 2015; Smith and Knapp 2011).

Kolb's Experiential Learning Cycle

David Kolb's (1984) Experiential Learning Cycle explains the process by which learning happens in experiential education. As shown in figure 1, learning requires cycling between four stages. While it is possible to begin learning at any point on the cycle, experiential education programs are often designed to begin with a *concrete experience*: the students' active participation in an activity. For example, the concrete experience may be students doing work at an international internship or engaging in community service efforts as part of an international service-learning program.

The next stage of the cycle is *reflective observation*. In this stage, students take note (in writing, in their minds, or in some other format) of what happened during the concrete experience. They may focus on particular interactions that they found confusing or significant. They begin to identify patterns that they have observed.

In the stage that follows, *abstract conceptualization*, students theorize on possible meanings and explanations for the patterns they observed. They connect their individual experiences with theories and research that they have been exposed to in the past or in the experiential education program curriculum.

In the next stage of the cycle, *active experimentation*, students devise plans for how they will test their new understanding for accuracy. They may make plans for how to handle particular situations in the future. As students continue to have concrete experiences, such as through their ongoing internship or service work, they try out their newly devised

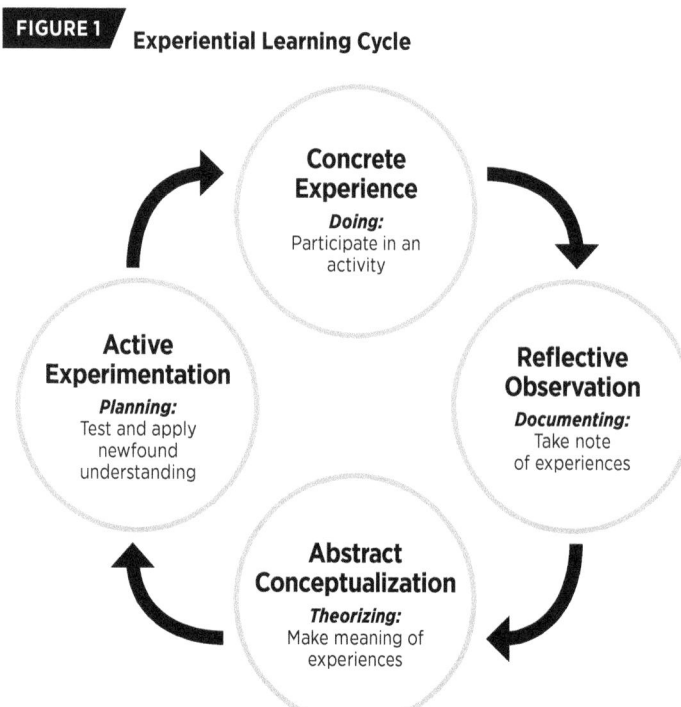

FIGURE 1 Experiential Learning Cycle

Concept Source: Kolb (1984).

plans then reflect on how well the new approaches worked, and the cycle continues. Learning happens as the cycle is repeated and learning is refined (Jacoby 2018; Kolb and Kolb 2017; Kolb 1984).

Experiential Learning Cycle in Practice

Roberts (2015) distinguishes between learning from life experience and experiential education. He offers the example of a university coach running athletes through drills. These students are learning by doing, but this does not fit the experiential education model because of the absence of reflection, theorizing, and planning. In contrast, an internship curriculum (see table 1) with

TABLE 1 Experiential Learning Cycle in Practice

	Example 1	Example 2	Example 3
Program Type	Student internship with government agency	Students offer service in local area after natural disaster temporarily closes university	Large-scale online simulation game
Preparation	Student develops reading list and learning goals related to public health and environmental justice.	No advance student preparation because event was unanticipated. University fast-tracks approval of the service-learning course and enrolls interested student volunteers.	Faculty members develop complex online game set in watershed ecosystem. Students are assigned roles as farmers, watermen, land developers, etc.
Concrete Experience	Participates in internship work.	Engage in heavy labor, shovel dirt and debris, distribute food and water to the elderly, etc.	Play online game in a large room with all 100 students.
Reflective Observation	Engages in periodic check-ins with faculty adviser. Prepares substantive public presentation about the internship to be delivered after return home.	Respond to online reflection questions.	Discuss with each other the patterns they are observing regarding consequences of their actions on the socioecological health of the watershed.
Abstract Conceptualization	Integrates readings with personal observations in preparation for public presentation on intersections of public health, environmental issues, and public policy.	Use online readings to help place their individual experiences in context, focusing on how collaboration happens and how communities function.	Identify patterns of behavior that are detrimental to the virtual ecosystem and economy.
Active Experimentation	During presentation, student answers questions about how experience affects understanding of the field, career goals, and intersections of race, class, inequity, and own research.	Students consider how their new understanding of community systems can apply to their ongoing service. Program strengthens campus-community connections and student engagement in university.	Collectively, players (without prompting from faculty) exchange information, negotiate, and try to optimize positive benefits for the whole ecosystem, even when individuals could benefit more from noncollaborative strategies.

Source: Roberts (2015).

learning goals, defined internship projects, required synthesis of the learning experience with readings/theories, and a final presentation by students on lessons learned and plans for the future incorporates the stages of the Experiential Learning Cycle.

The phases of the Experiential Learning Cycle can be used to guide program design, though it must be noted that the model is an idealization. In reality, students may move back and forth between stages of the model and will vary in their preferred points of entry to the cycle. Some students may enjoy starting with a hands-on experience, while others may prefer to observe first, for example. In table 1, Roberts (2015) offers three examples of how the Experiential Learning Cycle may operate in practice. These scenarios demonstrate the diversity of opportunities that may be experiential: in this case, an individual internship, a large group service-learning project, and a large online simulation game.

In experiential education, the focus is on teaching people, rather than on teaching content. Students are thought of holistically as not only brains, but also physical, emotional, and spiritual beings (Roberts 2015). Experiential education tends to be less teacher centered, meaning that the teacher is not primarily delivering content to the students. Instead, the teacher organizes the learning, facilitating the students' progress through the learning cycle by structuring the experience, reflection, theorizing, and planning stages (Roberts 2015). Experiential education programs are pragmatic, connecting the curriculum to real-world problem-solving, a key tenet of adult learning theory (Merriam and Bierema 2014).

Sometimes rooted in Freire's critical pedagogy, in critical race theory, and in feminist theory, among others, experiential education programs may also emphasize the importance of working to identify and dismantle inequitable power structures in society for the explicit goal of social justice (Chambers and Lavery 2018; Jacoby 2018; Smith and Knapp 2011).

History of International Experiential Education

The NAFSA: Association of International Educators publication *Internships, Service Learning, and Volunteering Abroad: Successful Models and Best Practices* (Nolting et al. 2013) explores the history of international experiential education programs. Highlights from that account are offered here:

Within international education, experiential education programs have existed for more than a hundred years. One of the oldest international experiential education programs, Princeton in Asia, was founded in 1898. Fulbright teaching programs started in 1946. Cultural Vistas was founded in 1949 to offer international work experience to farmers, businesspeople, and engineers in order to rebuild post–WWII Europe. Also started in the aftermath of the war, Association Internationale des Etudiants en Sciences Economiques et Commerciales (AISEC) offered business traineeships for international students, while the International Association for the Exchange of Students for Technical Experience (IASTE) offered international internships in science

(continued on next page)

History of International Experiential Education (continued)

and engineering. All of these organizations continue to operate today, managing programs in countries around the world.

The U.S. Peace Corps was established in 1961 to send young people around the world to serve in developing countries while simultaneously learning about other cultures. In 1962, BUNAC formalized agreements for U.S. and UK students to work in the other country on short work exchanges. In 1963, Stanford University began offering summer student volunteer programs in Hong Kong through an organization known today as VIA. Starting in 1965, Council on International Educational Exchange (CIEE) offered short-term job placements for undergraduate students in Europe. Shortly after that, CIEE began publishing books and creating resources for college staff members who were advising on overseas work opportunities.

International service-learning programs grew rapidly in number beginning in the late 1960s and throughout the 1970s and 1980s. In 1968, Goshen College launched service-learning programs that lasted a full academic term. In the 1970s, IES Abroad added international internships to its portfolio of education abroad programs. In 1975, NAFSA's first publication, *SECUSSA Sourcebook: A Guide for Advisers of U.S. Students Planning an Overseas Experience* was released, covering both study abroad and international experiential education programs.

The International Partnership for Service-Learning was established in 1982. By the 1980s and 1990s, education abroad offices at many U.S. universities were running for-credit and noncredit international experiential education programs and advising on a wide range of international education opportunities beyond study abroad. Most education abroad provider organizations began adding international internship and service-learning programs to their collection of program offerings. Over the last few decades, the division between study abroad and experiential education programs has blurred as experiential education approaches have been applied to study abroad programs. Many programs under the broad heading of "education abroad" now include both classroom and experiential education components (Nolting et al. 2013).

Benefits of Participation

The National Survey of Student Engagement (NSSE) offers insight into the benefits of participation in international experiential education activities. More than 6 million students have taken the NSSE survey since 2000, creating a very large data set. The survey examines the relationship between the time and effort students put into their education and how institutions organize the curriculum, use resources, and structure learning opportunities. Among the findings, NSSE identified six high-impact education practices that result in greater student engagement:

- Learning communities in which groups of students take two or more classes together;
- Courses that include a community-based project (service-learning);
- Work with a faculty member on a research project;

- Internship, co-op, field experience, student teaching, or clinical placement;
- Study abroad; and
- Culminating senior experience (capstone course, senior project or thesis, comprehensive exam, portfolio, etc.).

These six high-impact practices share several characteristics: They demand time and effort, involve learning outside of the classroom, entail meaningful interaction between students and faculty, encourage collaboration with diverse others, and provide frequent and substantive feedback (NSSE 2018).

High-impact practices, such as those found in international experiential education programs, increase student engagement. Increased student engagement, in turn, is shown to have positive benefits for cognitive development, college adjustment, moral and ethical development, skills development, accrual of social capital, psychosocial development, positive racial and gender identity formation, positive self-image, increased grade point average, and increased graduation rate (Quaye and Harper 2015). Further, research has shown that underserved students benefit even more in these areas than does the general population when exposed to high-impact practices such as those found in experiential programs (Roberts 2015).

International Experiential Education

Many universities design and run their own international experiential education programs through the education abroad office, an internship center, a career center, a civic engagement program, an academic department, or a collaboration between these or other departments. Institutions may also support students' participation in programs run by education abroad program providers. This support can range from making providers' information available to students (posting flyers and having brochures available) at the lowest level of institutional commitment, up to contracting with providers to develop and deliver programs specifically for the institutions' students at the highest level of engagement. In the middle of the range, institutions may invite providers to campus career fairs and study abroad fairs. Universities may host information sessions with education abroad program providers for prospective students. Universities may also facilitate student participation by establishing a list of experiential education programs that are preapproved for academic credit transfer.

Definitions and Terminology

Numerous education sectors, including international education, utilize the philosophy of experiential education. Among them are adventure education, career and technical education, environmental education, outdoor education, service-learning, and vocational education

(Roberts 2015). As discussed in previous chapters, many key terms in international education do not have agreed upon definitions and there is debate over which terms are ideal. Experiential education is no exception. Roberts (2015, 30) describes "a haze around experiential education as used in the literature…more descriptors and terms appear seemingly overnight."

International Experiential Education: Related Terms

Key terms related to international experiential education are described in table 2.

TABLE 2 — Key Terms in International Experiential Education

Term	Description
Adult Learning	Distinguishing the education of adults from the education of children, adult learning theory emphasizes that adults should know why content is being taught; adults should be involved in directing their own learning; learning should connect to adults' prior experiences; and learning should be applicable to adults' current goals and needs (Merriam and Bierema 2014).
Alternative Break	Alternative breaks "are opportunities for small groups of students to travel to a different city, state, or country to participate in a service-learning project during their academic break" (Niehaus and Kurotsuchi Inkelas 2015, 134).
Civic Engagement	Civic engagement may be an outcome of experiential education. Civic engagement is defined as "acting upon a heightened sense of responsibility to one's communities through both political and non-political means" (Jacoby 2015, 4). Civic engagement may also be referred to as "active citizenship" or "democratic participation" (Jacoby 2015).
Educational Travel	Educational travel refers to travel for primarily recreational purposes, with an educational component such as a lecture series. Often, lectures and excursions are organized around a theme.
Faith-Based Programs	These programs are rooted in the values of religious faiths. They may be organized by religious colleges and universities, religious institutions, or nonprofit organizations. The term may also be used to describe mission trips.
Gap Year	The gap year refers to a hiatus year between high school and university or between higher education and professional life. Students sometimes use a gap year for international work, internships, volunteering, or study (The Forum on Education Abroad 2017).
Co-ops	Cooperative education (co-ops) "are paid work programs that are usually integrated into a university-level degree, in which terms of study and degree major-related work are alternated. They tend to be in the technical, business, and healthcare fields" (Nolting et al. 2013, pp. 1–2).
WIVA	WIVA is an acronym for "work, intern, and volunteer abroad." Nolting et. al (2013) argue that the WIVA acronym is used for convenience and is meant to encompass all types of related international experiential education programs, including international service-learning.
WIVRA	WIVRA is an acronym for "work, intern, volunteer, and research abroad."

Overlapping terms include active learning, adult learning, civic engagement, collaborative learning, community-based learning, experiential learning, simulation- and game-based learning, hands-on learning, holistic education, integrative learning, inquiry-based learning, place-based learning, problem-based learning, and project-based learning (Kolb and Kolb 2017; Roberts 2015).

Size of the Sector

There are no comprehensive data available on the number of international experiential education programs that exist or the number of participants in such programs. However, some data points help to indicate the immense size and scope of this sector of the international education field.

The website GoAbroad.com includes listings and reviews for 17,634 education abroad programs, as of February 2019. GoOverseas.com lists more than 14,000 programs. Both websites provide profiles of programs and reviews posted by past participants. While it should be noted that a single program may be listed in more than one category, in February 2019, GoOverseas.com offered the following number of program listings for each program type:

- Volunteer abroad: 3,766
- Study abroad: 3,738
- Intern abroad: 1,824
- Language schools: 1,456
- Gap year: 1,352
- Teach abroad: 1,005
- Tours and trips: 847
- High school abroad: 955
- Teaching English as a foreign language (TEFL) courses: 521

A key source for data on international volunteering is a Washington University in St. Louis analysis of census data from approximately 60,000 U.S. households (Lough 2015). From those responses, Lough (2015) was able to extrapolate that 800,000 to 1,100,000 people in the United States volunteered internationally each year between 2004 and 2014. Looking at the demographics of these volunteers, the researcher found that participants were disproportionately young, white, married college graduates with higher incomes. Most did not have minor children living at home. Slightly more women (52 percent) than men (48 percent) volunteered (Lough 2015). According to the study, this gender gap is smaller than the gender difference for domestic volunteering.

Lough (2015) found that the participants spanned all age groups, with those aged 15 to 24 the most likely to volunteer abroad. Data on the more recent years showed an increase in the number of participants aged 65 and older. Among those 16 to 24 years old, 55 percent of the volunteers were students (Lough 2015). The largest group of respondents (44 percent) volunteered with a religious organization (Lough 2015). Social and community organizations received 11 percent of the volunteers and health care organizations received 10 percent (Lough 2015). The most common volunteer activities did not require advanced skills; most common were tutoring or teaching (28 percent), general labor (27 percent), and mentoring youth (26 percent) (Lough 2015). Nearly 45 percent of these individuals participated in programs of 2 weeks or less in length (Lough 2015). The survey does not provide any data on whether the volunteering was accompanied by any curriculum or structured educational content.

There is general consensus across the field that many U.S. university students participate in international experiential education programs; however, the programs may not be organized by their university, which impacts the data collected. Even if students do participate in programs through the university, if the program is not credit bearing, the institution may not maintain records of the number of students participating. Beginning with the 2012–13 annual *Open Doors* report, the Institute of International Education (IIE) began to collect data on student participation in noncredit work, internships, and volunteer programs abroad. For the 2016–17 academic year, 414 U.S. higher education institutions reported that a total of 32,975 students participated in such programs abroad (IIE 2018). In terms of program region, the reported numbers (IIE 2018) were:

- Latin America and the Caribbean: 14,895 (40.3 percent)
- Europe: 8,372 (22.6 percent)
- Asia: 4,860 (13.1 percent)
- Sub-Saharan Africa: 2,561 (6.9 percent)
- Unknown destinations: 2,372 (6.4 percent)
- North America 2,225 (6.0 percent)
- Middle East and North Africa 1,142 (3.1 percent)
- Oceania 530 (1.4 percent)
- Antarctica 17 (0.0 percent)

Because the *Open Doors* data are self-reported by universities and many universities do not collect data on noncredit-bearing programs, it is reasonable to assume that these figures underestimate actual participation rates.

Program Types

International experiential education programs may last anywhere from a week to several years. Programs may be designed so that each student participates individually in the international experience, or they may be designed for a group of students (Mlyn and McBride 2013).

Many education abroad offices design and administer international experiential education opportunities for their students. Even if they are not actively running their own programs, they likely refer students to education abroad program providers. In either case, university education abroad advisers will definitely find themselves advising students who have returned home from these programs, passionate about the experience and eager for ideas on how to get more international experience. For this reason, education abroad advisers at universities should be aware of international experiential education programs beyond those offered through their institution.

This section offers an introduction to some of the most prominent international experiential education program types. It should be noted that, depending on the curriculum and teaching methodologies used, individual programs may or may not qualify as experiential education. For example, a program that sends students to work or volunteer overseas but offers no goal-setting, training, incorporation of theoretical materials, or structured reflection would not qualify as experiential education. Participants can certainly learn through life experience; however, experiential learning theory and abundant research emphasize that learning is maximized with intentional, thoughtful design and facilitated reflection (Roberts 2015).

Organizations that offer international experiential programs should be able to tell prospective participants about the types of projects they will work on; the training and mentoring they will receive; the amount of independent work versus group work; hours per week of work/service; program length; and what skills, qualifications, language skills, and academic background are required. Additionally, logistical arrangements should be transparent: the estimated cost of living in the local area, housing options, distance to emergency medical care, whether there will be a person in the local area as an emergency contact, and the visa arrangements (NAFSA WIVA Subcommittee 2012).

Intern Abroad

Some educators contest the idea of granting academic credit for internships, arguing that internships are professional rather than academic endeavors. In recent years, however, there has been gradual acceptance of the idea that credit can be granted for internships, not in acknowledgment of the professional work done, but in recognition of the academic work that elicits meaning and learning from the work activities. In other words, the experiential education elements of internships are increasingly being recognized and valued within higher education. With the rise in education abroad programs, alongside the growing recognition of the educational value of internships, interest in international internships has flourished in recent decades (DeWinter and Rumbley 2010; McFarland 2017).

Many universities and most education abroad program providers now offer intern abroad programs. These may be full-time or part-time internships, may be paid or unpaid, may be in any part of the world, and may be in any professional field. Sometimes, the internships are paired with study abroad programs; two of the most common models are (a) part-time internships completed concurrently with study abroad programs, and (b) full-time internships following the completion of study abroad programs. Students' motivations to participate are typically career oriented, either exploring a potential career or gaining experience in a chosen field. Selection for these programs may be competitive, and students may be required to have advanced foreign language skills (Nolting et al. 2013).

Work Abroad

In a global world that is growing ever more connected, it is becoming increasingly likely that graduates will have international careers, even if they are based in their home country. Graduates "will use technology to customize products and services for clients worldwide, communicate with suppliers, collaborate on projects with overseas offices, and cooperate with colleagues whose first language is not English. New graduates will be immersed in many foreign cultures as part of their jobs—sometimes without ever setting foot overseas" (Nolting et al. 2013, 63). With this expectation in mind, many students are interested in pursuing opportunities to gain international career experience during and after their university education (American Council on Education, Art & Science, and College Board 2008; Punteney 2012). In parallel, employers are seeking graduates with international experience, for both their industry-specific skills as well as cross-cultural skills (Nolting et al. 2013).

There are many possible types of work abroad. One option is short-term work abroad. This is often temporary work, such as restaurant work, though some students are able to find professionally relevant options. Because their fellow employees are usually local, students can use the opportunity to engage in cultural learning (Nolting et al. 2013). Popular destinations for short-term work abroad include Canada, Australia, and New Zealand, as well as some countries in Europe. Several countries have facilitated this type of experience by providing a work-travel visa category specifically for short-term work abroad combined with cultural exploration.

Visas and work permits are one of the most challenging aspects of work (and intern) abroad programs. Visa rules vary by country, vary by type of position, and change frequently. It is very difficult for an education abroad adviser to stay informed of each country's regulations. Both the students and university education abroad advisers find that one of the key benefits of working with education abroad program providers is the assistance they provide with navigating visa and work permit processes. If the student can enroll in an internship course, or otherwise get credit for the work, it may enable the student to qualify for a student visa (Nolting et al. 2013).

A common approach is for students to use a work permit program such as BUNAC. These programs and organizations provide work permits and offer some assistance with job searches—though students are ultimately responsible for finding jobs. Fees for this type of service will typically be lower than for job placement. In some cases, students may search for a job once they arrive in-country. An in-person job search may be more effective than applying remotely, but the uncertainty can be a deterrent to students and parents, and students will not be able to begin working until they have the appropriate visa or work permit (Nolting et al. 2013).

Teach Abroad

Teaching abroad is a subcategory of work abroad. Some students teach abroad to meet a professional practice requirement as they work to earn a degree in education or a teaching credential. (Chapter 8, "International Schools," discusses these teacher education programs in greater depth.) For many other recent graduates, teaching abroad is one of most accessible long-term (1 to 2 years) work abroad opportunities. There are also some summer positions available. While most opportunities are in East Asia and Europe, there are some in Africa and Latin America as well. The majority of positions are focused on teaching English and usually require a bachelor's degree. Though not required, it is ideal to have previous teaching or tutoring experience because limited training is provided. Positions in affluent countries can pay well. In developing countries, pay will likely be high by local standards, but low by U.S. standards.

Much of the workday is spent using English, so this is a difficult way to improve foreign language skills. Teaching abroad does allow for cultural immersion into a local educational system (Nolting et al. 2013). Well-known government-sponsored programs include the Japan Exchange and Teaching Program (JET), the English Program in Korea (EPIK), the Fulbright English Teaching Assistant (ETA) Programs, and the Teaching Assistant Program in France (TAPIF). Additionally, many education abroad program providers offer teach abroad programs, and many private language schools hire recent graduates.

Research Abroad

While graduate students studying international topics have long conducted research overseas (Hoffa 2007), it is becoming increasingly common for undergraduates to do so as well (DeWinter and Rumbley 2010). McFarland (2017) identifies four types of undergraduate research programs:

- Nationally sponsored projects not affiliated with an institution, such as National Science Foundation (United States) or Research in Science and Engineering (Germany) programs;

- Independent study alongside a home or host institution faculty member who is conducting research;

- Undergraduate programs facilitated by education abroad program providers; and

- Independent research in which students travel alone and collect data, often with a faculty mentor back home.

Having the opportunity to conduct research alongside a faculty member is recognized as a high-impact practice, strengthening students' engagement in their education (McFarland 2017; NSSE 2018). Cross-national research collaboration continues to increase (Altbach and de Wit 2018), which is likely to significantly expand the number of opportunities for student research abroad.

Volunteer Abroad

Many U.S. higher education institutions have seen a steady rise in the number of students participating in some form of service abroad (Mlyn and McBride 2013). Programs can range from a week in length to as long as multiple years (for example, the U.S. Peace Corps) (Nolting et al. 2013). Volunteer abroad programs recruit students, professionals, and retirees to participate. For some people, volunteer abroad programs can offer an opportunity to explore a career field of interest. For other participants, the motivations may be contributing to society and seeing another part of the world. There are countless programs offered around the world. Programs typically provide grassroots, direct service to local people. The service given may require some professional skills or may involve unskilled labor (Nolting et al. 2013). Because these volunteer programs allow for extensive interaction with local people, there is the potential for deep cultural immersion.

The programs are often, but not exclusively, offered in developing countries (Nolting et al. 2013). Living in a low-income country can be a challenge for some participants from the United States and other wealthy countries. If it is a participant's first major exposure to poverty, the individual may need a lot of support to process his or her feelings and experiences. Participants may also find themselves struggling mentally and emotionally if they are in refugee camps, communities recovering from conflict, or places recovering from natural disasters. The scope of the challenges and the participants' general inability to make major changes can be disheartening for some. Participants who are successful in these programs usually have both an altruistic goal and a personal goal, such as wanting to learn about another culture (Nolting et al. 2013).

International Service-Learning

Service-learning programs combine study with community service. It is "a form of experiential education in which students engage in activities that address human and community needs, together with structured opportunities for reflection designed to achieve desired learning outcomes" (Jacoby 2015, pp. 1–2). Like experiential education, service-learning is both a program type and a methodology. It is an educational method used all around the world and at all age levels (Chambers and Lavery 2018).

While some people consider only for-credit programs to be service-learning, other people consider noncredit-bearing programs to be service-learning if they incorporate an intentional learning structure, reflection, and reciprocity with community partners (Jacoby 2015). Among the diverse variety of programs, some emphasize the service activities and add complementary curricular content, some programs focus on the students' educational experience with a modest service component, and other programs aim for approximately equal emphasis on both the service activity and the curricular learning (Jacoby 2018). Within higher education, most international service-learning falls within one of three types: (a) direct service incorporating personal contact with people in need; (b) indirect service working on societal issues rather than with individuals, such as doing research in the community on an area of concern; or (c) advocacy to mitigate the cause of a problem (Chambers and Lavery 2018).

Like volunteer abroad programs, international service-learning opportunities are characterized by extensive community engagement. These programs are available in almost every part of the world, with participants performing wide-ranging types of services, from skilled to unskilled (Nolting et al. 2013). However, service-learning is distinguished from volunteerism by the presence of an intentionally designed and facilitated curriculum. Jacoby (2015, 71) emphasizes that service-learning is different from volunteering because "opportunities for learning and reflection are fully integrated into the structure of the [service-learning] program or course. Service-learning is explicitly designed to promote learning about the historical, economic, political, and cultural contexts that underlie the needs or issues the students address." While the distinction between volunteer abroad and international service-learning are clear in theory, in practice, the distinction is more muddled. Programs that characterize themselves as volunteer abroad may incorporate intentional use of the Experiential Learning Cycle, including reflection, while programs that characterize themselves as international service-learning may have varying amounts of structured learning.

Learning outcomes for international service-learning may be intellectual, social, civic, ethical, moral, spiritual, intercultural, career, or personal (Jacoby 2018). The learning may focus on "deepening understanding of academic content, applying theory to practice, increasing awareness of the complexity of social issues, understanding human difference and commonality, exploring options for future individual and collective action to solve community problems, and developing a wide range of practical skills" (Jacoby 2018, 71). Grusky (2000) suggests that many international service-learning programs raise profound questions in students about why poverty exists and how injustice may contribute to inequity. These are questions that can be explored through the course content and structured reflection and analysis.

Reciprocity is a key principle in the success of service-learning programs. "Reciprocity means that we, as service-learning educators, relate to the community in the spirit of partnership, viewing the institution and the community in terms of both assets and needs" (Jacoby 2018, 71). Each participant should serve and be served; each should contribute and receive contribution (Jacoby 2018). Educators are often primarily focused on the experience of their students, and there is a risk that programs will be designed more to suit student interests than to meet community needs. A strong focus on reciprocity counters this tendency, ensuring that service project development is led by community groups to meet needs that they identify (Jacoby 2018).

Global Health

Global health programs are a subset of international service-learning programs. They may also be considered as intern abroad programs if the student is earning a degree in a medical or health-related field. Graduate students studying in health-related fields are typically required to gain hands-on experience, and many students may have the option to complete these experiences internationally through global health programs. Such work can include clinical work, research, community engagement, and health policy studies. Through these programs, participants may be able to earn some of their required hours of observation. Other programs may be geared more toward undergraduates who are exploring their career options.

Whatever the population of students who participate, particular care needs to be taken with training before and during the program. Students must understand the health risks posed by infectious diseases. Additionally, ethical issues must be emphasized in the training. This includes the principles of not performing medical care that goes beyond the participant's level of qualification, recognizing and respecting cultural differences in the approaches to health care, and ensuring that participants do no harm (McFarland 2017; Pinto and Upshur 2009).

Partnerships

Experiential education is not possible without partnerships. This section explores the partnerships between education abroad organizations—whether they are universities or program providers—and the community-based organizations that host students for international experiential education programs. In all of the types of experiential education programs described in this chapter, students contribute their labor and receive learning opportunities. This is true for work abroad, intern abroad, teach abroad, research abroad, volunteer abroad, international service-learning, and global health programs. For this discussion of partnerships, the programs are loosely sorted into two broad categories: work-based and service-based. While acknowledging the overlap between categories, "work-based" refers to those programs that emphasize developing the students' professional skills, while "service-based" refers to those programs that emphasize social issues and community service.

Experiential education programs involve many stakeholders, each with varied, and sometimes conflicting, goals (Grusky 2000). Students may participate because of a desire for travel or adventure, altruism, curiosity, interest in broadening their perspectives on the world, desire to develop language skills, or as career preparation. Faculty may be involved to further their own research, to travel, or because of a commitment to experiential pedagogy. Universities and education abroad program providers may be interested in developing the global competence of participants and fulfilling their organizational mission, while at the same time seeking to advance their financial and reputational interests. Companies and other professional organizations may participate in order to develop a talent recruitment pool or to give back to the community. Charities may host students for heightened visibility, the opportunity to develop new contacts, in expectation of donations, or in a desire to receive the service provided by the students. Staff and clients of both host professional organizations and host service organizations may, as individuals, feel an affinity for and welcome the participating students, or they may wish the students were not there. With so many individual and organizational goals simultaneously in existence, ensuring that all stakeholders contribute and benefit equitably is the primary challenge in managing partnerships.

Because the building of relationships and trust over time is so essential to successful partnerships, it is best if there is continuity of leadership. A faculty or staff member leading the program year after year in partnership with a capable on-site coordinator can work effectively together, adjusting to each other's work styles over time. The usual division of tasks is that the on-site coordinator handles the logistics for the service project, while the campus-based person handles the implementation of the curriculum (McFarland 2017).

With partnerships for international experiential education, there is the added complexity of intercultural relations and varying cultural norms related to time, decisionmaking, communication, priorities, and more. In order to maintain warm relations between the education abroad organization and the community-based organization, it is essential to have bilingual and bicultural staff members on the program to bridge the differences and be able to explain to each group what the expectations of the other stakeholders might be (Morales and Barron 2014). These staff members can work to ensure that respect, commitment, communication, and sustainability are the explicitly enacted values within the program and the partnership (Jacoby 2018).

Work-Based Partnerships

Work-based programs, such as intern or work abroad, need many partner organizations to host students because, typically, only one or a few students can be hosted by a single organization at a time. For this reason, a university or provider will probably need to develop relationships with a relatively large number of host organizations (e.g., corporations, small companies, nonprofit organizations, etc.) in one or more countries. Universities may decide that establishing their own partnerships is too labor-intensive and instead choose to partner with a provider that already has a network of partners around the world.

Development of Work-Based Partnerships

It typically takes 2 to 12 months to establish a relationship with a potential partner and get an internship or job defined and made available to students. For that reason, in the first year or two of a new intern abroad or work abroad program, there may not be that many options for students. By the third year, however, based on the investment of time in the first 2 years, the options begin to be more robust. Education abroad organizations considering developing these programs should be prepared for the investment of resources and be willing to make a long-term commitment to their partnerships (Nolting et al. 2013).

There are a range of sources for finding host organizations for work-based partnerships (NAFSA WIVA Subcommittee 2012; Nolting et al. 2013), including:

- Existing relationships (check with career center and others to see what already exists);
- Partner universities;
- Faculty connections;
- Education abroad program providers;
- Chambers of commerce;
- Government departments of economic development;
- Students find their own (especially at the graduate level); and
- Alumni networks.

Once potential partners are identified, representatives from both organizations should discuss the interests and constraints of the host organization. At the same time, the students' learning goals, the connection between the internship and the home university curriculum, and the support and mentoring that is desired by students should be discussed. Logistics related to language of work, housing, transportation, cost of living, visas, and other pragmatic matters should also be explored. If, after extensive discussion, both parties think that the partnership would be beneficial, an agreement may be signed.

Management of Expectations

In all experiential education programs, one of the key roles of the program facilitator is managing conflict. In the case of work-based partnerships, the most common conflict is between a student (or group of students) and an employer. Often, these conflicts are rooted in the parties holding different expectations of the experience. Accordingly, a priority in partnership management is for facilitators to proactively establish and manage expectations.

NAFSA offers some advice for facilitators on managing student expectations for an intern abroad program (NAFSA WIVA Subcommittee 2012):

- Meet with all students before they submit an application. Assess their expectations through an in-person conversation.

- Provide a health, safety, and cross-cultural orientation, discussing expectations to have as intern. Bring former interns to the session to share their experiences.

- Connect outgoing interns with previous interns who were at the same company. If that is not possible, at least try to connect the outgoing interns with someone who went to the same region or country.

- Recommend that students have previous co-op or internship experience in the United States before doing international internships.

- Recommend that students have previous language or in-country experience.

- Have students write a cover letter that discusses their interest in working for the company.

- Have students complete a phone or Skype interview with the employer.

- Emphasize to students that the success of their experience is highly dependent on their attitude and that they should be flexible.

At the same time that student expectations are being managed, it is also essential to proactively manage the expectations of the employers. Giving the employer detailed information on the student's coursework and degree plan will help the organization to understand the level of the student's expertise and potential areas of contribution (Nolting et al. 2013). NAFSA offers advice to facilitators on managing employer expectations (NAFSA WIVA Subcommittee 2012):

- Ask the employer about past experiences working with interns when establishing the internship.

- Provide the employer with student and employer testimonials from past internships at other organizations.

- Provide the employer with examples of projects that students have completed in the past to demonstrate the capabilities of the typical student.

- Work with the employer to develop a clear job description that lets prospective students know what the internship will focus on.

- Suggest that the employer conduct phone or Skype interviews with a few prospective students.

- If possible, have a representative of the host organization interview students on campus.

- Have the employer and selected student(s) work together to complete a goal-setting document at the beginning of the internship.

- Ask the employer to complete an evaluation at the completion of the internship so that advisers can offer prospective students more details in the future.

Partnership management for work-based experiential education programs involves facilitators' dedication to cultivating the initial partnerships, managing relationships between individual students and employers, and constantly monitoring the partnerships and making the necessary adjustments.

Service-Based Partnerships

Service-based partnerships include international service-learning, global health, and volunteer abroad programs. Mlyn and McBride (2013, pp. 44–45) argue that "the most important distinction between traditional study abroad and international service is the presence of the community as a partner in the service and learning endeavor. Working with community partners in a responsible, ethical, and reciprocal way, usually presents as many challenges as it does rewards. . . . the introduction of the community partner into the already complicated international educational endeavor introduces a variable with great changeability." This section of the chapter explores good practices in working with community partners in order to maximize positive outcomes for all stakeholders.

Partnering directly with a local community organization to establish service-based programs offers several advantages, not the least of which is that the local organization has expertise on local issues and long-standing community relationships (Mlyn and McBride 2013). This allows the university or provider to ensure that the work that the students are contributing is relevant to the local needs and that the services delivered are culturally appropriate. Partnering with a local organization also allows the university or provider access to a network of local contacts that may be able to provide support with other parts of the program such as housing, language education, excursions, etc., or may allow for the program to be expanded to multiple partner organizations in the same community if the program grows.

Challenges of Service-Based Partnerships

Despite the benefits that service-based partnerships can bring to the local community, there are a number of challenges as well. Due to the nature of experiential education programs, which are often shorter in length than some of the yearlong study abroad programs, cases happen where the students arrive to do a program, do their service project for a few weeks, and then they leave. This may be more of a hinderance than a value for local community organizations if it disrupts their long-term efforts. For this reason, community organizations need to be a part of the program design process from the very beginning to ensure that the time-limited work done by students complements the ongoing work of the organization and helps it to achieve its objectives (Mlyn and McBride 2013).

Another big challenge of service-based partnerships is navigating power inequities (Carrington and Kimber 2018). Experiential programs such as international service-learning are a product of Western culture and are based on Western values. The university or provider, in some ways, plays the role of the donor to a charity, holding the funding and, with it, the ability to decide how and for how long the community organization will benefit financially from the relationship (Enos 2015; Halverson-Wente and Halverson-Wente 2014). This inherently unequal power relationship exists even when the university or provider is trying to be supportive and sensitive to the position of the community organization (Halverson-Wente and Halverson-Wente 2014; Johnson 2014).

Effective Service-Based Partnerships

While these power dynamic issues may not ever be fully resolved, positive outcomes can still result from the partnership that benefit the students and the community organization in different ways. The program planners and the community organization representatives should work together to design the international experiential education so that the partnership is deep and sustainable (Mlyn and McBride 2013). There are several key recommendations for building effective service-based partnerships (Halimi et al. 2014, pp. 64–65):

- Intentionally select and closely collaborate with community partners.

- Pay close attention to, and try to align with, the local political, economic, cultural, social, and organizational context.

- Use a collaborative process to build consensus at all stages, focusing on coproduction and codelivery of the program.

- Establish a facilitating entity with enough administrative, faculty, and financial support.

- Begin with a small collaboration and seek early wins in order to build trust and momentum.

- Create a pathway for senior administrators and influential faculty to participate.

- Involve local political leaders early on in the process, create opportunities for them to have a say in the design and to offer public support.

- Collaboratively assess program progress.

- Work to ensure ongoing, valuable benefits for both partners.

- Share lessons learned in an atmosphere of scholarship by producing joint publications, presenting at conferences, etc.

- Publicize the program. Disseminate results, tell stories, and attract the media. Do so early, often, and broadly.

- Expect problems and learn from challenges and successes. In working through the issues, honor multiple perspectives.

- Share power and build trust. Listen carefully to all key stakeholders.

Jacoby (2018) recommends researching potential partners, determining if there is compatibility, and carefully considering the commitment. Once a partnership is formed, she emphasizes staying in touch, asking questions, determining how the effectiveness of the partnership will be assessed, and celebrating the successes. In order for partnerships to be effective and sustainable, they need to be strategic, long-term, multifaceted, developmental for all stakeholders, contextualized with consistent attention to historical and cultural understanding, reciprocal, and focused on building capacity for community change (Johnson 2014).

Management Roles and Responsibilities

International experiential education programs may be managed by universities or education abroad program providers (Mlyn and McBride 2013). The management of international experiential programs has many similarities with the management of study abroad programs (see chapter 4). Many of the key job functions described in chapter 4 are also found among the roles and responsibilities of international educators in the management of experiential education programs, including advocacy, partner and stakeholder relationships, development and implementation of programs, marketing and recruitment, admissions, student advising, orientation, housing, group dynamics, reentry, data collection, funding and financing, and risk prevention and crisis management. This section focuses on a few areas in which experiential education programs have their own considerations, beyond those discussed in the previous chapter.

Advocacy

Convincing stakeholders, such as senior administrators, faculty, and parents, of the educational value of international experiential education programs may be even more difficult than it is for study abroad. Some individuals may see experience and reflection as less academically rigorous than traditional classroom-based coursework and may view the programs as little more than vacations (Mlyn and McBride 2013). International educators need to invest time and energy in communicating the benefits and effectiveness of experiential programs to stakeholders in order to overcome this resistance. Failure to do so may result in not having enough students, staff, or funding to sustain the programs (Nolting et al. 2013).

Awarding of Credit

Awarding credit for experiential education programs can be contentious, depending on the institutional history and culture. McFarland (2017) offers some practical considerations in exploring the possibility of awarding credit for an experiential education program:

- What are the criteria for course approval at the institution?

- Do noncredit-bearing experiences have to go through an approval process?

- In addition to practical experience, does the program offer any formal academic component that engages students in theoretical or literary work that would look familiar to stakeholders?

- If credit is not offered, does an employee have to go with the students abroad? Can students travel alone?

- Will a faculty member be overseeing the student's work?

- Can staff members from the career center teach an online course for international internships, or are only faculty members allowed to oversee and grade courses?

- Will program cost (tuition fees) deter students from participating in valuable experiential education abroad if they cannot access financial aid?

- Are there budget implications with lost tuition revenue if there is no credit?

- How are noncredit-bearing experiences tracked by the international office (e.g., applications, program fees, payments to vendors, orientation, etc.)?

- How will student performance in this program be evaluated?

If the program is designed to be credit bearing, there will likely need to be a syllabus, stated learning outcomes, assignments, grading policies, assessment of learning, etc., to comply with campus requirements (McFarland 2017).

Funding

As with study abroad, there are a number of potential funding models for international experiential education. The initial costs of developing a program will typically be borne by the university or the provider. The costs of student participation may be covered by financial aid (for credit-bearing programs), or the student may pay from personal or family funds. In the case of work-based programs, the employer may pay the student a salary or pay for some of the student's expenses. In the case of service-based programs, additional funding can come in the form of government and foundation support, donations, and fundraising outcomes (Nolting et al. 2013).

On-Campus Partnerships

In order to implement international experiential education programs in a university context, the education abroad office staff will need to work with many other campus departments. These may include the career center, internship office, academic departments, risk management office, the health and safety committee, institutional research office, and alumni office (Nolting et al. 2013). Legal counsel will need to be involved from the initial stages of program planning to handle international contracts, waivers, the tax status of employees, and educating students about risk (Mlyn and McBride 2013).

The campus may have a tradition of domestic service-based programs, which may be organized by a center for civic engagement or a service-learning office (Nolting et al. 2013). Offering international service-based experiential education programs may work most effectively as a collaboration between these units and the education abroad office. Work-based experiential education programs will likely necessitate added collaboration with the campus career center (McFarland 2017). Students will need support from career center staff with résumé critiques and interview preparation. Staff in both the career center and the education abroad office will need to be able to advise students about cultural differences in the job search process and workplace norms (Nolting et al. 2013).

Program Assessment

Institutions offering international experiential education programs will want to record quantitative data for reporting, including participant numbers and demographics, types of programs, program countries, and compensation data (Nolting et al. 2013). Above and beyond collecting basic participation data, international educators must make developing a rigorous plan for the assessment of learning a priority; this is necessary not only to guide program improvement, but also to demonstrate the impact of the programs as part of advocacy efforts (Mlyn and McBride 2013).

While assessment of learning is very important in study abroad, the nature of international experiential education programs and the emphasis on partnerships makes the assessment process more complex. In experiential education, it is essential to measure not only the effects of the program on students' growth, but also the effects of the program on local communities and host organizations. In order to know if a partnership is effective, data should be collected on the impacts for all partners (Grusky 2000; Mlyn and McBride 2013).

University Responsibility to Evaluate Program Quality

Universities are expected to do some vetting to ensure that any outside programs they refer students to are reputable. The degree of vetting typically correlates to the degree to which the university is involved in the partnership with the education abroad program provider. If the education abroad advisers are only posting some flyers, it may be enough to ensure that the provider is a legitimate entity and does not have a negative reputation within the international education field. At the opposite end of the spectrum, if the university is partnering with a provider and offering credit for program participation, the university has a higher level of responsibility. At this level of engagement, the university is expected to do site visits, compare the merits of the program to competitor programs, talk with program alumni, ensure that crisis response plans are in place, and more. Some questions that education abroad advisers (and prospective students) should be asking of providers include (Nolting et al. 2013, 33):

- What kinds of experiences are available?
- Where are the placements located?
- What is the program fee? What is included?
- How many students typically use the provider's services each year?
- What have been the experiences of past participants from this institution?
- Does the provider have protocols in place for good practices for health and safety?
- What is the reputation of the provider in the education abroad field?
- Where is the provider's headquarters?
- How does the provider monitor overseas partners?
- Does the provider have on-site staff?

Facilitation of Experiential Education

The learning that happens in international experiential education programs is not solely a product of the experience abroad. Instead, the learning is the result of the students' processing of the experience, guided by a skilled facilitator using structured reflection activities. The facilitator could be a faculty member or a staff member, an individual, a pair, or a team. The facilitator could be a citizen of the host country or from elsewhere. Whatever the facilitator's background, Roberts (2015) identifies four important principles of facilitating experiential education programs:

- Teach people, not content. The facilitator should consider learners holistically, not just as brains, but as physical, emotional, and spiritual beings. The facilitator needs to focus more on the learners and learning, and less on getting through a prescribed amount of course content.

- Less is more. Experiential education requires that students have dedicated time to investigate, consider, and apply what they are learning, so facilitators should not overpack the course with content.

- Learn together. Rather than thinking of the teacher as the expert with the right answers, there must be a commitment among students and the facilitator to learn together.

- Experience before labeling. The traditional lecture style of teaching provides vocabulary and schema for understanding abstract and complex concepts. In experiential education, the complex, messy, and unscripted experiences must have primacy. Students must be able to engage in questioning, experimenting, constructing meaning, being creative, and solving problems. The facilitator must be careful not to construct the course in such a way that it takes this sense-making role away from students by providing labels and schema too early in the process.

Abiding by Roberts's principles for experiential education is not an easy task for facilitators. But doing so is important to creating an optimal environment for student sharing and learning.

Facilitation Skills

Roberts (2015) identifies four skills that facilitators of experiential education programs must have: tone-setting, processing, differentiation, and group dynamics. Roberts (2015) describes techniques for each of the skills:

TONE-SETTING: ESTABLISHING THE ATMOSPHERE

- Facilitate a consensus-oriented discussion on ground rules and individual and community expectations.

- Do not promise that people will be comfortable.

- Promise to monitor conversations to ensure that everyone is empathetic, caring, respectful, and appropriate.

- Allow enough time for the formulation of personal and group goals.

- Give explicit attention to group norms that celebrate both similarities and differences.

- Accept healthy conflict as well as strategies, structures, and methods for conflict resolution.

- Do not equate a "safe atmosphere" with not challenging students.

- Create structured feedback mechanisms on what is working and what can be improved (instructor to student and student to student).

PROCESSING: ENCOURAGING ACTIVE REFLECTION

- Commit to making enough time for reflection.

- Establish clear objectives for all reflection activities.

- Encourage students to plan, reflect, describe, analyze, and communicate about experiences before, during, and after the program.

- Use "I wonder" questions to set an invitational tone.

- Build up to the big questions using follow-up questions such as: So what? Now what?

- Use a range of questions to seek clarification, probe assumptions, ask for reasons and evidence, explore viewpoints, consider implications.

DIFFERENTIATION: DESIGNING AND MONITORING ACTIVITIES FOR THE OPTIMAL BALANCE OF COMFORT AND CHALLENGE

- Balance ritual and novelty, aiming for approximately 60 percent ritual (traditions, patterns, and other constants) and 40 percent novelty (intrigue, playfulness, surprise, and other creative forms of expression).

- Read the mood of the group to see if they are energized, stressed, tired, etc., and then adjust accordingly.

- Ask for periodic student feedback on what the group should continue to do, what the group should start doing, and what the group should stop doing.

- Check in with individual students to monitor their engagement and perceived level of challenge.

- Allow options in the program and facilitation design to increase the challenge level for some students and lower it for others.

GROUP DYNAMICS: SHAPING THE PATTERNS OF INTERACTION

- Explain to students Tuckman's (1965) stages of group development:
  - Form: group is established;
  - Storm: disagreements arise;
  - Norm: disagreements get resolved;
  - Perform: work gets completed; and
  - Adjourn: group is disbanded.

- Help students to identify the stage of group development that the group is in.

- Help students to be more comfortable with being uncomfortable.

- Anticipate conflict with the goal of identifying and moving through it, not avoiding it.

- Address conflicts rooted in group dynamics by focusing on goals and roles, tone-setting, and situational support.

Roberts (2015) emphasizes that facilitators need to continually work on practicing and refining their skills in these four areas so that they can support students in processing experiences and learning. This section discusses essential elements that contribute to the design of structured reflection that can facilitate students' movement through the Experiential Learning Cycle.

Discomfort and Emotion

Grusky (2000) argues that students' international experiences are not meant to be life-enriching, but rather complacency-shattering or soul-searching. Emotional responses to an experience or topic are often a signal to both the student and the facilitator that there is a topic to be explored and discussed. Johnson (2014, 2) concurs, recommending that students and facilitators "explore the terrain illuminated by discomfort." Recognizing and considering emotional reactions can serve to reveal deeper meanings that might be missed in a purely intellectual consideration of an experience (Johnson 2014).

In describing her experience leading international service-learning programs in Latin America, Grusky (2000) identifies seven topics that often elicit emotional reactions in students and provide learning and reflection opportunities:

- Students interacting with beggars and street peddlers can lead to discussions about poverty and government policies that might perpetuate poverty.

- Female students receiving catcalls and lewd comments can lead to discussions about double standards of female liberation and sexual availability.

- Students receiving romantic interest from local people can lead to discussions about exoticizing others and economic and cultural tropes about being taken to a land of opportunity.

- Students responding happily to how cheap everything is (for them) in the host country can lead to discussions about why currency values differ and how the students might be inadvertently offending local peers and their host families with their carefree spending.

- Students making donations, or being asked to make donations, can lead to discussions about the politics of charitable giving, the perception of U.S. people as resources, the politics of foreign aid, and the power of economic privilege.

- Students reacting to social issues can lead to discussions about their assumptions of U.S. superiority, the complexity of social issues, and why local communities are best suited to address local problems.

- Students encountering others who know more about U.S. foreign policy than they do as U.S. residents can lead to discussions about the role of the U.S. government in the host country.

These and other learning opportunities, often triggered by students' emotional reactions, can spark conversations that facilitate students' exploration of complex issues and contradictions in the United States and around the world.

Educational theories and research by Sanford, Vygotsky, Dewey, and others clearly document that students need to face some discomfort in order to learn. At the same time, they need support to grow. If students face too much discomfort, they will resist or reject the learning. Yet, if they are too comfortable, they will not be motivated to learn. The role of the facilitator is to manage the balance between challenge and support, keeping students in an optimal emotional space for learning (Jacoby 2018; Roberts 2015). Roberts (2015) illustrates this concept with an activity: Students stand in a circle and are asked to throw foam balls straight up into the air. Students are told that they can step back or stay still as the balls land on or near them. Most students remain still. The exercise is repeated with tennis balls, and a few students move out of the way before the balls come back down to hit them. The exercise is repeated with water balloons, and many students move out of the way. A final round is conducted with more water balloons that Roberts (falsely) informs students are filled with really cheap perfume. All but one or two students avoid the falling balloons. Roberts uses this exercise to show that among a group of students, there are varying levels of risk tolerance. Roberts (2015) argues that it is up to the facilitator to judge how much to challenge students in order to keep them in the space between comfort and discomfort for optimal learning. Roberts (2015) reports that in discussing the activity with students and asking why they made the choices that they did, the students cite the power of the peer group to influence individual behavior. This peer effect is something that facilitators should keep in mind when managing group dynamics. The facilitator must be constantly monitoring and adjusting activities to ensure, for the group and individuals, that the level of challenge is appropriate so that the group behaviors and attitudes support learning for all.

Importance of Reflection

In the Experiential Learning Cycle, reflection and observation follow an experience (see figure 1). The reflection stage should focus on description. It may include recognizing emotions, describing key interactions, or beginning to identify patterns in observations. Students may be asked to acknowledge the expectations and beliefs that they had, and what happened that was or was not as they expected (Jacoby 2015). After robust reflection and observation, the Experiential Learning Cycle moves into abstract conceptualization (see figure 1). At this stage, students begin the process of sense-making by connecting their observations with theories or models. These theories may come from their past knowledge or from content provided by the facilitator of the experiential education program. Whether the experiential education program is for credit or not for credit, intentional thought must be given to providing theoretical content to support the abstract conceptualization stage of the Experiential Learning Cycle. This content may come from a wide variety of sources including academic readings, popular media articles or videos, lectures, guest speakers, etc. In the active experimentation stage of the cycle, students use their new understandings to construct hypotheses of how they should engage in future interactions. With the next concrete experience, they will be able to test their new understandings and the cycle will continue.

While the Experiential Learning Cycle theory names the stage immediately after the concrete experience as "reflective observation," in professional practice, "reflection" is the word most commonly used to describe the structures that the facilitator puts in place to lead students through the three stages that follow the experiential activity. In this section, the term "reflection" is used in this broader sense, referring to the process of intentionally guiding students through all of the stages of the Experiential Learning Cycle.

Activities for Structuring Reflection

Using reflection to help students to progress through the Experiential Learning Cycle stages is the role of the facilitator, who, as discussed, might be a faculty member, a staff member, or a team of people. It is essential that the facilitator intentionally develop a reflection process that is continuous, challenging, and appropriate in the cultural context (Roberts 2015).

The situations that students encounter while abroad are often unfamiliar, complex, and intense, making it challenging for students to process their international experiential education interactions on their own. Failure to provide a structure for reflection may push students too far into discomfort and hopelessness, causing them to retreat into stereotypes and simplistic conclusions to restore their comfort. The antidote to this risk is to provide ongoing structured reflection opportunities, challenging students while keeping their discomfort within manageable levels (Jacoby 2018).

Jacoby (2018) describes many ways to structure reflection, individually or in groups. While small group and large group discussions are common forms of spoken reflection, other options include presentations, interviews, storytelling, debates, poetry readings, artwork, or performances and plays. Written reflections allow students to organize their thoughts in order to make arguments. Journaling and responding to reflection questions are perhaps the most common forms of written reflection, but other options include writing essays, press releases, letters to oneself, letters to the editor, and letters to officials, as well as responding in written form to problem analysis prompts, case studies, and drafted legislation. Activity-based approaches to reflection can include team-building activities, role-plays, and simulations. Media-based reflection can include artistic creations, photo and video essays, and musical compositions. Roberts (2015) adds the options of one-on-one meetings with the facilitator, digital platforms, fishbowl exercises, world café activities, and cooperative jigsaw activities. These diverse forms of expression can appeal to students' varied talents and may be used to create a permanent record of student learning and growth (Jacoby 2018).

Critical Reflection

Some international educators may be tempted to ignore the more uncomfortable discussions of power and structural inequities in society, instead assuming that merely learning about other cultures and getting to know people from other cultures will result in just and equitable relationships (Andreotti, Biesta, and Ahenakew 2015; Goren and Yemini 2017; Mannion et al. 2011). However, critical reflection focused on power relationships and patterns of inequity plays an important role in experiential education.

Students are asked to explore the history and structures of economic and political inequality, often eliciting discussions of cultural arrogance, racism, stereotypes, and privilege (Grusky 2000). Through critical reflection, students challenge simplistic conclusions, compare perspectives, investigate causality, and raise more provoking questions for continued reflection. The result is often new self-awareness of the student's own ways of perceiving, knowing, and acting (Jacoby 2018). Students need to go beyond learning about the dominant culture of the host country; they must also be able to recognize subordinate cultures and identify how members of subordinate cultural groups conform to, navigate, or resist the dominant cultural norms (Punteney 2016).

The power dynamics within the volunteer and service-learning experiential education programs will typically be a needed area of focus for critical reflection. In fact, the very idea of traveling to another country to interact with those who are less well-off in order to have a life-enriching experience for oneself carries with it all kinds of troubling implications. If critical reflection is not undertaken, the program can become little more than tourism, and the privilege of being able to travel becomes tacit acceptance of economic disparity (Grusky 2000). While reciprocity is the goal of these experiential education partnerships, it is not always achieved (Grusky 2000). In fact, the host organization is often offering more of a service to the students than it is receiving a benefit. Recognizing this dynamic can prompt students to overcome cultural arrogance, paternalism, and naïve ideas of charity (Grusky 2000; Mlyn and McBride 2013).

There is a mostly unquestioned belief that service is good, which needs to be explored through critical reflection (Enos 2015). Students may, consciously or unconsciously, hold the belief that they have the knowledge and skills to bring transformative change to people and communities that they perceive as needy (Aktas et al. 2017). Students with this belief may see a deficit or need in the local community and attempt to fix the need with money, training, etc. Defining those participating in service as "helpers" and those being served as "needing help" is problematic because it undermines collaboration and reciprocity (Halverson-Wente and Halverson-Wente 2014; Mellom and Herrera 2014).

An antidote is to explicitly utilize an Asset-Based Community Development approach that emphasizes the resources, talents, and understandings in a community and expects decisions about actions to come from the community itself (Jacoby 2018; Morales and Barron 2014). Students can then work alongside local people to carry out some of the work that the community has identified. As this crucial understanding of community development has become more widespread, more and more organizers of service-based international experiential programs see themselves in solidarity with host communities, participating in programs more as learners than as helpers (Nolting et al. 2013). Within the experiential education program, there should be an emphasis on the development of cultural humility and learning from others, rather than doing things for others (Harris 2014; Murray-Garcia and Tervalon 2017).

Follow-Up and Outcomes

Reflection should happen not only during the program, but also after students return home, so that students can continue to process and learn from their experiences (Mlyn and McBride 2013). Returning home can be a difficult transition for some students. Through their engagement with the experiential education program, students may have changed personally, intellectually, morally, spiritually, culturally, and/or politically (Carrington and Kimber 2018). As students attempt to reconcile international and local issues, experiential learning with traditional classroom learning, and their "old" selves with their "transformed" selves, ongoing structured reflection will encourage students to continue to grow personally and professionally (Mlyn and McBride 2013).

Research shows that experiential education programs can result in personal development such as greater self-esteem, emotional maturity, values clarification, and confidence (Jacoby 2018). Programs can also improve individuals' interpersonal skills, intercultural awareness, communication, and leadership skills (Chambers and Lavery 2018). Experiential education programs can prepare individuals to live in a multicultural society by promoting tolerance, empathy, and intercultural understanding. Students can learn to appreciate multiple perspectives, reflect on their own perspectives, and understand the reciprocal nature of relationships (Chambers and Lavery 2018; Jacoby 2018).

Another outcome may be a greater understanding of the impact of individuals on local and global communities and a commitment to social responsibility and active citizenship (Chambers and Lavery 2018; Jacoby 2018). Experiential education also benefits students' career and professional development and degree attainment (Chambers and Lavery 2018; Jacoby 2018). Through skillfully facilitated reflection, international experiential education programs can help learners to increase their knowledge, develop skills, clarify values, and increase their capacity to contribute to their communities (Roberts 2015).

Conclusion

The design and facilitation of experiential education centers on moving students through the four stages of the Experiential Learning Cycle: concrete experience, reflective observation, abstract conceptualization, and active experimentation. With this theory serving as the backbone of many intern abroad, work abroad, teach abroad, research abroad, volunteer abroad, international service-learning, and global health programs, participating students gain such benefits as cognitive development, skill development, positive self-image, increased grade point average, and increased graduation rate.

In order to reach such outcomes and develop cultural humility, students must engage in critical reflection that focuses on an awareness of power dynamics and their own place in a global system that perpetuates inequity. Facilitators can guide students through their process of learning to help them to grow as individuals and future professionals. To that same end, facilitators must commit the time and energy into developing and managing partnerships with host organizations that are reciprocal relationships and work to bridge intercultural differences.

Resources

READINGS:

- Green, Patrick M., and Matthew Johnson. 2014. *Crossing Boundaries: Tension and Transformation in International Service-Learning.* Sterling, VA: Stylus Publishing.

- Jacoby, Barbara. 2015. *Service-Learning Essentials: Questions, Answers, and Lessons Learned.* San Francisco, CA: Jossey-Bass.

- Kolb, Alice Y., and David A. Kolb. 2017. *The Experiential Educator.* Kaunakakai, HI: Experience Based Learning Systems, Inc.

- McFarland, Miko. 2017. "Alternative Program Types." In *The Guide to Successful Short-Term Programs Abroad, Third Edition*, eds. Lisa Chieffo and Catherine Spaeth. Washington, DC: NAFSA: Association of International Educators.

- Nolting, William, Debbie Donohue, Cheryl Matherly, and Martin Tillman, eds. 2013. *Internships, Service Learning, and Volunteering Abroad: Successful Models and Best Practices.* Washington, DC: NAFSA: Association of International Educators.

- Roberts, Jay W. 2015. *Experiential Education in the College Context: What It Is, How It Works, and Why It Matters.* New York, NY: Routledge.

ORGANIZATIONS AND RESOURCES:

- Association for Experiential Education www.aee.org/
- Break Away alternativebreaks.org
- Building Bridges Coalition buildingbridgescoalition.org/
- Campus Compact compact.org/
- NAFSA WIVA Resources www.nafsa.org/findresources/default.aspx?catId=429109
- WIVRA-L listserv groups.google.com/a/discussions.umich.edu/forum/#!forum/wivra-l

References

Aktas, Fatih, Kate Pitts, Jessica C. Richards, and Iveta Silova. 2017. "Institutionalizing Global Citizenship: A Critical Analysis of Higher Education Programs and Curricula." *Journal of Studies in International Education* 21, 1:65–80. https://doi.org/10.1177/1028315316669815.

Altbach, Philip G., and Hans de Wit. 2018. "Are We Facing a Fundamental Challenge to Higher Education Internationalization?" *International Higher Education* 93:2–4.

American Council on Education, Art & Science, and College Board. 2008. *College-Bound Students' Interest in Study Abroad and Other International Learning Activities*. Washington, DC: American Council on Education.

Andreotti, Vanessa, Gert Biesta, and Cash Ahenakew. 2015. "Between the Nation and the Globe: Education for Global Mindedness in Finland." *Globalisation, Societies and Education* 13, 2:246–259. https://doi.org/10.1080/14767724.2014.934073.

Association for Experiential Education. n.d. "What Is Experiential Education?" Denver, CO: Association for Experiential Education. http://www.aee.org/what-is-ee.

Carrington, Suzanne, and Megan Kimber. 2018. "International Service-Learning: Preparing Teachers for Inclusion." In *Service-Learning: Enhancing Inclusive Education*, eds. Shane Lavery, Dianne Chambers, and Glenda Cain. Bingley, United Kingdom: Emerald.

Chambers, Dianne, and Shane Lavery. 2018. "Introduction to Service-Learning and Inclusive Education." In *Service-Learning: Enhancing Inclusive Education*, eds. Shane Lavery, Dianne Chambers, and Glenda Cain. Bingley, United Kingdom: Emerald.

DeWinter, Urbain J., and Laura E. Rumbley. 2010. "The Diversification of Education Abroad across the Curriculum." In *A History of U.S. Study Abroad: 1965–Present*, eds. William W. Hoffa and Stephen C. DePaul. Carlisle, PA: Frontiers: The Interdisciplinary Journal of Study Abroad and The Forum on Education Abroad.

Enos, Sandra L. 2015. *Service-Learning and Social Entrepreneurship in Higher Education: A Pedagogy of Social Change*. New York, NY: Palgrave Macmillan.

The Forum on Education Abroad. 2017. "Glossary." Carlisle, PA: The Forum on Education Abroad. https://forumea.org/resources/glossary/.

Goren, Heela, and Miri Yemini. 2017. "Global Citizenship Education Redefined – A Systematic Review of Empirical Studies on Global Citizenship Education." *International Journal of Educational Research* 82 (Supplement C):170–183. https://doi.org/10.1016/j.ijer.2017.02.004.

Grusky, Sara. 2000. "International Service Learning: A Critical Guide from an Impassioned Advocate." *The American Behavioral Scientist* 43, 5:858–867.

Halimi, Shpresa, Kevin Keckes, Marcus Ingle, and Phung Thuy Phong. 2014. "Strategic International Service Learning Partnership: Mitigating the Impact of Rapid Urban

Development in Vietnam." In *Crossing Boundaries: Tension and Transformation in International Service-Learning*, eds. Patrick M. Green and Mathew Johnson. Sterling, VA: Stylus Publishing.

Halverson-Wente, Lori, and Mark Halverson-Wente. 2014. "Partnership Versus Patronage: A Case Study in International Service-Learning from a Community College Perspective." In *Crossing Boundaries: Tension and Transformation in International Service-Learning*, eds. Patrick M. Green and Mathew Johnson. Sterling, VA: Stylus Publishing.

Harris, Anita. 2014. "Generation G, Global Connectedness & Global Responsibility." International Education Association of Australia. https://www.ieaa.org.au/documents/item/292.

Hoffa, William W. 2007. *A History of U.S. Study Abroad: Beginnings to 1965*. Carlisle, PA: Frontiers: The Interdisciplinary Journal of Study Abroad and The Forum on Education Abroad.

Institute of International Education (IIE). 2018. *Open Doors Report on International Educational Exchange*. Institute of International Education. https://www.iie.org/opendoors.

Jacoby, Barbara. 2015. *Service-Learning Essentials: Questions, Answers, and Lessons Learned*. San Francisco, CA: Jossey-Bass.

Jacoby, Barbara. 2018. "Integrating Service-Learning into Student Affairs Pedagogy." In *Learning Everywhere on Campus: Teaching Strategies for Student Affairs Professionals*, eds. Jane Fried and Ruth Harper. New York, NY: Routledge.

Johnson, Mathew. 2014. "Introduction." In *Crossing Boundaries: Tension and Transformation in International Service-Learning*, eds. Patrick M. Green and Mathew Johnson. Sterling, VA: Stylus Publishing.

Kolb, Alice Y., and David A. Kolb. 2017. *The Experiential Educator*. Kaunakakai, HI: Experience Based Learning Systems, Inc.

Kolb, David A. 1984. *Experiential Learning: Experience as the Source of Learning and Development*. Upper Saddle River, NJ: Prentice Hall.

Lough, Benjamin J. 2015. "A Decade of International Volunteering from the United States, 2004 to 2014." Center for Social Development Research Brief 15–18. Washington University in St. Louis Center for Social Development. https://openscholarship.wustl.edu/cgi/viewcontent.cgi?article=1014&context=csd_research.

Mannion, Greg, Gert Biesta, Mark Priestley, and Hamish Ross. 2011. "The Global Dimension in Education and Education for Global Citizenship: Genealogy and Critique." *Globalisation, Societies and Education* 9, 3–4:443–456. https://doi.org/10.1080/14767724.2011.605327.

McFarland, Miko. 2017. "Alternative Program Types." In *The Guide to Successful Short-Term Programs Abroad, Third Edition*, eds. Lisa Chieffo and Catherine Spaeth. Washington, DC: NAFSA: Association of International Educators.

Mellom, Paula J., and Socorro Herrera. 2014. "Power Relations North and South: Negotiating Meaningful 'Service' in the Context of Imperial History." In *Crossing Boundaries: Tension and Transformation in International Service-Learning*, eds. Patrick M. Green and Mathew Johnson. Sterling, VA: Stylus Publishing.

Merriam, Sharan B., and Laura L. Bierema. 2014. *Adult Learning: Linking Theory and Practice*. San Francisco, CA: Jossey-Bass.

Mlyn, Eric, and Amanda Moore McBride. 2013. "Administering a Volunteer or Service-Learning Program Abroad for Civic Engagement." In *Internships, Service Learning, and Volunteering Abroad: Successful Models and Best Practices*, eds. William Nolting, Debbie Donohue, Cheryl Matherly, and Martin Tillman. Washington, DC: NAFSA: Association of International Educators.

Morales, Marisol, and Arturo Caballero Barron. 2014. "Asset-Based Community Development and Integral Human Development: Two Theories Undergirding an International Service-Learning Program." In *Crossing Boundaries: Tension and Transformation in International Service-Learning*, eds. Patrick M. Green and Mathew Johnson. Sterling, VA: Stylus Publishing.

Murray-Garcia, Jann, and Melanie Tervalon. 2017. "Rethinking Intercultural Competence: Cultural Humility in Internationalising Higher Education." In *Intercultural Competence in Higher Education: International Approaches, Assessment and Application*, eds. Darla K. Deardorff and Lily A. Arasaratnam-Smith. London, United Kingdom: Routledge.

NAFSA WIVA Subcommittee. 2012. *Best Practices on Vetting Partners and Developing Opportunities for Work, Internships and Volunteering Abroad (WIVA)*. Washington, DC: NAFSA: Association of International Educators. https://www.nafsa.org/uploadedFiles/NAFSA_Home/Resource_Library_Assets/Networks/AREA1/Best_Practices_on_How_to_Vet_Partners.pdf.

National Survey of Student Engagement (NSSE). 2018. "High-Impact Practices." Bloomington, IN: Indiana University Center for Postsecondary Research. http://nsse.indiana.edu/html/high_impact_practices.cfm.

Niehaus, Elizabeth, and Karen Kurotsuchi Inkelas. 2015. "Exploring the Role of Alternative Break Programs in Students' Career Development." *Journal of Student Affairs Research and Practice* 52, 2:134–148. https://doi.org/10.1080/19496591.2015.1020247.

Nolting, William, Debbie Donohue, Cheryl Matherly, and Martin Tillman, eds. 2013. *Internships, Service Learning, and Volunteering Abroad: Successful Models and Best Practices*. Washington, DC: NAFSA: Association of International Educators.

Pinto, Andrew D., and Ross E. G. Upshur. 2009. "Global Health Ethics for Students." *Developing World Bioethics* 9, 1:1–10. https://doi.org/10.1111/j.1471-8847.2007.00209.x.

Punteney, Katherine. 2012. "International Careers: The Gap Between Student Interest and Knowledge." *Journal of Studies in International Education* 16, 4:390–407.

Punteney, Katherine. 2016. "Deliberations on the Development of an Intercultural Competence Curriculum." *Intercultural Education* 27, 2:137–150. https://doi.org/10.1080/14675986.2016.1145457.

Quaye, Stephen John, and Shaun R. Harper. 2015. *Student Engagement in Higher Education: Theoretical Perspectives and Practical Approaches for Diverse Populations, 2nd ed*. New York, NY: Routledge.

Roberts, Jay W. 2015. *Experiential Education in the College Context: What It Is, How It Works, and Why It Matters*. New York, NY: Routledge.

Seaman, Jayson, and Matthew Gingo. 2011. "Lev Vygotsky: Experiential Education - A View from the Future." In *Sourcebook of Experiential Education: Key Thinkers and Their Contributions*, eds. Thomas E. Smith and Clifford E. Knapp, New York, NY: Routledge.

Smith, Thomas E., and Clifford E. Knapp. 2011. *Sourcebook of Experiential Education: Key Thinkers and Their Contributions*. New York, NY: Routledge.

Tuckman, Bruce. 1965. "Developmental Sequence in Small Groups." *Psychological Bulletin* 63, 6:384–399.

Chapter 6

International Enrollment Management

Many colleges and universities in the United States and around the world have sophisticated and strategic enrollment management plans. These plans align campuswide marketing, recruitment, admissions, enrollment, and student support services to work toward achieving institutional goals. Enrollment management includes not only the processes of attracting students to an institution and enrolling them, but also the support they receive during their studies and the institutions' ongoing relationship with alumni. Figure 1 illustrates the enrollment management cycle.

Enrollment management goals specify clear targets for the overall number of students to be enrolled. Additionally, there may be secondary target goals for diversifying student demographics (e.g., geographic regions, majors, and other characteristics of the students to be enrolled). Attainment of these enrollment goals often has a financial impact on the institution because budgets and investments in recruitment are developed based on predictions about enrollment numbers and the associated tuition revenue. Beyond the financial effect, the enrollment management plans also strengthen other campus initiatives, such as diversity and inclusion goals and aims to expand particular academic programs (Prieto 2014; Adams, Leventhal, and Connelly 2012).

International enrollment management (IEM) is the subset of enrollment management initiatives focusing on the recruitment and enrollment of international students. The ability to meet international enrollment targets impacts both the campus's internationalization initiatives

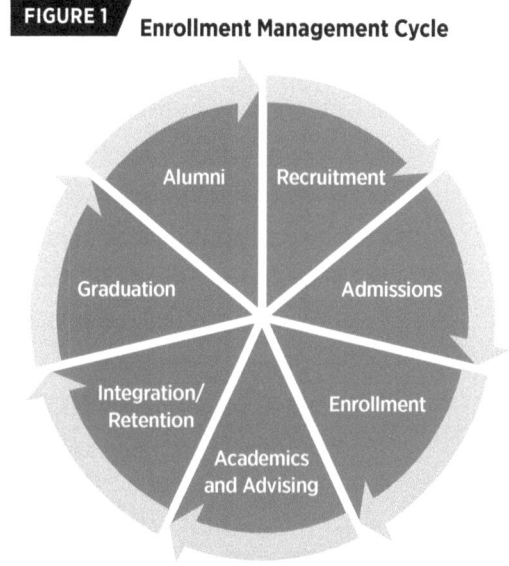

FIGURE 1 **Enrollment Management Cycle**

Source: NAFSA: Association of International Educators (2018b).

and its finances. Institutions vary in the degree to which they invest resources in IEM. At some institutions, the IEM department is highly professionalized, making use of targeted marketing, customer relationship management (CRM) technologies, and extensive data analytics (Adams, Leventhal, and Connelly 2012). In other cases, IEM may be an additional responsibility assigned to an already busy admissions or international education professional who, given the lack of time and resources, has to make ad hoc attempts at international student recruitment (Dunnett 2017). And, of course, many institutions are somewhere between these two poles. While the role and level of emphasis on IEM varies from institution to institution, an increasing number of places are establishing strategic IEM priorities and plans. In addition to four-year universities, numerous community colleges, graduate programs, and intensive English programs are also actively engaged in IEM (Kraft and Redman 2017; Fradkin 2017; Elliot 2017).

This chapter explores many of the issues, considerations, and challenges involved in the recruitment of international students. It examines the role of national governments in promoting and aiding in the recruitment of international students, the IEM strategic planning process, and international student recruitment methods. The U.S. context is given particular attention, with a presentation of the demographics of international students studying in the United States, the history of IEM in the country, and information on U.S. visa types and immigration regulations as they relate to international students. Specializations within IEM are explored, including marketing and brand management, international student admissions, and international student retention. The chapter concludes with suggested resources for further study.

International Students in the United States

Globally, there are more than 5 million higher education students studying outside of their home country; the growth has been rapid, rising from 2.1 million in 2001 (Institute of International Education 2018b). The British Council is predicting that enrollment in international higher education will increase to 6 million students by 2020 (Dunnett 2017). While internationally mobile students constitute only 6 percent of enrollment in higher education worldwide, the proportion increases as the education level goes up; at the doctoral level, 26 percent of students are international students (Organisation for Economic Co-operation and Development 2018). Key decisionmaking factors for international students about where to study are the cost, perceived quality of instruction, perceived value of host institutions, and language of instruction (Organisation for Economic Co-operation and Development 2018).

Demographics

The United States is the most popular destination for international students, hosting 22 percent of students (Institute of International Education 2018b). As of March 2018, there were 1.2 million F-1 (academic student) and M-1 (vocational student) nonimmigrants studying in the United States

(Student and Exchange Visitor Program 2018). The F-1 visa is the more common of the two visa types, used for students studying in degree and English language programs in the United States. The M-1 visa is used for students at a smaller number of institutions offering programs specifically designated as vocational education, such as cosmetology, aviation, and acupuncture schools. (For additional information on these two visa types, see "SEVIS and Admissions" on pages 209–210. In terms of the scope of these programs, a few key statistics from 2018 (Student and Exchange Visitor Program 2018; Institute of International Education 2018a) include:

F-1 AND M-1 STUDENTS:

- Just over 1 million students were enrolled in higher education degree programs.
- Approximately 200,000 students were enrolled in K–12 education, language training programs, and nondegree programs.
- 8,744 schools (including colleges and universities) were certified to host students.
- 75 percent of schools host 50 or fewer students.
- 19 percent of schools host 51 to 500 students.
- 5 percent of schools host more than 500 students.
- The most common majors are:
    - Engineering (21.3 percent);
    - Business and management (17.9 percent); and
    - Math and computer science (17.0 percent).

In addition to F-1 and M-1 nonimmigrants, there were more than 200,000 J-1 exchange visitors in the United States in March 2018 (Student and Exchange Visitor Program 2018). The J-1 visa is used for degree and nondegree programs that have an emphasis on cultural exchange. The visa is issued to individuals for a range of program categories including college and university students, interns, visiting professors, visiting researchers, and short-term scholars (Student and Exchange Visitor Program 2018). (For additional information on this visa type, see "SEVIS and Admissions" on pages 209–210, as well as chapter 9, "Citizen Diplomacy.")

Value of International Students

International students and scholars contribute greatly to the U.S. economy and job market. NAFSA: Association of International Educators identifies the economic value of international students to the United States by calculating their tuition and fee payments, plus living expenses and other funds brought into local communities, and subtracting estimated funding from U.S. scholarships, sponsors, and employment. For the 2017–18 academic year, NAFSA found that international students contributed $39 billion to the U.S. economy (NAFSA 2018a). That inflow into the economy helped create or support 455,622 jobs in a wide range of fields, including higher education, housing, dining, retail, transportation, etc. (NAFSA 2018a).

While the United States remains the most popular destination for international students, the nation is gradually losing its market share to its competitors. As other countries are aggressively recruiting international students, developing desirable programs, and facilitating international student visas and work authorization, an increasing number of international students are choosing destinations for study other than the United States. Enrollment growth in the United States between 1999 and 2005 was 17 percent, while it was 81 percent in France, 46 percent in Germany, 42 percent in Australia, and 29 percent in the United Kingdom during the same period (Dunnett 2017). The United States hosted 28 percent of all international students in 2001, and only 22 percent in 2018 (Institute of International Education 2018b).

Despite the decline, many U.S. institutions are becoming more strategic in their efforts to recruit more international students, as well as diversify the student populations that they are enrolling. The American Council on Education's study, *Mapping Internationalization on U.S. Campuses*, found that 75 percent of U.S. institutions awarding 20 or more doctorate degrees have an international student recruitment plan (Helms and Brajkovic 2017). By contrast, only 33 percent of two-year colleges have such plans (Helms and Brajkovic 2017). Data from that survey, collected in 2016, indicate that Brazil, China, India, Japan, Saudi Arabia, South Korea, and Vietnam were geographic recruitment targets for more than 30 percent of the U.S. institutions surveyed (Helms and Brajkovic 2017).

History of International Enrollment Management

Dunnett (2017) identifies key economic and geopolitical factors that have shaped the international enrollment management field. The highlights are presented in table 1.

TABLE 1 Key Economic and Geopolitical Factors Impacting International Enrollment Management in the United States

1960s–1970s	▪ As economies develop around the world, more international students have the means to study in the United States.
	▪ Institutions seek to mitigate the decline in domestic enrollments by increasing international recruitment.

(continued on next page)

History of International Enrollment Management (continued)

1970s–1980s	▪ Educational agents seize the business opportunity, and the number of agents increases rapidly. (For more information on agents, see "Agent Debate" on pages 198–199.)
	▪ In 1980, at the Wingspread Colloquium, a set of ethical principles for recruitment is developed. These principles serve as the basis of current codes of ethics.
	▪ The Wingspread Colloquium recommends not paying commission to agents on a fee-per-enrolled-student basis.
	▪ Educational fairs and tours are organized by the Institute of International Education. Later, other organizations such as European Council of International Schools, College Information Exchange, and Linden Educational Services develop their own fairs.
1980s–1990s	▪ Promotional materials begin to be produced specifically for international students.
	▪ The number of university fairs, school networks, and agents increases.
	▪ Faculty and international alumni begin to get involved in overseas recruitment.
	▪ Databases and tracking systems start to be used.
	▪ Internationalization begins to be part of institutional visions, with the recruitment of international students as a key strategy.
	▪ Large numbers of international science, technology, engineering, and mathematics (STEM) students are recruited because there are not enough qualified U.S. students in STEM graduate programs.
	▪ Enrollment management offices are increasingly under the purview of a senior administrator.
1990s–2000s	▪ The 1998 Asian financial crisis shakes up institutions, highlighting how dependent they have become on international student enrollment.
	▪ The September 11, 2001, terrorist attacks prompt the U.S. government to tighten student visa controls and background checks, slowing growth in international recruitment (though the government has since improved processing times).
	▪ Affluent Asian countries invest in their higher education systems and become competitors for U.S. higher education.
	▪ China, France, Germany, and others begin to offer degrees in English, increasing competition.
	▪ Australia, Canada, and others actively recruit international students. Some countries give international students the right to work part time off campus and offer a pathway to apply for permanent residence.
2000s–2010s	▪ During and after the recession of 2008, U.S. state governments struggle with their budgets and cut higher education budgets by as much as 30 to 40 percent.
	▪ U.S. universities become more aggressive in their international student recruitment to increase revenue. Tuition rates increase.
	▪ U.S. regulations are changed to allow international students completing certain STEM majors to apply for permission to participate in Optional Practical Training for an additional 2 years (see chapter 7).
2010s	▪ The United States remains the number one destination for international students. However, the United States is gradually losing its market share as other countries become more attractive to international students.

Source: Dunnett (2017).

National Enrollment Management Policies

Around the world, many national governments are aiming to maintain or increase their global market share of internationally mobile students by implementing targeted IEM plans and policies (British Council 2017). For example, Australia's aggressive recruitment strategies have led to positive outcomes, with 32 percent of all higher education students in Australia coming from another country (Institute of International Education 2018b). Census data show that among many groups of skilled workers, including accountants, doctors, engineers, and information technology professionals, more than 40 percent were born overseas, and most were hired while they were living in Australia (Hawthorne 2010). This demonstrates the effectiveness of the "two-step migration" policy that facilitates the conversion of international students into workers (Hawthorne 2010). The Australian government has taken specific steps to encourage international student enrollment by vigorously marketing the country's programs and by actively working to make enrollment easier, for example, by experimenting with waiving English language testing (Hawthorne 2010; Dunnett 2017).

Canada, France, Germany, and the United Kingdom have also been aggressively recruiting international students to their institutions of higher education. Some countries have added government subsidies and specialized programming to appeal to international students. Some have made employment possible for enrolled students, as well as simplified postgraduation pathways to employment (Dunnett 2017). Countries with significantly cheaper tuition rates than the United States often use their cost-competitiveness to their advantage. For example, tuition at French universities, which is considerably less than in the United States, is set by law and applies to all students, domestic and international. International students are beginning to recognize that they can receive a high-quality education at a more affordable cost if they consider a broad range of countries (Becker and Kolster 2012; Dunnett 2017; James-MacEachern 2018).

In the United States, some federal agencies have made efforts to continue their support of international students in the country. The Department of State's EducationUSA network runs more than 425 advising centers in more than 175 countries (U.S. Department of State n.d.). These centers promote U.S. higher education by providing information to prospective students to help them find institutions that are a good fit, navigate the admissions and visa processes, and prepare for departure to the United States (U.S. Department of State n.d.). The U.S. Commercial Service also supports institutions in their international marketing and recruitment efforts (U.S. Department of Commerce 2018). Despite the important work of these two agencies, there is not a "nationally/federally" coordinated U.S. IEM policy. Instead, efforts are left largely to the discretion of individual universities, though there are consortia and regional initiatives, including more than 30 statewide consortia (Kacenga 2019; Punteney and Wei 2018). An example of an initiative is Study California, a nonprofit member-based organization that promotes study at California colleges and universities through the use of a website and recruitment fairs (Study California 2019).

Responsibility for International Enrollment Management

The responsibility for IEM issues may be housed within an institution's enrollment management/admissions office, or it may be housed within the international education office. Oftentimes, there is some degree of collaboration between the two offices. Di Maria (2017) describes four potential models to organize IEM efforts:

- Ad hoc. In this model, IEM is no one's job in particular, but rather an added duty for someone with an already busy job. The end result of the ad hoc model is usually limited, disorganized efforts with curtailed results.

- International student recruitment specialist. In this model, one individual is assigned responsibility for international recruitment. That person may be housed within the admissions office or international education office. The individual is responsible for recruitment efforts but may not be situated highly enough in the organization to be able to make strategic policy positions.

- International recruitment committee. This model reflects a desirable level of broader cross-campus participation and shared decisionmaking. However, it is likely that international recruitment is only a small part of the job duties for the individuals involved, running the risk that it will not be given much attention.

- Central recruitment office. In this model, IEM is a unit within that office. It can be structured in one of three ways:

    - International recruitment responsibilities are taken on by everyone in the admissions office;

    - International recruitment is assigned to a team within the admissions office or international education office; or

    - An autonomous office focused on international recruitment and admissions is established.

The central international recruitment office model is rare, but highly effective. It is characterized by shared responsibility across professional domains, rather than as an assignment to a group of specialists. It is the most difficult model to implement because all stakeholders have to develop capacity for international dimensions of their work. These stakeholders may be from admissions, the registrar, financial aid, or marketing/communications, and they may include international student advisers, faculty and department heads, academic and career advisers, housing staff, graduate coordinators, and senior administrators. This model requires the greatest institutional commitment, but also offers the greatest opportunity for strategic action.

The model that an institution chooses depends on the vision, mission, values, executive commitment, organizational culture, and current state of cooperation on international recruitment within an organization (Di Maria 2017).

International Enrollment Management Competencies

The *NAFSA International Education Professional Competencies* framework identifies specific skills and knowledge needed by IEM professionals, including international student and scholar recruitment, admission, and placement; English as a second language (ESL) program administration; IEM planning strategies; preparation of international students and scholars for study in the United States; and comprehensive internationalization (NAFSA 2015). Additionally, as described in the introduction to this book, NAFSA recommends that all professionals, in IEM and other international education sectors, have a set of cross-cutting competencies that include advocacy, communication with stakeholders, financial stewardship, human resources, information technology, intercultural communications, leadership, and strategic planning (NAFSA 2015).

Furthermore, IEM professionals must follow codes of ethics designed to guide good practice and approaches to international enrollment management. Three key documents can provide some guidance (Ott 2017):

- Council of International Schools's *Guiding Principles for Higher Education*
- NAFSA's *Statement of Ethical Principles*
- National Association for College Admission Counseling's *Code of Ethics and Professional Practices*

Each of these documents prioritizes the needs and well-being of international students. The standards urge institutions to align their enrollment management plans with their institutional missions, remain legally compliant, and communicate with transparency (Ott 2017; Heaney and Ott 2009).

International Enrollment Management Strategic Planning

The process of developing an IEM plan is, in many ways, similar to the strategic planning process discussed in chapter 3 on "Internationalization." Similarities include the emphasis on understanding the status quo, collaborating across campus, setting measurable goals, and building stakeholder support. IEM strategic planning also shares some similarities to the backward design process introduced in chapter 4, "Education Abroad," in terms of the focus on identifying goals and then working backward to identify tactics and assessment methods.

First, in order to develop an IEM plan, it is essential to assess the status quo internal to the institution and in the external market. Beatty (2014) and Ghandi (2014) offer some suggestions: Internally, the analysis must focus on the mission, institutional strategic plan goals, institutional brand and reputation/rank, current student demographics, budgetary targets, and capacity for international support services such as housing, intensive English programs, academic support, cross-cultural support, immigration advising, etc. It is also important for IEM planners to identify what international partnerships already exist and where there are international alumni. Meeting with a wide range of stakeholder groups and campus departments for input can help planners to look at the larger picture.

Regarding the external assessment, it is essential that IEM planners are familiar with global trends in higher education and academic mobility. It is important to know the chief factors for students choosing to study in a foreign country for each target market, as well as the cultural norms related to higher education admission and the use of agents in those countries. Planners should explore marketing principles, partnership options, and industry norms. Familiarity with sponsored student programs (described later in the chapter) is a requirement, as is knowledge of the services available through government agencies such as EducationUSA and the U.S. Commercial Service. Figure 2 illustrates the way in which the internal and external assessments can be synthesized to develop the IEM strategy.

FIGURE 2 Development of an International Enrollment Management Strategy

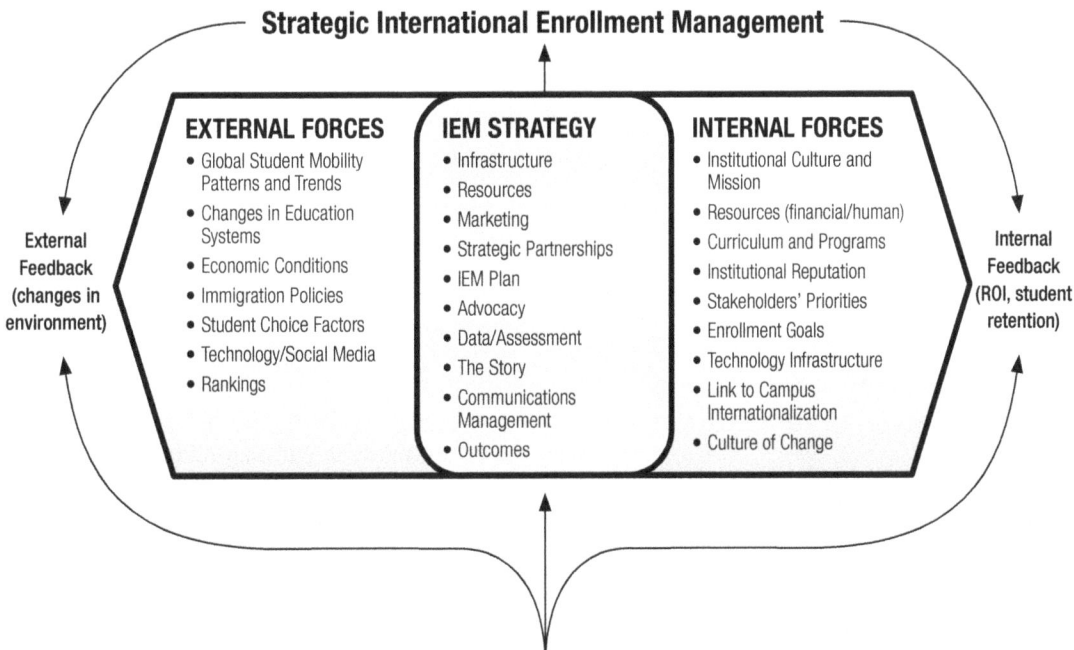

Source: Sinclair and Croom (2017). Reprinted with permission from Julie Sinclair and Fanta Aw.

The second stage of the strategic planning process involves identifying the IEM goals based on the institutional mission and guided by the constraints revealed in the internal and external assessments. IEM planners should identify key performance indicators that are measurable and will signal both progress toward and achievement of goals. Example performance indicators might include the number of international students applying from a particular country, the GPA or Test of English as a Foreign Language (TOEFL) English proficiency scores of the incoming class of international students, the cost to recruit a student from a particular country, international student graduation rates, or results from surveys of international student satisfaction (Beatty 2014).

In the third stage of the IEM strategic planning process, planners should develop and implement a plan with specific tactics that aim to achieve the identified key performance indicators. The tactics should be measurable and include timelines and budgets. Unlike domestic recruitment plans, an international plan must take into account the social, cultural, and linguistic differences between the institution and the international students' home country (Beatty 2014). For example, the role of parents in international students' decisionmaking processes should be considered, particularly for prospective undergraduates (Ghandi 2014). Throughout the implementation of the plan, it is necessary to continually build institutional support by providing a channel of dialogue with senior administrators and key department heads (Ghandi 2014).

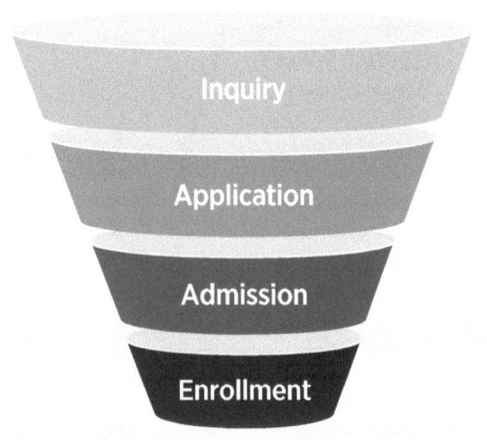

FIGURE 3 Student Recruitment Funnel

The written IEM plan document will likely include many components, such as the history of international recruitment at the organization, the goals of the plan, strategic alignment with institutional priorities and other internationalization goals, resource allocation, process changes (such as instituting new software or improving admissions response times), the target markets (geographic or student type), the recruitment methods for each market, timelines, stakeholders, plans to manage risk, and methods to assess the effectiveness of the plan (Sinclair and Croom 2017; Boutsis 2017).

The next step in implementing the IEM strategic plan is to continuously monitor enrollment data. The student recruitment funnel shown in figure 3 illustrates a classic enrollment management concept. As shown in the figure, a broad number of prospective students may be at the right point in their lives to consider further education. Of those, only a portion of students will show interest in an institution by investigating its programs online or making an inquiry requesting information. From the group that shows interest, a smaller group of students will actually apply. From that group, only a fraction of students will be admitted. And finally, from those who are admitted, only a percentage of students will choose to enroll. Thus, there are fewer and fewer prospective students at each stage of the process.

Regular (daily, weekly, or monthly) reports are important in tracking and comparing the number of students at each level (inquiry, application, admission, and enrollment) and the percentage of prospects who move from each level to the next (Hansen 2016). In addition to looking at institution-wide data, data on individual academic programs, recruitment channels, and applicant country can be tracked. Such data can be compared year to year to determine the effectiveness of changes in marketing and recruitment methods. Based on the data, decisions can be made to boost current recruitment efforts in one area or another, adjust enrollment predictions, or update the strategic IEM plan for future recruitment cycles.

The fifth stage in the IEM strategic planning process is reviewing and revising the plan. The IEM plan is a working document and should be updated often to incorporate new ideas and information. Target countries and groups may need to be adjusted from year to year to respond to shifts in the global market (Beatty 2014). Both internal and external factors may prompt a need to readjust the plan. These could include new programs launching on a campus, demographic shifts, institutional budget cuts, changes in foreign scholarship funding, natural disasters, or government initiatives (Ghandi 2014; Choudaha, Chang, and Kono 2014; Sinclair and Croom 2017). Creating the IEM plan is both a science and an art. It is a science because it is data based, and it is an art because it requires creativity and adaptability (Sinclair and Croom 2017).

International Student Recruitment Methods and Channels

A key responsibility of IEM professionals, and a primary goal of IEM strategic plans, is the recruitment of international students. Choudaha (2017a) warns institutions against using the following ineffective approaches to international student recruitment:

- Blanket approach: Assuming that what worked at other institutions will work for every institution.

- Trial and error: Haphazardly trying a slew of approaches just to see if any work.

- Gut feeling: Using pure instinct on what may feel like it could possibly work.

Instead of these ineffective approaches, Choudaha (2017a) urges institutions to be intentional, strategic, and ethical, developing a customized recruitment plan that represents the institution accurately and positively. Specifically, Choudaha, Chang, and Kono (2014) recommend using the following three tools to facilitate successful international student recruitment:

- Real-time research. Data analysis can be used to determine where to focus efforts and to measure return on investment.

- Technology. Technology should be used to reach target markets more efficiently and economically. This may include hosting online information sessions, participating in virtual study abroad fairs, and translating the institution's website.

- Partnerships. Partnerships with third-party organizations or other institutions can help to create sustainable connections to new markets.

These are just a few tools that can be used to maximize recruitment initiatives. There may be some effective methods that are used for domestic student recruitment that can be adapted for international student audiences. Efforts for international student recruitment and domestic student recruitment should be viewed as complementary, rather than in opposition to each other (Sinclair 2010). IEM professionals should look for synergies between the two plans in order to make the best use of resources.

Recruitment Methods

There is no standard set of recruitment practices across U.S. institutions; instead, how the recruitment is undertaken depends on the organization (Adams, Leventhal, and Connelly 2012). Ozturgut (2013) surveyed the 40 U.S. institutions that, at the time of the study, hosted the largest number of international students and asked about their international student recruitment methods. Ozturgut (2013) found that the most prevalent methods of recruitment were participation in international recruitment fairs, the development and distribution of marketing materials, alumni involvement in outreach, promotions by faculty and staff directly to international students (see chapter 3), and the provision of support and resources (see chapter 7) such as international student advising and scholarships to international students.

Recruitment Fairs

One long-standing method of international student recruitment is participation in recruitment fairs. These events offer institutions the chance to build pools of prospective students and create opportunities for focused follow-up. Recruitment fairs can increase exposure and brand recognition, reinforce the interest of prospective students, and possibly attract new students (Smith 2017). From the student and parent perspective, these fairs grant students more personalized exposure to the institution through individual appointments and give parents the place to ask questions and voice concerns.

Recruitment fairs may be held in hotel ballrooms, schools, cafeterias, exhibition halls, or online. A fair may be a single event or part of a series of fairs organized in a particular geographic region. The advantages for participating institutions are that the fairs offer increased access to a large pool of students at once, a lot of progress can be made in a short period of time, and the handling of the logistics is usually done by other people. One potential challenge is that fair participation may cost between $10,000 and $20,000 and it might not include round-trip airfare, shipping, visas, etc.

Some well-known fair organizers are Council of International Schools, Linden Educational Services, U.S. Educational Group, KIC UnivAssist, and Chegg (Boutsis 2017). Virtual fairs are becoming more common as a way to reduce the costs of international travel. Smith (2017) finds that today, with so much information readily available online, students research the institutions in advance of attending the fair and then, at the event, they seek out the specific schools that are of interest to them. Generally speaking, students are less inclined to develop new interest at a fair, though it is possible. While there is no predicting the actual outcomes of participation in fairs, many institutions continue to attend in hopes of reaching and attracting new students to meet their enrollment goals. Fairs can be especially enlightening experiences for those professionals who are new to the recruitment field (Boutsis 2017).

International Travel

As an alternative to recruitment fairs, small groups of IEM recruiters from nearby institutions may choose to travel together and share the related costs of international school visits in order to pull a larger attendance without having to pay for fair participation fees. Individual travel, on the other hand, may be most appropriate when working closely with partner organizations, for example if setting up a memorandum of understanding with a partner (Boutsis 2017). In addition to the recruiter, overseas recruitment efforts may involve alumni, faculty, agents, and education abroad center staff (Boutsis 2017).

Institutions engaging in international travel may benefit from creating a travel calendar. Most travel takes place from August to mid-November and then from February to May; the travel calendar needs to consider both the home institution calendar and the calendars of the target countries (Boutsis 2017).

International travel requires research, resources, time, and flexibility. Boutsis (2017, 107) points out that "relationship-building continues to be a cornerstone of our work. Personal connections are what make our institutions real for everyone involved (the counseling community, the student, and the family). In person, we offer a voice of reassurance, empathy, and understanding and are able to establish a bond that might help to make the decision to study abroad easier." The results of this relationship building may take a few years to manifest, so institutions need to make a long-term commitment to measure the true effectiveness of international travel (Boutsis 2017).

Print and Digital Materials

To support and supplement international travel, most organizations use print and digital communication in their recruitment efforts (Kraft and Redman 2017). Print communication may include brochures and posters. Digital materials will certainly include the institution's website, as well as email campaigns, online advertisements, and more. Institutions may use social media ads targeted at specific demographics or at users who follow particular organizations that are relevant to the program for which they are recruiting.

Organizations may buy lists of prospective students' contact information from the companies administering tests such as the SAT, GRE, TOEFL, and the International English Language Testing System (IELTS) (Iverson 2017). Recruiters may also send more focused content to the prospective students whom they met at the recruitment fairs to build on those initial connections.

Alumni Engagement

Alumni may be formally engaged in international recruitment activities, such as representing the institution at recruitment fairs, inviting prospective students to organized alumni chapter events, having individual conversations with prospective students, and interviewing applicants. These alumni should be carefully selected, trained, and supported in order to represent the university effectively and ethically (Zdawczyk 2017).

The Agent Debate

The use of agents in international student recruitment has long been a topic of debate. "An agency is defined as an organization, company, or association that recruits and places nonresident U.S. students into accredited colleges, universities, and other education institutions on a commercial 'fee for service' basis" (Bridge Education Group 2016, 10). Agents may be self-employed, or they may work for incorporated businesses with multiple employees.

Agents can provide a range of services, including helping students to identify best-fit universities and navigate the application process, as well as providing coaching on essay writing, test preparation, visa applications, and travel assistance (Scoby 2017). Some agents are compensated by the students, while others receive payment from the universities for the students that the agents enroll (Bridge Education Group 2016; Crawley 2017). The source of payment and, thus, whose interest the agent is serving, leads to many discussions of ethics. Some international educators question whether the agent is acting in the students' best interest or in the agent's own interest when recommending a particular higher education institution.

The National Association for College Admissions Counseling (NACAC) is a leading influencer on

(continued on next page)

The Agent Debate (continued)

undergraduate admissions and recruitment policies in the United States. Up until 2013, NACAC members were not allowed to use agents for recruitment purposes because NACAC had deemed the use of agents to be unethical (Dunnett 2017). While this policy was not controversial for domestic recruitment, it was more contested in international recruitment. In many countries, it is commonplace for agents to assist students and families in managing the higher education admissions process. Many international enrollment professionals found that working with agents was a cost-effective means of recruiting qualified international students.

NACAC now allows institutions to use agents in the recruitment of international students if specific guidelines to ensure accountability, integrity, and transparency are followed (Dunnett 2017; Bridge Education Group 2016). Organizations such as the American International Recruitment Council (AIRC) and ICEF certify agencies that meet quality standards (AIRC n.d.; ICEF n.d.). If institutions choose to use agents, it is essential that the agencies are carefully vetted, relationships are effectively managed, and expectations are made transparent (Crawley 2017).

In the United States, 37 percent of higher education institutions use international student recruitment agents, and an estimated 22 percent of international students are enrolled through agencies (Bridge Education Group 2016). While U.S. institutions hold a mixed stance on the use of agents, countries like Australia, Canada, New Zealand, and the United Kingdom have national policies governing the ethical use of agents, and the use of agents is quite robust. In Canada, for example, 69 percent of higher education institutions use agents for the recruitment of international students (Bridge Education Group 2016; Crawley 2017).

Agents can provide an efficient, cost-effective method for entering new markets and recruiting students, while helping institutions to diversify their campuses. Effective agents are familiar with the international students' culture, family structure, and local language, and they are knowledgeable about the program offerings of the institutions they represent. Agents are based in-country, in the local time zone, and are readily available to provide face-to-face guidance and support that a university employee usually cannot offer without traveling. In this way, agents can bridge the needs of the students and the institutions (Bridge Education Group 2016; Scoby 2017).

Recruitment Channels

Recruiting international students individually can be a labor-intensive and costly way to meet IEM goals. Most institutions try to complement their efforts to recruit individual students with the creation of channels that allow a wider reach. This section explores some of the most common approaches.

Conditional Admission

Insufficient foreign language proficiency can be a barrier to admission for international students who wish to study outside their home country. In the United States, many intensive English programs (IEPs) help students to develop the academic English skills they need to enroll in U.S. higher education institutions. Partnerships between institutions and IEPs can be an effective recruitment channel (Choudaha, Chang, and Kono 2014).

Oftentimes, the partnership is structured as a conditional admission agreement. With conditional admission, a student is offered admission to an IEP and a higher education institution at the same time. This is an appropriate course of action if the student lacks the necessary English language proficiency but meets all other academic admissions criteria (Hansen 2017; Crawley 2017). If the student completes a specified course level in the IEP program, he or she will then be able to begin degree studies, often without taking English language proficiency exams (Crawley 2017).

A higher education institution may have a conditional admission agreement with an IEP located on its own campus or an independent IEP. Conditional admission benefits the students because they know they have a path to university admission. The agreement also benefits the IEP and higher education institution because it allows them to recruit more students. For this reason, conditional admission options are actively marketed to prospective students (Crawley 2017).

Bridge Programs

Bridge programs are also designed for international students who need additional development of their language proficiency before beginning university studies. For many institutions, these programs serve as a viable recruitment channel. As the name implies, these programs present a "bridge" from intensive language study to full-time academic study (Crawley 2017).

In the United States, bridge programs provide students with English language courses prior to full matriculation in the degree program. The courses also incorporate lessons on some of the skills needed for college success, such as time management, study skills, academic integrity, acculturation, presentation skills, etc. (Crawley 2017). Such support and preparation may be an attractive option for many prospective students.

Pathway Programs

The terms "pathway program" and "bridge program" are sometimes used interchangeably in the international education field. In this book, the term "bridge program" refers to a type of program offered before beginning a university degree, while "pathway program" refers to a foundation year or a year of concurrent enrollment in which students are enrolled in both language courses and academic courses after matriculation into the university. In pathway programs, the academic courses, and sometimes the language courses, result in credit that is counted toward the degree (Dunnett 2017; Hovland, Ng Hartmann, and Schulte 2017; Baker 2017).

Pathway programs may be administered by university-run IEPs or by for-profit providers. In the case of a partnership with a provider, the provider may manage the recruitment, language instruction, student services, and staffing for the program. Some educators have raised concerns about the appropriateness of outsourcing the core educational functions of admission and instruction (Choudaha 2017b).

The American Council on Education's *Mapping Internationalization on U.S. Campuses* survey found that 31 percent of doctoral institutions have a bridge or pathway program operated by the university, while 10 percent have one operated by a third-party provider (Helms and Brajkovic 2017). An additional 13 percent of surveyed doctoral institutions were in the process of developing a bridge or pathway program, and 11 percent were considering developing one (Helms and Brajkovic 2017). In contrast, at baccalaureate and associate institutions, more than 50 percent did not have, were not building, and were not considering adding such a program (Helms and Brajkovic 2017).

A 2017 investigation into the use of third-party providers of pathway programs in the United States found that 45 U.S. institutions—roughly half of which were public institutions—were partnering with eight third-party pathway providers (Choudaha 2017b). Using focus groups and surveys, the study identified the following motivations for considering pathway providers (Choudaha 2017b):

- Gain access to their recruitment network;
- Expand enrollment at the bachelor's level;
- Improve yield of international enrollment; and
- Make up for lack of in-house expertise.

Additionally, the study identified the dominant reasons that institutions do not partner with pathway providers (Choudaha 2017b):

- Fear of loss of academic standards;
- Concern for loss of control over international admissions;
- University-governed IEP is working well;
- Undesirable terms of contract with provider (length, cost, etc.); and
- Preference to develop in-house expertise.

The report concludes that the number of international students studying in the United States on pathway programs is still relatively small. Further, each institution must consider its mission and context in order to determine if partnering with a third-party pathway provider is a strategic option for the institution and an appropriate recruitment channel.

Sponsored Student Programs

Being designated as an approved host institution for sponsored student programs is another way to create a recruitment channel that can bring in multiple students. A sponsored student is defined as "an individual who receives funding for the purpose of education, training, or professional development from a sponsor" (Schmiegel 2017, 138). Sponsoring organizations may be funding students' study in order to promote cultural exchange and international understanding. Many organizations also sponsor international students so that students can develop particular expertise that can be applied in the students' home country after graduation, thus improving capacity in the home country (Schmiegel 2017). Recent evidence suggests that students who return, as well as those who stay on in the host country, often actively contribute to the development of the home country (Campbell 2018). The governments of countries such as Brazil and Saudi Arabia offer scholarships for their students to study in the United States (Choudaha, Chang, and Kono 2014; Becker and Kolster 2012).

U.S. government programs such as Fulbright might bring only a few students into a given university, however, the student pool is typically very diverse and highly qualified. Getting on the list of approved institutions for foreign government scholarships can create a larger and steadier volume of students, though it may be difficult to get on the list (Schmiegel 2017). Still, hosting sponsored students can bring prestige to the host institution and can be an effective way to meet enrollment goals, such as adding diversity to the overall international student population.

At the same time, there is a level of risk involved when geopolitical changes cut off scholarship funds with little warning, which can affect revenues if a large portion of international student enrollments are facilitated through a particular sponsored student program (Schmiegel 2017). The Washington International Education Conference serves as an opportunity for IEM professionals to network with and ask questions of the foreign government personnel who oversee sponsored student programs (Schmiegel 2017).

Supporting sponsored students also brings increased administrative complexity because it involves many stakeholders, each with his or her own interests and priorities. The sponsor will have a set of rules and expectations that the host institution is required to observe. Regular communication is needed between the sponsor and the host institution to ensure that policies are abided. Often, there is a staff member who is the designated sponsored student coordinator who can help coordinate matters. This person should have strong people and communication skills and an attention to deadlines in order to navigate the policies of the sponsor and host institution and to develop creative solutions to working across the two infrastructures (Schmiegel 2017).

Joint and Double Degrees

The educational value of joint and double degrees, as discussed in chapter 3, "Internationalization," also makes them a key recruitment strategy. The degrees stem from partnership agreements between two or more institutions that have identified select courses that are complementary and are then combined into a cohesive curriculum. For example, two institutions in different countries may create a 4 + 1 program in which students complete 4 years of study in a particular major at an institution in their home country, and then complete 1 year of study in the partner institution abroad. The program enables students to earn two degrees in a shorter span of time than if the degrees were completed independently. In this case, the students graduate with a bachelor's degree from the first institution and a master's degree from the second institution.

Joint- and double-degree programs work well when the curricula of the two partnering institutions are well aligned. For the first institution, the built-in pathway to the partner institution's master's degree program helps to recruit students to the first institution's bachelor's degree program. For the second institution, it creates a pipeline for recruiting international graduate students.

The joint- and double-degree program may also result in students completing degrees in the usual amount of time, but in two different institutions. An example of this model is a 2 + 2 program in which the first 2 years of a bachelor's degree are completed in one institution and the next 2 years of the program are completed in the partner institution. Both institutions are better able to attract students because they are able to offer this degree option with an international study component. Other programs may include 3 + 1 or 3 + 2 models (Dunnett 2017). The condensed timelines, multiple degrees, and opportunities to study abroad combine to form an attractive offer for many students considering their higher education options.

Recruitment from Community Colleges

A potential pool of international student applicants can be found at community colleges across the United States (Hulstrand 2009; Hansen 2017). Many institutions have agreements in place to facilitate the transfer of students, domestic as well as international, from community colleges to four-year universities. Attending a community college prior to a four-year university can be a more affordable option for international students, so the possible path of enrolling at a community college and then a university is often marketed by both the community college and the university. Two-year and four-year institutions located in the same city are especially likely to partner in this way.

Recruitment from High Schools

An increasing number of international students are enrolling in U.S. high schools as a pathway to enrollment in U.S. universities. Many international students see the opportunity to engage in an international education experience during their secondary school years as a way to gain an advantage when applying to U.S. universities. International students in the United States can benefit from college counseling programs in U.S. high schools that help students to understand the U.S. higher education system and application process. Students who attend high school in the United States typically find the transition to a U.S. university to be a smoother process because they have already adjusted to U.S. culture, English language expectations, and teaching methods (Farrugia 2014; Sandberg 2017). For the enrollment professional, this means there is less work to do in orienting the prospective international students.

Because U.S. laws limit international student enrollment in public secondary schools to 1 year, most international students attend private schools (Farrugia 2014). Private schools are also more likely to have residence halls or other housing options available for international students. Many private secondary schools are actively recruiting international students, using similar methods to those described in this chapter.

For U.S. colleges and universities, recruiting international students who are already enrolled in the United States is significantly cheaper (Sandberg 2017). Recruiters can reach these students by attending college fairs within the United States and by hosting campus visits. Recruiters may also buy lists of students' contact information from companies that administer the PSAT and SAT (Sandberg 2017).

Marketing and Brand Management

While international students are not homogeneous, it is a fair generalization to say that the prestige, selectivity, and global rankings of institutions are important factors in students' enrollment decisions (Hazelkorn 2012). For this reason, institutions may be motivated to try to manage the perception of their brand through publicity efforts, as well as work to increase their ranking on global indexes. Campuses create print and digital content that shape how they are viewed by prospective students, carefully selecting the text and images that most appeal to students and parents.

An understanding of the push and pull factors described in chapter 3, "Internationalization," as well as the dynamics of student choice in each target market segment can help institutions to customize the brand messaging for maximum effectiveness (Sinclair 2010; Bodycott 2009). Cultural factors should be taken into account; for example, a survey of international students from China, India, Indonesia, and Taiwan revealed that the recommendation of a parent or relative played a key role in the student's selection of an institution, second only to the reputation of the institution (Mazzarol and Soutar 2002). Some institutions provide resources specifically geared toward parents and families, addressing their most pressing questions and concerns.

In an international market, digital marketing often plays an essential role in recruiting students. Waxman and Andrews (2017) recommend a four-step process to the digital marketing plan: measure the institution's digital footprint, develop content, disseminate that content, and implement the plan. Measuring the digital footprint refers to auditing the institution's existing digital marketing, i.e., website, email, and social media. Data should be looked at according to target market segments, and analytics should be examined where available. Surveys can be done of current students to augment the available data. The analysis should identify strengths and gaps in the digital marketing materials and create a foundation for content creation.

Content creation may include websites, videos, webinars, e-newsletters, email campaigns, social media campaigns, and more. The content, language, and images must be carefully selected and be in line with the institution's brand. Translation of the materials may be required, as well as localization of the materials to adapt them to the culture of particular target markets.

During the content dissemination phase, the materials are shared and there is careful tracking of data and the recording of contact information of prospective students. Through the digital software, information on how many times content is viewed, how many times links are clicked, and how many times images are shared can easily be compiled into reports for analysis.

The implementation phase requires coordinating the staffing, funding, and technology needed to enact, track, and modify the digital marketing plan. Social media campaigns, especially given the wide range of platforms used by students today, depend on an investment in time and energy. Staff members must engage with and respond to students' inquires in a timely manner to demonstrate the institution's commitment.

Given the advances in technology and the interconnected nature of the world today, many institutions are putting more resources toward their digital marketing and recruiting strategies. The reach and impact of digital materials can often be far spread and may result in increased enrollment. IEM professionals can work with the marketing and communications departments on campus to coordinate messages, increase outreach, and enhance the overall institutional brand.

International Student Admissions

In addition to marketing and recruitment, a key function within IEM is international student admissions, which comprises the setting of admissions standards and the review of individual student applications. An international admissions professional typically works with recruitment staff, communicates with prospective students, manages application files and data, makes or communicates admissions decisions, and guides students on the process of applying for a visa and traveling to the institution. This section provides an overview of these and other related admissions responsibilities.

Applications

Admissions professionals must be organized and detail-driven in order to maintain all of the digital and paper files that comprise student applications. Application requirements may include the submission of transcripts, test scores, portfolios, personal essays, auditions, and personal interviews (Hansen 2017). International student applications should be reviewed according to the same academic admissions standards that are applied to domestic students, to the extent possible. Some of the differences may relate to the availability of exams such as the SAT and ACT in the student's home country; whether or not high schools and universities in the student's country have the practice of sending sealed, certified transcripts (some countries give students only one original transcript, which the student will, quite reasonably, not want to mail to institutions); and whether or not it is possible to access online fee payment systems (Morawski 2017; Hansen 2017).

International admissions personnel may receive some documents through an online application system and others through the mail. As the different application components arrive, the documents need to be logged into a system in order to be able to send reminders to the students who are missing elements, as well as to notify the admissions professional when a file is complete and ready for review.

Depending on institutional policy, the admissions professional may be responsible for reviewing the application materials and determining whether or not the student meets the admissions requirements, or the admissions professional may compile the application materials and send the file to a faculty department head or committee to make the admissions decision. For either scenario, the admissions professional will communicate the decision to the student in writing. If the student is admitted, he or she will be sent information on accepting or declining the admissions offer, travel, the visa, the academic calendar, orientation dates, class enrollment procedures, cross-cultural information, and more.

Responsive, clear, and warm communication from admissions personnel, and a quick admissions decision, may make an international student more inclined to choose one institution over others. Thus, the effectiveness of the international admissions professional is crucial, not only to the students' experience but also to the institution's ability to meet its IEM goals.

Language Proficiency

For university admission, it is often necessary to ensure that international students have the foreign language proficiency to complete the academic work in a language other than their own (Hansen 2017). In the United States, universities generally accept transcripts that show that students completed high school or university degrees in an English-speaking country. In other cases, students will likely be asked to take English language proficiency examinations, such as TOEFL or IELTS (Hansen 2017).

Each institution sets its own minimum required scores for admission. Graduate-level degrees, as well as certain undergraduate majors, may require higher test scores than the average undergraduate degree. Students with scores near the minimum requirement may be required to take courses in academic English that are designed for international students and other non-native English speakers. Applicants with scores below the required level may be directed to IEPs.

Credential Evaluation

A specialty field within international admissions is credential evaluation. Credential evaluation is the process of determining equivalency of courses and degrees between two countries. For example, a credential evaluator in the United States might receive a student's undergraduate transcript from another country as part of an application to a master's degree program in the United States. The credential evaluator will research the educational system of the other country and produce an analysis of whether the studies on that transcript are equivalent to a U.S. bachelor's degree and what the grades on the transcript would be equivalent to based on the U.S. GPA model. The admissions professional uses this analysis to determine whether or not the student should be admitted to the master's program. Credential evaluation is necessary because educational systems and grading systems around the world vary significantly. The credential evaluator plays a crucial role in determining if the student is likely to be successful in the program to which he or she is applying (Morawski 2017).

Credential evaluation is more complicated than the mere translation of documents (though that may be needed, too). Organizations such as the National Association of Credential Evaluation Services (NACES) and the Association of International Credential Evaluators (AICE) ensure that their members maintain high ethical standards and up-to-date credentialing knowledge (Riley 2017; Morawski 2017).

Some institutions instruct applicants to send their credential documents directly to a credential evaluation agency, which are private companies with expertise in this area. The students request that an analysis be conducted and sent to the institution. The students pay a fee for this service, which is usually between $200 and $300 (Riley 2017).

Other institutions, particularly those with large international student populations, train their admissions personnel in credential evaluation. The advantage of performing credential evaluation in-house is that it is more cost-effective (for large operations), more customizable, and offers a quicker admissions decision turnaround time. However, building up the expertise (and a collection of resources) on educational systems around the world is costly, so this option requires a long-term commitment from the institution (Riley 2017). Organizations such as NAFSA and the American Association of Collegiate Registrars and Admissions Officers (AACRAO) provide resources and opportunities for professional development in this area.

Some institutions employ a hybrid model by using external evaluation agencies for university transcripts and internal evaluators for secondary school transcripts. Others might use evaluation agencies only for complicated cases (Riley 2017).

No matter the model, all credential evaluators must be on the alert for potential fraud. They must determine whether the documents belong to the applicant, examine the authenticity of the document, assess whether the institution that issued the document is accredited, and verify that the accrediting body is legitimate (Morawski 2017; Riley 2017). With the emphasis on investigating educational systems and the added element of watching for fraud, Riley (2017, 72) suggests that, "people who like to solve mysteries will find the field of foreign credential evaluation to be fun and rewarding. Endless opportunities to research foreign institutions and educational systems abound!"

Financial Aid

Another aspect of the international admissions sector that institutions must navigate is financial aid. International students are not eligible for U.S. federal aid, including federal loans, grants, or work-study. They can apply for private loans from U.S. banks, but the lack of a social security number, credit history, or U.S.-based cosigner makes international students likely to be ineligible (Brown 2017).

Institutional merit scholarships may be granted on the basis of SAT or ACT scores, GPA, or class rank. However, many international students may not have these scores and thus may be disqualified from some institutional scholarships (Brown 2017). Some institutions offer emergency funds, tuition discounts, or tuition installment plans to help international students fund their education and manage short-term financial difficulties (Brown 2017).

Among international students studying in the United States, 58.6 percent are primarily supported by personal and family funds, 18.8 percent by current employment (almost entirely through Optional Practical Training, which is introduced in chapter 7), 15.8 percent by the U.S. college or university, 5.2 percent by a foreign government or university, and less than 1 percent by private sponsors, the U.S. government, or international organizations (Institute of International Education 2018a). Finances are a major barrier for many students who wish to study internationally. Any steps an institution can take to create financial aid eligibility for international students will help advance IEM goals.

SEVIS and Admissions

Almost all international students studying in the United States are on one of three nonimmigrant visa types: F-1, M-1, or J-1. The F-1 student category is for international students in the United States who are pursuing an educational objective. This may be at any level, from primary school up to the doctoral and professional degree levels, and it includes certificate, nondegree, pathway, and language learning programs (such as intensive English programs). The M-1 vocational student category is for international students studying at approved vocational schools in the United States, such as cosmetology schools, aviation schools, and computer technology institutes. The J-1 exchange visitor category has a wide range of subcategories, including professor, research scholar, short-term scholar, intern, secondary school student, college and university student, camp counselor, au pair, teacher, summer work travel, and alien physician (Bureau of Educational and Cultural Affairs 2018). Table 2 provides a summary of the nonimmigrant visa categories and related information. F-2, M-2, and J-2 categories are for the spouses and minor children who accompany or follow to join the F-1, M-1, and J-1 principal students in the United States.

The Student and Exchange Visitor Information System (SEVIS) is the U.S. Department of Homeland Security database used to collect and monitor information on F, M, and J students and exchange visitors. Institutions apply to be certified schools to host students on F and M visas. Approved schools have one principal designated school official (PDSO) and multiple designated school officials (DSOs). The PDSO and DSOs can access their students' records in SEVIS.

Colleges and universities, as well as nonprofit organizations, can apply to host J-1 exchange visitors. These organizations are referred to as "exchange visitor program sponsors." Approved sponsors have one responsible officer (RO) and multiple alternate responsible officers (AROs). The RO and AROs can access the SEVIS records of exchange visitors who are participating in their programs.

Admitted students who apply for an F or M student visa, or otherwise acquire F or M nonimmigrant status, must submit proof to the school that they have funding to cover at least their first year of tuition and living expenses. This proof is most often in the form of bank statements or sponsorship/scholarship letters. The PDSO or DSO also requests a copy of the student's passport and certain personal information. The PDSO or DSO then creates a new record in SEVIS for the admitted student. The SEVIS record includes the student's full name, date of birth, country of citizenship, country of residence, home country address, names and information of any spouse or minor children who will accompany the student to the United States, and information on sources of funding. The program information, such as educational level, major, the cost of tuition and living expenses, and program start and end dates, are also entered into SEVIS. Once all of the information is in SEVIS, the PDSO or DSO submits the information and then prints the Form I-20 Certificate of Eligibility document. The Form I-20 is signed by the PDSO or DSO before it is mailed to the international student. If the international student applies to multiple institutions, the student will receive a Form I-20 from each school that offers admission. The student signs the Form I-20 for the school that is ultimately chosen.

The Form DS-2019 Certificate of Eligibility for J nonimmigrants is the equivalent to the Form I-20 for F and M nonimmigrants. To be eligible for the J-1 exchange visitor category in the college or university student subcategory, the student must show proof of funding for the entire length of the program. J-1 college or university student funding often comes from the institution itself, the U.S. government, a foreign government, or another entity or organization.

(continued on next page)

SEVIS and Admissions (continued)

TABLE 2 U.S. Nonimmigrant Visa Categories

	U.S. NONIMMIGRANT VISA CATEGORY		
	F-1 Category: Academic Students	**M-1 Category:** Vocational Students	**J-1 Category:** Exchange Visitors
Category	N/A	N/A	College and university students
Host Organization	"School" certified by the U.S. Department of Homeland Security	"School" certified by the U.S. Department of Homeland Security	"Program sponsor" designated by the U.S. Department of State
Authorized to Access Student's SEVIS Records	Principal designated school official (PDSO)/ designated school official (DSO)	Principal designated school official (PDSO)/ designated school official (DSO)	Responsible officer (RO)/ alternate responsible officer (ARO)
Certificate of Eligibility Form	I-20	I-20	DS-2019
Funding Source	Any source	Any source	Substantially from sources other than personal or family funds, unless coming pursuant to a written agreement

A student whose support consists primarily of personal or family funds is not eligible for the J-1 college or university student subcategory unless the study is carried out pursuant to a written agreement between U.S. and foreign academic institutions, a U.S. academic institution and a foreign government, or a U.S. state or local government and a foreign government. If the student appears to be eligible to participate in the institution's J-1 exchange visitor program, the RO or ARO creates a new record in SEVIS for the student. The J-1 SEVIS record includes the student's personal information, information on sources of funding, and program information. The Form DS-2019 Certificate of Eligibility document is generated through SEVIS, printed and signed by the RO or ARO, and mailed to the exchange visitor.

In some institutional configurations, the personnel who create the initial I-20 and DS-2019 documents in SEVIS are part of the admissions office. In other cases, the admissions office refers the files of admitted students to the international student and scholar services office, and staff there create the student records in SEVIS. International education professionals such as international admissions coordinators and international student advisers may, in addition to using their job title, refer to their SEVIS role, such as DSO or ARO.

For all three visa categories, the person applying for the visa pays a SEVIS fee and visa fees and uses the Form I-20 or DS-2019 to apply for the visa to enter the United States. International students need to maintain their Form I-20 or DS-2019, and work with their PDSO/DSO or RO/ARO to keep their SEVIS record up to date throughout their stay in the United States.

International Student Retention

Retention refers to the goal of ensuring that students remain enrolled in the institution and are making progress toward their degrees. One aspect of retention efforts is to make sure that students' needs and expectations are met, regarding the quality of instruction delivered, housing options, food services, and student life (Prieto 2014; Mamiseishvili 2011). Chapter 7, "International Student and Scholar Services," explores the types of support that campuses can provide to international students.

Within the enrollment management context, retention is often assessed as a way to measure the success of recruitment efforts. It would generally be considered a waste of resources to dedicate effort and money to recruit international students only to have them return home or transfer to another institution. Retention data are often analyzed to answer questions such as: Were students recruited who were academically prepared for the program? Were expectations managed so that students knew what to expect? In general, did English proficiency exam scores correlate to students' GPA or retention? It can also be useful to analyze whether students recruited from particular countries or through particular recruitment channels were more or less successful in terms of grades earned and degree completion, as well as in relation to student satisfaction (Mamiseishvili 2011; Choudaha 2017a). This analysis helps to refine and strengthen IEM plans and inform international student services.

Considerations for International Enrollment Management

The IEM field is ever-changing, influenced by global geopolitical trends, movements in the workforce, and shifts in students' needs and interests. IEM professionals must remain cognizant of some of the risks and challenges currently facing the field, and ones that may emerge in the future, in order to better manage enrollment.

Risks

With the increasing institutional emphasis on IEM, there is also added risk. There is a risk that enrollment targets will not be met and institutions will face revenue shortfalls. Additionally, if international students are recruited from just a few countries, a geopolitical change may leave institutions vulnerable to the risk of a sudden, unanticipated decline in international student enrollments (Dunnett 2017; Kraft and Redman 2017; Barrett 2014). Barrett (2014) identifies several other categories of IEM risk:

- Strategic: failure to act in a coherent, future-oriented way.
- Environmental: failure to understand external risks.
- Structural: failure to create systemic, consistent, and comprehensive policies.

- Reputational (partners): damage to reputation and ability to control brand.

- Reputational (communication): damage related to internal and external communication.

- Program management: loss of ability to maintain robust academic and support services standards.

- Financial: damage to the institution's financial health.

Each of these areas of potential risk must be considered by IEM professionals. Staying informed about external trends, diversifying recruitment channels, nurturing partnerships, monitoring operations, and updating and adapting the strategic IEM plan can all help to mitigate the risks.

Another IEM-related risk is the possible effect on international students if institutions are overly dependent on that revenue. Will institutions emphasize quantity over quality? Will international students be exploited for the higher tuition and fees that they pay? This could happen if an institution admits underqualified students just to meet enrollment targets, or admits large numbers of students without adequate services in place for their cultural integration and academic success (Ott 2017; Dunnett 2017; Fradkin 2017).

Countermeasures to this risk are providing adequate support services to international students and making sure that marketing information about the campus and community is accurate. These two actions can help students make informed decisions about the best-fit institution. Students need to have realistic and complete information about academics, housing, campus life, financial aid, visas, health care, work opportunities, and the local community, even if some of it is not as ideal as might be desired (Ott 2017). If agents are being used to recruit students, it is essential that they have an accurate understanding of these topics and are transparent in their communications with students and families (Ott 2017). The worst-case scenario is to have an agent or staff member promise an international student something that cannot be delivered by the institution. The student may feel as though he or she has been taken advantage of and that may damage the institution's reputation and future enrollment plans.

Diversity

A growing challenge that has affected IEM, and education in general, is the tension that exists between access and exclusivity. Many of the policy goals in education, particularly public education, are focused on ensuring that individuals from all demographics of society have access to education. At the same time, institutions compete to recruit students, striving to stand out in global rankings and other markers of exclusivity (Hazelkorn 2012). Questions about diversity and access to education are not only relevant to the domestic context, but also critical in international education.

Institutions have to ask themselves if they are recruiting international students from a range of nationalities, linguistics groups, socioeconomic backgrounds, etc., and whether their answer is aligned with their organizational mission. In many cases, institutions may find that their international student recruitment targets are not as diverse as they could be.

Iverson (2017) offers some suggested steps for diversifying international student enrollments:

- Conduct self-evaluation of the institution.

- Conduct market evaluation.

- Incorporate diversity goals into internationalization and recruitment plans.

- Use virtual recruitment methods not restricted by international travel budgets.

    – Purchase contact information for SAT or TOEFL test takers in nontraditional locations and send out email campaigns.

    – Enlist the help of current students and alumni for social media or online information sessions.

    – Participate in virtual fairs.

- Travel to nontraditional locations.

- Award more scholarship funds to students from underrepresented countries.

- Reconsider admissions policies, such as simplifying requirements and eliminating application fees.

- Develop relationships with professionals in organizations that run sponsored student programs.

Iverson (2017) also recommends that when overseas, recruiters should offer information sessions on the U.S. higher education system, specific parts of the application process, or other general topics in order to draw larger audiences than an information session specifically about one institution or program.

Conclusion

As international student enrollment has become an increasingly important source of revenue for institutions, IEM has become more professionalized and sophisticated. It is now common to have specialists in marketing, recruitment, admissions, and credential evaluation on the IEM team. Strategic plans are developed, different recruitment channels are employed, and software and data analyses are utilized to measure marketing and recruiting effectiveness and to manage communications with prospective students.

However, as with the broader field of education, the questions, challenges, and concerns affecting IEM change with the times. There are questions regarding who benefits from recruitment, and how. There are the challenges of navigating the geopolitical landscape that can quickly veer enrollment numbers off course. There are also concerns that international students could be exploited, misinformed, or unsupported once enrolled. Professional organizations in international education offer resources, training, and codes of ethics to mitigate these risks so that campuses can benefit from a rich mix of students from a wide range of countries and backgrounds.

Resources

READINGS:

- Di Maria, David L., ed. 2017. *Managing a Successful International Admissions Office*. Washington, DC: NAFSA: Association of International Educators.

- Sandberg, Jessica Black, ed. 2017. *NAFSA's Guide to International Student Recruitment, Third Edition.* Washington, DC: NAFSA: Association of International Educators.

CODES OF ETHICS:

- Council of International Schools's *Guiding Principles for Higher Education* www.cois.org/colleges-and-universities/guiding-principles-for-higher-education

- NAFSA: Association of International Educators's *Statement of Ethical Principles* www.nafsa.org/About_Us/About_NAFSA/Leadership_and_Governance/NAFSA_s_Statement_of_Ethical_Principles/

- National Association for College Admissions Counseling's *Code of Ethics and Professional Practices* www.nacacnet.org/advocacy--ethics/NACAC-Code-of-Ethics/

ASSOCIATIONS:

- American Association of Collegiate Registrars and Admissions Officers (AACRAO) www.aacrao.org/

- International Association for College Admission Counseling www.internationalacac.org/

- NAFSA International Enrollment Management Resources www.nafsa.org/professional-resources/browse-by-interest/international-enrollment-management

CREDENTIAL EVALUATION RESOURCES:

- AACRAO Electronic Database for Global Education (AACRAO Edge) www.aacrao.org/resources/AACRAO-International/about-edge

- AACRAO *Guide to Bogus Institutions and Documents* www4.aacrao.org/publications/catalog.php?item=4008

- ENIC-NARIC Country Profiles and Tools www.enic-naric.net/index.aspx

- NAFSA Admissions and Credential Evaluation Network www.nafsa.org/Connect_and_Network/Networking_with_NAFSA/Professional_Networks/IEM_KC/International_Enrollment_Management_Knowledge_Community/

- NAFSA's Guide to Educational Systems Around the World www.nafsa.org/GES

- World Higher Education Database www.whed.net

References

Adams, Tony, Mitch Leventhal, and Stephen Connelly. 2012. "International Student Recruitment in Australia and the United States: Approaches and Attitudes." In *The SAGE Handbook of International Higher Education*, eds. Deardorff, Darla K., Hans de Wit, John D. Heyl, and Tony Adams. Thousand Oaks, CA: Sage Publications.

American International Recruitment Council (AIRC). n.d. "About AIRC." Bethesda, MD: American International Recruitment Council. https://www.airc-education.org/about-airc.

Baker, Peter. 2017. "Bridge and Pathway Programs." In *Managing A Successful International Admissions Office*, ed. David L. Di Maria. Washington, DC: NAFSA: Association of International Educators.

Barrett, Pamela Kay. 2014. "A Strategic Approach to Risk in International Enrollment Management." In *International Enrollment Management Strategic Planning: An Integrated Approach*, ed. Julie Sinclair. Washington, DC: NAFSA: Association of International Educators.

Beatty, Matthew R. 2014. "Creating an IEM Recruitment and Retention Plan." In *International Enrollment Management Strategic Planning: An Integrated Approach*, ed. Julie Sinclair. Washington, DC: NAFSA: Association of International Educators.

Becker, Rosa, and Renze Kolster. 2012. *International Student Recruitment: Policies and Developments in Selected Countries*. The Hague, Netherlands: Netherlands Organization for International Cooperation in Higher Education.

Bodycott, Peter. 2009. "Choosing a Higher Education Study Abroad Destination." *Journal of Research in International Education* 8, 3:349–374.

Boutsis, Stavroula. 2017. "International Recruitment Travel." In *NAFSA's Guide to International Student Recruitment, Third Edition*, ed. Jessica Black Sandberg. Washington, DC: NAFSA: Association of International Educators.

Bridge Education Group. 2016. *Pace of Adoption of International Student Recruitment Agencies by U.S. Institutions*. Denver, CO: Bridge Education Group, Inc. https://www.bridge.edu/assets/bridge-edu.pdf.

British Council. 2017. *10 Trends: Transformative Changes in Higher Education*. British Council.

Brown, Blair. 2017. "International Admissions: Financing Higher Education." In *Managing a Successful International Admissions Office*, ed. David L. Di Maria. Washington, DC: NAFSA: Association of International Educators.

Bureau of Educational and Cultural Affairs. 2018. "J-1 Visa Exchange Visitor Program." Washington, DC: Department of State Bureau of Educational and Cultural Affairs. https://j1visa.state.gov/wp-content/uploads/2018/03/J1VIsa-fact-sheet-2018.pdf.

Campbell, Anne C. 2018. "'Giving Back' to One's Country Following an International Higher Education Scholarship: Comparing In-Country and Expatriate Alumni Perceptions of Engagement in Social and Economic Change in Moldova." *Compare: A Journal of Comparative and International Education*, 1–19. https://doi.org/10.1080/03057925.2018.1540925.

Choudaha, Rahul. 2017a. "Assessing Return on Investment in International Student Recruitment." In *NAFSA's Guide to International Student Recruitment, Third Edition*, ed. Jessica Black Sandberg. Washington, DC: NAFSA: Association of International Educators.

Choudaha, Rahul. 2017b. *Landscape of Third-Party Pathway Partnerships in the United States*. Washington, DC: NAFSA: Association of International Educators.

Choudaha, Rahul, Li Chang, and Yoko Kono. 2014. "International Student Mobility Trends 2013: Towards Responsive Recruitment Strategies." SSRN Scholarly Paper ID 2275946. Rochester, NY: Social Science Research Network. https://papers.ssrn.com/abstract=2275946.

Crawley, Jim. 2017. "Recruiting via Conditional Admission and Pathway Programs." In *NAFSA's Guide to International Student Recruitment, Third Edition*, ed. Jessica Black Sandberg. Washington, DC: NAFSA: Association of International Educators.

Di Maria, David L. 2017. "Developing Human Resource Capacity for International Recruitment." In *NAFSA's Guide to International Student Recruitment, Third Edition*, ed. Jessica Black Sandberg. Washington, DC: NAFSA: Association of International Educators.

Dunnett, Stephen C. 2017. "A History of International Recruitment in U.S. Higher Education." In *NAFSA's Guide to International Student Recruitment, Third Edition*, ed. Jessica Black Sandberg. Washington, DC: NAFSA: Association of International Educators.

Elliot, William. 2017. "International Recruitment for Graduate Programs." In *NAFSA's Guide to International Student Recruitment, Third Edition*, ed. Jessica Black Sandberg. Washington, DC: NAFSA: Association of International Educators.

Farrugia, Christine A. 2014. *Charting New Pathways to Higher Education: International Secondary Students in the United States*. New York, NY: Institute of International Education.

Fradkin, Marci. 2017. "Making the Case for International Recruitment at Community Colleges." In *NAFSA's Guide to International Student Recruitment, Third Edition*, ed. Jessica Black Sandberg. Washington, DC: NAFSA: Association of International Educators.

Ghandi, Miloni. 2014. "Implementing an IEM Strategic Plan." In *International Enrollment Management Strategic Planning: An Integrated Approach*, ed. Julie Sinclair. Washington, DC: NAFSA: Association of International Educators.

Hansen, Mandy. 2016. "Best Practices for Projecting International Enrollment." *NAFSA IEM Spotlight Newsletter* 13, 3:1–5. Washington, DC: NAFSA: Association of International Educators. https://www.nafsa.org/professional-resources/browse-by-interest/best-practices-projecting-international-enrollment.

Hansen, Mandy. 2017. "International Undergraduate Admissions Issues." In *Managing A Successful International Admissions Office*, ed. David L. Di Maria. Washington, DC: NAFSA: Association of International Educators.

Hawthorne, Lesleyanne. 2010. "How Valuable Is 'Two-Step Migration'? Labor Market Outcomes for International Student Migrants to Australia." *Asian and Pacific Migration Journal* 19, 1:5–36. https://doi.org/10.1177/011719681001900102.

Hazelkorn, Ellen. 2012. "The Effects of Rankings on Student Choices and Institutional Selection." In *Access and Expansion Post-Massification: Opportunities and Barriers to Further Growth in Higher Education Participation*, eds. Benjamin W. A. Jongbloed and Johan J. Vossensteyn. London, United Kingdom: Routledge.

Heaney, Linda, and Panetha Theodosia Nychis Ott. 2009. "Ethics in International Student Recruitment." In *NAFSA's Guide to International Student Recruitment, Second Edition*, ed. Linda Heaney. Washington, DC: NAFSA: Association of International Educators.

Helms, Robin Matross, and Lucia Brajkovic. 2017. *Mapping Internationalization on U.S. Campuses: 2017 Edition*. Washington, DC: American Council on Education. https://www.acenet.edu/news-room/Documents/Mapping-Internationalization-2017.pdf.

Hovland, Kevin, Joann Ng Hartmann, and Sheila Schulte. 2017. "Foreword." In *Landscape of Third-Party Pathway Partnerships in the United States*, by Rahul Choudaha. Washington, DC: NAFSA: Association of International Educators.

Hulstrand, Janet. 2009. "International Students at Community Colleges." *International Educator* XXVIII, 3:94–98.

ICEF. n.d. "ICEF Agents." ICEF. http://www.icef.com/icef-agents/.

Institute of International Education. 2018a. *Open Door Report on International Education Exchange*. Institute of International Education. http://www.iie.org/opendoors.

Institute of International Education. 2018b. "Project Atlas 2018 Infographics." Institute of International Education. https://www.iie.org/en/Research-and-Insights/Project-Atlas/Explore-Data/Current-Infographics.

Iverson, Ben. 2017. "Exploring Diversity Beyond the Big 3: China, India, and South Korea." In *NAFSA's Guide to International Student Recruitment, Third Edition*, ed. Jessica Black Sandberg. Washington, DC: NAFSA: Association of International Educators.

James-MacEachern, Melissa. 2018. "A Comparative Study of International Recruitment – Tensions and Opportunities in Institutional Recruitment Practice." *Journal of Marketing for Higher Education* 28, 2:1–19. https://doi.org/10.1080/08841241.2018.1471014.

Kacenga, George. 2019. "On the Rise: State Consortia." *International Educator* XXVIII, 1:40–43.

Kraft, Lisa, and Nadia Redman. 2017. "Recruitment Strategies for Intensive English Programs." In *NAFSA's Guide to International Student Recruitment, Third Edition*, ed. Jessica Black Sandberg. Washington, DC: NAFSA: Association of International Educators.

Mamiseishvili, Ketevan. 2011. "International Student Persistence in U.S. Postsecondary Institutions." *Higher Education* 64, 1:1–17.

Mazzarol, Tim, and Geoffrey N. Soutar. 2002. "'Push–Pull' Factors Influencing International Student Destination Choice." *International Journal of Educational Management* 16, 2:82–90. https://doi.org/10.1108/09513540210418403.

Morawski, Aleksander. 2017. "Foreign Credit Evaluation." In *Managing a Successful International Admissions Office*, ed. David L. Di Maria. NAFSA: Association of International Educators.

NAFSA: Association of International Educators. 2015. *NAFSA International Education Professional Competencies*. Washington, DC: NAFSA: Association of International Educators.

NAFSA: Association of International Educators. 2018a. "Benefits from International Students: The United States." Washington, DC: NAFSA: Association of International Educators. https://www.nafsa.org/policy-and-advocacy/policy-resources/nafsa-international-student-economic-value-tool.

NAFSA: Association of International Educators. 2018b. "International Student Recruitment: Methods and Strategies." Washington, DC: NAFSA: Association of International Educators.

Organisation for Economic Co-operation and Development. 2018. *Education at a Glance 2018: OECD Indicators*. Paris, France: Organisation for Economic Co-operation and Development. https://read.oecd-ilibrary.org/education/education-at-a-glance-2018_eag-2018-en#page3.

Ott, Panetha Theodosia Nychis. 2017. "Ethics in International Student Recruitment." In *NAFSA's Guide to International Student Recruitment, Third Edition*, ed. Jessica Black Sandberg. Washington, DC: NAFSA: Association of International Educators.

Ozturgut, Osman. 2013. "Best Practices in Recruiting and Retaining International Students in the U.S." *Current Issues in Education* 16, 2:1–22.

Prieto, Eduardo. 2014. "Inserting IEM into the Institution." In *International Enrollment Management Strategic Planning: An Integrated Approach*, ed. Julie Sinclair. Washington, DC: NAFSA: Association of International Educators.

Punteney, Katherine, and Yilin Wei. 2018. "Dynamics of Internationalization in U.S. and Chinese Higher Education." In *The Rise of China-U.S. International Cooperation in Higher Education: Views from the Field*, eds. Christopher J. Johnstone and Li Li Ji. Leiden, The Netherlands: Brill Sense.

Riley, Linda. 2017. "Building Foreign Educational Credential Evaluation Expertise." In *NAFSA's Guide to International Student Recruitment, Third Edition*, ed. Jessica Black Sandberg. Washington, DC: NAFSA: Association of International Educators.

Sandberg, Jessica Black. 2017. "Recruiting International Students at U.S. High Schools." In *NAFSA's Guide to International Student Recruitment, Third Edition*, ed. Jessica Black Sandberg. Washington, DC: NAFSA: Association of International Educators.

Schmiegel, Gabriele. 2017. "It Takes a Village: Recruiting, Enrolling, and Supporting Sponsored Students at Your Institution." In *NAFSA's Guide to International Student Recruitment, Third Edition*, ed. Jessica Black Sandberg. Washington, DC: NAFSA: Association of International Educators.

Scoby, Stephanie. 2017. "Partnering with Agents." In *NAFSA's Guide to International Student Recruitment, Third Edition*, ed. Jessica Black Sandberg. Washington, DC: NAFSA: Association of International Educators.

Sinclair, Julie. 2010. *International Enrollment Management: Framing the Conversation*. Washington, DC: NAFSA: Association of International Educators.

Sinclair, Julie, and Patty Croom. 2017. "Creating an International Recruitment Plan." In *NAFSA's Guide to International Student Recruitment, Third Edition*, ed. Jessica Black Sandberg. Washington, DC: NAFSA: Association of International Educators.

Smith, Marjorie S. 2017. "Recruitment Fairs." In *NAFSA's Guide to International Student Recruitment, Third Edition*, ed. Jessica Black Sandberg. Washington, DC: NAFSA: Association of International Educators.

Student and Exchange Visitor Program. 2018. *SEVIS By the Numbers: Biannual Report on International Student Trends*. Washington, DC: U.S. Department of Homeland Security.

Study California. 2019. "About." 2019. Study California. http://studycalifornia.us/about/.

U.S. Department of Commerce. 2018. "Global Education and Training Services Team." Washington, DC: U.S. Department of Commerce. https://2016.export.gov/industry/education/.

U.S. Department of State. n.d. "About EducationUSA." Washington, DC: United States Department of State EducationUSA. https://educationusa.state.gov/about-educationusa.

Waxman, Ben, and Cathryn Andrews. 2017. "Effective Marketing Practices for International Student Recruitment: Simplifying the Complexity of Academic Global Branding." In

NAFSA's Guide to International Student Recruitment, Third Edition, ed. Jessica Black Sandberg. Washington, DC: NAFSA: Association of International Educators.

Zdawczyk, Aaron. 2017. "Alumni Involvement in International Recruitment Initiatives." In *NAFSA's Guide to International Student Recruitment, Third Edition*, ed. Jessica Black Sandberg. Washington, DC: NAFSA: Association of International Educators.

Chapter 7

International Student and Scholar Services

While international students have been studying in the United States in sizable numbers since the mid-1800s (Bevis and Lucas 2007), enrollment has risen rapidly in recent decades. In 1950, there were just over 25,000 international students studying in the United States; today, there are more than 1 million (Glass, Wongtrirat, and Buus 2015; Institute of International Education 2018). This growth reflects both the global increase in the number of students pursuing higher education outside of their home country and the efforts that U.S. colleges and universities are making to recruit international students as part of their enrollment management and internationalization plans. In fact, international students now constitute 5.5 percent of all U.S. higher education enrollment (Institute of International Education 2018).

In addition to students, higher education institutions often host international professors, researchers, postdocs, and other scholars. The Institute of International Education (IIE)'s *Open Doors* report shows that 134,379 scholars traveling on temporary nonimmigrant visas were hosted by U.S. colleges and universities for the 2016–17 academic year (IIE 2018).

Working or studying in a foreign country, and often in a foreign language, is not an easy endeavor. In making the choice to live in the United States, particularly for programs that may take years to complete, international students and scholars display dedication, ambition, talent, and a sense of adventure. They utilize these strengths to adapt to the differences they will encounter in many spheres: academic, cultural, linguistic, and logistical, among others. Having invited and admitted the international students and scholars to campus, it is the ethical responsibility of higher education institutions to provide resources to support them in achieving academic and professional success (Akanwa 2015; Glass, Wongtrirat, and Buus 2015; Shapiro, Farrelly, and Tomaš 2018; Mamiseishvili 2011). The responsibility of supporting international students and scholars is shared across institutions. The support services are often coordinated by international educators working in the international education field, typically in an office dedicated to international student and scholar services (ISSS).

In its exploration of the ISSS field, this chapter focuses on international students and scholars studying at U.S. colleges and universities on nonimmigrant visas (specifically F-1, J-1, and M-1, see chapter 6 for more information). It should be noted that some ISSS offices provide support for other groups as well. They may include undocumented students, permanent residents who are recent immigrants, faculty and staff on H1-B specialty worker visas, and others. While students and scholars on nonimmigrant visas are the focus of this chapter, the discussions of cultural adjustment, advising, and programming may be applicable to these other groups as well.

This chapter introduces areas of cultural differences that often affect international students and scholars and describes the acculturation process that many experience. The chapter examines the role of ISSS professionals in providing support through advising, several essential advising topics and approaches, as well as support programs that can be offered. Select immigration regulations affecting international students and scholars are also introduced. Finally, considerations for practitioners are explored.

Benefits of Hosting International Students and Scholars

Recruiting international students and scholars is a prominent strategy in most campus internationalization plans. International scholars can bring a global perspective to their classrooms and research (Theobald 2013). Hosting international students can help all students to develop their global competence through the richness of cross-cultural dialogue both within and beyond the classroom. Though Knight (2011) cautions that the mere presence of international students on campus does not automatically result in intercultural competence for all, there is evidence that this benefit may be experienced by some students.

For those domestic students who frequently interact with international students, research has shown that they are more likely to seriously reflect on their own beliefs about politics, religion, and people with ethnicities or sexual orientations different from their own (Luo and Jamieson-Drake 2013). Domestic students who interact frequently with international students have been reported to have higher skill levels in speaking foreign languages, formulating creative solutions, synthesizing ideas and information, understanding the role of science and technology, developing quantitative skills, and utilizing computer skills (Luo and Jamieson-Drake 2013). While this evidence does not suggest that the mere presence of international students automatically leads to these benefits for domestic students, it does suggest that campuses have an opportunity to intentionally cultivate structures and opportunities for meaningful cross-cultural interactions that may benefit both international and domestic students.

Adjustments to the United States

As is true for anyone who moves to a new country, international students and scholars generally face a sometimes lengthy and complex process of adjustment. They must adjust to the U.S. academic system, social and cultural norms, and the structures of daily living. This section introduces a few of the many areas that may require adjustment on the part of international students and scholars. These topics are much more complex than can be fully addressed here. Resources for further exploration of these topics are listed at the end of the chapter.

Academic Norms

Academic cultures typically reflect the dominant values of a society. International students and scholars may find that expectations surrounding learning, teaching, and student-professor relationships are significantly different compared with the norms of their home country. For example, a significant structural difference found between U.S. higher education and many other countries' educational systems is the amount of decisionmaking power that students hold in the academic setting. Students in the United States have many options when selecting a college, choosing (and changing) a major, identifying courses to take, and even picking assignment topics; this is in contrast to many other educational systems in which admissions is more correlated with test scores and curricula are more prescribed (Nathan 2006; Shapiro, Farrelly, and Tomaš 2018). Furthermore, the U.S. educational structure requires general education coursework (taking a sampling of courses from a range of fields) even in higher education, which is surprising to many international students whose home educational systems may end general education with the completion of secondary school, expecting higher education students to focus solely on the study of their specific discipline (Althen and Bennett 2011).

Academic Expectations

Classroom environments and teaching methods vary culturally. In some countries, strong emphasis is placed on learning from specialists, such as published experts and course professors. In this setting, students might be expected to read the material, listen to lectures, and demonstrate their learning through memorization and recitation (Althen and Bennett 2011; Shapiro, Farrelly, and Tomaš 2018). By contrast, in the United States, there is a common belief that much potential knowledge is not yet known. Education thus focuses on experimentation, analysis, creativity, and questioning. Students are encouraged, and often required, to contribute their own perspectives and opinions to expert knowledge; in this way, U.S. education tends to be more active than receptive (Shapiro, Farrelly, and Tomaš 2018; Althen and Bennett 2011; Lipson 2008). Learning in the United States is generally considered to be most worthwhile if it is practical and can be applied professionally (Althen and Bennett 2011).

Another key value in U.S. academic writing, and speaking, is the importance of extensive and careful citation. As an individualistic society, there is a belief in the United States that ideas and words are the intellectual property of individuals. Accordingly, failing to cite ideas or data is considered "theft" of someone else's property and has serious consequences (Shapiro, Farrelly, and Tomaš 2018; Lipson 2008). This is in contrast to cultures that are more collectivist and expect students to build their arguments based on the ideas of experts; in this case, plagiarism or the lack of citations might be considered sloppy, but not an egregious wrong. International students and scholars may need explicit information on U.S. expectations of academic honesty in order to avoid any pitfalls (Shapiro, Farrelly, and Tomaš 2018).

Classroom Behaviors and Expectations

International students and scholars may be surprised about aspects of what they observe in terms of classroom behaviors and student-teacher interactions. International students sometimes remark with disbelief that U.S. students eat, drink, sleep, put their feet up, and even wear pajamas in class (Nathan 2006). International students also report that, in general, U.S. faculty are friendly, approachable, and interested in helping students; they often note that the interactions between students and professors seem informal and egalitarian (Nathan 2006; Shapiro, Farrelly, and Tomaš 2018). The challenge is that there are cultural differences in how respect is signaled; while international students may perceive U.S. students to be interacting with U.S. professors as peers, international students may not observe some of the more nuanced differences in what words are used with the professor, which nonacademic topics can be discussed, tone, etc. (Shapiro, Farrelly, and Tomaš 2018).

There are also differences regarding communication styles and expectations. Communication in the United States is usually fairly direct, and arguments tend to be linear. When writing or giving a presentation, it is expected that the main point will be stated very quickly, evidence and support will be offered, and then the main point will be repeated. By contrast, in some other cultures, a persuasive argument is made by gradually building up to the main point. Unfortunately, this difference in communication styles can lead some U.S. instructors to think that international students' assignments are illogical or disorganized (Shapiro, Farrelly, and Tomaš 2018).

Other key differences in academic culture relate to assignments and grading. International students are sometimes surprised to find that U.S. classes have frequent assignments, including, potentially, small homework assignments and credit for required class attendance and participation (Shapiro, Farrelly, and Tomaš 2018; Lipson 2008). International students may not recognize the importance of the course syllabus, which serves as a sort of contract between students and professors in the U.S. academic system (Nathan 2006). International students may also be taken aback by the amount of group work assigned to them and the notion that the group members may earn the same grade even if they do not contribute equally to the assignment (Nathan 2006). Finally, international students and scholars may be astonished to find that it is common for students to evaluate their professors through course evaluations, which reflects the U.S. emphasis on choice and personal expression (Nathan 2006).

Similar to international students, visiting scholars who teach at U.S. colleges and universities may face a language barrier if English is not their native language. Beyond language, there are some cultural adjustments that international scholars must manage, including learning the cultural norms of the classroom and how to navigate university politics, academic governance, promotion systems, and more (Yudkevich, Altbach, and Rumbley 2017; Foote 2013).

Social and Cultural Norms

International students and scholars must also adapt to a broad range of differences related to social and cultural values and behaviors. These beliefs and customs affect all facets of life, including work life, job searches, friendships, dating, family life, recreation, political engagement, hygiene, health care, driving, shopping, and more (Althen and Bennett 2011). Social norms also guide the nuances of every interaction, including verbal and nonverbal communication presented through gestures, facial expressions, word choice, tone, and posture. Social norms help individuals to know when to be serious or lighthearted, when and how it is appropriate to interrupt, which greetings are appropriate, how to proceed in interactions between supervisors and employees, what time to arrive at an event, how to accept or refuse invitations, when and how to give gifts, how to offer and accept compliments, and myriad other areas that affect interpersonal dynamics (Gebhard 2010).

The boundlessness of the list of cultural norms that an individual needs to learn in a new country can be overwhelming. With potential language and cultural barriers, students and scholars may find that they are unable to express their personalities as they would in their home country, for example as a leader, or humorous, or nurturing (Young and Althen 2013). Being unable to feel fully like oneself can be unsettling and further impact the transitional experience.

Friendships

One area that many international students and scholars find difficult in the United States is making friends. Research shows that more than one-third of international students have no close U.S. friends, and other students may report having only one or two U.S. friends (Gareis 2012). While not the case for every student, many international students report dissatisfaction with the number and depth of their friendships with U.S. students. International students frequently observe that U.S. people show relatively little interest in international students' home culture, and may even have a general ignorance about life outside the United States (Gareis 2012; Nathan 2006).

The process of building friendships can be frustrating. In particular, many international students express surprise and hurt that casual invitations such as "We should get lunch sometime" are not often followed by concrete invitations and, further, that coffees and other informal meetings do not consistently lead to deeper friendships (Glass, Wongtrirat, and Buus 2015; Gareis 2012). International students and scholars often observe that U.S. people ask "How are you?" without waiting for an answer, which can feel uncaring to the international individual (Nathan 2006). International students and scholars may also be surprised by the degree to which friendships are compartmentalized in the United States; for example, roommates may be strictly roommates, without being friends. While not true in every situation, it is common for adults not to know their friends' families. U.S. people may have work friends, school friends, workout friends, families, and other groups of friends, without much overlap between groups. For some international students and scholars, this is very surprising (Nathan 2006).

Many international students find that they develop the deepest friendships and support networks among other international students (Glass, Wongtrirat, and Buus 2015). Some of the most effective strategies for making friends include joining student organizations, participating in on- and off-campus events, finding employment, and volunteering (Jean-Francois 2017). Each of these provides a structure for repeated interaction with the same people, allowing friendships an opportunity to grow. Being away from their normal support system of friends and family, some international students and scholars may struggle with loneliness, isolation, and depression if they are unable to develop friendships in the United States (Glass, Wongtrirat, and Buus 2015).

Physical and Logistical Challenges

While academic and sociocultural challenges can be complex, the toll of adapting to a new physical environment should not be underestimated. International students and scholars have to get used to new weather patterns, sights, sounds, and smells, which can affect physical comfort and sleep. Many international students who live in residence halls struggle with the food choices available in dining halls, finding that the foods might upset their stomachs or simply not bring them the comfort that their native foods bring (Ammigan and Jones 2018; Gebhard 2010; Young and Althen 2013). Students and scholars may not be able to find the ingredients they need to cook the foods they want. Additionally, medicines and home remedies that they are used to may not be available in the United States.

Other physical and logistical challenges include knowing where to go to buy particular items, knowing the legalities and expectations of renting an apartment or house, and figuring out transportation options. International students and scholars are not eligible for social security numbers unless they are employed, so they often arrive needing to set up phone service, bank accounts, utilities, and similar services, but may encounter roadblocks because they do not have a social security number or a credit history. Obtaining a phone and perhaps a driver's license will often be early priorities. Throughout their stay, and particularly at the beginning, international students and scholars will have many questions about how and where to buy goods and access services. While they may have individuals around them who are able to help, the ISSS office can also be instrumental in providing support and guidance.

Acculturation Process

Acculturation is the process of questioning and letting go of some aspects of one's own culture and gradually adopting elements of another culture. Kim (2001) refers to individuals who have traveled to a new culture metaphorically as "strangers." She describes the process of acculturation:

> Encounters with a new culture bring many surprises, large and small. Some of the surprises may awaken or shake strangers' previously taken-for-granted self-concepts and collective ethnic identity and bring the anxiety of temporary rootlessness. Strangers in a new environment are confronted with situations in which their mental and behavioral habits are called into question, and they are forced to suspend or even abandon their identification with the cultural patterns that have symbolized who they are and what they are. Such inner conflicts, in turn, make individuals susceptible to external influence and compel them to learn the new cultural system. This activity of learning is the very essence of *acculturation.* (Kim 2001, 50)

Figure 1 illustrates Kim's acculturation model. The model shows that an individual starts out (in Time 1) with characteristics of his or her home culture. After traveling to a new culture, the individual starts to adopt a few of the beliefs, behaviors, and values of the host culture (Time 2). Over time, if the individual remains in the host culture, he or she increasingly adopts more and more of the beliefs, behaviors, and values of the host culture, while always maintaining some elements of the original culture (Time 3).

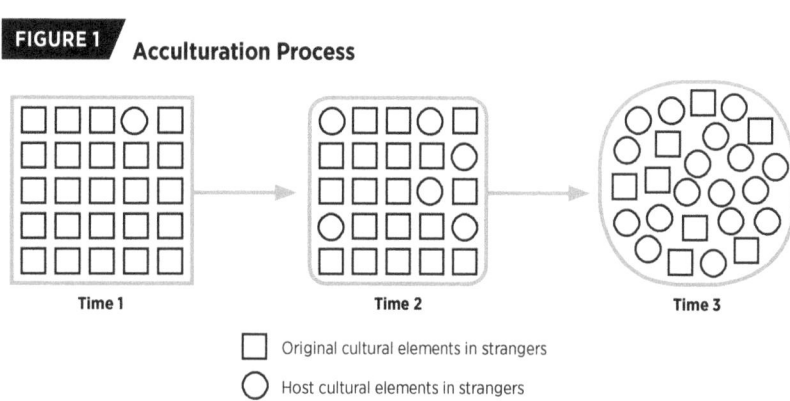

FIGURE 1 Acculturation Process

☐ Original cultural elements in strangers
○ Host cultural elements in strangers

Source: Republished with permission of Kim (2001); permission conveyed through Copyright Clearance Center, Inc.

Kim (2001) acknowledges that the acculturation process looks different based on both the personality traits of the individual and the circumstances of traveling to another culture. The length of time that an individual is away and the motivation for going also affect the acculturation process. A refugee and a student studying abroad may have very different experiences in part due to the differences in reasons for transitioning across cultures and the length of stay. Kim (2001) suggests that some individuals resist the acculturation process by trying to cling to their home cultural elements and avoiding adapting to the local culture, perhaps by isolating themselves from host culture nationals to the extent possible. This is both stressful and ineffective. Another way that individuals may unknowingly resist is by "going native" and trying to fully adopt the host culture characteristics. This denial of the culture of origin is bound to fail and create pain for the individual. Those individuals who are self-reflective, open to the process, and active in observing similarities and differences between the home and host cultures will generally move through the transition more effectively.

Tran and Vu (2017) point out that international students may feel varied degrees of responsibility to their home and host cultures. They may feel a need to accurately and respectfully represent their home country. At the same time, they may feel a pressure, internal or external, to conform to the expectations of the host country and an obligation to blend into the host country and adhere to the host cultural expectations. International students may even feel a responsibility to assist other international students in trying to have authentic, respectful interactions with host country people. International students may hold some or all of these intentions to varying degrees, depending on the individual student (Tran and Vu 2017).

Support Services

Universities have a responsibility to international students and scholars to ensure that they are integrated into the campus community and that they receive the support they need to be able to succeed in their academic and professional goals. While much of the coordination for this work is done by the ISSS office, it is the shared responsibility of the whole institution. Each unit of the university should assess its programs and services to determine how well it serves diverse campus groups, including international students and scholars.

ISSS professionals should ensure that all of their work enhances learning, supports achievement, and deepens the cross-cultural experience of the international members of the campus community. They should strive to make campus internationalization efforts function in ways that result in international visitors being integral to campus life—though that is easier said than done (Glass, Wongtrirat, and Buus 2015). Initiatives to support international students and scholars may be divided into two categories: advising and programming. Advising refers to support provided to individuals, most often in one-on-one, face-to-face meetings. Programming refers to initiatives that provide support for groups of students and scholars, and their family members. These may take the form of workshops, courses, events, programs, etc. Beyond advising and programming, ISSS offices also provide information on campus and community resources. This section of the chapter introduces ISSS advising, followed by some effective advising approaches.

Advising

Individual advising is a critical component of the work performed by ISSS offices. In these one-on-one advising sessions, an international educator meets with a student or scholar to discuss the specifics of the person's situation. The topics of advising meetings are likely to fall into one or more of these categories: logistics, academics, careers, personal issues, or immigration regulations, all of which are discussed below. Throughout this section, the international educator who meets with the student or scholar is referred to as an "adviser," though, as explored later in the chapter, professionals with a variety of job titles may engage in this work.

Logistics Advising

Logistical conversations often involve the student or scholar asking the adviser for information on a campus or community process, such as how to apply for a driver's license, where to find a dentist, or what the process is for changing a major. These tend to be relatively transactional conversations, focused on the exchange of information. The adviser will either be able to answer the questions or will direct the student or scholar to an appropriate location to find an answer. Occasionally, the adviser may have to research the question and get back in touch with the student or scholar, rather than answering immediately.

Academic Advising

Academic advising is primarily for students. It focuses on course selection and ensuring that the student is on track to meet graduation requirements, as well as conversations related to the skills and habits needed for academic success. In some institutional structures, staff in the ISSS office might be tasked with providing the academic advising for international students, which would involve meeting with the students to discuss their academic and career interests, helping them to select courses, and explaining academic policies related to satisfactory grades, general education requirements, etc. In most cases, however, academic advising is the responsibility of an academic advising office at a college or a university. ISSS advisers may collaborate with the academic advising office or provide a second layer of academic advising support for international students.

It is common for ISSS advisers to meet with students who are struggling in their classes. The advising sessions may arise from a range of prompts: at the student's request, because a faculty member alerted the adviser that the student seemed to be struggling, following an adviser asking a student how classes are going, or because a student earned unsatisfactory grades and the adviser requested a meeting. The ISSS adviser may talk with the student about support services available on campus, such as faculty office hours and writing or tutoring centers. The adviser may discuss cultural differences related to class discussion, student-instructor relationships, how arguments are made in written papers, etc. If needed, the ISSS adviser may also discuss campus policies for dropping courses, maintaining a satisfactory GPA, etc.

Depending on how the conversation unfolds, the adviser might also segue the discussion into the connections between enrollment and immigration regulations, or into personal topics such as mental health support. In many cases, the adviser will introduce these topics and also make a referral to another campus office such as academic advising or the counseling center.

Career Advising

Career advising may be closely linked with academic advising. Discussion of majors and courses to take may relate directly to students' career goals and plans for future degrees. Scholars such as visiting professors and postdoc researchers may also seek career advising as they are considering their next career opportunity. While much of the career advising is done by staff in the campus career center, ISSS professionals may also engage students and scholars in discussions of their career interests and goals, resources available, and cultural norms regarding résumés, cover letters, networking, interviewing, and salary negotiations in the United States.

Personal Advising

Personal advising can focus on any range of personal issues that international students and scholars find challenging. These could be related to adjustments to the culture, homesickness, roommate problems, or difficult relations with an instructor or peers. Advisers often find that students and scholars will want to talk when something is going on at home with their family. For example, the death of a relative can result in both loneliness and guilt at being away. Some students and scholars have left their spouse and children at home and struggle with the distance. Others bring their spouse and children to the United States and find it difficult to offer logistical and practical support to their family members while they themselves are overwhelmed with the cultural transition. Students and scholars may seek out ISSS advisers for guidance on a cross-cultural topic that has them confused. Advisers can provide support by listening, by directing them to information, by helping them to choose a path of action, and by making referrals to campus departments and community organizations that can offer additional support.

Being away from the comfort and familiarity of their normal support networks of family and friends, some international students and scholars may find that mental health issues arise or are exacerbated. These may be previously diagnosed issues that flare up in a stressful period, or undiagnosed issues that the individuals are unaware of. ISSS advisers will find that some of the international student and scholar population, like the domestic student and scholar population, struggle with issues such as depression, anxiety, mood disorders, eating disorders, etc. Advisers can create an environment in which individuals feel comfortable sharing and are supported. It is important to note that in some countries, seeking help or counseling may have some negative stigmas attached; advisers should commend the student or scholar for putting his or her health first. Additionally, advisers will need to recognize when the issue goes beyond their professional scope and should be referred to appropriate professionals.

Immigration Advising

Immigration advising is one of the primary responsibilities of ISSS offices and, often, the focus of much of an ISSS adviser's workload. U.S. immigration regulations are complex and govern the type of activities that an international student or scholar can undertake in the United States. These federal regulations relate to length of stay in the United States, course enrollment, employment restrictions, information that must be reported to the government, transfer process to a new institution, changes to a new immigration status, and more.

Failure to abide by the regulations can have serious ramifications for an international student or scholar. Even unintentional violations of the regulations may prevent students and scholars from continuing or extending their stay in the United States, from visiting the United States in the future, or from future U.S. employment. ISSS advisers often meet with students and scholars to explain the regulations and answer questions, helping students to complete application paperwork for employment authorization or changes in immigration status. While students and scholars are ultimately responsible for complying with the regulations, receiving correct, clear, and timely information from advisers is essential. ISSS advisers are also responsible for ensuring that their institution remains compliant with immigration regulations and continues to be able to enroll and host international students and scholars. This process requires making timely updates to the Student and Exchange Visitor Information System (SEVIS) (see chapter 6).

International Student Immigration Regulations

Colleges and universities in the United States are granted authorization to admit international students by the Department of Homeland Security and Department of State. The students and the institutions are required to comply with rules detailed in the U.S. Code of Federal Regulations. The immigration regulations are lengthy and complicated. This section offers a brief introduction to a few areas of the regulations that apply to international students on F-1, M-1, and J-1 visas at the college or university level. (For more information on the visa categories, see chapter 6.) However, the specifics of each situation vary from student to student, from visa type to visa type, and from institution to institution, so it is essential that individual students always consult with an ISSS professional. NAFSA: Association of International Educators offers detailed instruction and resources to ensure that advisers have up-to-

(continued on next page)

International Student Immigration Regulations *(continued)*

date knowledge of the regulations (see resources at the end of this chapter).

Duration of Status

Duration of status is an important concept in international student regulations. When international visitors in other visa categories are given permission to enter the United States, a date is written in their passport and on their entry documents that says by what date they must depart the United States. International students instead have the notation "D/S" written on their documents, which represents "duration of status." Duration of status means that an international student can legally remain in the United States as long as the individual is abiding by the regulations governing his or her status.

Full-Time Enrollment

International students, and all visitors, are expected to pursue the purposes for which they were admitted to the United States. For international students, this means they need to be primarily engaged in their studies. Students with F-1 and M-1 visas must be enrolled full time in courses. For F-1 students, the regulations require that undergraduates be enrolled in at least 12 credits each academic term. F-1 graduate students must be enrolled full time according to the institution's definitions. In English as a second language (ESL) and language programs, the F-1 requirement is to be enrolled a minimum of 18 clock hours per week in classroom-based programs and 22 clock hours per week in laboratory-based programs. M-1 regulations are similar to F-1, but with some additional options that give a little more flexibility for the institution to define "full time" for the nature of the program. Of the three visa statuses, the J-1 visa provides the most flexibility, allowing the institution to define "full-time enrollment."

Employment

The regulations provide strict guidance on employment opportunities for international students. F-1 students have the opportunity to work on campus for up to 20 hours per week while school is in session and full time during school breaks. J-1 students can work on campus with advance permission from the ISSS adviser. M-1 students cannot work on campus.

Off-campus work is allowed only as authorized practical training for F-1 and M-1 students. For F-1 students, practical training is further divided into Curricular Practical Training (CPT) and Optional Practical Training (OPT). J-1 students have a similar form of off-campus work authorization called "Academic Training." Practical training and academic training work authorization make it possible for students to undertake internships and gain experience in their fields to complement their coursework. The rules and regulations related to employment authorization are highly complex. Interested students and scholars should always ensure that they receive their information from an ISSS professional.

Advising Approaches

International student and scholar offices may have one adviser or several, depending on the number of international students and scholars that they serve. ISSS offices structure their advising in a variety of ways. They may have assigned advisers for students and scholars based on academic department, nationality, immigration status, or even the first letter of the last name. Alternatively, certain advisers may be appointed to work on particular types of issues, with the senior advisers handling the more complex cases. Regardless of the structure of the office, generally, advisers are available to see students and scholars by appointment, during drop-in office hours, or through a combination of these methods.

Some international students and scholars will want and need a lot of support during their stay in the country. Others may require very little from the ISSS office, either because the transition comes easily to them or because they are getting support from other sources. For those who seek it, individual support is often provided through advising. McClellan and Moser (2011) suggest that the typical advising session has seven phases:

1. Preparation. The adviser reviews any email correspondence from the student or scholar, past advising session notes, and other relevant records (e.g., student's transcripts).

2. Welcome. The advisee is greeted in a welcoming manner and environment.

3. Rapport building. The adviser and advisee take the time to continue to get to know each other, which contributes to building trust.

4. Exploration and clarification. The adviser uses verbal and nonverbal cues to ensure understanding of the advisee's questions and the specifics of the situation.

5. Advising. The adviser addresses the questions and concerns.

6. Wrap-up. The adviser summarizes the outcome and identifies next steps and the person responsible.

7. Follow-up. The adviser and advisee each complete any tasks that they agreed to take on, including scheduling a follow-up advising appointment.

Young and Althen's (2013) *The Handbook of International Student Advising* discusses the welcome and rapport-building stages in detail, offering recommendations on greetings, office decor, and small talk topics to help put international students and scholars at ease. A discussion of the attitudes that the adviser brings to her or his advising and the challenges of intercultural communication in the advising context are also included in the book, with implementable guidance offered to advisers.

While McClellan and Moser's (2011) seven-phase model provides an outline for an advising session, it does not, by itself, describe what could or should happen in phase 5: Advising. The following section describes different approaches that advisers can take regarding the advising phase.

Prescriptive Advising

Prescriptive advising is a broad category of advising in which communication is primarily unidirectional, with the adviser telling the advisee what to do, and the advisee doing what he or she is told to do. In prescriptive advising, advisers may do things for students and scholars such as informing them about deadlines and following up to make sure work is done (Missouri State 2013; Stockwell 2015). While there may occasionally be times when ISSS advisers do dictate policies in this way, particularly in relation to immigration compliance, this mode of advising is viewed less favorably than developmental advising (Missouri State 2013).

Developmental Advising

Developmental advising is a broad category of advising that stresses helping advisees develop knowledge and skills to increase their self-sufficiency and academic and professional success. So, whereas in a prescriptive advising session, an adviser would give a student or scholar information about a campus policy, in a developmental advising session, the adviser would teach the student or scholar where to find the policy and then discuss with the individual how the policy applies to the specific situation. In developmental advising, there is greater emphasis on the student or scholar being responsible for making decisions and taking action, while the adviser takes on a coaching or teaching role. The specific approaches to advising introduced in the remainder of this section are typically developmental advising approaches.

Proactive Advising

Proactive advising, also sometimes known as "intrusive advising," highlights the role of the adviser in initiating advising sessions. It is widely used across student affairs departments, particularly with students considered to be at risk of not succeeding in school. These may be students on academic probation, for example. Proactive advising may even mandate that certain students engage in advising sessions.

Regular and early meetings can promote trust building so that the adviser is well positioned to help the student as issues arise later (Ohrt 2016). Because some international students and scholars are reluctant to seek out advising, ISSS advisers may wish to engage in proactive advising by setting up routine meetings with some or all advisees in order to create an opportunity to offer support before any situation becomes too serious.

Appreciative Advising

Appreciative advising focuses intentionally on positive dialogue about the advisee's strengths, dreams, and goals. It uses a structured format with six phases (Bloom and Martin 2002; Stockwell 2015):

1. Disarm. Make a warm first impression on the advisee.

2. Discover. Use positive open-ended questions to build rapport and learn about the advisee's strengths.

3. Dream. Elicit hopes and dreams by directing discussions toward the advisee's future.

4. Design. Create concrete, step-by-step plans for the future by working together, with the advisee ultimately taking ownership of the plan.

5. Deliver. Express confidence while the advisee takes responsibility for executing the plan.

6. Don't settle. Set high expectations and encourage the advisee's continued improvement.

While not all conversations can be positive, using the appreciative advising structure for as many advising interactions as possible helps to build trust and confidence in the relationship so that the student or scholar will be willing to talk with the adviser during difficult conversations as well.

Advising as Coaching

McClellan and Moser (2011) complement their seven-phase advising structure with their "advising as coaching" model. This model is built on theories of business executive coaching but is applied to educational settings. McClellan and Moser (2011) offer a six-step ADVISE model for the advising conversation:

1. (A) Actively listen. Throughout the advising session, the adviser should be primarily listening and asking questions.

2. (D) Determine the desire, dream, or problem. The adviser should ask many clarifying questions to ensure understanding of the advisee's goal and the specifics of the situation.

3. (V) Evaluate what has been done. The adviser should ask questions to find out what steps or solutions have already been tried or considered.

4. (I) Identify options. The adviser should help the advisee develop as many potential solutions as possible, without evaluating them.

5. (S) Select options. The adviser should help the advisee analyze the potential options, both rationally and emotionally, to find the one that is best for the individual.

6. (E) Engage in and evaluate the plan. The adviser should encourage the advisee to implement the plan and invite the individual to return to report on what happened.

The advising as coaching model can be used in both shorter and longer advising sessions.

Advising as Teaching and Learning

The advising as teaching and learning model emphasizes thinking of the adviser as a teacher and the student or scholar as a learner. This model asks advisers to think explicitly about what knowledge, skills, and attitudes they hope to cultivate in the advisee. Advisers who use this approach should be cognizant of student development theories (see table 3 in chapter 4) and think about how they can use advising sessions to help students to value the learning process, develop personally and professionally, and strengthen thinking and learning skills. As an advising team, the ISSS staff would likely develop a curriculum for advising (Stockwell 2015).

Other Advising Structures and Approaches

Advising approaches are influenced by a wide range of disciplines including psychology, philosophy, sociology, and student affairs. In addition to the models presented here, there are other advising theories and techniques that involve motivational interviewing, storytelling, constructivism, Socratic advising, and hermeneutic advising (Stockwell 2015).

It should also be noted that advising can happen in structures other than one-on-one meetings between an adviser and a student or scholar. Advisers might meet with small groups of students and still engage in the same type of advising approaches as they would if talking with one individual. Another commonly used advising structure is peer mentoring. In this model, peer students or scholars, with training and mentorship from advisers, conduct some advising sessions. This model is common across student affairs departments and often used in education abroad offices, particular with returned study abroad students and interested students.

Peer advising serves the very pragmatic function of expanding the capacity of the ISSS office to meet the needs of students and scholars. It also offers benefits in terms of rapport building because a student or scholar may be more willing to share doubts or concerns with a peer than with an adviser. In addition to supporting international students and scholars, the peer advisers typically find that they develop new skills and knowledge through these engagements (Stockwell 2015).

Referrals

An essential note related to advising is that advisers need to be aware of the limits of their knowledge and training. In the case of peer mentoring structures, there must be clear guidelines for the type of advising questions that need to be referred to an ISSS adviser. Similarly, when an ISSS adviser encounters an individual with a highly complex immigration situation, the adviser may need to refer the student or scholar to an immigration attorney. Additionally, when an adviser becomes aware that a student or scholar is struggling with a severe mental health issue, a referral needs to be made to a mental health professional.

ISSS offices must develop, in advance, policies related to when and how to make referrals. Many offices on campus may offer other support services, including the health center, counseling center, women's center, and campus police. Advisers should know their office locations, intake policies, and key people in the departments in advance of an emergency situations (Young and Althen 2013; Altbrecht 2015). ISSS offices must develop risk management and crisis response plans, including guidance on how to respond to a range of emergency situations. NAFSA offers several detailed resources for responding to crises regarding individual students as well as groups of students (see resources at the end of this chapter).

Supportive Programming

ISSS offices use campus programming to support international students and scholars in the many areas in which they must adapt to life in a new country. Some programs are wholly designed and facilitated by the ISSS office, some are created by other campus offices, and many are developed and offered in collaboration between ISSS and another office. ISSS professionals may find it helpful to think of programming in three broad categories: academic, social/cultural, and logistical.

Academic support might include programs on reading and note-taking skills, U.S. writing styles, academic honesty, citations, public speaking/classroom presentations, etc. Social and cultural programming might include workshops on cross-cultural topics, panel presentations, holiday programs, and programs that encourage interaction and friendship with U.S. individuals. Logistical support is a particularly important need when a student or scholar is newly arrived in the United States. This might include tutorials on opening a bank account, getting a phone, navigating public transportation, obtaining a driver's licenses, etc.

For an ISSS professional considering where to start in expanding support services, one recommendation is to ensure that programs are offered in all three categories: academic, social/cultural, and logistical. Another recommendation is to build on the existing strengths and initiatives of the institution to deepen, strengthen, and expand support (Glass, Wongtrirat, and Buus 2015). An important element in the planning process is to gather input from the international students and scholars themselves through focus groups or surveys. The strategic planning process described in chapter 3, "Internationalization," can be utilized to develop an ISSS plan, or the ISSS component of an internationalization plan.

Orientation Programs

Orientation is one of the most common components of support offered to new international students and scholars. In fact, the U.S. Code of Federal Regulations requires that students and scholars on J-1 exchange visitor visas be provided an orientation on life and customs in the United States, community resources, and health care and health insurance. These topics, and many others, including campus tours, academic norms, immigration regulations, and campus and community activities, are commonly covered in orientation sessions for international students and scholars with any visa type. Because many international students and scholars come from countries with more emphasis on ceremony than the United States, it is advisable to arrange for a high-ranking university official to offer a welcome to the new members of the campus community (Young and Althen 2013).

International students and scholars often arrive in the United States just in time for orientation programs. A typical orientation might be held in a large lecture hall, with the participants listening to presenter after presenter speak about a wide range of topics. Unfortunately, newly arrived international students and scholars are often experiencing severe jet lag at that time, having difficulty adapting to the accents of the U.S. presenters, and are perhaps worried about finding housing or other logistical matters, thus making it difficult for them to concentrate and retain all of the information at once (Young and Althen 2013; Jean-Francois 2017).

There are two solutions to this challenge. One is to strengthen the orientation session by keeping information concise and reinforcing the information with written handouts (Young and Althen 2013). Advisers can also enhance the orientation program by making it interactive with activities and lively discussions. If possible, the academic departments and student organizations should be involved (Young and Althen 2013). Students and scholars could be taken to various departments on campus such as the health center, tutoring center, campus police, etc., rather than having presenters from each department come to the lecture hall. Not only does this keep the students and scholars active and awake, it helps them to learn the location of campus services. During orientation, it is important to ensure that there is enough free time in the schedule for students to explore, be able to attend to their logistical needs, and interact with each other.

The second solution to the inundation of orientation content is to intentionally extend the program to include prearrival and ongoing orientation sessions (Forbes-Mewett and Sawyer 2016). Many campuses offer webinars, videos, and written materials to international students and scholars prior to arrival. This allows students and visitors to learn more about the campus and community prior to arrival and at a pace that suits them (Jean-Francois 2017). Many institutions also provide ongoing orientation opportunities. One option for ongoing orientation is sharing access to a robust collection of resources, such as a collection of videos on practical and cultural topics, that students and scholars can retrieve when they need it. Another common approach to ongoing orientation is to present a series of workshops throughout the year on a range of cultural topics, allowing students and scholars to participate in the sessions that most interest them, at a time when they might be most able to utilize the information. A variation on the idea of a series of workshops is to offer a credit-bearing course that allows students to explore U.S. culture and academic success skills over a full semester period (Geary 2016). The possibility to earn course credit can motivate student enrollment and ensure higher participation rates.

Logistical Support

At the beginning of each academic term, new international students and scholars will have many logistical needs to which they need to attend. Offering shuttle services to stores that sell groceries and household goods will be greatly appreciated. Additionally, a schedule of outings led by ISSS staff or campus volunteers could be offered in the weeks just before and after the start of the term. These might include going to a bank to open an account, going to cellular phone retailers, riding public transit together to a shopping center, campus tours, city tours, etc.

Academic Success Support

Programs for academic support for international students and scholars are often best provided by departments outside of the ISSS office. These may include libraries, tutoring centers, writing centers, ESL departments, judicial affairs (for workshops related to academic honesty and citations), academic advising offices, and academic departments. The ISSS office may be approached by any of these offices to discuss how to better serve international students, or perhaps the ISSS office might reach out to develop a collaborative partnership.

While the academic success of international students can be supported with programming from these different departments, the most essential support factor is the faculty. Faculty members can play an important role in guiding students by helping them to normalize their difficulties and find ways to navigate cultural differences and the university structure (Glass, Wongtrirat, and Buus 2015). Some of the things that faculty members can do to support international students in the classroom include (Shapiro, Farrelly, and Tomaš 2018):

- Establish a community of learners
    - Utilize icebreakers
    - Learn students' names

- Be explicit about expectations
    - Expected background knowledge
    - Learning goals
    - Classroom expectations
    - Instructor and student roles (name, how to contact, availability, etc.)
    - How classroom participation will be assessed
    - Teaching philosophy
    - Academic integrity
    - Classroom policies for attendance, tardiness, late work, technology use, etc.

- Encourage participation in discussion
  - Ask students to discuss a topic in pairs and then share with the larger group
  - Invite students to contribute a perspective from their culture
  - Post discussion questions in advance so that students can prepare their thoughts

- Be conscientious of cultural references
  - Give context for pop culture references
  - Be aware of cultural assumptions
  - Give students options for assignments
  - Incorporate diverse cultural perspectives in curricular content

- Be an academic and cultural mentor
  - Provide clear feedback on what is culturally appropriate
  - Offer help before students ask
  - Encourage students

When faculty members use these practices to ensure that international students are integrated into the classroom, it helps to support students' academic and professional success. In fact, research shows that having interactions with peers related to academic matters is one of the factors that contributes to international students continuing their studies in the United States (Mamiseishvili 2011). ISSS staff can work with faculty members to incorporate these inclusive practices into classrooms.

Career Support

International students and scholars may be unfamiliar with U.S. customs related to the job search process, including résumés, cover letters, networking, interviewing, and salary negotiations. These are skills that international students and scholars may need if they are looking for work during their program, or if they hope to remain in the United States to work after their program (Arthur 2007).

In addition to helping students and scholars learn about the cultural norms in the U.S. career search, ISSS advisers should be familiar with the value of global competence in the contemporary job market. They can offer programs to help international students (and students returning from education abroad) learn to articulate the strengths that their international experience has given them that would be of value to employers (Arthur 2007).

Residence Life Support

Integrating domestic students and international students in residence halls or apartments, if done well, has the potential to help all of the students learn from each other's cultural background (Jean-Francois 2017). "International" theme residence halls (or floors) are a common approach to creating an impactful living learning community. By housing students of diverse backgrounds together, and structuring meaningful opportunities for communication and engagement, everyone has an opportunity to learn. International students often find that these interactions help them to acclimate to life in the United States in fun and relaxing ways, while the domestic students are given the chance to learn about other cultures and develop their global competence. This social and cultural integration is a key factor in the students' academic success and social development (Geary 2016).

For international scholars, particularly those accompanied by families, the ISSS office or a campus housing office may be able to offer support with finding apartments. Some campuses have graduate student housing, usually in the form of apartments, that may meet the needs of scholars. Other times, ISSS offices may be able to work with apartment complexes directly to ensure that rental units are available when needed.

Because international students and scholars often do not leave the United States during shorter holiday breaks in the school year, staff from the ISSS and Residential Life offices might join efforts to ensure that housing is open during the breaks. This is also an excellent time to organize programming and integrate international and domestic students and scholars who remain on campus. Another potential collaboration is that the ISSS advisers may be able to provide cross-cultural training to the residence life staff, particularly the resident assistants who likely have the most direct contact with international students.

Friendship and Peer Mentor Programs

A survey of more than 400 undergraduate and graduate international students studying at U.S. colleges and universities found that 38 percent had no U.S. friends, 17 percent had one U.S. friend, 18 percent had two U.S. friends, and only 27 percent reported having three or more U.S. friends (Gareis 2012). The data showed that students from Europe and English-speaking countries most often reported having two or more U.S. friends, while students from East Asian countries most often reported having no U.S. friends (Gareis 2012).

One way that colleges and universities can try to assist students and scholars in developing intercultural friendships is by coordinating friendship programs (sometimes known as "buddy programs") and peer mentoring programs. In these programs, U.S. and international individuals are paired together for conversation and social activities. In the case of peer mentoring, the role of the U.S. participant as a supporter and adviser to the international participant is made explicit.

Friendship and peer mentor programs have varying levels of structure. Some programs involve only a few meetings over the course of the semester, without any oversight to see if the meetings actually take place. Other programs include organized group and pair activities, structured conversation topics, or a reporting structure for accountability to try to ensure meaningful engagement between partners.

Recruiting U.S. partners for these programs can be a challenge for some ISSS offices, while interest from international students and scholars is usually quite high. Some institutions have built the programs into relevant course curriculum, such as courses on intercultural communication, international studies, or leadership, in order to incentivize participation (Geary 2016; Campbell 2012). For institutions aiming to internationalize their curriculum, this approach can contribute to both internationalizing the curriculum and integrating international students into the campus and community.

A variation on peer mentor programs is to create opportunities for international students to meet with faculty and staff, for example by arranging an event early in the semester where new international students and scholars have lunch with faculty members from across campus (Forbes-Mewett and Sawyer 2016). Faculty and staff can also be asked to volunteer to host students and scholars for holiday meals (such as Thanksgiving) or to help with early semester logistical support, such as escorting newly arrived groups on excursions to buy household goods. Many faculty and staff enjoy the opportunity to get to know smaller groups of students and scholars and help in this tangible way. At the same time, the international students and scholars begin to build networks on campus.

Spouse and Family Programs

International students, and particularly international scholars, may bring their spouse and children with them to the United States. Within the immigration regulations, these individuals are referred to as "dependents" because their permission to reside in the United States is dependent upon the student or scholar maintaining immigration status. The U.S. Department of State reported that in 2017, it issued 27,435 F-2 visas for the spouses and children of F-1 student visa holders, 395 M-2 visas for the spouses and children of M-1 vocational student visa holders, and 39,354 J-2 visas for the spouses and children of J-1 exchange visitor visa holders (U.S. Department of State 2018).

At the same time that the student or scholar is adjusting to life in the United States, the spouse and children are also adjusting. This adjustment includes all of the social, cultural, and logistical areas discussed earlier in the chapter. Additionally, while the student or scholar often has sufficient English language skills for daily interactions, the spouse and children may not. Although youth can enroll in public schools for their academic needs, there are some restrictions on the ability of spouses to work and study. Many spouses have left their own careers at home and may struggle with isolation and loneliness without the support networks of friends and family that would be present for them at home (Chittooran and Sankar-Gomes

2007). International students and scholars often feel the added pressure of supporting the family's adjustment while undergoing their own.

Many ISSS offices provide programming not just for students and scholars, but for spouses and children as well. These may be social activities, cultural outings, or assistance with logistical matters such as K–12 school enrollment. In response to the limitations on staff time in most ISSS offices, and because it is more effective and sustainable, the spouses are often encouraged to help organize these programs. A spousal group or committee might be formed to take a leadership role for organizing regular, ongoing programming such as social gatherings, children's play groups, language lessons, and cross-cultural activities.

Campus and Community Engagement Programs

Staff in the ISSS office may want to partner with other campus offices such as the civic engagement or service-learning office to provide opportunities for international students and scholars to get involved in the broader campus community. Participation in these ongoing projects not only creates opportunities for students and scholars to make friends, it also gives them a broader understanding of the United States beyond the sometimes insular bubble of a higher education institution.

ISSS advisers may also want to distribute information on student clubs and organizations, local religious institutions, local hobby groups, and other groups that might welcome students and scholars to their events and help to build networks. Information on these organizations may be shared through a website, social media, or email, along with any flyers that may be posted in the ISSS office.

Professional Skills and Specialties

The structure of ISSS offices can vary from institution to institution, depending on the size of the international population (Ammigan and Jones 2018). ISSS professionals working in small institutions may have responsibilities in international admissions and international student and scholar support, including orientation, advising, programming, and SEVIS reporting. At larger institutions with more international students and scholars, the work is likely to be divided among many professionals. Some institutions have staff who work only on programming and are not involved with immigration advising and SEVIS. Others have staff assigned to both advising and programming. An institution may have one set of professionals supporting international students and another set supporting international scholars.

With this wide range of functions and responsibilities, ISSS professionals need a diverse set of knowledge and skills. As already discussed, they need to be familiar with different advising approaches and good practices in programming. Young and Althen (2013) list some of the knowledge and skills that are essential for ISSS advisers:

KNOWLEDGE:

- Self-knowledge
- Institutional knowledge
- Community knowledge
- Professional colleagues
- External agencies (including immigration agencies)
- Students' and scholars' backgrounds
- Current affairs

SKILLS:

- Communication
- Administration
- Administering an office
- Education and training
- Advising
- Referring
- Following through
- Saying no
- Crisis management

The *NAFSA International Education Professional Competencies* (2015), which was developed based on the input of international educators in the field, identifies eight cross-cutting competencies that apply to most, if not all, positions within the international education field. The *Competencies*, along with NAFSA's Career Print self-assessment tool, can help prospective and current ISSS professionals to identify areas of strength and areas for further professional development. These knowledge and skill sets can be gained through graduate study, NAFSA workshops and trainings, books and resource materials, and interactions with colleagues. Several other professional associations provide opportunities for training and networking to help ISSS practitioners to continue their professional development. At the end of this chapter, some resources for professional development are recommended.

Considerations for Practitioners

ISSS professionals need to balance many considerations as they work across all sectors of the campus to provide support and guidance for international students' and scholars' productive experiences. Considerations that are of particular concern to ISSS practitioners are discussed in this section.

Campus Community Readiness and Involvement

Hosting international students and scholars on campus involves the whole institution taking on the ethical responsibility to ensure that they are welcomed and supported. Beyond ethics, faculty and staff need to assist international students and scholars during their cultural transition to contribute to international student retention efforts, thus helping the institution to achieve its larger enrollment management and internationalization goals (Mamiseishvili 2011).

An ISSS office does not have the capacity to provide all the necessary support to students and scholars on its own. In response, ISSS office staff can offer intercultural training programs for faculty and staff so that they are better equipped to address issues surrounding the acculturation process and offer guidance to international members of the campus. Through cross-cultural events and training, participants should become aware of cross-cultural differences in daily life, academia, and the workplace. Faculty should learn how to how to make the curriculum and communication accessible for non-native speakers of English, how to help international students and scholars successfully navigate U.S. academic culture, and how international members of the community can be assets for internationalization (Shapiro, Farrelly, and Tomaš 2018).

It is important to increase awareness among the faculty and staff working with international students on the dangers of stereotypes and generalizations about international students' backgrounds (Jean-Francois 2017). One of the most effective ways to achieve this is by involving international students and scholars in developing and delivering the trainings. Most campus community members will be open to hearing the stories and experiences of international individuals, and through listening to the stories, will develop greater awareness, and, hopefully, sensitivity.

Domestic students must also be encouraged to engage with international students and scholars. This is not only important for supporting the international individuals, but also for the personal and professional development of the domestic students who will be graduating and entering a workforce that is more global than ever. Glass, Wongtrirat, and Buus (2015) emphasize that campuses must pay attention to "the actual readiness of domestic students to create a tolerant and welcoming context for international students." It is an unfortunate reality that international students may still face stereotyping, prejudice, and discrimination (Jean-Francois 2017; Bonazzo and Wong 2007) because, ultimately, changing campus culture is easier said than done. However, purposeful, structured engagement in courses, housing, and extracurricular activities can help to promote international student integration.

Professional Philosophy

There is some debate among ISSS professionals about the type of support that international students and scholars need. Some practitioners warn against deficit thinking, which assumes that the international individuals are lacking in some way and need bolstering, perhaps in terms of language skills or U.S. cultural knowledge (Killick 2018). Marginson (2013, 23), instead, contends that "International Students are not weak or in 'deficit.' They are strong self-determining human agents, involved in complex self-formation through education and global mobility." These scholars might argue that international students and scholars should be treated the same as domestic students and scholars.

Other scholars suggest that international students and scholars have a few special needs that must be accommodated, such as immigration advising, but should, in most ways, be treated like any other students and scholars. Still, other international educators would regale listeners with tales of the complexities of cultural adjustment and intercultural communication and suggest that robust support structures should be in place to ensure that international students and scholars achieve their academic and professional goals. While there is not a right or wrong answer in this debate, and it might vary from case to case, practitioners are advised to be aware of the assumptions that they and others are making so that they can be thoughtful and intentional in their work (Young and Althen 2013).

Institutional Position

A challenge facing many ISSS practitioners is that they are leading from the middle. While they have authority due to their knowledge of intercultural issues and immigration regulations, they generally are not in a position to set campus priorities. ISSS advisers have many diverse functions and answer to many stakeholders, including government agencies, academic departments, and the students and scholars that they support (Young and Althen 2013). ISSS professionals often find themselves serving as the literal and metaphorical bridge:

- Between the government and the institution;
- Between the institution and the students/scholars;
- Between the students/scholars and the local community; and
- Between the students/scholars and the government.

Functioning effectively through these complex situations requires skills and fluency in both immigration matters and intercultural communication (Young and Althen 2013). Suggestions for balancing the demands of the many stakeholders include (Glass, Wongtrirat, and Buus 2015):

- Connect international initiatives with institutional strategic priorities, such as student success or student engagement.
- Expand initiatives that are already purposeful and effective.
- Invest in faculty learning and development.

- Partner with other offices on collaborative programs and to advocate for international students and scholars.

- Collaborate with international students and scholars.

- Focus on sustained multiyear efforts.

- Conduct continuous, data-driven decisionmaking with these caveats:

    - Do not treat international students or international scholars as one group in assessment;

    - Focus on analysis of data already collected, not collecting more data;

    - Assign someone to share key findings with stakeholders; and

    - Weave illustrative stories in with the data when communicating points.

These recommendations can help ISSS professionals extend their influence on campus in order to better serve international students and scholars.

Conclusion

International students and scholars enrich the diversity of higher education campuses, helping to achieve internationalization goals for the benefit of all students. ISSS offices play a crucial role in supporting students and scholars through the process of adjusting to U.S. culture, which happens within social, cultural, academic, and logistical spheres. Support is offered through individual advising and group programming, on a wide range of topics and with a wide range of collaborators across campus. ISSS professionals need to be knowledgeable and thoughtful about advising models and approaches, immigration regulations and advising, and their own beliefs about their professional roles.

ISSS professionals have the opportunity to use their knowledge and skills to make a difference in the lives of international students and scholars. They incorporate technical skills, educational knowledge, administrative skills, people and communication skills, and intercultural knowledge in positions that are challenging, dynamic, and rewarding.

Resources

READINGS:

- Altbrecht, Teri, ed. 2015. *Crisis Management in a Cross-Cultural Setting: International Student and Scholar Services.* Washington, DC: NAFSA: Association of International Educators.

- Gareis, Elisabeth. 2012. "Intercultural Friendship: Effects of Home and Host Region." *Journal of International and Intercultural Communication* 5, 4:309–328.

- Glass, Chris R., Rachawan Wongtrirat, and Stephanie Buus. 2015. *International Student Engagement: Strategies for Creating Inclusive, Connected, and Purposeful Campus Environments*. Sterling, VA: Stylus Publishing.

- Shapiro, Shawna, Raichle Farrelly, and Zuzana Tomaš. 2018. *Fostering International Student Success in Higher Education*. Alexandria, VA: TESOL Press and NAFSA: Association of International Educators.

- Young, Nancy E., and Gary Althen. 2013. *The Handbook of International Student Advising, Third Edition*. Portland, OR: Intercultural Interaction.

PROFESSIONAL DEVELOPMENT:

- NAFSA Core Education Program Workshops on Advising, Programming, and Immigration Regulations www.nafsa.org/Professional_Resources/Learning_and_Training/Workshops/NAFSA_Core_Education_Program_(CEP)_Workshops/

- NAFSA e-Learning Courses www.nafsa.org/elearningcourses

- U.S. Department of Homeland Security Online Training for Designated School Officials studyinthestates.dhs.gov/2013/10/online-training-for-designated-school-officials

References

Akanwa, Emmanuel E. 2015. "International Students in Western Developed Countries: History, Challenges, and Prospects." *Journal of International Students* 5, 3:271–284.

Altbrecht, Teri, ed. 2015. *Crisis Management in a Cross-Cultural Setting: International Student and Scholar Services*. Washington, DC: NAFSA: Association of International Educators.

Althen, Gary, and Janet Bennett. 2011. *American Ways: A Cultural Guide to the United States of America, Third Edition*. Boston, MA: Intercultural Press.

Ammigan, Ravichandran, and Elspeth Jones. 2018. "Improving the Student Experience: Learning From a Comparative Study of International Student Satisfaction." *Journal of Studies in International Education* 22, 4:283–301. https://doi.org/10.1177/1028315318773137.

Arthur, Nancy. 2007. "International Students' Career Development and Decisions." In *A Handbook for Counseling International Students in the United States*, eds. Helma D. Singaravelu and Mark Pope. Alexandria, VA: American Counseling Association.

Bevis, Teresa Brawner, and Christopher J. Lucas. 2007. *International Students in American Colleges and Universities: A History.* New York, NY: Palgrave Macmillan.

Bloom, Jennifer L., and Nancy Archer Martin. 2002. "Incorporating Appreciative Inquiry into Academic Advising." *The Mentor: An Academic Advising Journal* 4. https://dus.psu.edu/mentor/old/articles/020829jb.htm.

Bonazzo, Claude, and Y. Joel Wong. 2007. "Japanese International Female Students' Experience of Discrimination, Prejudice, and Stereotypes." *College Student Journal* 41, 3:631–639.

Campbell, Nittaya. 2012. "Promoting Intercultural Contact on Campus: A Project to Connect and Engage International and Host Students." *Journal of Studies in International Education* 16, 3:205–227. https://doi.org/10.1177/1028315311403936.

Chittooran, Mary M., and Anita Sankar-Gomes. 2007. "The Families of International Students in U.S. Universities: Adjustment Issues and Implications for Counselors." In *A Handbook for Counseling International Students in the United States*, eds. Helma D. Singaravelu and Mark Pope. Alexandria, VA: American Counseling Association.

Foote, Ken. 2013. "Supporting and Mentoring International Faculty: Issues and Strategies." In *International Students and Scholars in the United States: Coming from Abroad*, eds. Heike C. Alberts and Helen D. Hazen. New York, NY: Palgrave Macmillan.

Forbes-Mewett, Helen, and Anne-Maree Sawyer. 2016. "International Students and Mental Health." *Journal of International Students* 6, 3:661–677.

Gareis, Elisabeth. 2012. "Intercultural Friendship: Effects of Home and Host Region." *Journal of International and Intercultural Communication* 5, 4:309–328.

Geary, Danielle. 2016. "How Do We Get People to Interact? International Students and the American Experience." *Journal of International Students* 6, 2:527–541.

Gebhard, Jerry G. 2010. *What Do International Students Think and Feel?* Ann Arbor, MI: University of Michigan Press.

Glass, Chris R., Rachawan Wongtrirat, and Stephanie Buus. 2015. *International Student Engagement: Strategies for Creating Inclusive, Connected, and Purposeful Campus Environments.* Sterling, VA: Stylus Publishing.

Institute of International Education (IIE). 2018. *Open Doors Report on International Educational Exchange.* New York, NY: Institute of International Education. https://www.iie.org/opendoors.

Jean-Francois, Emmanuel. 2017. "Exploring the Perceptions of Campus Climate and Integration Strategies Used by International Students in a US University Campus." *Studies in Higher Education* December:1–17. https://doi.org/10.1080/03075079.2017.1416461.

Killick, David. 2018. *Developing Intercultural Practice*. New York, NY: Routledge.

Kim, Young Yun. 2001. *Becoming Intercultural: An Integrative Theory of Communication and Cross-Cultural Adaptation*. Thousand Oaks, CA: Sage Publications.

Knight, Jane. 2011. "Five Myths about Internationalization." *International Higher Education* 62. https://doi.org/10.6017/ihe.2011.62.8532.

Lipson, Charles. 2008. *Succeeding as an International Student in the United States and Canada*. Chicago, IL: The University of Chicago Press.

Luo, Jiali, and David Jamieson-Drake. 2013. "Examining the Educational Benefits of Interacting with International Students." *Journal of International Students* 3, 2:85–101.

Mamiseishvili, Ketevan. 2011. "International Student Persistence in U.S. Postsecondary Institutions." *Higher Education* 64, 1:1–17.

Marginson, Simon. 2013. "Equal or Others? Mobile Students in a Nationally Bordered World." In *International Students Negotiating Higher Education: Critical Perspectives*, eds. Silvia Sovic and Margo Blythman. New York, NY: Routledge.

McClellan, Jeffrey, and Clint Moser. 2011. "Advising as Coaching." Manhattan, KS: NACADA Clearinghouse. http://www.nacada.ksu.edu/Resources/Clearinghouse/View-Articles/Advising-as-coaching.aspx.

Missouri State. 2013. "Theories of Advising." In *Missouri State Policy Library Master Advisor Handbook*. Missouri State University. https://www.missouristate.edu/policy/Op3_26_4_AdvisingTheories.htm.

NAFSA: Association of International Educators. 2015. *NAFSA International Education Professional Competencies*. Washington, DC: NAFSA: Association of International Educators. http://www.nafsa.org/competencies.

Nathan, Rebekah. 2006. *My Freshman Year: What a Professor Learned by Becoming a Student*. London, United Kingdom: Penguin Books.

Ohrt, Elizabeth Kalinowski. 2016. "Proactive Advising with First-Generation Students: Suggestions for Practice." *The Mentor: An Academic Advising Journal.* January 31, 2016. https://dus.psu.edu/mentor/2016/01/proactive-advising-first-generation-students/.

Shapiro, Shawna, Raichle Farrelly, and Zuzana Tomaš. 2018. *Fostering International Student Success in Higher Education*. Alexandria, VA: TESOL Press and NAFSA: Association of International Educators.

Stockwell, Kathy. 2015. "Academic Advising Approaches." Presented at the NACADA Academic Advising Summer Institute. https://www.nacada.ksu.edu/Portals/0/Events/SummerInst/2015/Powerpoints/W4-Approaches-LA-KS.pdf.

Theobald, Rebecca. 2013. "International Faculty: A Source of Diversity." In *International Students and Scholars in the United States: Coming from Abroad*, eds. Heike C. Alberts and Helen D. Hazen. New York, NY: Palgrave Macmillan.

Tran, Ly Thi, and Thao Thi Phuong Vu. 2017. "'Responsibility in Mobility': International Students and Social Responsibility." *Globalisation, Societies and Education* 15, 5:561–575. https://doi.org/10.1080/14767724.2016.1195729.

U.S. Department of State. 2018. "Table XVI(B) Nonimmigrant Visas Issued by Classification (Including Border Crossing Cards) Fiscal Years 2013–2017." Washington, DC: U.S. Department of State. https://travel.state.gov/content/dam/visas/Statistics/AnnualReports/FY2017AnnualReport/FY17AnnualReport-TableXVIB.pdf.

Young, Nancy E., and Gary Althen. 2013. *The Handbook of International Student Advising, Third Edition*. Portland, OR: Intercultural Interaction.

Yudkevich, Maria, Philip G. Altbach, and Laura E. Rumbley, eds. 2017. *International Faculty in Higher Education: Comparative Perspectives on Recruitment, Integration, and Impact*. New York, NY: Routledge.

Chapter 8

International Schools

While international schools once predominately served the children of elite, globally mobile families, it has become increasingly common for local neighborhood schools to embrace the same mission of preparing youth for professional and civic engagement in a global world. Worldwide, kindergarten through twelfth grade (K–12) education is being re-envisioned within a global context that is dominated by a flattening economy, unprecedented global migration, and greater communication connectivity than ever before. National educational systems are progressively emphasizing the internationalization of school curricula and the development of students' global competence. This shift aims to meet the educational needs of students, families, and societies; prepare students to engage across national and cultural boundaries; gain or maintain national competitiveness in the global economy; and ensure a more peaceful world.

This chapter opens with an exploration of the historical development of international schools, types of international schools, and the political contexts that constrain and promote the proliferation of international schools. The chapter then shifts to look at the rapid growth of international schools within national public school systems, with particular focus on the International Baccalaureate curriculum. Moving to the institutional level, the chapter addresses strategies for internationalizing a school in the form of curriculum internationalization, language education, partnerships, technology, youth mobility, extracurricular programs, and assessment. Approaches for internationalizing teacher training and teacher development are also introduced. The chapter concludes with critiques of the current trajectory of international school development and projections about the future of international schools.

History of International Schools

Some of the oldest international schools, such as the International School of Geneva and the Tanglin Trust School in Singapore, were developed in the aftermath of World War I at a time when the international community was striving to promote tolerance and understanding among nations to prevent future conflict. It was hoped that an international education would enable children of diverse cultures to live in harmony with one another (Hallgarten, Tabberer, and McCarthy 2015; Tate 2016).

Following World War II, fervor for international education surged again and more international schools were established around the world. These schools were characterized by having an international mix of students enrolled, an internationally minded set of teachers, an international curriculum, and international governance (meaning that they were outside of the national systems of oversight and accreditation) (Hallgarten, Tabberer, and McCarthy 2015). Many of these international schools did and continue to accept and promote the (arguably Western) values from the 1948 United Nations's Universal Declaration of Human Rights, which include individualism, freedom, democracy, egalitarianism, rationalism, optimism, and universalism (Tate 2016). Variances in the scope of the curriculum among different international schools have led to some ambiguity in terms of their relationship with the community and government.

Since the beginning, national governments have viewed and responded to international schools in different ways. Some take a hands-off approach, allowing international schools to function as independent private schools with little oversight. The number of such private schools are small, and the students' families are typically influential, so it may not seem worthwhile for governments to spend time regulating them, particularly if the public school system needs attention and effort toward improvement.

Other countries take a more regulatory approach, limiting the number of schools and setting requirements with which schools have to comply (Calliods 2008). Some national governments may even view international schools as a competitive threat to the national educational system. In Indonesia, for example, the government required that all school teachers (including at international schools) be proficient in Indonesian, forbid schools from being fully owned by foreign stakeholders, and required all schools to drop the word "international" from their school name (Bunnell, Fertig, and James 2016).

Despite the varied government relationships and responses, in recent decades, the number of international schools has continued to expand dramatically around the world, resulting in not only many more schools, but also schools with a greater range of missions and more diversified student bodies. International schools are increasingly becoming accessible educational opportunities for students of all socioeconomic backgrounds.

Growth of International Schools

Hallgarten, Tabberer, and McCarthy (2015) report that the number of international schools has grown sevenfold in the last 25 years. According to data collected by the International

School Consultancy (ISC), private international schools brought in a total fee income of USD$37.9 billion in 2015 and, by 2025, are projected to reach USD$65 billion (Hallgarten, Tabberer, and McCarthy 2015). ISC also reports that there were more than 7,545 international schools in January 2015, serving 3.92 million children (Hallgarten, Tabberer, and McCarthy 2015). Projecting growth in both public and private international schools, ISC anticipates that by 2025, student numbers will reach 8.26 million, teacher numbers will hit 734,000, and the number of international schools will soar to 15,100 (Hallgarten, Tabberer, and McCarthy 2015). This would be bigger than the school system, public and private, of the whole of England (Hallgarten, Tabberer, and McCarthy 2015).

One important caveat is that ISC defines an "international school" as any school teaching in English in a non-English-speaking country, regardless of whether the curriculum is international in any aspect beyond the language of instruction (Bunnell, Fertig, and James 2016). While fewer than 0.5 percent of the world's school-aged population is being educated in international schools, the sector is rapidly growing in size and impact (Tate 2016).

United World Colleges

The United World Colleges (UWC) is a well-known group of international schools founded in 1962 to bring together "young people from areas of post-war conflict to act as champions of peace through an education based on shared learning, collaboration, and understanding" (UWC 2017). Today, UWC continues to welcome students from multiple countries to study and live together for 2 years before beginning university, with the goal of overcoming intercultural barriers and misunderstandings (Hayden and Thompson 2016). UWC program values include international and intercultural understanding, celebration of difference, personal responsibility, compassion and service, respect for the environment, and more.

Since opening the first campus in South Wales, United Kingdom, UWC has established 17 sites around the world, enrolling students from more than 155 countries. While some campuses serve only students in their final 2 years of secondary education, others serve children of all ages. Boasting a diverse student body—in terms of culture, nationality, and socioeconomic status—some of the students receive scholarships, while others are fee paying. More than 60,000 students from over 180 countries have participated in UWC programs since its founding (UWC 2017).

Definitions and Types of International Schools

International schools vary greatly in scope and range. They may be residential or day schools; they may be coeducational or single sex; they may serve 20 students or 4,500; and they may enroll students from kindergarten through 12th grade or just cover one age range. Students may be primarily of one nationality or students may be diverse across nationalities. While most international schools use the English language, some teach in the local language or in other languages (Bates 2011b; Hayden 2006; Hayden and Thompson 2016).

Given the diversity of schools, it is challenging to define an international school. Historically, international schools have had three main characteristics: (a) they offer a curriculum other than the one of the host country; (b) they enroll a large percentage of students who are not host country nationals; and (c) teachers and administrators are mostly expatriates (Hayden and Thompson 2016). This definition is now being challenged as more and more public schools, under the auspices of the national or local governments, are becoming international schools that serve local populations.

As international schools have proliferated, scholars have attempted to explain the variance in type and mission. Skelton (2016), for example, offers a four-part categorization of international schools:

- The first category comprises those schools that are monocultural but exist outside the home country, for example, a school teaching the Japanese national curriculum to Japanese students in London, England.

- The second category includes those schools serving students of many nationalities, such as the many international schools serving a diverse range of expatriate children.

- The third category of schools is organized around a values system/ethos of internationalization.

- The fourth category of schools is reserved for those that have the word "international" added to their name for reputational purposes with little other change.

Hayden and Thompson (2016, 2013) also attempt to organize the diversity of international schools by proposing three categories:

- Type A: The traditional form of international schools (described above) that caters to the globally mobile elite;

- Type B: Ideologically focused schools that are founded for that particular purpose and not created to respond to a market need; and

- Type C: A newer, nontraditional type of international school aimed largely at host country nationals, particularly the aspirational middle class in the developing world, hoping to garner advantage for their children. Very often, these schools teach in English and the schools are operated on a more commercial footing than has tended to be the case for Type A and Type B schools. This might include groups of commercially operated schools as well as satellite campuses of prestigious schools.

These categorization systems attempt to classify international schools based on mission, curriculum, and student demographics. However, neither Skelton nor Hayden and Thompson put much emphasis on one key group that is now being increasingly served by international schools, namely, the local children of all socioeconomic class backgrounds who are being educated by local public schools that are internationalizing.

International Schools in Public Education

Around the world, nations are actively reforming their public education systems to make certain that their graduates are part of an educated citizenry, which can ensure countries' economic competitiveness, peace and understanding across cultures, and solutions to complicated global problems (Smink 2007; Suarez-Orozco and Qin-Hilliard 2004). In the United Kingdom, the government is instituting the Global Partnership Schools program, linking UK schools to schools around the world; Sweden has emphasized preparing students and teachers to understand countries of strategic importance; and India's national curriculum calls for promoting national identity and unity while also promoting peace among nations (Boix Mansilla and Jackson 2011). Brazil, Chile, China, Jordan, Russia, and South Africa are also reforming their national educational systems in order to prepare students to compete in the global economy (Smink 2007).

In many countries, governments are not the only proponents of internationalization. Increasingly, there is consumer demand for international schools. Dissatisfied with the standard offerings of national educational systems, parents and students from the socioeconomic middle class are seeking out international schools as a means of upward mobility (Doherty 2009; Hayden and Thompson 2008; Parker 2009). The result of this pressure is rapid growth over the past few decades, not of international schools for the mobile elite (the number of such schools is relatively stable), but rather of local schools, public and private, that are offering an international curriculum (Hayden and Thompson 2008).

International Baccalaureate

The International Baccalaureate (IB) system has been at the forefront of the transformation of local schools into international schools. The IB offers curricula that can be adopted by schools, and the schools then become part of the IB network of schools. It is now the world's largest group of international schools.

History of the International Baccalaureate

The IB was founded in Geneva, Switzerland, in 1968. The IB programs were originally designed to meet the needs of international diplomats and international businesspeople who wanted their children to have a high-quality secondary education that would enable them to gain admission to prestigious universities in their home country. Referred to as "third culture kids" or "global nomads," these children grow up in one or more countries abroad due to their parents' work and often do not feel truly at home in either their passport country or the country in which they are living. Instead, many feel most at home in the multicultural, cosmopolitan environment of the international school where international mobility is the norm (Pollock and Reken 2009).

Private IB international schools have met that need. As the IB system developed, and more and more international schools around the world adopted the IB curriculum, it allowed students to move from posting to posting with their family, maintaining a coherent educational experience and quickly integrating into an educational community abroad. The IB curriculum, like many international schools established in this era, prioritizes international understanding, international mindedness, intercultural awareness, respect for difference, tolerance, equality, education for peace, and the development of global citizenship (Tate 2016).

Expansion of the International Baccalaureate

In the half-century since its establishment, the IB system has grown considerably, including expanding into public schools. The IB system currently offers programs for students ranging from 3 to 19 years old. Perhaps the most well-known IB program is the Diploma Programme (DP), which is delivered during the last 2 years of secondary school, serving students aged 16 to 19 (International Baccalaureate n.d.).

As of March 2017, 4,655 schools worldwide were offering IB programs (International Baccalaureate n.d.), and almost 60 percent of schools that have adopted the IB curriculum are public schools (Bunnell 2011). The United States is home to more than 1,800 schools offering the IB curriculum (International Baccalaureate n.d.). Over 1,600 of these are public schools, in some cases offering the IB program as a track for selected students, and in other cases enrolling all students in the school in the program. Students enrolled in the IB program are not necessarily from upper socioeconomic levels. Half of the U.S. schools offering the IB Primary Years Programme, which serves students aged 3 to 12, are schools in which 40 percent or more of the school's students are from low-income families (Bunnell 2011).

The United States is the largest host country for the IB program by far (International Baccalaureate n.d.). One reason that the IB has been able to proliferate in the United States is that the standards (adopted by the majority of U.S. states) for English language and mathematics education, called the "Common Core State Standards," are flexible enough that teachers can easily incorporate content that develop students' global competence (Boix Mansilla and Jackson 2011) and classes can meet the IB requirements.

Publicly funded local IB international schools are particularly prolific in countries such as the United States, England, and Australia, where college admissions processes are less standardized and universities have the opportunity to determine which academic credentials to accept (Bunnell, Fertig, and James 2016; Bunnell 2011; Resnik 2012). Together, the United States, Canada, England, and Australia host more than half of all IB schools, making English the dominant language of the IB—though all IB materials and services are also available in French and Spanish (International Baccalaureate n.d.). Outside of English-speaking countries, the IB is increasingly being offered in public schools in Ecuador, Japan, Malaysia, and other countries. It is much easier for the IB program to expand into countries where there is not a rigid national curriculum or system of education (Bunnell 2011). The IB curriculum, while still used in schools for expatriate children, offers a prominent example of the internationalization of local public schools.

The International Baccalaureate Curriculum

The IB approach to education is considered to be holistic and balanced, with a focus on interdisciplinary learning and whole person development. The programs are widely respected for being rigorous and academically challenging (Bunnell 2011; Doherty 2009). The first and most well-known IB program, the Diploma Programme, was based on elements of the French, British, and German educational systems and offers a balance between breadth and specialization (Resnik 2012).

The IB curriculum is composed of four programs: The Primary Years Programme serves students aged 3 to 12; the Middle Years Programme serves students aged 11 to 16; and the Diploma Programme serves students aged 16 to 19. The newest program, the Career-Related Programme, is also designed for students aged 16 to 19. The Career-Related Programme includes elements of the Diploma Programme, such as language learning, personal reflection, and service-learning, combined with courses focused on workplace skills development (International Baccalaureate n.d.).

The IB pedagogy is based on the work of progressive education thinkers such as John Dewey, Jean-Jacques Rousseau, and Jean Piaget, and it encourages discussion, debate, collaboration, and inquiry, rather than memorization and reproduction of what was memorized (Tate 2016). The IB learner profile (International Baccalaureate 2015, 2) states that "the aim of all IB programmes is to develop internationally minded people who, recognizing their common humanity and shared guardianship of the planet, help to create a better and more peaceful world." To this end, IB programs try to give students the knowledge and tools to be:

- Inquirers
- Knowledgeable
- Thinkers
- Communicators
- Principled
- Open-Minded
- Caring
- Risk-Takers
- Balanced
- Reflective

In the Diploma Programme (DP), students must take courses in languages and literature, language acquisition (study of a foreign language), individuals and societies, sciences, mathematics, and the arts. Additionally, students take three hallmark courses: (1) "Theory of Knowledge," which helps students to reflect on the nature of knowledge and how claims of truth are evaluated; (2) "The Extended Essay," which is an independent, interdisciplinary research project designed and conducted by each student and documented in a 4,000-word paper; and (3) "Creativity, Activity, and Service," which requires each student to engage in a personally challenging project in the area of arts, athletics (or other active project), or community service. Throughout the project, students reflect on the outcomes of the project and their personal learning (International Baccalaureate n.d.).

International mindedness is cultivated through the study of foreign language, an emphasis on and ethos of global focus, and the celebration of cultural diversity (Doherty 2009; Tate 2016). Research shows that the IB curriculum has a positive effect on students' global mindedness and that DP graduates are well prepared for the research and writing tasks they will encounter in university. Further, IB students are reported to outperform non-IB students in mathematics, reading, narrative writing, and expository writing (International Baccalaureate 2014).

Rationales for Adopting the International Baccalaureate Curriculum in Public Education

National educational systems have long served to reinforce loyalty, patriotism, and a national culture (Doherty 2009; Resnik 2012). Thus, it may be surprising that some national governments would allow an organization such as the IB, which promotes global citizenship, to be incorporated into the public education system. The desire to do so stems from governments, schools, students, and parents.

Government Motivations

Rationales for why host nations are willing to adopt the IB curriculum in their public schools include the strategic goal of increasing the number of graduates who speak English, improved opportunities for graduates to gain admission to prestigious higher education institutions, and the hope that graduates with a global outlook will bolster the country's economic competitiveness. Nations may also be trying to use the IB to improve educational outcomes for disadvantaged youths (Doherty 2009). Research from the IB organization shows that the IB has been successful at challenging and motivating students from disadvantaged backgrounds (Doherty 2009).

Political Ideologies

Two often-competing political ideologies come together to support the inclusion of IB. One dominant political ideology argues for the benefits of a competitive marketplace and is promoted by the education policies of the World Bank and the Organisation for Economic Co-operation and Development (OECD). This outlook suggests that the more choices that consumers have in regard to education, the more that the competition will force improvements in the educational system as a whole. Market-driven schools, such as magnet schools, fit well within this paradigm, and the IB has been very effective at expanding within this sector (Doherty 2009; Doherty et al. 2012; Resnik 2012).

At the same time, other ideologies push for greater standardization and quality control across education, with an emphasis on the importance of external examinations. The IB's compulsory course structure, reputation for academic rigor, and mandated exams are appealing to proponents of this ideology. Both of these ideologies have supported the adoption of the IB curricula within national systems of public education around the world (Doherty et al. 2012; Doherty 2009).

Institutional Reasons

The reasons for adopting the IB curriculum vary by individual school. Some data are available from Sperandio's (2010) analysis of schools' written applications for the IB Middle Years Programme, which serves students aged 11 to 16. In Sperandio's (2010) study, the most prominent reasons that schools cited for wanting to adopt the IB program were the appeal of the program elements, to complement other IB programs (such as the Primary Years Programme and/or Diploma Programme), as a good fit with the existing school mission, to increase international awareness, for the rigor of the program, and for the prestige that IB brings.

More specifically, in schools where there was a mandate to improve performance, the perceived ability of the IB to affect educational outcomes was most important (Sperandio 2010). Where there was no such mandate, the IB program philosophy was the most important consideration for schools (Sperandio 2010). Similarly, Hayden and Thompson (2008) contend that some public schools adopt the IB because of the academic rigor and prestige that comes from offering this program to gifted and talented students. Other public schools often adopt IB because they have high immigrant populations and they welcome the international curriculum.

Parent and Student Demand

Around the world, parents seek advanced opportunities for their children, wanting their children to have a high-quality education and strong future prospects for higher education and careers. Many parents and students consider IB schools to be a viable pathway to such prestigious academic and professional options (Doherty 2009; Marshall 2011; Resnick 2012).

In fact, many colleges and universities privilege IB graduates in the admissions process or offer advanced credits for completion of the Diploma Programme (Culross and Tarver 2011). This consumer demand has aligned with government and school goals, as well as receptive political ideologies, to support the adoption of the IB curricula within different national systems of public education (Doherty et al. 2012; Doherty 2009).

Internationalization in the United States

The internationalization of U.S. primary and secondary education is gaining momentum, and it is not limited to just adoption of the IB curriculum. Walter Payton College Preparatory High School (WPCP) in Chicago, Illinois, is an example of an international public school that serves students from the local community. Working through the Sister Cities International program, WPCP connects with schools around the world, bridging classrooms through videoconferencing and other technology that allow students to work together on projects and engage in cross-cultural discussion. WPCP is also a host site for a Chinese government-funded Confucius Institute, which teaches Chinese language and culture (Kisch 2010; Asia Society and The George Lucas Foundation 2007).

Another example is the College of Staten Island High School for International Studies (CSIHSIS), which is a public high school for high-achieving students that is supported by partnerships with Asia Society and the College of Staten Island. The school has an explicitly international mission statement. All CSIHSIS students are required to take 4 years of Mandarin, Spanish, or Japanese language. Service-learning is also required and often focuses on global issues such as AIDS, child soldiers, or human trafficking. Study abroad is encouraged, and even the school newspaper has an international focus (Kisch 2010).

The internationalization of public education is not limited to high school. The John Stanford International School (JSIS) is a public elementary school in Seattle, Washington, that covers kindergarten through the fifth grade. The campus features a dual-language immersion program in which students spend half of their day studying in English and the other half studying in either Spanish or Japanese. In addition to language classes, other subjects such as science and math are also taught in the foreign language, offering students greater immersion. A sizable number of the students at JSIS are recent U.S. immigrants learning English, and the fact that everyone is struggling to learn a language helps to create a culture of empathy and tolerance. The school has international sister school relationships, organizes visits to the sister school in Mexico, and is supported through partnerships with organizations such as the University of Washington, the Sister City Council, the Trade Development Alliance, and the Mexican Council (Asia Society and The George Lucas Foundation 2007; Seattle Public Schools 2019).

In response to the rise in international schools, Asia Society's International Studies Schools Network (ISSN) offers services to schools wishing to internationalize, including professional development modules; resources and tools for curriculum, instruction, and assessment; study tours to see ISSN schools; international study tours to learn about other countries' educational systems; an annual conference; and an electronic platform for teacher collaboration (Asia Society 2018).

Internationalization Strategies

While there are many goals motivating internationalization, questions remain as to whether these outcomes are achieved (Tate 2016). It is not clear, for example, whether implementation of the IB curriculum in some schools contributes to increasing the quality of public education as a whole (Tate 2016). It is also not clear from current research the *degree* to which the content being taught is "international." There are some critiques that international schools, IB and others, may not always fully internationalize their curriculum despite calling themselves "international schools" (Skelton 2016).

To counter such critiques, comprehensive internationalization must be undertaken. Internationalization and global learning must become part of the ethos of the school. While updating the curricular content is perhaps the most obvious way to work toward the development of students' global competence, schools have many more options available to them. These strategies (Hobert 2013; Oxfam 2015; Uraneck 2002) might include:

- Restructuring the curriculum schoolwide;
- Infusing global content into courses;
- Expanding world language and English as a second language (ESL) offerings;
- Developing international partnerships, such as school-to-school links and international collaborations on projects;
- Emphasizing the use of global technology;
- Encouraging study abroad and international exchange for both teachers and students;
- Sponsoring service-learning related to global problems;
- Launching ethnic heritage programs to connect to local neighborhoods; and
- Enhancing the campus climate.

Schools that are truly international, and not just international in name only, must ensure that an international focus is fundamental in all aspects of the school's work. International schools should adopt most, if not all, of the strategies described in this section of the chapter.

Internationalizing the Curriculum

As discussed in earlier chapters of this book, the first step in internationalizing the curriculum is determining the global learning outcomes. One of the leading global competence models aimed at school-aged youth that can be used to support the curriculum internationalization process is presented in the publication *Educating for Global Competence: Preparing Our Youth to Engage the World*, which was developed collaboratively by Asia Society and the Council of Chief State School Officers (Boix Mansilla and Jackson 2011). The model offers a holistic set of four learning outcomes: ability to investigate the world, recognize perspectives, communicate ideas, and take action (Boix Mansilla and Jackson 2011). (For more information on this global competence model, see chapter 2 of this book.)

Another prominent model that identifies specific global competencies for youth is the United Nations Educational, Scientific and Cultural Organization (UNESCO)'s Global Citizenship Education model. The *Global Citizenship Education: Topics and Learning Objectives* document (UNESCO 2015) describes several essential learning outcomes:

- Learners develop skills for critical thinking and analysis.

- Learners develop attitudes of empathy, solidarity, and respect for differences and diversity.

- Learners experience a sense of belonging to a common humanity, sharing values and responsibilities, based on human rights.

- Learners acquire knowledge and understanding of local, national, and global issues and the interdependency of different countries and populations.

- Learners develop motivation and willingness to take necessary actions.

- Learners act effectively and responsibly at local, national, and global levels for a more peaceful and sustainable world.

Available online, this document emphasizes the interaction between the cognitive, socioemotional, and behavioral domains of learning. UNESCO argues that learners must be (a) informed and critically aware; (b) socially connected and respectful of diversity; and (c) ethically responsible and engaged (UNESCO 2015). The appendix of the document offers specific learning objectives and topics in each of the three areas, broken down by age group: lower primary (ages 5 to 9), upper primary (ages 9 to 12), lower secondary (ages 12 to 15), and upper secondary (ages 15 to 18) (see UNESCO 2015).

After the learning objectives are defined, the next phase of curriculum integration is that teachers develop course content that will facilitate students' achievement of the learning outcomes. Extensive resources exist for teachers who wish to internationalize the content of their individual courses (see resources at the end of this chapter). There are also existing internationalized curricular programs that schools can adopt, including Advanced Placement (AP), Cambridge IGSCE, Advanced International Certificate of Education, French Baccalaureat Option Internationale, European Baccalaureate, International Baccalaureate (Primary Years Programme, Middle Years Programme, Diploma Programme, and Career-Related Programme), International Primary Curriculum, and Cambridge International Primary Programme (Hayden 2006).

Internationalization of the curriculum can happen at the course, department, or school level. Uraneck (2002) discusses the three levels of integration:

1. Curriculum enrichment. Curriculum integration involves the addition of an international project to enrich a unit of study. It is performed by individual teachers.

2. Curriculum integration. Curriculum integration involves the restructuring of department- or school-wide curricula to center around global themes, to involve other colleagues and disciplines, and to collaborate with schools in the United States and abroad. It is performed by teams of teachers and the administration.

3. School restructuring. School restructuring involves going beyond curriculum integration to center the school around a multicultural and international vision, changing policies and practices of staffing, instruction, and outreach. It is performed by principals and administrators, the school board, the entire teaching staff, and the community.

While advocates for global competence would appreciate any achievement at any of these levels, many people would argue that only those schools that achieve all three can truly be considered as international schools.

At the curriculum enrichment level, Boix Mansilla and Jackson (2011) offer five broad approaches teachers can take to internationalize the content within their unit of study or course:

A. Provide global context to the topics studied.
B. Have students address global challenges.
C. Connect course content to universal themes.
D. Focus on the global history of knowledge.
E. Advance learning through international collaboration.

Teachers seeking to internationalize their courses may wish to incorporate all of these methods into their course design and facilitation.

Emphasizing Language Education

Language learning is a core component of global competence, and it is one of the most effective strategies for internationalizing schools. It is recognized as a key factor in developing students' intellectual, cultural, and social skills, enabling students to see things from multiple perspectives and worldviews (Tate 2016). Beyond the benefits of the process of learning a language, reaching proficiency in a language allows students to engage more meaningfully with people from cultural backgrounds that are different from their own.

This emphasis on language learning is recognized as a strategic priority in most public education systems around the world. In China, students learn English from a young age; in Australia, 25 percent of students are learning an Asian language on top of a European language; and throughout much of Europe, studying two foreign languages is recommended (Stewart 2012). The UK government has set a goal that 75 percent of students will learn a foreign language at the General Certificate of Secondary Education (GCSE) level by 2022 (Civinini 2018). Promoting language learning is central to what nations can do to help make their students and societies globally competitive (Stewart 2012).

Unfortunately, in the United States, only 30 percent of secondary school students are enrolled in a foreign language course; in some states, enrollments are below 10 percent (Boix Mansilla and Jackson 2011). From 1997 to 2008, the proportion of U.S. middle school students taking a foreign language declined from 75 to 58 percent, and the proportion in primary school declined from 31 to 19 percent (Stewart 2012). The low enrollments in language education have significant impacts not only for the students' future careers, but also on the economy. Research suggests that U.S. corporations lose more than $2 billion per year due to inadequate linguistic and cross-cultural guidance (Stewart 2012).

Approaches to Language Education

Recognizing the benefits, most international schools emphasize the study of languages. In fact, international educators generally agree that it is best that language education start at a young age and that middle school and high school programs offer intermediate and advanced courses to allow for continuous instruction (Hobert 2013; Boix Mansilla and Jackson 2011; Tate 2016), allowing students to develop proficiency in one or more languages beyond their primary language.

Language learning should be integrated with learning about cultures, and it can be done in ways that are fun and engaging for youth. Ideas for instruction (Asia Society 2009; Hobert 2013) include:

- Using media, such as film, music, photography, and even international commercials, to attract student attention;
- Labeling school spaces such as the gym and cafeteria with a variety of languages;
- Having students research the names of local streets, towns, and other places;
- Using poems and simple rhymes from other languages;

- Playing with language through games;
- Going on field trips; and
- Participating in a digital pen pal program.

Video conferencing and social media technology can also be used to connect students to peers in other countries who speak the target language, making the learning more authentic and meaningful (Boix Mansilla and Jackson 2011).

Research into language teaching and learning demonstrates that it is more effective to teach school subjects (i.e., science, math, art, etc.) using a foreign language as the medium of instruction, rather than having a stand-alone foreign language course (Boix Mansilla and Jackson 2011; Tate 2016). This method of foreign language teaching is called "content-based instruction" (CBI). Studies in research fields as diverse as language acquisition, cooperative learning, metacognition, reading, educational psychology, cognitive psychology, cognitive learning theory, motivation, and others support the power of this methodology (Grabe and Stroller 1997). Grabe and Stroller's (1997) review of the research shows that CBI:

- Is a student-centered approach to teaching;
- Makes learning more contextual and interconnected, resulting in increased student motivation;
- Creates authentic opportunities for students to use the language they are learning;
- Offers a flexible teaching methodology, able to be adapted to many learning approaches;
- Results in students learning both the language and the subject content; and
- Results in increased student motivation.

The example of John Stanford Elementary School shared earlier in the chapter demonstrates the application of this model of language learning, where instructors teach half of the school subjects in a foreign language, rather than having a separate language course.

Developing Partnerships

The internationalization of schools can be widely supported by partnerships, which often fall into two primary categories: (a) partnerships with local community organizations, and (b) partnerships with schools in other countries. Both types of partnerships have the potential to expand the services and resources of the school, as well as provide opportunities for students to have interactions with people of varying ages, nationalities, and cultural backgrounds.

Local Partnerships

A local partnership might entail a partnership between a school and a nearby university. For example, in the case of the College of Staten Island High School for International Studies (CSIHSIS), the high school students are able to utilize the College of Staten Island (CSI)'s campus library, language laboratories, and other facilities, and have the opportunity to take college classes. Additionally, CSI college professors teach at the high school, while the college students offer tutoring to the students (Kisch 2010). Through this partnership, the CSIHSIS students have the chance to work with and learn from a wider pool of resources.

International School Manila, a private K–12 day school located in the Philippines, offers an additional example as it works with local partner organizations, including nonprofits, schools, and community groups, to conduct service-learning programs that teach students about the interconnections between human activity and environmental sustainability (International School Manila 2019).

Other potential local partners might include businesses, museums, embassies and consulates, humanitarian organizations, heritage or immigrant associations, labor groups, faith-based groups, volunteer organizations, and local World Affairs Councils (Asia Society 2009; Uraneck 2002). These groups might assist with guest speakers, collaborate on a classroom project, offer tours of their organizations, host interns, share educational materials, or sponsor programs.

International Partnerships

In addition to finding partners in the local community, it is essential that international schools have international partners to advance internationalization efforts. International partnerships often take the form of school-to-school connections. Classrooms in the partner schools may collaborate on a project, with students in both schools using technology to work together through research, writing, multimedia production, debate, or other forms of engagement (Stewart 2012). On a higher level, the partnership may provide the pathway for students, teachers, and administrators to visit each other's school to learn about other educational systems. The benefit comes not just from the experience abroad, but also in the learning opportunities implicit in hosting visiting students and teachers in short-term programs and, potentially, in homestays.

In some cases, national governments are encouraging and supporting these partnerships. In the United Kingdom, the Department for International Development has created the Global Partnership Schools Program, connecting UK schools with schools in Africa, Asia, the Caribbean, and Latin America (Boix Mansilla and Jackson 2011). A former UK secretary of state even advocated for every school in England to establish an overseas partnership (Bunnell 2010).

In Sweden, the students, teachers, and administrators can learn about Sweden's strategic partner countries through the Global Citizen Program. Partnerships with schools in China and India are expected to help prepare Swedish graduates to engage with these two rising global powers in the areas of sustainable development, corporate social responsibility, and economics (Boix Mansilla and Jackson 2011).

Advances in technology make the connections between schools in different countries more feasible than ever before. Videoconferencing and other technological innovations can greatly facilitate the internationalization of K–12 education, offering the opportunity for authentic engagement between students without the expense of study abroad. The Aquila School in Dubai offers an example. The school is part of the International Schools Partnership, which is a group of international schools that strive to support each other through partnerships related to curriculum, quality assurance, and governance. The Aquila School in Dubai specializes in science, technology, engineering, art, and math and is able to use technology to connect with students at its partner institutions around the world on projects in those subject areas (The Aquila School n.d.). This type of direct interaction is significant in connecting with students and motivating them to learn languages, travel, and study abroad (Boix Mansilla and Jackson 2011).

Though there are certainly global inequities, many students around the world now have access to computer-linked projectors, videoconferencing, course websites, vast internet resources for research, and, of course, instant communication between individuals (Hobert 2013; Wylie 2011). Youth can use technology to consume information, for individual one-on-one communication, and to produce content for others.

Technology to Connect Classrooms

Lindsay and Davis's (2012) book *Flattening Classrooms, Engaging Minds* offers a template for teachers who want to implement collaborative projects with international partner schools. They present a taxonomy of collaboration and recommend starting with the simplest (first level) and moving toward the most complex (fifth level).

- Level 1: Intraconnection (within a single classroom)
- Level 2: Interconnection (within one school district)
- Level 3: Managed global connection
- Level 4: Student to student connection (with teacher management)
- Level 5: Student to student connection (with student management)

Lindsay and Davis (2012) suggest that the teacher starts by having all the students in the class work on a collaborative project such as writing a class wiki (a website that allows multiple collaborative writers) to develop skills related to respectfully editing each other's work (Level 1). Then, the students can work with students from another classroom at a school in the same district on an online asynchronous project so that they experience working in a fully mediated (not in person) environment and learn how important it is to stick to the agreed timeline and to communicate well between the two classrooms (Level 2). At Level 3, Lindsay and Davis (2012) recommend that the students join an existing international project with a built-in infrastructure, most likely involving classes around the world posting to a common

(continued on next page)

Technology to Connect Classrooms (continued)

website and perhaps offering comments on each other's work (see iearn.org for options). At Level 4, students from two classrooms in different countries can develop their own joint project, with the two teachers coordinating the process. At Level 5, the students in the two (or more) countries take over the coordination of the project, and the teachers serve more as coaches.

Lindsay and Davis's book offers extensive advice on timelines, communication, technology, existing projects that can be joined, potential pitfalls, and more. Citing a study by Heidi Everett-Cacopardo, Lindsay and Davis (2012) recommend the following practices when engaging in a global collaboration:

- Join with a teacher who is more experienced in online projects for the first several online collaborative projects between classrooms in different countries.
- Plan projects sufficiently far in advance to permit all partners to prepare.
- Ensure commitments from project partners.
- Communicate regularly between teachers.
- Have clear timelines in advance.
- Use multiple communication tools in addition to email, such as wikis, blogs, and videoconferencing.
- Use a project website to showcase students' work and help to engage other classrooms in collaboration.

Lindsay and Davis (2012) assert that technology is not a topic to be included in the curriculum, but rather a pedagogical approach. They argue that global collaboration between students should not be viewed as a bonus or filler activity, but a core part of the mission of any school that aspires to develop globally competent graduates.

Creating Opportunities for Student Mobility

Another internationalization strategy is creating more opportunities for study abroad, which can be a highly impactful experience for youth. As discussed in chapter 4 of this book, study abroad programs can result in a deepened understanding of the students' own country, a stronger sense of the rights and responsibilities of individuals in societies, greater tolerance for difference, lessening of stereotypes, improved leadership skills, enhanced intercultural communication skills, greater recognition of the spectrum of mobility from tourism to acculturation, and heightened confidence in their ability to have a positive impact on their local and global communities (Fayez and Prinzing 2010; Fordham 2006; U.S. Department of State 2009). Youth study abroad and exchange programs are likely to include homestays, further extending the impact of the program beyond the student to both the home and host families as well (Fayez and Prinzing 2010).

The American Council on Education (ACE) surveyed 1,509 U.S. youths and found that 85 percent expressed an interest in study abroad, although that particular survey was limited to college-bound students (ACE 2008). The study found high levels of interest among college-bound high school students in international learning, including language learning, and that students were motivated to expand their horizons by living in another culture (ACE 2008). It is especially important that all youth have the opportunity to learn about world regions and global issues and the chance to develop their intercultural communication and world language skills.

Data on Youth Study Abroad

Comprehensive data on the number of youths participating in study abroad are largely unavailable. Tracking of study abroad participant numbers is typically based on immigration data regarding visas issued and border crossings by visa holders. The majority of countries do not track these data, and when they do, they define the data in such different ways that the data are impossible to collate. For example, some countries count the number of international students studying in their countries, while other countries count the number of foreign students (all noncitizens, including immigrants who are permanently residing in the country). These two groups are clearly not the same, and adding the numbers up does not give an accurate view of how many students are studying abroad. Also, many youth study abroad programs are short term, lasting just a few weeks. Youth typically utilize tourist visas for these short-term programs, so these numbers are not included in national tallies of study abroad students either, further skewing the data (Macready and Tucker 2011).

A few discrete data points are available. U.S. Immigration and Customs Enforcement reports show that in July 2016, 4,846 students were studying in the United States on F-1 visas at the primary school level and 46,454 students were studying in the United States at the secondary school level (Student and Exchange Visitor Program 2016). However, students may also enter the United States in visitor visa categories if they are participating in a short recreational course of study that is not being used as credit toward a degree. Data from a June 2010 study listed 24,988 secondary students in the United States on visitor visas in June 2010 (Macready and Tucker 2011).

The Council on Standards for International Educational Travel (CSIET) is an organization that identifies and evaluates programs that facilitate international exchange and travel for secondary school-aged youth, both those coming into the United States and those going out of the United States. CSIET has developed quality standards for exchange programs that all of its members agree to comply with, and it evaluates members on the degree to which they are in compliance with those standards. For their 2014–15 semester and academic year study abroad programs, CSIET member organizations reported that they sent a total of 988 U.S. students abroad and received 32,663 international students in the United States (Olivetti and Hsiao 2015). By state, California hosted the largest number of international youths at 2,798, while the Midwest was the region that hosted the largest number of students on J-1 visas and the Northeast region hosted the largest number of students on F-1 visas (Olivetti and Hsiao 2015). Based on the state population, Idaho had the largest number of exchange students as a percentage of the high school population at 0.72 percent (Olivetti and Hsiao 2015). Germany and Italy were the top two sending countries for youth on J-1 visas, while China was the top sender of youth on F-1 visas (Olivetti and Hsiao 2015).

The U.S. government does not track the purposes for which its citizens leave the country, so any data on outbound U.S. students would need to be collected from the countries to which the students traveled. Australia is one example of a country that keeps detailed data on international students (both youth and university students). In 2017, it was reported that 25,762 international youths were enrolled in schools in Australia; the top sending countries were China, Vietnam, and South Korea (Australian Government 2017).

While most international educators support the expansion of study abroad and international travel opportunities, the students who study abroad are still a relatively elite group. In the United States, students of color and students from low socioeconomic backgrounds are generally underrepresented in youth study abroad programs (McLellan 2011; Seifert 2009). McLellan (2011) surveyed organizations that run youth exchange programs and found that most of the organizations were not even tracking student demographics, so they had no way of knowing if they were serving (or failing to serve) underrepresented groups.

Internationalizing Extracurricular Programming

Beyond the formal education curriculum, global competence can be developed in after-school and extracurricular programs. These nonformal learning opportunities can be fun and engaging, getting students excited about learning. At their best, these programs can increase students' self-confidence and social skills while building students' commitment to global citizenship and their social capital (Cieslik and Simpson 2013). Asia Society (2009) points out that after-school programs can:

- Expose young people to in-depth content about global issues as well as cultures, countries, and languages;

- Provide young people with opportunities to develop and use media literacy and technology skills to conduct research and communicate effectively on global topics;

- Enable social and emotional development critical to cross-cultural understanding, communication, and collaboration;

- Develop leadership and civic participation by empowering young people to take action on issues of both local and global relevance; and

- Engage young people in learning about international possibilities in college and future careers.

Asia Society (2009) elaborates that extracurricular programs can be structured in four different ways, which may or may not directly involve the school:

A. As an after-school program seamlessly connected with the school instruction;

B. As an after-school program that is separate from, but complementary to, the school instruction;

C. As an after-school program with distinct objectives that are completely separate from school instruction; and

D. As a summer program.

Regarding summer programs, Smink (2007) identifies three ways in which extracurricular programs can enhance formal schooling through meaningful, engaging experiences:

- Engagement. Students find something that interests them and develop a specialized skill or talent.

- Exploration. Students try something new or experiment with hands-on, outdoor, or project-based activities.

- Enrichment. Students participate in field trips, art, music, international studies, or other activities not found in the formal education curriculum.

Studies have shown that it may be advantageous for schools to offer after-school and summer programs. Research indicates that many students drop out of school because they are unengaged, and also that students often forget what they have learned over the summer; lower-income students are disproportionately affected by these trends (Smink 2007). Unequal access to enriching informal learning over the summer has been shown to account for as much as two-thirds of the achievement gap between privileged and underprivileged students (Smink 2007). Conversely, high-quality educational opportunities can allow students to explore music, arts, nature, world languages, and more (Smink 2007). Extracurricular programs can be particularly effective at reaching youths from low-income and minoritized backgrounds (Asia Society 2009).

The hallmarks of the most successful after-school programs are, not surprisingly, well suited toward the development of global competence: an asset-based approach, the involvement of families and communities, the use of interdisciplinary themes, project-based learning, and real-world connections to learning (Asia Society 2009). Asia Society (2009) recommends that when designing extracurricular programs to develop students' global competence, start with students' identity and heritage, introduce cultures, move from the familiar to the universal, promote multiple perspectives, and support intercultural communication opportunities.

Extracurricular Programs

There are many fun, interactive extracurricular programs that are intended to help to develop the global competence of youth:

- **Concordia Language Villages.** These are summer camps for students of all ages, focusing on fun and cultural learning through language immersion. www.concordialanguagevillages.org/

- **Global Glimpse.** It is a two-year leadership program for students in San Francisco, California; New York City, New York; and Chicago, Illinois, that includes after-school workshops, weekend summits, and a summer international travel experience. It serves many low-income youths. www.globalglimpse.org

- **Global Kids.** Global Kids organizes in-school, after-school, and summer programs in New York City and Washington D.C., primarily for students from underserved communities. Programs focus on global education in a human rights framework. www.globalkids.org

- **Global Young Leaders Conference.** High school students are able to participate in this 10-day conference focusing on developing global competence through interactions with students and leaders from around the world. www.envisionexperience.com/explore-our-programs/global-young-leaders-conference

- **Global Youth Village.** It is a summer camp for high school-aged youth, with approximately half of the participants from the United States and half from around the world. www.globalyouthvillage.org/

- **John Hopkins Center for Talented Youth.** It offers summer programs for students in the United States and abroad. Some of the programs focus on global issues. cty.jhu.edu/summer/grades7-12/leadership/catalog/curriculum.html

- **Model United Nations.** Students form teams representing different nations and attend conferences to debate global issues in the manner of the United Nations. There are various regional and national conferences. bestdelegate.com/model-un-conferences-database/

- **OneWorld Now!** It is an after-school program focusing on global citizenship for Seattle, Washington, high school students by providing Arabic, Chinese, and Korean instruction; leadership coursework; and study abroad. Evaluations show that students experienced increased levels of global citizenship upon completing the program (Thier et al. 2016). oneworldnow.org/

- **WE.** WE is a global movement dedicated to making a difference in the world. It offers in-school and after-school programs, including experiential service-learning and a guest speaker program. www.we.org

Extracurricular programs are well positioned to incorporate the diversity of the local community into the design. Students and parents may be recent immigrants willing to share their cultural heritage, or they may have connections through family, religion, or professional life to other parts of the world. Community members who are active in addressing global issues within the local area may be eager partners in internationalization efforts (Asia Society 2009).

Parents can also contribute to students' global development with games, food, media, holidays, discussion, and more (see Tavangar 2009 for detailed recommendations for parents; also see "Extracurricular Programs" on page 276).

Developing Global Outcomes and Assessment

Because international schools are often outside of national accreditation systems and have less oversight, there is a risk that the quality of education provided will be poor. Thus, there is strong pressure on international schools to demonstrate their effectiveness (Hayden and Thompson 2008). As with the internationalization of higher education, the emphasis and strategy of the internationalization of primary and secondary education is typically focused on developing students' global competence in measurable and demonstrable ways. This assessment of learning can be accomplished only with careful articulation of the intended learning outcomes. In other words, it is essential to know what the program leaders want students to learn before they are able to consider how to teach the content and how to measure student learning.

With international schools, parents want reassurance that students are developing the global knowledge and skills that have been promised. Therefore, international schools are under pressure to not only assess student learning in core subjects such as math and language, but also measure students' global competence. International standardized tests such as the SAT, AP tests, and GCSE do not test for international mindedness, making it harder for international schools to demonstrate their comparative value (Boix Mansilla and Jackson 2011; Bates 2011a). (Some of the international curricula that are available, such as the International Baccalaureate Diploma Programme, may test for international mindedness [Bates 2011a]).

If global competence is not measured through standardized testing, it must be measured through project-based work. Asia Society has developed the Graduation Performance System (formally known as the "Graduation Portfolio System"), in which teachers use Asia Society (2009) rubrics to assess student work against each of the four learning outcomes introduced earlier in the chapter: students' ability to investigate the world, recognize perspectives, communicate ideas, and take action. Teachers use the rubrics to identify the students' work as emerging, developing, proficient/college ready, or advanced in each of these areas and offer feedback to students on areas for growth (Asia Society 2011; Boix Mansilla and Jackson 2011).

In addition to attempting to measure and document student learning, international schools typically emphasize the college and career benefits for students. For example, the IB organization has agreements with almost 2,000 universities that they will accept the IB Diploma Programme for admissions purposes and, in many cases, will even offer students some credits toward their first year of college (Bates 2011a).

Teacher Training and Development

It is certain that students will be hindered in the development of their global competence if their teachers are not globally competent as well. For this reason, the development of teachers' global competence is an essential precursor to internationalizing schools. A crucial and urgent task of university colleges of education is that they internationalize their teacher training programs. This is also the responsibility of schools, districts, and governments offering continuing professional development opportunities for teachers. Intercultural training and international experience can occur during any phase of a teacher's education and career—during the bachelor's degree program, student teaching, master's degree program, or while working as a professional (West 2013).

Globally Competent Teachers

While many organizations have worked to articulate the knowledge, skills, and attitudes that are held by globally competent students, less has been done to identify the knowledge, skills, and attitudes of globally competent teachers (West 2013). Boix Mansilla and Jackson (2011) argue that teachers should be able to identify engaging topics of local and global significance, focus on global competence outcomes, design activities that allow students to practice and expand their global competence, and assess students' global competence.

At the 2012 NAFSA: Association of International Educators Colloquium on Internationalizing Teacher Education, the following global competencies were drafted by teams of teacher educators (NAFSA 2012):

KNOWLEDGE:

- Understand fundamental concepts of culture, globalism, and intercultural communication.
- Maintain an awareness of world and current events.
- Identify topics of global significance within content areas.
- Know one's own cultural construct.
- Know how to identify culturally and age-appropriate resources.
- Understand anticipated student outcomes for global competence and how to assess them.

SKILLS:

- Promote active listening, critical thinking, and perspective recognition.
- Promote global engagement, respect for diversity, and conflict resolution.

- Promote content-appropriate investigations of the world.

- Facilitate learning experiences in which students effectively communicate ideas to local and global audiences.

- Use technology to connect across classrooms, nations, and cultures.

- Assess students' global competence development.

DISPOSITIONS:

- Demonstrate an interest in and engagement with the world.

- Continue active learning about cultures, communities, and global concerns.

- Be reflective about one's own strengths and weaknesses in cultural awareness, knowledge, and pedagogical competence.

- Recognize multiple perspectives and respect other ways of knowing.

- Prioritize the development of students' global competence.

- Advocate for global education and social justice.

Working with a small group of Portuguese secondary school teachers, Bastos and Araújo e Sá (2015) developed an intercultural communicative competence training design. Through their experience and discussions with the participants, they posit that the best way to develop global competence is to begin with the affective component, promoting empathy and positive attitudes toward others and self, and toward intercultural and multilingual contexts. Bastos and Araújo e Sá (2015) contend that teachers value the coexistence of theoretical and practical application as well as self-reflection in training programs.

The reflection aspect of professional development is emphasized by the Globally Competent Learning Continuum developed by the Longview Foundation and LEARN NC. This tool identifies 12 teacher disposition, knowledge, and skill areas and offers a description of each at the nascent, beginning, progressing, proficient, and advanced levels (ASCD 2017). Teachers and student teachers can self-assess their level of proficiency on each of the 12 items and identify professional development opportunities to help them continue to develop their global competence.

Teacher Education Programs

While offering professional development for working teachers is important, there must also be a stronger focus on internationalizing teacher education programs. Colleges of education need to ensure that their faculty are themselves globally competent and able to help foster global competence in the teachers they are training (Longview Foundation 2008; West 2013). Unfortunately, colleges of education are typically among the least internationalized departments of universities (Schwarzer and Bridglall 2015). The transformation of a teacher education program may start with a single faculty member who is committed, with the deliberate introduction of globally oriented coursework or curriculum, or with a desire to embark on high-profile international projects and research (West 2012).

Biases in Classroom Materials

No educator can be knowledgeable about every culture, religion, historical era, political issue, and environmental issue. So, teachers will often find themselves teaching content that they have only introductory knowledge of, leaving them highly dependent on the curricular materials they are using to be detailed and accurate. Unfortunately, in this setting, there is a high risk that teachers will inadvertently reinforce biases or stereotypes. Uraneck (2002) advises on the careful adoption of classroom materials by offering descriptions of common biases:

- Regional or genre imbalance. Examples:
  - Using only folktales from a certain culture, giving an impression of quaintness rather than contemporary life
  - Having fewer books about the Middle East than Europe
- Broad labels and generalizations. Examples:
  - Having books about "Africa" as a category and not distinguishing the many nations and cultures
  - Having books about China that do not include China's many minority ethnic and religious groups
  - Focusing on only the grim topics associated with one country or continent (e.g., African poverty or Middle Eastern terrorism)

- Social and ethnic diversity neglected. Examples:
  - Having materials that show only the exotic examples and ignore the mainstream or everyday examples
  - Focusing too much on one group, such as the Maasai people of East Africa
- Stereotypes in environmental topics. Examples:
  - Emphasizing wild animals too much, while distorting ecology by omitting the human role
  - Presenting Africa as a landscape of wild animals and ignoring the cities and people
- Fiction with "colonial" mindsets. Examples:
  - Having adventure novels with harsh, exotic settings
  - Having materials that convey the idea that indigenous people cannot look out for themselves
- "Western" biographies and heroes. Examples:
  - Having stories of Western explorers, missionaries, humanitarians, and others that depict them as "saving" local people from their own weaknesses
  - Ignoring biographies of opposition leaders

(continued on next page)

Biases in Classroom Materials (continued)

- Overuse of fiction with rural or premodern settings. Examples:
  - Having stories set in rural areas that reinforce the ideas that other societies are quaint
  - Having stories set in rural areas that ignore contemporary urban problems

- Illustrations that reinforce stereotypes. Examples:
  - Overemphasizing polar bears in Alaska or elephants in Africa
  - Minimizing depiction of modern architecture and technology in developing countries

There are three primary approaches to internationalizing teacher education programs (West 2012):

A. Promote study abroad opportunities for student teachers. The transformative experience can motivate and increase one's understanding.

B. Focus on comparative education research and literature and explore educational practices from around the world in order to improve one's own practice.

C. Take a global studies approach and learn about global issues/topics in the content areas one will be teaching.

Like all approaches to internationalization, the internationalization of teacher education is best served by adopting a multipronged approach. Using West's (2012) threefold approach, this would mean promoting study abroad, offering courses in comparative education, and helping future teachers learn about international topics related to their teaching specialties.

West (2012) offers some strategies that universities can implement to internationalize their teacher education programs:

- Collectively determine priorities in curricular transformation and set a timeline for change.

- Budget necessary resources for curricular and cocurricular transformation and professional development.

- Develop and follow through with a plan for the coordination of international initiatives across the program, in collaboration with other related units on campus.

- Develop and implement a plan for assessment of outcomes of new programs and courses.

- Review teacher preparation programs that are further along in their internationalization initiatives to acquire ideas, good practices, and expert advice.

- Articulate ways that global competence fits into existing state and national standards and programs.

- Inspire faculty commitment to internationalization, and encourage, facilitate, and reward faculty growth in global awareness and cross-cultural theory and skill.

- Recruit faculty members with international expertise and a commitment to preparing globally competent teachers.

- Facilitate cross-cultural learning among teacher candidates and faculty members with international students and scholars on campus and with local immigrant communities to help build knowledge and appreciation of other cultures.

- Learn about existing technology on campus to determine how it might be used to create or enhance international, cross-cultural learning and partnership opportunities.

- Showcase accomplishments in curricular transformation and faculty and student growth.

Internationalization of Teacher Education Programs

Many colleges of education around the world have made significant strides in internationalizing their teacher education programs. In Toronto, Canada, York University conducted a survey of undergraduate education majors, and 63.8 percent said they were interested in teaching internationally when they graduate (West 2013). As a result, York developed several new internationally focused courses to add to its offerings: "Preparing to Teach Internationally," "Internationalizing Your Curriculum," "Teaching Internationally and Interculturally," "Reflecting on and Interpreting the International Education Experience," and "Teaching English in International Contexts." York is also offering a specialization in international education as part of its bachelor's degree program (West 2013).

The School of Leadership and Education Sciences (SOLES) at the University of San Diego (USD), located in San Diego, California, has taken more of a multipronged approach to internationalizing a teacher education program that is focused on globalizing. USD internationalized the curriculum, developed overseas partnerships and student teaching sites, and created a series of video case studies. The program curriculum includes an international experience requirement; while it can be fulfilled without traveling abroad, it must include the opportunity for reflection and the processing of cultural learning (Longview Foundation 2008; West 2012).

Many professional associations have created resources to support the internationalization of teacher educator programs as well. The NAFSA myCAP tool offers an online survey of 18 questions regarding attitudes about culture, global context, and the impact of culture on teaching (for more information, visit www.nafsa.org/mycap). The tool is recommended for use before and after a course or other learning experience so that changes in awareness and perspectives can be measured. It is set up for education faculty to register their students and for whole classes to take the survey. Both individual and class reports are generated for assessment (NAFSA 2018).

Study Abroad for Student Teachers

Beyond internationalizing the curriculum, providing opportunities for firsthand international experience is essential for developing globally competent international educators. Colleges of education can help meet this need by offering both study abroad and teach abroad opportunities. One of the logistical challenges is that it is often difficult for education majors to go abroad because of rigid licensure mandates and restrictive curricula determined by state, university, and professional accreditation bodies. For this reason, education is one of the least represented majors among study abroad participants (Cushner and Chang 2015).

Despite the underrepresentation of education majors, both study and teach abroad experiences can help student teachers to become more comfortable and competent working in cultural contexts other than their own, to work more effectively with diverse peers and students, and to gain more knowledge about the world (Cushner and Chang 2015). Cushner and Chang (2015) conducted a study focused on student teachers abroad. Their findings correspond with extensive research in education abroad. They found that simply going abroad to do student teaching is not sufficient for strengthening global competence; the intercultural learning must be intensive and planned, and the faculty and local mentors need to be interculturally competent (Cushner and Chang 2015).

Several organizations can help facilitate opportunities for student teaching abroad. Through the Global Gateway for Teachers Program (formerly known as "Cultural Immersion Projects") at Indiana University-Bloomington, students live in the community where they are teaching and complete a service-learning project while they are there. There are structured reflection activities, and a mentor classroom teacher travels overseas with the student teachers for support (West 2013; Indiana University 2019).

Additionally, the Consortium for Overseas Student Teaching (COST) is an association of U.S. colleges and universities with partnerships around the world that can provide opportunities for overseas student teaching (West 2013; Grand Valley State University 2019). The University of Kentucky (UK), for example, participates in COST and has two exchange programs that allow the school to host student teachers from partner institutions.

UK also has a visiting faculty-in-residence program. Prior to going abroad to teach, University of Kentucky students take a three-credit course titled "Culture, Education and Teaching Abroad," which introduces intercultural theory and practice, as well as teaching with a global perspective. Students study the educational system of the place where they will be going and submit two structured reflections while abroad. After the program, they receive a final evaluation from their host teacher, debrief upon return, and complete a survey 1 year later (West 2013).

Teacher candidates from the United States who have studied abroad have been generally highly sought-after when it comes to the job marketplace. For example, at Western Kentucky University, data show that about 25 percent of all teacher candidates participate in the international program, and those candidates had a 100 percent postgraduation employment rate (West 2013).

Short courses abroad can also have a strong impact on participants. Brendel et al. (2016) describe a study in which eight German and eight Turkish student teachers took a course together on sustainable development, doing fieldwork in multicultural groups. The reflection activities took place first with those from the same group, and later in groups of mixed nationality (and language). Brendel et al. (2016) found that through these short-term collaborative projects, the student teachers became aware of how different educational systems socialized students, they learned how to overcome stereotypes, and they became more empathetic to language learners.

Considerations for Practitioners

With varied types of international schools serving students within many different national, cultural, political, and economic contexts, it is impossible to identify one set of concerns that apply to all international schools. Instead, this section describes critiques of international schools that may apply to *some* schools. Students, parents, educators, accreditors, and others must assess each case in order to determine which considerations and challenges are relevant to an individual school or group of schools.

International in Name Only

One of the concerns about international schools is that some are operating more like corporations than educational institutions. Designating a school as an "international school," in some cases, is considered a branding tactic and a carefully calibrated marketing strategy that may come with very little real internationalization of the educational content. From this perspective, international schools are treated as products and the students and parents as customers, using the lens of global business to define and run the school, rather than using a lens of public service and considering the needs of the local or international community (Bunnell 2011; Doherty 2009; Resnik 2012; Tate 2016).

Western Emphasis

Another concern about some international schools is that the values, educational content, pedagogies, and assessment of learning may be Western in origin and do not allow for other cultural ways of knowing (Bates 2011b, 2011a; Bunnell 2011; Skelton 2016; Fail 2011). For example, Western values related to individualism and capitalism may lead to a school focus on entrepreneurship and place less emphasis on being a socially responsible citizen, something that might be prioritized within a more collectivist culture (Marshall 2011).

The current dominant approach to schooling originated in individualistic Western countries. It is typically characterized by having children divided by age groups, working on the same projects at the same time, following an inflexible daily schedule under the direction of a single teacher. In contrast, alternative approaches to education could include multigrade classrooms, students working at their own pace, peer tutoring with older children helping younger children, and the free flow of children and adults between the school and the community (Farrell 2008).

The teachers and curriculum developers working in international education tend to be from Western countries and, therefore, teach in the ways that they have been trained (Fail 2011; Hayden and Thompson 2008). Wylie (2011) argues that even in international partnerships, schools dominated by Western culture often prefer to connect with other schools with Western cultures. Yet, to be truly international, programs need to include voices from students, teachers, and curriculum developers from all parts of the world (Wylie 2011). For example, the subject area of history can vary greatly in different national cultures, yet because most teachers are Western, it is usually Western interpretations of history that are taught (Hayden and Thompson 2008; Sakhiyya 2011). In this way, the ideas of internationalization may also be very one-directional, flowing from the west to the east, or from developed countries to developing countries, when internationalized schools should intentionally adopt a wide diversity of views (Sakhiyya 2011).

The languages taught in educational systems around the world often incite fierce political battles. In international schools, the most common language of instruction is English, and when foreign languages (languages other than the official language of the host country) are taught, they are most often Western languages as well (Doherty 2009; Hayden and Thompson 2008). For internationally mobile students, this is often the most pragmatic situation. However, it also exacerbates global inequities.

For some students, gaining proficiency in English and other dominant world languages can improve social and career capital and provide future job opportunities (Marshall 2011; Resnik 2012). However, for other students, they have little access to formal instruction in their heritage languages. While there are practical reasons for focusing on Western languages in international schools, it is also an impediment to diversity that so few world languages are taught and that the curriculum does not seem to value all languages equally (Doherty 2009; Hayden and Thompson 2008; Tate 2016).

Reinforced Inequities

Another common concern about international schools is that they are too elite and serve to reinforce inequities in society. Many governments around the world seek to reduce societal inequities by providing educational opportunities that offer people the chance to achieve an above average livelihood. However, there is a paradox: Above average livelihoods (salaries, perks, etc.) are given to people with credentials and skills that are in demand and scarce in society. So, the more educational opportunities created, the less scarce the credentials become and the less that people warrant an above average livelihood. An important attraction of international schools that are perceived to be elite is that "they offer social status and lifestyles that are in short supply. They are sought after because they are exclusive rather than inclusive" (Bates 2011a, 150).

Doherty (2009, 5) suggests that the IB curriculum "seems to be associated as much with vertical mobility and class politics as with horizontal or spatial mobility." Indeed, one of the reasons why many parents choose to enroll their children in international schools is because of the social and economic advantages they hope their children will gain (Doherty 2009; Hayden 2006). In an examination of IB enrollment in Australia, Doherty et al. (2012) found that parents with higher incomes and postgraduate degrees were the most likely to enroll their children in IB programs. In this way, international schools may sometimes be reinforcing existing stratification within societies, bolstering local elites at the expense of the wider local population (Bunnell 2011; Resnik 2012; Tate 2016). Yet the "eliteness" of international schools may be waning in at least some regions, such as the United States and the United Kingdom, where the majority of IB international schools are public schools serving local students (Bunnell 2011).

Values Deficit

A final concern about some international schools is that in their attempt to be unbiased and nonjudgmental of cultural viewpoints, there may be a deficit of values taught. With a belief that all values and perspectives are equally valid, an unfortunate lack of morality can be inculcated based on the idea that nothing is inherently wrong (Fail 2011). An approach to developing students' global competence that is strongly focused on interpersonal understanding and common humanity might have this unintended result. The remedy is to also include an emphasis on critical global citizenship focused on mitigating global inequities of power (Harris 2014).

Future Trends

Hobert (2013) estimates that as many as 90 percent of schools are adding the words "international," "global," or "world" into their mission statements, and it is likely that many schools will gradually follow that step with the internationalization of their curriculum, professional development for teachers, establishment of international partnerships, increased student mobility, and more. With this growth comes increasing numbers of job opportunities for international educators trained in both education and international/intercultural studies (Hallgarten, Tabberer, and McCarthy 2015).

On a policy level, it is expected that governments will continue to grapple with the place of international schools in national educational systems. Governments will proceed to create opportunities for improved access to education for their citizens, to prepare graduates to be competitive in the global economy, and to ensure high-quality outcomes for students. Some of the stakeholders in and around government will argue that international schools can help achieve these goals, while others will contest that international schools are a hindrance. Some will maintain that international schools offer marketplace alternatives, improving the quality of all education through competition. Others will suggest that international schools are elitist institutions reinforcing social inequities. The reality is likely a combination of both.

In an analysis of rhetoric related to U.S. public schools becoming international schools and arguments in favor of international education, Parker (2009) found messages of hope that students will know and care about people everywhere, messages of fear that the United States is losing its competitive advantage, and messages of exaggeration, for example, that education is the key to the nation's economic salvation. While there are many allies to be found, educators seeking to internationalize the K–12 curriculum may face resistance from their colleagues and other stakeholders. Hobert (2013) argues that the resistance is often couched in one of the following questions and statements:

- What is global competence?

- There are already too many things we need to teach our students.

- Students are busy with homework in their other subjects. This will take time away from the things that are more important.

- What about students who already struggle with school? School is hard enough already.

- With the pressures of standardized testing, there isn't enough time in the day.

- Where is the funding for teaching this?

- The town/board/community will never approve.

Each of these areas of resistance reinforces the idea that global competence is an optional add-on to the curriculum and that it is less important than other types of learning.

The movement to convince all stakeholders of the importance of developing the global competence of youth is by no means complete. International educators must continue to advocate for changes to educational policies and practices. To maximize the benefits of internationalization, *all* students in *all* schools need to develop global competence, not just those in international schools (Mansilla and Jackson 2011; Skelton 2016). This will require overcoming political conflicts to collaborate on policy changes at the district, state, and national levels. Specifically, Boix Mansilla and Jackson (2011) propose four policy priorities:

- Making world languages a core component of the K–12 curriculum;

- Redefining expectations and high school graduation requirements to include global competence;

- Providing greater opportunities for students to connect worldwide; and

- Increasing educators' capacity to teach about the world.

Also essential for policy advocacy is ensuring that there is funding for the internationalization of curricula and for travel of both teachers and students. Teacher education programs at universities need to be internationalized so that K–12 teachers are, themselves, globally competent (Boix Mansilla and Jackson 2011; West 2013; Yemini and Fulop 2015; NAFSA 2012).

Conclusion

While there are some critiques of international schools, there continues to be strong demand from students and parents, as well as high regard for the educational, social, and professional outcomes. Because of these anticipated benefits, the growth in the number of international schools and the trend toward internationalization will likely carry on for the foreseeable future.

In the coming decades, however, as local public schools internationalize, it is expected that the distinction between international schools and other schools will diminish, with international schools looking less different from their local counterparts (Hallgarten, Tabberer, and McCarthy 2015; Resnik 2012; Grand Valley State University 2019; Cambridge 2011). International schools will enroll and influence a greater diversity of students. At the same time, international school curricula and pedagogies will influence and shape teaching and learning within national educational systems, benefiting all youth and the global society.

Resources

READINGS:

- Boix Mansilla, Veronica, and Anthony Jackson. 2011. *Educating for Global Competence: Preparing Our Youth to Engage the World*. New York, NY: Asia Society and Council of Chief State School Officers. https://asiasociety.org/files/book-globalcompetence.pdf.

- Lindsay, Julie, and Vicki A. Davis. 2012. *Flattening Classrooms, Engaging Minds: Move to Global Collaboration One Step at a Time*. Boston, MA: Pearson.

- Pollock, David C., and Ruth E. Van Reken. 2009. *Third Culture Kids: Growing Up Among Worlds, Second Edition*. Boston, MA: Nicholas Brealey America.

- Tavangar, Homa Sabet, and Becky Mladic-Morales. 2014. *The Global Education Toolkit for Elementary Learners*. Thousand Oaks, CA: Corwin.

- United Nations Educational, Scientific and Cultural Organization (UNESCO). 2015. *Global Citizenship Education: Topics and Learning Objectives*. Paris, France: United Nations Educational, Scientific and Cultural Organization. http://unesdoc.unesco.org/images/0023/002329/232993e.pdf.

RESOURCE WEBSITES FOR TEACHERS:

- Asia Society Center for Global Education Educator Resources asiasociety.org/education/educators

- Edutopia Global Education Resource Roundup www.edutopia.org/article/global-education-resources

- Global Teacher Education Approaches and Preparation www.globalteachereducation.org/category/583d2c0a542190008b3c8073

- iEARN iearn.org/

- NAFSA: Association of International Educators Resources for Teachers www.nafsa.org/professional-resources/browse-by-interest/internationalizing-teacher-education-online-resources

- National Education Association Global Education Resources www.nea.org/home/37409.htm

- National Geographic Society Classroom Resources www.nationalgeographic.org/education/teaching-resources/
- Oxfam Global Citizenship Guides www.oxfam.org.uk/education/global-citizenship/global-citizenship-guides
- Peace Corps Educator Resources www.peacecorps.gov/educators/resources/
- UNICEF Kid Power School Program schools.unicefkidpower.org/

INTERNATIONAL SCHOOL ASSOCIATIONS:

- Academy for International School Heads www.academyish.org
- Alliance for International Education www.intedalliance.org
- Association for the Advancement of International Education www.aaie.org
- Association of American Schools in Mexico www.asomex.org
- Association of American Schools in South America www.aassa.com
- Association of American Schools of Central America www.aascaonline.net
- Association of American Schools of Central America, Colombia – Caribbean and Mexico www.tri-association.org
- Association of Boarding Schools www.boardingschools.com
- Association of China and Mongolia International Schools www.acamis.org
- Association of Christian Schools International www.acsi.org/
- Association of German International Schools www.agis-schools.org
- Association of International Schools in Africa www.aisa.or.ke
- Boarding Schools' Association (UK) www.boarding.org.uk
- British Schools in the Middle East www.bsme.org.uk
- Central and Eastern European Schools www.ceesa.org
- Council of British International Schools www.cobis.org.uk
- Council of International Schools www.cois.org

- East Asia Regional Council of Schools www.earcos.org
- Educational Collaborative for International Schools www.ecis.org
- Federation of British International Schools in Asia www.fobisia.org
- International Baccalaureate Schools and Colleges Association of the UK and Ireland www.ibsca.org.uk
- International Schools Association www.isaschools.org
- International Schools Association of Thailand www.isat.or.th
- Latin American Heads Conference www.lahc.net
- Mediterranean Association of International Schools www.mais-web.org
- Middle East International Baccalaureate Association www.meibaschools.org
- National Association of British Schools in Spain www.nabss.org
- National Association of Independent Schools (U.S. and International) www.nais.org
- Near East South Asia Council of Overseas Schools www.nesacenter.org
- Rome International Schools Association www.romeschools.org
- Swiss Group of International Schools www.sgischools.com
- U.S. Department of State Office of Overseas Schools www.state.gov/m/a/os

OTHER:

- Asia Society International Studies Schools Network https://asiasociety.org/international-studies-schools-network
- Council of International Schools job board www.cois.org/international-education-careers/educator-vacancies
- International School Community online forum internationalschoolcommunity.com/loginmember.php
- *International Schools Journal* www.johncattbookshop.com/books/international-schools-journal

- International Schools Services www.iss.edu/

- *International Teacher Magazine* consiliumeducation.com/itm/

- NAFSA: Association of International Educators myCAP www.nafsa.org/mycap

- University of Northern Iowa Overseas Recruiting Fair www.uni.edu/placement/overseas/fair

- U.S. Department of State, Office of Overseas Schools www.state.gov/bureaus-offices/under-secretary-for-management/bureau-of-administration/office-of-overseas-schools/

References

American Council on Education (ACE). 2008. *College-Bound Students' Interests in Study Abroad and Other International Learning Activities*. Washington, DC: American Council on Education. http://www.acenet.edu/news-room/Documents/2008-Student-Poll.pdf.

The Aquila School. n.d. "About Us." Dubai, United Arab Emirates: The Aquila School. https://www.theaquilaschool.com/about-us/.

ASCD. 2017. "The Globally Competent Learning Continuum." Alexandria, VA: ASCD. http://globallearning.ascd.org/lp/editions/global-continuum/index.html.

Asia Society. 2009. *Expanding Horizons: Building Global Literacy in Afterschool Programs*. Washington, DC: Asia Society. http://asiasociety.org/files/Expanding%20Horizons%20guidebook.pdf.

Asia Society. 2011. "Asia Society's Graduation Portfolio System (GPS): Global Leadership Rubric." New York, NY: Asia Society. http://asiasociety.org/files/issn-glpo.pdf.

Asia Society. 2018. "Our Services." Asia Society. https://asiasociety.org/international-studies-schools-network/our-services.

Asia Society and The George Lucas Foundation. 2007. *A World-Class Education: Volume 2*. DVD. Asia Society and The George Lucas Foundation.

Australian Government. 2017. "End of Year Summary of International Student Enrolment Data - Australia - 2017." Australian Government Department of Education and Training. https://internationaleducation.gov.au/research/international-student-data/pages/default.aspx.

Bastos, Mónica, and Helena Araújo e Sá. 2015. "Pathways to Teacher Education for Intercultural Communicative Competence: Teachers' Perceptions." *The Language Learning Journal* 43, 2:131–147. https://doi.org/10.1080/09571736.2013.869940.

Bates, Richard. 2011a. "Assessment and International Schools." In *Schooling Internationally: Globalisation, Internationalisation and the Future for International Schools*, ed. Richard Bates. Abingdon, Oxon, United Kingdom: Routledge.

Bates, Richard. 2011b. "Introduction." In *Schooling Internationally: Globalisation, Internationalisation and the Future for International Schools*, ed. Richard Bates. Abingdon, Oxon, United Kingdom: Routledge.

Boix Mansilla, Veronica, and Anthony Jackson. 2011. *Educating for Global Competence: Preparing Our Youth to Engage the World*. New York, NY: Asia Society and Council of Chief State School Officers. https://asiasociety.org/files/book-globalcompetence.pdf.

Brendel, Nina, Fisun Aksit, Selahattin Aksit, and Gabriele Schrüfer. 2016. "Multicultural Group Work on Field Excursions to Promote Student Teachers' Intercultural Competence." *Journal of Geography in Higher Education* 40, 2:284–301. https://doi.org/10.1080/03098265.2016.1140731.

Bunnell, Tristan. 2010. "The Momentum Behind the International Primary Curriculum in Schools in England." *Journal of Curriculum Studies* 42, 4:471–486. https://doi.org/10.1080/00220272.2010.487315.

Bunnell, Tristan. 2011. "The International Baccalaureate: Its Growth and Complexity of Challenges." In *Schooling Internationally: Globalisation, Internationalisation and the Future for International Schools*, ed. Richard Bates. Abingdon, Oxon, United Kingdom: Routledge.

Bunnell, Tristan, Michael Fertig, and Chris James. 2016. "What Is International about International Schools? An Institutional Legitimacy Perspective." *Oxford Review of Education* 42, 4:408–423. https://doi.org/10.1080/03054985.2016.1195735.

Calliods, Francoise. 2008. "Preface." In *International Schools: Growth and Influence*, eds. Mary Hayden and Jeff Thompson. Paris, France: UNESCO: International Institution for Educational Planning. http://unesdoc.unesco.org/images/0018/001803/180396e.pdf.

Cambridge, James. 2011. "International Curriculum." In *Schooling Internationally: Globalisation, Internationalisation and the Future for International Schools*, eds. Richard Bates. Abingdon, Oxon, United Kingdom: Routledge.

Cieslik, Mark, and Donald Simpson. 2013. *Key Concepts in Youth Studies*. London, United Kingdom: Sage Publications.

Civinini, Claudia. 2018. "UK: Gap Widening in Foreign Language Learning." *PIE News*. June 27, 2018. https://thepienews.com/news/gap-foreign-language-learning/.

Culross, Rita, and Emily Tarver. 2011. "A Summary of Research on the International Baccalaureate Diploma Programme: Perspectives of Students, Teachers, and University Admissions Offices in the USA." *Journal of Research in International Education* 10, 3:231–243.

Cushner, Kenneth, and Shu-Ching Chang. 2015. "Developing Intercultural Competence through Overseas Student Teaching: Checking Our Assumptions." *Intercultural Education* 26, 3:165–178. https://doi.org/10.1080/14675986.2015.1040326.

Doherty, Catherine. 2009. "The Appeal of the International Baccalaureate in Australia's Educational Market: A Curriculum of Choice for Mobile Futures." *Discourse: Studies in the Cultural Politics of Education* 30, 1:73–89. https://doi.org/10.1080/01596300802643108.

Doherty, Catherine, Allan Luke, Paul Shield, and Candice Hincksman. 2012. "Choosing Your Niche: The Social Ecology of the International Baccalaureate Diploma in Australia." *International Studies in Sociology of Education* 22, 4:311–332. https://doi.org/10.1080/09620214.2012.745346.

Fail, Helen. 2011. "Teaching and Learning in International Schools." In *Schooling Internationally: Globalisation, Internationalisation and the Future for International Schools*, ed. Richard Bates. Abingdon, Oxon, United Kingdom: Routledge.

Farrell, Joseph P. 2008. "Teaching and Learning to Teach; Successful Radical Alternatives from the Developing World." In *Comparative and International Education: Issues for Teachers*, eds. Karen Mundy, Kathy Bickmore, Ruth Hayhoe, Meggan Madden, and Katherine Madjidi. New York, NY: Teachers College Press.

Fayez, Sherifa M. B. E, and Dan Prinzing. 2010. "Promoting U.S.-Middle Eastern Cultural Understanding Through Youth Exchange." In *Innovation Through Education: Building the Knowledge Economy in the Middle East*, eds. Daniel Obst and Daniel Kirk. New York, NY: Institute of International Education.

Fordham, Traci. 2006. "Pedagogies of Cultural Change: The Rotary International Youth Exchange Program and Narratives of Travel and Transformation." *Journal of Tourism and Cultural Change* 3, 3:143–159. https://doi.org/10.1080/14766820608668492.

Grabe, William, and Fredericka L. Stroller. 1997. "Content-Based Instruction: Research Foundations." In *Content-Based Instruction in Foreign Language Education: Models and Methods*, eds. Stephen R. Stryker and Betty Lou Leaver. Washington, DC: Georgetown University Press.

Grand Valley State University. 2019. "Consortium for Overseas Student Teaching." Allendale, MI: Grand Valley State University. https://www.gvsu.edu/cost/.

Hallgarten, Joe, Ralph Tabberer, and Kenny McCarthy. 2015. *3rd Culture Schools: International Schools as Creative Catalysts for a New Global Education System*. London, United Kingdom: ECIS. https://www.thersa.org/globalassets/pdfs/reports/third-culture-schools-report.pdf.

Harris, Anita. 2014. "Generation G, Global Connectedness & Global Responsibility." International Education Association of Australia. https://www.ieaa.org.au/documents/item/292.

Hayden, Mary. 2006. *Introduction to International Education: International Schools and Their Communities*. London, United Kingdom: Sage Publications.

Hayden, Mary, and Jeff Thompson. 2008. *International Schools: Growth and Influence*. Paris, France: UNESCO: International Institution for Educational Planning. http://unesdoc.unesco.org/images/0018/001803/180396e.pdf.

Hayden, Mary, and Jeff Thompson. 2013. "International Schools: Antecedents, Current Issues and Metaphors for the Future." In *International Education and Schools: Moving Beyond the First 40 Years*, ed. Richard Pearce. New York, NY: Bloomsbury Publishing.

Hayden, Mary, and Jeff Thompson. 2016. *International Schools: Current Issues and Future Prospects*. Oxford, United Kingdom: Symposium Books.

Hobert, Carl. 2013. *Raising Global IQ: Preparing Our Students for a Shrinking Planet*. Boston, MA: Beacon Press.

Indiana University. 2019. "Global Gateway for Teachers." Indiana University. https://education.indiana.edu/programs/global-gateway/index.html.

International Baccalaureate. n.d. "About the IB." International Baccalaureate Organization. https://www.ibo.org/about-the-ib.

International Baccalaureate. 2014. "Key Findings from Global Research on the Impact of IB Programmes." International Baccalaureate Organization. https://www.ibo.org/globalassets/publications/ib-research/globalkeyfindingssheeten.pdf.

International Baccalaureate. 2015. *Education for a Better World*. International Baccalaureate Organization. https://www.ibo.org/globalassets/digital-tookit/brochures/corporate-brochure-en.pdf.

International School Manila. 2019. "Service Learning Program." Taguig City, Philippines: International School Manila. https://www.ismanila.org/learning-at-ism/service-learning-program.

Kisch, Marian. 2010. "Opening Young Eyes." *International Educator* XIX, 5:22–30.

Lindsay, Julie, and Vicki A. Davis. 2012. *Flattening Classrooms, Engaging Minds: Move to Global Collaboration One Step at a Time.* Boston, MA: Pearson.

Longview Foundation. 2008. *Teacher Preparation for the Global Age: The Imperative for Change.* Silver Spring, MD: Longview Foundation. http://www.acenet.edu/news-room/Documents/Teacher-Prep-for-Global-Age.pdf.

Macready, Caroline, and Clive Tucker. 2011. *Who Goes Where and Why? An Overview and Analysis of Global Educational Mobility.* Washington, DC: Institute of International Education. https://www.iie.org:443/en/Research-and-Insights/Publications/Who-Goes-Where-and-Why.

Marshall, Harriet. 2011. "Instrumentalism, Ideals and Imaginaries: Theorising the Contested Space of Global Citizenship Education in Schools." *Globalisation, Societies and Education* 9, 3–4:411–426. https://doi.org/10.1080/14767724.2011.605325.

McLellan, Carlton E. 2011. "International Education Travel and Youth of Color: College Is Too Late!" *Education and Urban Society* 43, 2:244–265. https://doi.org/10.1177/0013124510379874.

NAFSA: Association of International Educators. 2012. "Knowledge, Skills, and Dispositions of Globally Competence Teachers at the Proficiency Level." Washington, DC: NAFSA: Association of International Educators. https://www.nafsa.org/_/File/_/colloquium12_draft_rubic.pdf.

NAFSA: Association of International Educators. 2018. "myCAP Suite of Resources." Washington, DC: NAFSA: Association of International Educators. http://www.nafsa.org/mycap.

Olivetti, Nina, and Chung Yang Hsiao. 2015. *International Youth Exchange Statistics 2014–2015 Academic Cycle.* Alexandria, VA: Council on Standards for International Education Travel.

Oxfam. 2015. *Education for Global Citizenship: A Guide for Schools.* Oxford, United Kingdom: Oxfam.

Parker, Walter C. 2009. "'International Education' in US Public Schools." *Globalisation, Societies and Education* 9, 3–4:487–501.

Pollock, David C., and Ruth E. Van Reken. 2009. *Third Culture Kids: Growing Up Among Worlds, Second Edition.* Boston, MA: Nicholas Brealey America.

Resnik, Julia. 2012. "The Denationalization of Education and the Expansion of the International Baccalaureate." *Comparative Education Review* 56, 2:248–269. https://doi.org/10.1086/661770.

Sakhiyya, Zulfa. 2011. "Interrogating Identity: The International Standard School in Indonesia." *Pedagogy, Culture & Society* 19, 3:345–365. https://doi.org/10.1080/14681366.2011.607841.

Schwarzer, David, and Beatrice L. Bridglall, eds. 2015. *Promoting Global Competence and Social Justice in Teacher Education: Successes and Challenges within Local and International Contexts*. Lanham, MD: Lexington Books.

Seattle Public Schools. 2019. "About John Stanford." Seattle, WA: Seattle Public Schools. https://stanfordes.seattleschools.org/about/about_john_stanford.

Seifert, Kim. 2009. "'Colored Glasses': Moving Intercultural Exchange into the Classroom." *Intercultural Education* 20, sup1:S143–149. https://doi.org/10.1080/14675980903371043.

Skelton, Martin. 2016. "What Should Students Learn in International Schools?" In *International Schools: Current Issues and Future Prospects*, eds. Mary Hayden and Jeff Thompson. Didcot, Oxford, United Kingdom: Symposium Books.

Smink, Jeffrey D. 2007. "Summer Learning Programs and Student Success in the Global Economy." *New Directions for Youth Development* 2007, 116:35–48. https://doi.org/10.1002/yd.232.

Sperandio, Jill. 2010. "School Program Selection: Why Schools Worldwide Choose the International Baccalaureate Middle Years Program." *Journal of School Choice* 4, 2:137–148. https://doi.org/10.1080/15582159.2010.483916.

Stewart, Vivien. 2012. *A World-Class Education: Learning from International Models of Excellence and Innovation*. Alexandria, VA: ASCD.

Student and Exchange Visitor Program. 2016. *SEVIS By the Numbers: July 2016*. Washington, DC: U.S. Immigration and Customs Enforcement. https://www.ice.gov/sites/default/files/documents/Document/2016/SEVP_SBTN_JUL2016.pdf.

Suarez-Orozco, Marcelo, and Desiree B. Qin-Hilliard, eds. 2004. *Globalization: Culture and Education in the New Millennium*. Berkeley, CA: University of California Press.

Tate, Nicholas. 2016. "What Are International Schools For?" In *International Schools: Current Issues and Future Prospects*, eds. Mary Hayden and Jeff Thompson. Oxford, United Kingdom: Symposium Books.

Tavangar, Homa Sabet. 2009. *Growing Up Global: Raising Children to Be At Home in the World.* New York, NY: Ballantine Books.

Thier, Michael, Richie Thomas, Jennifer Tanaka, and Lokela Alexander Minami. 2016. "Global by Design: Participatory Evaluation of a Global Citizenship After-School Program." *Journal of Research in Curriculum & Instruction* 20, 3:220–231.

United Nations Educational, Scientific and Cultural Organization (UNESCO). 2015. *Global Citizenship Education: Topics and Learning Objectives.* Paris, France: United Nations Educational, Scientific and Cultural Organization. http://unesdoc.unesco.org/images/0023/002329/232993e.pdf.

United World Colleges (UWC). 2017. "About." London, United Kingdom: United World Colleges. https://www.uwc.org/about.

Uraneck, Madeline. 2002. *Planning Curriculum in International Education.* Madison, WI: Wisconsin Department of Public Instruction.

U.S. Department of State. 2009. *Evaluation of Youth Exchange & Study Program: Final Report.* Washington, DC: U.S. Department of State.

West, Charlotte. 2012. "Toward Globally Competent Pedagogy." Washington, DC: NAFSA: Association of International Educators.

West, Charlotte. 2013. *Global Classrooms, Global Teachers: Building Cross-Cultural Competence through Experiences Abroad.* Washington, DC: NAFSA: Association of International Educators.

Wylie, Michael. 2011. "Global Networking and Education." In *Schooling Internationally: Globalisation, Internationalisation and the Future for International Schools*, ed. Richard Bates. Abingdon, Oxon, United Kingdom: Routledge.

Yemini, Miri, and Alexandra Fulop. 2015. "The International, Global and Intercultural Dimensions in Schools: An Analysis of Four Internationalised Israeli Schools." *Globalisation, Societies and Education* 13, 4:528–552. https://doi.org/10.1080/14767724.2014.967185.

Chapter 9

Citizen Diplomacy

Citizen diplomacy emphasizes the collective power of individual interactions to create shared understanding across cultures. The Center for Citizen Diplomacy (2017) defines citizen diplomacy as "the concept that every global citizen has the right, even the responsibility, to engage across cultural differences and create shared understanding through person-to-person interactions." Citizen diplomats are the individuals who engage in these one-on-one interactions. They may be teachers, students, professionals, retirees, athletes, artists, humanitarians, and others who feel a responsibility to engage culturally different others in meaningful dialogue (The Center for Citizen Diplomacy 2017).

Citizen diplomats help to build cross-cultural understanding by listening to others with an open mind; learning about other histories, cultures, and ways of life; respecting others' right to think differently; looking for opportunities to interact with people from around the world; and working to make positive differences in the global community (The Center for Citizen Diplomacy 2017). Through sharing their culture and perspectives, and learning from others, citizen diplomats build individual and collective global competence, which, in turn, promotes global economic growth, problem-solving on global issues, and greater world peace (The Center for Citizen Diplomacy 2017). For this reason, many citizen diplomacy programs are funded by national governments.

Citizen diplomacy is often discussed as a form of soft power. In the international relations field, "hard power" refers to the use of military or economic power to pressure foreign governments to act in ways desired by the nation wielding the power. In contrast, "soft power" refers to efforts to influence foreign governments through the development of positive relations, cultivated by initiatives that highlight the attractiveness of a country's culture, values, and political ideals (Nye 2004). Soft power helps nations to achieve their goals in that international people and governments admire a nation's ideas and want to emulate the example (Atkinson 2010).

International education programs may be considered soft power initiatives because they foster the sharing of norms, customs, ideas, and values (Atkinson 2010). International education programs that highlight the power of individual interactions across cultures to further positive relations between cultural groups and between nations may be self-designated or described by others as "citizen diplomacy programs." Yang (2018, 4) suggests that "university activities such as enrolled international students, foreign scholars in-residence, and academic exchange, may reinforce official policy goals. The millions of people who have studied in other countries constitute a remarkable reservoir of goodwill for those host countries." Because of the overlapping goals of international education and international diplomacy, some of the citizen diplomacy programs described in this chapter may also be classified as education abroad, international student programs, or youth international education programs.

This chapter explores the goals of citizen diplomacy programs, citizen diplomacy in the United States, program models, and citizen diplomacy outcomes. The role of professionals in administering and leading such programs is introduced. And the challenges of assessment are explored, as are considerations for practitioners working in this sector.

Public Diplomacy

Public diplomacy is closely related to citizen diplomacy. Some writers use the term "public diplomacy" synonymously with "citizen diplomacy." Others use the term to describe government-funded citizen diplomacy programs. The most common use of the term comes from the international relations field. In this sphere, public diplomacy is a broad concept that conveys all of the ways in which governments seek to shape their reputation as perceived by the everyday people of the world (the global public). Used in this broader sense, public diplomacy may be defined as "international political communication aimed at creating mutually beneficial relations with the public abroad in order to support the communicator's objectives" (Ociepka 2018, 290). While historical efforts may have involved unidirectional propaganda campaigns, contemporary efforts are more likely to involve interactive media campaigns, cultural events, and citizen diplomacy programs (Cull 2009; Ociepka 2018; CPD Advisory Board 2017).

History of U.S. Citizen Diplomacy

The political will to support citizen diplomacy often surges in reaction to the devastation of war. Just as many international education and citizen diplomacy organizations were founded following World War I and World War II, so too has legislation promoting citizen diplomacy been passed in response to the horrors of these global events (Deardorff 2017; Hoffa 2007). Whether in legislation or in the launch of programs, the underlying assumption is that ensuring peace is not just the role of governments, but also the goal and responsibility of individuals (Deardorff 2017).

U.S. President Dwight D. Eisenhower, a U.S. army general who served as supreme commander of the allied forces in Western Europe in World War II, was a strong proponent of the idea that national security depended not only on military might, but also on the rapport between people of the United States and other nations. Eisenhower launched the People-to-People Program in 1956 with the idea that "ordinary people could serve as ambassadors of the American way of life and spread American values and goodwill to other countries just by being themselves" (Hoffa 2007, 119).

In 1961, U.S. President John F. Kennedy established the U.S. Peace Corps with the goal of sending the best and brightest U.S. volunteers overseas to serve as individual ambassadors to communities in need (Hoffa 2007; Bridgeland et al. 2011). Two of the three Peace Corps goals explicitly relate to citizen diplomacy: "helping promote a better understanding of Americans on the part of peoples served" and "helping promote a better understanding of other peoples on the part of Americans" (Bridgeland et al. 2011, 3).

Also in 1961, the Mutual Education and Cultural Exchange Act, commonly known as the "Fulbright-Hays Act," created educational exchanges between the United States and other countries to promote understanding and strengthen peaceful relationships (Mutual Educational and Cultural Exchange Program 1961). Philanthropic foundations such as Ford, Carnegie, and Danforth provided further support for citizen diplomacy programs in the 1960s (Hoffa 2007).

In the United States, by the mid-1960s, resistance to the Vietnam War, and the growing U.S. civil rights movement, shifted national sentiment. While some people argued that these events illustrated the need for global engagement, many began to feel that U.S. resources should be focused domestically, causing support for citizen diplomacy efforts to lessen (Hoffa 2007). Then, in 1967, a news story revealed that the U.S. Central Intelligence Agency (CIA) was secretly funding many cultural and educational exchanges. The CIA's goal was to counter pro-communist groups. Many educators were alarmed by this revelation and became concerned about the U.S. government co-opting the legitimate academic interests of faculty and students. After the covert funding was exposed, much of the support was made overt and support for educational and cultural programs came to be funded through the Bureau of Educational and Cultural Affairs (ECA) (Keller and Frain 2010).

The U.S. perception of the urgency of citizen diplomacy decreased after the 1991 collapse of the Soviet Union. The United States Information Agency, which had been tasked with promoting democracy and U.S. values around the world was abolished (Ociepka 2018; Epstein 2005). After the September 11, 2001, terrorist attacks, the United States reinvigorated efforts to promote its values, establishing new programs concentrated on the Middle East (Peterson 2002; Dutta-Bergman 2006). The Cultural Bridges Act of 2002 argued for the need to promote national security between the United States and countries with significant Muslim populations through international educational and cultural exchange (Kennedy 2002). This act created the Kennedy-Lugar Youth Exchange and Study (YES) Program, which allows youths from the Islamic world to attend public secondary schools in the United States while living with a host family for 1 academic year, with the specific purpose of promoting greater understanding of U.S. and Islamic values and cultures (Kennedy 2002).

In 2012, the U.S. Department of Education established its first ever, fully articulated international strategy. It centers on three goals: increasing students' global competence, learning from other countries, and engaging in education diplomacy. The priorities of education diplomacy are described as "expanding higher education partnerships, increasing international exchange, and promoting equity in education" (U.S. Department of Education 2012, 12).

U.S. Exchange Visitor Visa (J-1)

The U.S. J-1 visa was created in 1961, under the Mutual Educational and Cultural Exchange Act, commonly known as the "Fulbright-Hays Act." The preamble to the act (Mutual Educational and Cultural Exchange Program 1961) explicitly describes the citizen diplomacy goals of the program:

> The purpose of this chapter is to enable the Government of the United States to increase mutual understanding between the people of the United States and the people of other countries by means of educational and cultural exchange; to strengthen the ties which unite us with other nations by demonstrating the educational and cultural interests, developments, and achievements of the people of the United States and other nations, and the contributions being made toward a peaceful and more fruitful life for people throughout the world; to promote international cooperation for educational and cultural advancement; and thus to assist in the development of friendly, sympathetic, and peaceful relations between the United States and the other countries of the world. (22 U.S.C. § 2451).

The act refers to J-1 visa holders as "exchange visitors," stressing that it is a temporary (nonimmigrant) visa granted for the purpose of cross-cultural exchange. The J-1 exchange visitor visa has multiple categories (Bureau of Educational and Cultural Affairs 2018j) that are described in table 1.

TABLE 1 J-1 Exchange Visitor Visa Categories

Alien Physicians	Foreign medical graduates undertaking graduate medical education or training at an accredited school of medicine or scientific institution, or pursuing professional activities involving observation, consultation, teaching, or research.
Au Pairs	Young adults experiencing U.S. culture while living with a host family for up to 12 months, providing child care and taking courses at an accredited U.S. postsecondary institution.
Camp Counselors	Postsecondary students, youth workers, teachers, and others with specialized skills overseeing American youths at U.S. camps.
College and University Students	Students studying in a degree or nondegree program at a U.S. college or university.

(continued on next page)

U.S. Exchange Visitor Visa (J-1) (continued)

Government Visitors	International visitors developing and strengthening professional and personal relationships with their counterparts in U.S. federal, state, and local government agencies.
International Visitors	Participants in exchange programs sponsored and funded by the U.S. Department of State.
Interns	College and university students or recent graduates gaining exposure to U.S. culture and business practices in their chosen professional field.
Professors/Research Scholars	Individuals engaging in work focused on the exchange of ideas and research that strengthens connections between research and academic institutions.
Secondary School Students	Students studying at an accredited public or private high school and living with an American host family or at a boarding school.
Short-Term Scholars	Professors, scholars, and other accomplished individuals who are on a short-term visit (6 months or less) to teach, research, consult, train, or demonstrate special skills at U.S. research and academic institutions, museums, and libraries.
Specialists	Experts in a field of specialized knowledge who observe U.S. organizations and practices and share their knowledge with U.S. colleagues.
Summer Work Travel Program	College and university students from foreign universities working in seasonal or temporary jobs and exploring the United States during their summer vacation.
Teachers	Educators teaching full time at an accredited U.S. kindergarten, primary, or secondary school.
Trainees	Professionals with a degree, professional certificate, or relevant work experience gaining exposure to U.S. culture and business practices through a guided work-based program.

Each of these categories has regulations that are written and overseen by the U.S. Department of State. The goals of each are explicitly related to cross-cultural engagement and the sharing of knowledge and perspectives between U.S. people and exchange visitors. The Department of State designates universities, nonprofits, and other organizations as "program sponsors" of the J-visa program. More than 1,500 for-profit, nonprofit, and federal, state, and local government entities have received designation as program sponsors (Bureau of Educational and Cultural Affairs 2018j). This designation gives the organization the right to host programs and exchange visitors within the categories designated for that organization. The organization works to ensure positive intercultural exchange and learning within the regulatory framework established by the Department of State.

Size of the Sector

There are no comprehensive data on the number of citizen diplomacy programs or participants. It is surely a much smaller number than the 5 million higher education students that the Institute of International Education (IIE) reports are studying outside of their home country

(IIE 2018). Statistics of particular programs offer some sense of the scope of the citizen diplomacy sector:

- The Chinese government was offering more than 22,000 scholarships per year to international students to study in China, as of 2010 (Mawer 2017). China's 2012 expenditure on foreign scholarships is estimated at US$416 million (Balfour 2016).

- As of 2016, there were 511 Confucius Institutes established in 140 countries and regions. They have hosted 46,000 Chinese and overseas full-time and part-time teachers, enrolled 2.1 million students, hosted cultural events of many types, and received a total of 13 million participants (Yang 2018).

- The King Abdullah Scholarships (Saudi Arabia) funded 185,000 Saudi students to study internationally in 2014 (Mawer 2017). This number has declined in recent years.

- The Brazilian Science Without Borders Program supported 100,000 Brazilian students between 2011 and 2014 (Mawer 2017).

- The U.S. Fulbright Program operates in more than 160 countries, and there have been approximately 360,000 Fulbright participants since the program began in 1946 (Bureau of Educational and Cultural Affairs 2018c). Approximately 8,000 grants are awarded annually (Bureau of Educational and Cultural Affairs 2018c).

- 3,000 scholarships are awarded each year for the U.S. Benjamin A. Gilman International Scholarship Program (Bureau of Educational and Cultural Affairs 2018c).

- 85,000 participants attended a concert and/or interacted with American Music Abroad musicians in 2016 (Bureau of Educational and Cultural Affairs 2018c).

- Almost 5,000 professionals per year come to the United States on the International Visitor Leadership Program (Bureau of Educational and Cultural Affairs 2018i).

- More than 55,000 participants travel overseas through U.S. Department of State-funded exchange programs each year (Bureau of Educational and Cultural Affairs 2018c).

- More than 300,000 participants from almost every country in the world come to the United States on J-1 visas each year. Eighty-six percent are 30 years of age or younger. Fifty-five percent are women or girls (Bureau of Educational and Cultural Affairs 2018j).

- There are 1 million alumni of U.S. Bureau of Educational and Cultural Affairs exchange programs (Bureau of Educational and Cultural Affairs 2018c).

For more information on several of these programs and scholarships, see "Cultural Diplomacy Programs" and table 2 below.

Program Models

There are many different types of citizen diplomacy programs. Some are government sponsored and some are nongovernmental initiatives. The scope of the programs may range from language study to cultural exchange to economic development of host communities. What they each have in common is that they emphasize individual engagement, with the goal of promoting mutual understanding, awareness of shared values, and the exchange of knowledge (Bhandari and Belyavina 2011). Citizen diplomacy programs are likely to be designed in one (or more) of these five overlapping program models: exchange programs, scholarship programs, professional training, cultural diplomacy programs, or sports diplomacy programs.

Exchange Programs

Exchange programs are one model of citizen diplomacy programs. As described in chapter 4, "Education Abroad," exchange programs are characterized by students from two countries visiting the other country. In almost all cases, one of the primary goals of exchange programs is learning about the other culture. While most education abroad exchange programs are exchanges between two education institutions (or perhaps a consortium of institutions), citizen diplomacy exchange programs are often based on agreements between governments.

The funding for the Fulbright Program comes from both the United States and foreign governments. The program, among its many offerings, supports international students to earn degrees in the United States, while also supporting U.S. students and recent graduates to complete research or English teaching abroad. Around 4,000 international students are sponsored to study in the United States each year, while approximately 1,900 U.S. students receive Fulbright awards to go abroad (Bureau of Educational and Cultural Affairs 2018d). Most exchange programs are designed for youths and young adults. It is hoped that they will become future leaders of their nations and carry with them a fondness and desire to cooperate with their former host nation once they are in professional positions in government, business, science, media, the arts, etc.

Scholarship Programs

Scholarships for international study are offered by a wide variety of governments, quasi-governmental organizations, foundations, and private companies. Awards are offered for vocational, undergraduate, and graduate study, and, in small numbers, for K–12 study (Kent

2017). Many of the scholarship programs aim to offer international education opportunities to students who would otherwise be unable to access them (Mawer 2017; Kent 2017). These scholarship programs were referred to in chapter 6, "International Enrollment Management," from the perspective of the receiving institutions, as sponsored student programs. In this chapter, they are discussed from the perspective of the sponsors and the participants as scholarship programs.

Scholarship sponsors may be entities that provide development aid to developing countries. Developed countries give much of their overseas development assistance in the form of scholarships, as a means of both cultural influence and development aid (Abimbola et al. 2016). Beyond creating access to higher education, scholarships given as aid are expected to lead to improvements in civic governance, health care, and economic development, among other benefits (Mawer 2017). This form of development aid is considered to be so effective that the United Nations Educational, Scientific and Cultural Organization specifically calls for substantial expansion of the number of these scholarships in its Sustainable Development Goal Target 4.b (Campbell 2018).

Each scholarship provider has its own goals that shape the criteria for selecting scholarship recipients, the choice of partner educational institutions, and the program requirements. The criteria may be centered on the development of basic skills, the development of advanced knowledge for capacity building in developing nations, the development of advanced knowledge for innovation and economic competitiveness, the promotion of democracy, or cross-cultural exchange (Balfour 2016; Baxter 2017; Bhandari and Belyavina 2011; Atkinson 2010; Mawer 2017). The goals and design of the program reflect the funder's priorities. For example, some U.S. government-funded programs focus on having participants learn about democracy (Atkinson 2010). Whereas the Brazilian Science Without Borders Program, which ended in 2015, prioritized capacity building by developing students' science and technology skills (ICEF 2017). Other programs may be directed at leadership, trying to select future leaders and offer them the opportunity to be exposed to diverse people and perspectives while abroad in order to equip them to address home country challenges in their future professional lives (Baxter 2017). It must be noted that not all international scholarship programs include objectives related to diplomacy or intercultural understanding among their goals. Thus, not all international scholarship programs would be characterized as citizen diplomacy programs.

Professional Training

While most international education programs are designed for students, some citizen diplomacy programs are designed for professionals. These programs may be structured as exchange programs, or groups of professionals from similar fields may travel together to explore their profession in another cultural context. These programs exist for teachers, artists, military personnel, and many others (Atkinson 2010; IREX 2018a; Bureau of Educational and Cultural Affairs 2018g).

The International Visitor Leadership Program (IVLP) is one well-known U.S. professional training program. International participants are selected based on their leadership potential, participating in thematic programs related to their profession for up to 3 weeks. These programs often involve visits to relevant companies and organizations, guest lectures connected to the group's professional field, and cultural excursions and activities that are supported by more than 90 volunteer-based community organizations in the United States (Bureau of Educational and Cultural Affairs 2018a). These organizations are all members of Global Ties U.S., which welcomes the visitors, arranges cultural activities, and provides home hospitality (Bureau of Educational and Cultural Affairs 2018i).

As another professional training opportunity, the Fulbright Distinguished Awards in Teaching Semester Research Program enables K–12 teachers to spend a few months in another country. There, the participants work on research and projects and interact with peers. The Fulbright Teachers for Global Classrooms Program engages teachers in a semester-long online course, paired with a two- to three-week international experience in which they learn about another country's educational system (IREX 2018a, 2018b).

Professional training programs have the potential to develop goodwill among future leaders, help individuals develop international professional networks, and expand individuals' understanding of their profession in an international context. The University of Southern California Center on Public Diplomacy (CPD) further argues that citizen diplomacy programs "that encourage entrepreneurship and job-related training substitute hope for frustration and are among the tools most likely to stifle the spread of extremism" (CPD Advisory Board 2017, 1).

Cultural Diplomacy Programs

Cultural diplomacy focuses on sharing cultural expressions such as art, music, dance, language, etc. Historically, cultural diplomacy centered on exporting and displaying or teaching these cultural features (Cull 2009). Recent efforts often also include an emphasis on collaboration, or on bringing attention to the minority cultures of a society (Trent 2016). The Alliance Française, the British Council, Confucius Institutes, the Goethe Institute, and the Italian Cultural Institute are examples of agencies that engage in cultural diplomacy (Yang 2018; Cull 2009). These organizations maintain cultural centers around the world to showcase their national heritage. The cultural centers may offer libraries, guest speakers, movie showings, language courses, and more. Center staff may also be involved in coordinating programs that promote cross-cultural dialogue.

Other cultural diplomacy efforts involve traveling groups of presenters or performers. For example, American Music Abroad is a program that the Association of American Voices administers on behalf of the Bureau of Educational and Cultural Affairs. In cooperation with the U.S. Department of State, American Voices will arrange a two-week international tour for U.S. musicians to offer public concerts, interactive performances with local traditional musicians, workshops, jam sessions, demonstrations, and media interviews with the goal of showcasing the United States's musical contributions (American Music Abroad 2018).

Sports Diplomacy Programs

Sports diplomacy involves coaches and skilled athletes traveling to play with teams around the world. The groups may also host workshops and teach their skills. The Bureau of Educational and Cultural Affairs refers to these participants as "sports envoys" and says that "sports diplomacy exchanges increase dialogue and cultural understanding between people around the world. The use of sports as a platform exposes international exchange participants to American culture while providing them with an opportunity to establish links with U.S. sports professionals and peers. In turn, Americans learn about other cultures and the challenges young people from other countries face today. Sports diplomacy exchanges have involved tens of thousands of people from more than 100 countries to do just this" (Bureau of Education and Cultural Affairs 2018l). The programs are coordinated in cooperation with the U.S. Olympic Committee, U.S. sport federations, and professional leagues (Bureau of Educational and Cultural Affairs 2018k).

In addition to top athletes, young nonelite athletes and their coaches from around the world are chosen to visit the United States to participate in two-week Sports Visitor Programs that highlight the importance of nutrition, strength and conditioning, gender equity in sports, sports and disability, and team building. These programs provide the chance for international youths to experience U.S. society and culture, while interacting with local youths. These programs are coordinated by a nonprofit organization, FHI360, through a cooperative agreement with the U.S. government (Bureau of Educational and Cultural Affairs 2018m). Sports diplomacy programs help to support U.S. international relations by connecting with harder-to-reach groups such as at-risk youths, women, minorities, people with disabilities, and non-English speakers (Bureau of Educational and Cultural Affairs 2018m).

Citizen Diplomacy Program Examples

As the global geopolitical context shifts and specific global issues rise to prominence, new citizen diplomacy programs are launched and old programs contract or close. This makes citizen diplomacy a very dynamic sector of the international education field. While some citizen diplomacy programs have lasted for decades, others may exist for only a few years.

Table 2 describes a few of the programs in existence, but it is in no way an exhaustive list. The website exchanges.state.gov offers a searchable database that can be used to find U.S. government-sponsored programs. Unfortunately, finding non-U.S. and privately funded programs requires additional online searches; starting points include the websites of government departments engaged in international affairs. Some, such as the German Academic Exchange Service, also offer searchable lists.

TABLE 2 Sample List of U.S. and International Government and Nongovernment Citizen Diplomacy Programs

	U.S. GOVERNMENT PROGRAMS
Fulbright Program	The Fulbright Program is the largest postsecondary exchange program sponsored by the U.S. government. It is active in more than 160 countries and includes the following programs and others (Bureau of Educational and Cultural Affairs 2018e): • Distinguished Awards in Teaching • Doctoral Dissertation Research Abroad Program • English Teaching Assistant Program • Foreign Language Teaching Assistant Program • Foreign Student Program • Fulbright-Hays Program for K–14 teachers and administrators • International Education Administrators Seminars • Specialist Program • U.S. Scholar Program • U.S. Student Program • Visiting Scholar Program
Future Leaders Exchange Program	The Future Leaders Exchange (FLEX) Program brings high school students from Europe and Eurasia to live in the United States with a host family and attend a U.S. high school for 1 year.
Gilman International Scholarship Program	The Gilman International Scholarship Program provides scholarships to U.S. undergraduates with financial need to support study abroad. Additional funding is available for Gilman recipients who are studying critical need foreign languages (U.S. Department of State 2018a.).
Global Sports Mentoring Program	The Global Sports Mentoring Program (GSMP) was developed as a joint collaboration between the U.S. Department of State and ESPN television network to sponsor month-long programs featuring women's empowerment. A key component of the program is mentorship of emerging women leaders from around the world by top U.S. female executives in the sports industry (Bureau of Educational and Cultural Affairs 2018f).
Hubert H. Humphrey Fellowship	The Hubert H. Humphrey Fellowship offers early and mid-career professionals 1 year of graduate study in the United States, along with leadership development and the opportunity to collaborate with U.S. colleagues (U.S. Department of State 2018b).
International Military Education and Training Program	The International Military Education and Training (IMET) Program is one of several military professional training exchanges that the United States has conducted with many other countries (U.S. Department of State 2018c). The U.S. military routinely enrolls military officers from many countries in its professional military schools (Atkinson 2010).

(continued on next page)

Table 2. Sample List of U.S. and International Government and Nongovernment Citizen Diplomacy Programs (continued)

International Visitor Leadership Program	The International Visitor Leadership Program (IVLP) brings professionals to the United States for three-week programs. Participants typically travel to four cities, exploring their profession in the U.S. context with cultural excursions. Activities may include guest lectures, industry site visits, and meetings with government officials (Bureau of Educational and Cultural Affairs 2018a).
Kennedy-Lugar Youth Exchange and Study Program	The Kennedy-Lugar Youth Exchange and Study (YES) Program provides scholarships for high-achieving, English-speaking high school students from countries with significant Muslim populations to live and study in the United States for an academic year (Kennedy-Lugar Youth Exchange and Study Program 2018).
Open World Leadership Center Programs	The Open World Leadership Center is an agency of the U.S. legislative branch. It serves the U.S. Congress by facilitating professional exchanges for current and future leaders from Eurasia. The Open World Program highlights U.S. values and democracy, while offering U.S. legislators the opportunity to meet with international colleagues (Open World Leadership Center n.d.).
TechWomen	TechWomen is an exchange and mentorship program sponsored by the U.S. Department of State. It brings emerging women leaders in science, technology, engineering, and mathematics fields to the United States from Africa, Central and South Asia, and the Middle East. Participants work on projects in San Francisco and Silicon Valley, in California, alongside a mentor (TechWomen 2018).
INTERNATIONAL GOVERNMENT PROGRAMS	
Bolashak International Scholarship Program	The Kazakh government started the Bolashak International Scholarship Program in 1993. It is a state-sponsored student mobility program that has provided approximately 12,000 Kazakh citizens with full scholarships to earn degrees abroad (Sordi 2018; U.S. Department of State 2016).
Chevening Scholarships and Fellowships	The United Kingdom offers Chevening Scholarships and Fellowships for future leaders from around the world. The program aims to support international students and mid-career professionals as they learn about UK culture and build professional networks within the United Kingdom (United Kingdom Foreign and Commonwealth Office 2015).
Chinese Bridge Summer Camp for American High School Students	The Chinese Bridge Summer Camp for American High School Students was created by former U.S. Secretary of State Hillary Clinton and Chinese Vice Premier Liu Yandong to promote cross-cultural exchange. Held around the United States, these summer camps teach Chinese language and culture (Ogden and Maske 2018; Confucius Institute Headquarters 2014).
Confucius Institutes	The Chinese government has established Confucius Institutes all over the world. These institutions promote Chinese language and culture by offering educational programs (Punteney and Wei 2018; Ogden and Maske 2018).
Erasmus+	While the European Union's Erasmus Program supports international study at higher education institutions in Europe, Erasmus+ provides opportunities for students, trainees/interns, academic staff, teachers, volunteers, and others (European Commission n.d.).
German Chancellor Fellowship	The German Chancellor Fellowship is for early and mid-career professionals who demonstrate leadership potential. It provides financial support to spend a year in Germany working with a mentor on a project of social significance that builds bridges between Germany and the participant's country (Alexander von Humboldt Foundation n.d.).

(continued on next page)

Table 2. Sample List of U.S. and International Government and Nongovernment Citizen Diplomacy Programs (continued)

Japan Exchange and Teaching Program	The Japan Exchange and Teaching (JET) Program brings participants from partner countries to serve as assistant language teachers. Additionally, a smaller number of participants serve as coordinators for international relations or as sports exchange advisers. The goal of the program is to introduce Japanese culture to international people, while introducing international cultures to Japanese people (Metzgar 2012; JET Program USA 2016).
Libyan-North American Scholarship Program	A collaboration between the Canadian Bureau for International Education and the Libyan Ministry of Higher Education and Scientific Research, this program brings Libyan students to host universities in Canada and the United States (Canadian Bureau for International Education 2018).
NONGOVERNMENTAL PROGRAMS	
Open Society Foundation Scholarship Programs	The Open Society Foundation has been funding higher education scholarships for more than 35 years. The scholarships aim to empower individuals to bring about social change in their home country by exposing them to democratic societies (Brogden 2017).
Rotary Youth Exchange	Rotary International is a nonprofit organization with more than 1 million members around the world working together to promote peace and support communities. Rotary Youth Exchanges may be weeks long or last an academic year. Largely supported by volunteers and host families, the emphasis is on learning about other cultures and becoming global citizens (Rotary International 2018).
Schwarzman Scholars Program	The Schwarzman Scholars Program funds a cohort of up to 200 U.S., Chinese, and international students annually to earn a master's degree in global affairs at Tsinguhua University in China. The program aims to bridge the academic and professional cultures and to educate students about China's global role (Schwarzman Scholars 2018).
Sister Cities International	Sister Cities International helps establish partnerships between cities around the world to foster collaboration, trade, and cultural exchange. Based on the belief that citizen diplomacy promotes peace, the nonprofit organization serves as a hub of information on sister city collaborations and coordinates exchange programs for youths, professionals, and civic leaders (Sister Cities International 2018).

As is evident in table 2, citizen diplomacy programs take a wide variety of forms and may support a few participants or thousands. They may be funded by governments or private entities, or they may be the result of public-private partnerships. The scope of each program reflects the policy goals of the sponsors.

Impact of Citizen Diplomacy Programs

Citizen diplomacy programs endeavor to deliver an ambitious set of outcomes. Individual programs likely include some combination of the following objectives:

- Create educational opportunities for underserved populations.
- Develop the participants' knowledge and skills.
- Share the host country's culture.

- Share the participants' culture.

- Influence the participants' values through exposure to the host country's ideals.

- Develop fondness for the host country among participants.

- Develop positive regard for the host country among participants' family, friends, and colleagues.

- Empower participants to contribute to their home country's economic development.

- Establish professional networks for future collaboration in trade, politics, media, research, policy, and other areas.

A small but growing body of research is working to assess the impact of citizen diplomacy programs in order to determine whether programs meet these goals and to what extent. Much of the citizen diplomacy research continues to focus on program alumni. These studies examine the educational achievement, career outcomes, or attitudes of past program participants. Unfortunately, there is limited research on the degree to which citizen diplomacy contributes to development in the participants' home country. In one study, Campbell (2018) reports that both those participants who return to live and work in their home country and those who live abroad perceive themselves to be contributing to their home country's development. However, the consensus among participants is that those who live in the home country have the greatest opportunity to contribute because they are able to be directly involved in policy decisions (Campbell 2018). Abimbola et al. (2016) add that program alumni need continued support after the program to best be able to influence development and governance reforms in their home country. With this in mind, studies must be done to determine how to extend the knowledge and skills, positive regard, and country values learned.

Career Impact

Research shows that citizen diplomacy programs can build the knowledge and skills of participants. Scholarship programs, in particular, concentrate on developing the skills and credentials of participants in ways that influence their career trajectories (Baxter 2017; SRI International 2005). Participation in citizen diplomacy programs may enhance career interest in the international sector. A Gilman Program evaluation survey of more than 1,500 alumni found that (Bureau of Educational and Cultural Affairs 2016):

- 73 percent reported that the program broadened the geographic locations in which they were willing to work.

- 67 percent said that program participation promoted a desire to work in a cross-cultural or international field.

- 59 percent said that program participation led them to apply for positions at companies with a cross-cultural or international focus.

- 54 percent of the survey respondents were actively working in a field with an international or cross-cultural component.

As in the case of the Gilman Scholarships, citizen diplomacy programs are often expected to help participants to expand their international professional networks of colleagues who can serve as future collaborators (Baxter 2017; SRI International 2005).

Positive Regard

As documented in multiple studies, citizen diplomacy programs often result in participants holding a more positive and nuanced view of the host country and the host country's people (Atkinson 2010; Intermedia 2009). This impact is not limited to the participants themselves, but also extends to their family, friends, and colleagues in their home country who are influenced by hearing about the participants' experiences and perspectives (Intermedia 2009; Fayez and Prinzing 2010; Kent 2017; Bhandari and Belyavina 2011). In a study of the YES Program, participants reported that their experience in the United States dispelled many negative stereotypes that they held prior to the program, and that they had made an effort to break down those stereotypes among their family, friends, and communities upon returning to their home country (Intermedia 2009). These positive reputational outcomes continue to be effective years after the programs take place (SRI International 2005).

Citizen diplomacy programs that bring mid-career professionals to the United States have been shown to increase positive feelings about the United States among participants (Atkinson 2010). In a study of military professional exchanges in the United States, Atkinson (2010) found especially strong results, concluding that the highly structured and integrated nature of the military exchange programs, which are characterized by a depth of interaction with the local community, may have helped foster the successful achievement of this outcome.

Country Values

Some programs aim to promote particular values, such as a commitment to democracy. U.S.-funded programs often have the goal of exposing participants to values such as freedom of speech and the press, democracy, and anticorruption (Atkinson 2010). Studies have shown that former participants are more likely to have high levels of civic engagement, and they often try to share what they have learned abroad to influence the governance of their own communities (Intermedia 2009; Campbell 2018; Martel and Bhandari 2016).

Administration of Citizen Diplomacy Programs

While governments and foundations fund most citizen diplomacy programs, the programs are typically administered by external organizations. In the United States, most government funding for citizen diplomacy comes from the Department of State and is managed by the Bureau of Educational and Cultural Affairs. The Bureau of Educational and Cultural Affairs contracts with nonprofit organizations to design and implement the programs. In the case of the International Visitor Leadership Program (IVLP), there are eight partner organizations: CRDF Global, Cultural Vistas, FHI360, Graduate School USA, Institute of International Education, Meridian International Center, Mississippi Consortium for International Development, and World Learning (Bureau of Educational and Cultural Affairs 2018b). Other organizations also administer Department of State-funded programs, including AMIDEAST, American Councils for International Education, and IREX. Local organizations such as the Northern California World Trade Center, World Affairs Council of St. Louis, WorldChicago, WorldDenver, and WorldOregon help to support IVLP and other citizen diplomacy programs. Many of these local organizations are affiliated with Global Ties U.S. (a member list is available on the Global Ties U.S. website). U.S. embassies, EducationUSA offices, and partner organizations, including binational centers, AMIDEAST, the Institute of International Education, and others, are involved in the promotion of citizen diplomacy programs overseas.

Proposals

Most of the contracts to administer citizen diplomacy programs are awarded through a grant-making process. In the case of most U.S. government-funded programs, the Bureau of Educational and Cultural Affairs publishes a Notice of Funding Opportunity on the grants.gov website. Each call for proposals offers detailed information on the goals of the program. The logistics of the program, such as the number of participants, length of the program, month(s) and year(s) that the program is to be offered, etc., are explained in the notice. The specific responsibilities that the organization will need to agree to if awarded the grant contract are also listed. Eligibility requirements for the grant recipients are explained in the announcement. In the case of citizen diplomacy exchange programs, the Bureau of Educational and Cultural Affairs usually limits eligibility to public and nonprofit organizations (Bureau of Educational and Cultural Affairs 2018h).

Interested organizations submit their proposals to the Bureau of Educational and Cultural Affairs. The Notice of Funding Opportunity specifies the information to be included in the proposal, along with instructions on formatting, proposal length, and other specifics. These instructions must be followed exactly to ensure that the proposal receives consideration. A proposal will typically contain background information on the organization, details of the program activities that the organization is proposing to implement in order to meet the stated program objectives, a program calendar, a program budget, the credentials of program managers, the credentials of instructors/experts involved in the program, a publicity plan, and an evaluation plan. Working within the specified format described in the notice, organizations must make a compelling case for the impactfulness and cost-effectiveness of the program design they propose, and why their organization is well qualified to implement the program. Arguing that the organization is well qualified may entail sharing the organization's past experience with similar activities, describing the professional or community networks that the organization can mobilize, or arguing for the merits of a particular geographic location.

Selection Process

Following the proposal submission deadline, the Bureau of Educational and Cultural Affairs reviews all submissions to ensure that the selected organization meets the eligibility requirements and that the proposal addresses the required proposal topics. If the proposal passes this initial review, it is distributed to regional bureaus, embassies, and other relevant sections of the Department of State for comment. Once comments are collected, a panel of employees reviews the proposals and makes a recommendation to the assistant secretary of the Bureau of Educational and Cultural Affairs about the organization that should receive the grant (Bureau of Educational and Cultural Affairs 2018h). Selection of grant awardees is highly competitive and even well-written and well-substantiated grant proposals may not be chosen.

Implementation

After the grant is awarded, the organization begins the detailed work of program planning. Often, the organization will, in turn, publish its own call for proposals, for example, to look for higher education institutions to host individual visiting scholars. A time-consuming element of the work involves securing placements for the participants with host families, schools, mentors, etc. Curriculum may need to be developed for the program; logistics such as transportation, housing, and food need to be planned and contracted; and experts and volunteers may need to be recruited. The organization may need to coordinate with overseas entities to advertise the program and select participants. Predeparture communications and orientation need to be created and delivered.

During the execution of the program, staff members will need to be on hand to support participants and coordinate the events. Expenditures need to be tracked. Publicity will need to be coordinated during the event. Data for program assessment need to be gathered, and formative evaluation may prompt the need for modification of the curriculum or logistics during the program. During and after the program, reports need to be submitted to the program funder.

Many of the grants are multiyear grants with multiple cohorts of participants. The planning and recruitment stages of the program may take a year or more before the first cohort arrives. Then, multiple cycles of the program may run over multiple years. Often, momentum builds as increasing numbers of participants are involved over the initial years of the program. After remaining steady for some time, the numbers may begin to wane as the program reaches its final year.

Working in the context of grant-funded programs, increasing numbers of staff may be added to a project as it grows in size, and then gradually transferred to other initiatives as the project begins to wrap up. Some of the organizations that do this work have more than 100 grant-funded projects underway at a time. Staff in organizations administering citizen diplomacy programs have the benefit, and challenge, of working in a dynamic context where they may change projects every few months or years, or may be working on multiple projects simultaneously. Also, the intensity and hours of work required may vary based on the stage of the project. Staff working with citizen diplomacy programs benefit from strong skills in grant writing, grant management, budgeting, accounting, curriculum design, event planning, intercultural communication, interpersonal communication, problem-solving, and program assessment.

Assessment of Citizen Diplomacy

Assessment is perhaps one of the most important, and most needed, duties of the citizen diplomacy sector. Assessment is crucial for advocating for citizen diplomacy program funding, as well as for determining the most impactful program designs. Most major programs now include analysis of outcomes and program assessment as standard protocol (Mawer 2017; Baxter 2017). Unfortunately, much of the assessment has been qualitative and anecdotal, focused mostly on self-reported measures of participant satisfaction (Bhandari and Belyavina 2011). There is a need for more rigorous, quantitative studies (Mawer 2017).

Much of the existing research centers on the direct impacts on participants. The studies have often been on participant satisfaction, career trajectories, educational attainment, and on community engagement. In addition to these data, there is a need for more analysis of the outcomes as they relate to the societal and policy objectives of the programs (Mawer 2017). The effect on the participant's home community is often measured in terms of the "multiplier effect" of the participant's positive attitudes toward the host country being shared with family, friends, and colleagues after returning home. While this is certainly one aim or benefit of citizen diplomacy programs, it still does not measure the full scope of social change that these programs hope to achieve (Wang and Nisbet 2018).

Like all assessment efforts, it is essential to begin with clearly articulated program goals. From those goals, an assessment plan should be developed prior to the start of the program and data collection should be built into the program design (Bhandari and Belyavina 2011; Mawer 2017). This avoids one of the common pitfalls of citizen diplomacy evaluation, which is the tendency to contract with an external evaluator in the final stages of a program to conduct the evaluation. Doing so leaves the evaluation with no baseline data by which to recognize any change that has occurred (Mawer 2017). Further, it is essential to use multiple measures of assessment, going beyond participants' self-reporting. Options could include instruments for measuring global competence (see chapter 2), reports from external observers, and data collected from social media, among many others (Deardorff 2017; Mawer 2017; Bhandari and Belyavina 2011).

Challenges of Program Assessment

The assessment of citizen diplomacy programs comes with particular challenges. One is that citizen diplomacy programs typically use a merit-based selection process. This, of course, means that participants are never randomly selected to participate or not participate in programs, thus, there is no control group for scientific study (Mawer 2017). There is already a selection bias built into the programs because those participants who engage in the programs likely already have an interest in international people and places.

Another challenge is that the societal changes that citizen diplomacy programs hope to promote are, by definition, long-term changes. Generally, it will take years, if not decades, for these changes to manifest (Bhandari and Belyavina 2011). There is a logistical difficulty in maintaining accurate contact information for participants over such long periods of time (Wilson 2017). Also, because most programs are grant funded, and the programs have long since been completed, there is often no organization invested in conducting the long-term assessment. Political and organizational leaders will likely have shifted in that time, and with them, the priorities will have shifted, leaving little incentive to fund an assessment effort for a program that aimed to achieve a previous policy objective (Mawer 2017; Kent 2017).

Even if the issues of funding and contact information are overcome, large challenges still prevail. During the postprogram years when participation is gradually showing its impact in communities, participants will have countless influences on their lives. For researchers, it becomes very difficult to determine whether any particular societal change was influenced by individuals' past participation in a citizen diplomacy program, whether another intervening influence was more important, or whether it is a particular combination of influences that makes the difference (Mawer 2017). Measuring these changes requires measuring beliefs, interactions, identities, contexts, and more, both during the citizen diplomacy program and in the following years. These are constantly changing abstractions that are highly difficult to reliably measure and track (Trent 2016).

There is a need for rigorous, longitudinal citizen diplomacy research that measures not only outcomes for participants, but also impacts on home country and host country communities (Mawer 2017; Bhandari and Belyavina 2011). Further research is needed on which program designs, or what aspects of programs, best lead to desired outcomes (Abimbola et al. 2016).

Additionally, researchers should strive to identify the relationship between individual change and societal change, as prompted by citizen diplomacy programs (Baxter 2017).

Considerations for Practitioners

Practitioners need to be aware of several considerations as they develop and facilitate citizen diplomacy programs. One consideration is the need for more research to substantiate, and deepen, current understandings of citizen diplomacy. There is a need for research to provide evidence of the claims made by citizen diplomacy advocates. Specifically, the field would benefit from empirical evidence supporting its claimed values: goodwill felt, positive attitudes cultivated, long-term professional networks established, and peace strengthened (Wilson 2017). Rather than assuming that exposure to people of other cultures will automatically lead to desired changes in attitudes among citizen diplomacy participants, additional research needs to be undertaken. For example, studies could explore the social contexts in which the programs take place, the role of identity, and the program designs that jointly influence the program outcomes (Wilson 2017; Trent 2016).

Another consideration in citizen diplomacy, as in all sectors of international education, is ensuring that there is access to opportunities for individuals of all backgrounds. There is a concern that citizen diplomacy programs often select individuals to participate who have already received many privileges in society (Kent 2017). Those individuals who are already well educated and those who have the social capital to hold high-level positions are those who are most likely to be identified as future leaders, a common selection criterion. In addition to diversifying application pools and selection criteria for international programs, using a wider range of modes of engagement means that a greater diversity of people are able to engage in, and benefit from, citizen diplomacy programs. While programs that transport people across national borders are by far the most common means of citizen diplomacy, it is not the only possibility. Other modes of engagement may include online programs with academic coursework, scientific collaboration, cross-cultural video gaming, and virtual reality experiences (Trent 2016).

Mirroring the concern about inequity among individuals, there is also concern about inequity between nations. Scholars have pointed out that developed countries tend to be sponsors of citizen diplomacy programs, while developing countries are usually the recipients. This pattern of giving may reinforce global inequities, rather than alleviate them (Baxter 2017). Some scholars warn that although the rationales for citizen diplomacy emphasize two-way cultural exchange and learning, the program funder's goals heavily influence the program design. The end result is that the participants in citizen diplomacy programs may learn more about the host culture and the values being promoted by the funder, than the host community learns from the participants (Yun 2015; Cull 2009). Designing programs so that they involve sending people both to and from the home and host countries, with meaningful two-way interactions, is an important design element to help mitigate the inequity (Baxter 2017).

A final consideration is the importance of planning for postprogram support to maximize impact. It is essential to ensure that alumni have ongoing means of engagement and support from each other and from the program administrators. Setting up social media networks, in-person gatherings, an online course, or projects to be completed after the international segment of the program are all options to increase the learning opportunities from the program. Campbell (2017) suggests that during programs, participants should be asked to identify and make a plan for the ways they want to contribute to social change after completion of the program. Sponsors and administering organizations should keep in touch with alumni to conduct assessments of the impacts of the programs over time, and then use these data to refine future programs (Bhandari and Belyavina 2011; Kent 2017; Mawer 2017).

Conclusion

Citizen diplomacy aims to contribute to intercultural understanding, economic development, and world peace through contact between individual members of the global public. Both governments and nonprofit organizations actively engage in citizen diplomacy, supporting efforts to foster people-to-people connections among students, teachers, professionals, artists, athletes, military, and others. While citizen diplomacy efforts are small in scope compared with other facets of the international education field, they still have the potential to affect both individuals and societies for the long term.

A wide range of organizations are active in the citizen diplomacy sector. While funding may come from governments or foundations, nonprofit organizations administer many of the programs. Supported by grant funding, these organizations are active in recruitment, admissions, orientation, program design, program planning, facilitation, and program assessment. The evaluation of the impacts of citizen diplomacy programs on both individual participants and society is an urgent task to be undertaken. Professionals working in citizen diplomacy need to ensure that issues of equity and mutual benefit are addressed in programs so that the goals of citizen diplomacy can be achieved.

Resources

READINGS:

- Bhandari, Rajika, and Raisa Belyavina. 2011. *Evaluating and Measuring the Impact of Citizen Diplomacy: Current Status and Future Directions*. New York, NY: Institute of International Education.

- Dassin, Joan R., Robin R. Marsh, and Matt Mawer. 2018. *International Scholarships in Higher Education: Pathways to Social Change*. New York, NY: Palgrave Macmillan.

- Mawer, Matt. 2017. "Approaches to Analyzing the Outcomes of International Scholarship Programs for Higher Education." *Journal of Studies in International Education* 21, 3:230–245. https://doi.org/10.1177/1028315316687009.

OTHER:

- The Center for Citizen Diplomacy www.centerforcitizendiplomacy.org/
- Global Ties U.S. www.globaltiesus.org/index.php
- University of Southern California Center on Public Diplomacy www.uscpublicdiplomacy.org/

References

Abimbola, Seye, Rose Amazan, Pavle Vizintin, Leanne Howie, Robert Cumming, and Joel Negin. 2016. "Australian Higher Education Scholarships as Tools for International Development and Diplomacy in Africa." *Australian Journal of International Affairs* 70, 2:105–120. https://doi.org/10.1080/10357718.2015.1119230.

Alexander von Humboldt Foundation. n.d. "The German Chancellor Fellowship for Tomorrow's Leaders." Alexander von Humboldt Foundation. http://www.humboldt-foundation.de/web/german-chancellor-fellowship.html.

American Music Abroad. 2018. "About American Music Abroad." St. Louis, MO: American Music Abroad. http://amvoices.org/ama/about/.

Atkinson, Carol. 2010. "Does Soft Power Matter? A Comparative Analysis of Student Exchange Programs 1980–2006." *Foreign Policy Analysis* 6, 1:1–22. https://doi.org/10.1111/j.1743-8594.2009.00099.x.

Balfour, Susan. 2016. "SDG Target 4b: A Global Measure of Scholarships [ED/GEMR/MRT2016/P1/10]. Paper Commissioned for the Global Education Monitoring Report 2016, Education for People and Planet: Creating Sustainable Futures for All." United Nations Educational, Scientific and Cultural Organization. http://unesdoc.unesco.org/images/0024/002455/245570e.pdf.

Baxter, Aryn. 2017. "The Benefits and Challenges of International Education: Maximizing Learning for Social Change." In *International Scholarships in Higher Education: Pathways* to Social Change, eds. Joan R. Dassin, Robin R. Marsh, and Matt Mawer. London, United Kingdom: Palgrave Macmillan.

Bhandari, Rajika, and Raisa Belyavina. 2011. *Evaluating and Measuring the Impact of Citizen Diplomacy: Current Status and Future Directions*. New York, NY: Institute of International Education.

Bridgeland, John M., Harris Wofford, Kevin F. F. Quigley, and Jessica A. Milano. 2011. "A Call to Peace: Perspectives of Volunteers on the Peace Corps at 50." Peace Corps.

Brogden, Zoe. 2017. "Case Study: Open Society Scholarship Programs." In *International Scholarships in Higher Education: Pathways to Social Change*, eds. Joan R. Dassin, Robin R. Marsh, and Matt Mawer. London, United Kingdom: Palgrave Macmillan.

Bureau of Educational and Cultural Affairs. 2016. *The Benjamin A. Gilman International Scholarship Program*. Washington, DC: U.S. Department of State Bureau of Educational and Cultural Affairs. https://eca.state.gov/files/bureau/gilman_infographic_report_-_2016.pdf.

Bureau of Educational and Cultural Affairs. 2018a. "About IVLP." Washington, DC: U.S. Department of State Bureau of Educational and Cultural Affairs. https://eca.state.gov/ivlp/about-ivlp.

Bureau of Educational and Cultural Affairs. 2018b. "Citizen Diplomacy | Bureau of Educational and Cultural Affairs." Washington, DC: U.S. Department of State Bureau of Educational and Cultural Affairs. https://eca.state.gov/ivlp/about-ivlp/citizen-diplomacy.

Bureau of Educational and Cultural Affairs. 2018c. "Facts and Figures." Washington, DC: U.S. Department of State Bureau of Educational and Cultural Affairs. https://eca.state.gov/impact/facts-and-figures.

Bureau of Educational and Cultural Affairs. 2018d. "The Fulbright Program." Washington, DC: U.S. Department of State Bureau of Educational and Cultural Affairs. https://eca.state.gov/fulbright.

Bureau of Educational and Cultural Affairs. 2018e. "The Fulbright Program: Frequently Asked Questions." Washington, DC: U.S. Department of State Bureau of Educational and Cultural Affairs. https://eca.state.gov/fulbright/frequently-asked-questions.

Bureau of Educational and Cultural Affairs. 2018f. "Global Sports Mentoring Program." Washington, DC: U.S. Department of State Bureau of Educational and Cultural Affairs. https://eca.state.gov/programs-initiatives/initiatives/sports-diplomacy/global-sports-mentoring-program.

Bureau of Educational and Cultural Affairs. 2018g. "Implementing Partnerships." Washington, DC: U.S. Department of State Bureau of Educational and Cultural Affairs. https://eca.state.gov/ivlp/about-ivlp/implementing-partnerships.

Bureau of Educational and Cultural Affairs. 2018h. "Institutional Awards Process Explained." Washington, DC: U.S. Department of State Bureau of Educational and Cultural Affairs. https://eca.state.gov/organizational-funding/applying-grant/institutional-awards-process-explained.

Bureau of Educational and Cultural Affairs. 2018i. "The IVLP Experience." Washington, DC: U.S. Department of State Bureau of Educational and Cultural Affairs. https://eca.state.gov/ivlp/ivlp-experience.

Bureau of Educational and Cultural Affairs. 2018j. "J-1 Visa Exchange Visitor Program." Washington, DC: U.S. Department of State Bureau of Educational and Cultural Affairs. https://j1visa.state.gov/wp-content/uploads/2018/03/J1VIsa-fact-sheet-2018.pdf.

Bureau of Educational and Cultural Affairs. 2018k. "Sports Diplomacy." Washington, DC: U.S. Department of State Bureau of Educational and Cultural Affairs. https://eca.state.gov/programs-initiatives/initiatives/sports-diplomacy.

Bureau of Educational and Cultural Affairs. 2018l. "Sports Envoys and Sports Visitors." Washington, DC: U.S. Department of State Bureau of Educational and Cultural Affairs. https://eca.state.gov/programs-initiatives/initiatives/sports-diplomacy/sports-envoys-and-sports-visitors.

Bureau of Educational and Cultural Affairs. 2018m. "Sports Grants." Washington, DC: U.S. Department of State Bureau of Educational and Cultural Affairs. https://eca.state.gov/programs-initiatives/initiatives/sports-diplomacy/sports-grants.

Campbell, Anne C. 2017. "Influencing Pathways to Social Change: Scholarship Program Conditionality and Individual Agency." In *International Scholarships in Higher Education: Pathways to Social Change*, eds. Joan R. Dassin, Robin R. Marsh, and Matt Mawer. London, United Kingdom: Palgrave Macmillan.

Campbell, Anne C. 2018. "'Giving Back' to One's Country Following an International Higher Education Scholarship: Comparing In-Country and Expatriate Alumni Perceptions of Engagement in Social and Economic Change in Moldova." *Compare: A Journal of Comparative and International Education*, 1–19. https://doi.org/10.1080/03057925.2018.1540925.

Canadian Bureau for International Education. 2018. "Libyan-North American Scholarship." Canadian Bureau for International Education. https://cbie.ca/what-we-do/current-programs/libyan-north-american-scholarship/.

The Center for Citizen Diplomacy. 2017. "About Us." Washington, DC: The Center for Citizen Diplomacy. https://www.centerforcitizendiplomacy.org/about-us/.

Confucius Institute Headquarters. 2014. "'Chinese Bridge' Summer Camp." Beijing, China: Confucius Institute Headquarters. http://english.hanban.org/node_8073.htm.

CPD Advisory Board. 2017. "Making the Case for U.S. Public Diplomacy." Los Angeles, CA: University of Southern California Center on Public Diplomacy (CPD). https://www.uscpublicdiplomacy.org/sites/uscpublicdiplomacy.org/files/Making_the_Case_for_US_Public_Diplomacy_2017.pdf.

Cull, Nicholas J. 2009. *Public Diplomacy: Lessons from the Past*. CPD Perspectives on Public Diplomacy. Los Angeles, CA: Figueroa Press.

Deardorff, Darla K. 2017. "The BIG Picture: Reflections on the Role of International Educational Exchange in Peace and Understanding." In *International Education Exchanges and Intercultural Understanding: Promoting Peace and Global Relations*, ed. Julie Mathews-Aydinli. Cham, Switzerland: Springer International Publishing.

Dutta-Bergman, Mohan J. 2006. "U.S. Public Diplomacy in the Middle East: A Critical Cultural Approach." *Journal of Communication Inquiry* 30, 2:102–124. https://doi.org/10.1177/0196859905285286.

Epstein, Susan B. 2005. "U.S. Public Diplomacy: Background and the 9/11 Commission Recommendations." Washington, DC: Congressional Research Service.

European Commission. n.d. "Erasmus+ Opportunities for Individuals." European Commission. Accessed December 30, 2018. https://ec.europa.eu/programmes/erasmus-plus/opportunities/overview_en.

Fayez, Sherifa M. B. E., and Dan Prinzing. 2010. "Promoting U.S.-Middle Eastern Cultural Understanding Through Youth Exchange." In *Innovation Through Education: Building the Knowledge Economy in the Middle East*, eds. Daniel Obst and Daniel Kirk. New York, NY: Institute of International Education.

Hoffa, William W. 2007. *A History of U.S. Study Abroad: Beginnings to 1965*. Carlisle, PA: Frontiers: The Interdisciplinary Journal of Study Abroad and The Forum on Education Abroad.

ICEF. 2017. "Brazil Shutting down Science Without Borders." *ICEF Monitor - Market Intelligence for International Student Recruitment* (blog). April 22, 2017. http://monitor.icef.com/2017/04/brazil-shutting-science-without-borders/.

Institute of International Education (IIE). 2018. "Project Atlas 2018 Infographics." Institute of International Education. https://www.iie.org/en/Research-and-Insights/Project-Atlas/Explore-Data/Current-Infographics.

Intermedia. 2009. "Evaluation of the Youth Exchange & Study Program: Final Report." Washington, DC: U.S. Department of State Bureau of Educational and Cultural Affairs Office of Policy and Evaluation Division. https://eca.state.gov/files/bureau/youth-exchange-and-study-yes-full-report-aug-2009.pdf.

IREX. 2018a. "Fulbright Distinguished Awards in Teaching Semester Research Program for U.S. Teachers." IREX. http://www.irex.org/project/fulbright-distinguished-awards-teaching-semester-research-program-us-teachers.

IREX. 2018b. "Fulbright Teachers for Global Classrooms Program (Fulbright TGC)." IREX. http://www.irex.org/project/fulbright-teachers-global-classrooms-program-fulbright-tgc.

JET Program USA. 2016. "JET Program USA." JET Program USA. https://jetprogramusa.org/.

Keller, John M., and Maritheresa Frain. 2010. "The Impact of Geo-Political Events, Globalization, and National Policies on Study Abroad Programming and Participation." In *A History of U.S. Study Abroad: 1965–Present*, eds. William W. Hoffa and Stephen C. DePaul. Carlisle, PA: Frontiers: The Interdisciplinary Journal of Study Abroad and The Forum on Education Abroad.

Kennedy, Ted. 2002. Cultural Bridges Act of 2002. S. 2505.

Kennedy-Lugar Youth Exchange and Study Program. 2018. "About Us." Kennedy-Lugar Youth Exchange and Study Program. 2018. http://www.yesprograms.org/about/about-us.

Kent, Anna. 2017. "Recent Trends in International Scholarships." In *International Scholarships in Higher Education: Pathways to Social Change*, eds. Joan R. Dassin, Robin R. Marsh, and Matt Mawer. London, United Kingdom: Palgrave Macmillan.

Martel, Mirka, and Rajika Bhandari. 2016. *Social Justice and Sustainable Change: The Impacts of Higher Education.* Institute of International Education.

Mawer, Matt. 2017. "Approaches to Analyzing the Outcomes of International Scholarship Programs for Higher Education." *Journal of Studies in International Education* 21, 3:230–245. https://doi.org/10.1177/1028315316687009.

Metzgar, Emily T. 2012. *Promoting Japan: One JET at a Time*. Los Angeles, CA: Figueroa Press.

Mutual Educational and Cultural Exchange Program. 1961. Pub. L. 87–256. §2451. http://uscode.house.gov/view.xhtml?path=/prelim@title22/chapter33&edition=prelim.

Nye, Joseph S., Jr. 2004. *Soft Power: The Means To Success In World Politics*. New York, NY: PublicAffairs.

Ociepka, Beata. 2018. "Public Diplomacy as Political Communication: Lessons from Case Studies." *European Journal of Communication* 33, 3:290–303. https://doi.org/10.1177/0267323118763909.

Ogden, Anthony C., and Huajing Xiu Maske. 2018. "Leveraging Confucius Institutes for International Education and Exchange." In *The Rise of China-U.S. International Cooperation in Higher Education: Views from the Field*, eds. Christopher J. Johnstone and Li Li Ji. Leiden, The Netherlands: Brill Sense.

Open World Leadership Center. n.d. "About Us." Washington, DC: Open World Leadership Center. Accessed December 30, 2018. https://www.openworld.gov/about-us/about-us.

Peterson, Peter G. 2002. "Public Diplomacy and the War on Terrorism." *Foreign Affairs* 81, 5:74–94. https://doi.org/10.2307/20033270.

Punteney, Katherine, and Yilin Wei. 2018. "Dynamics of Internationalization in U.S. and Chinese Higher Education." In *The Rise of China-U.S. International Cooperation in Higher Education: Views from the Field*, eds. Christopher J. Johnstone and Li Li Ji. Leiden, The Netherlands: Brill Sense.

Rotary International. 2018. "Rotary Youth Exchange." Rotary International. https://www.rotary.org/en/our-programs/youth-exchanges.

Schwarzman Scholars. 2018. "Schwarzman Scholars." *Schwarzman Scholars* (blog). Schwarzman Scholars. https://www.schwarzmanscholars.org/program/.

Sister Cities International. 2018. "What We Do." Washington, DC: Sister Cities International. http://sistercities.org/what-we-do/.

Sordi, Adele Del. 2018. "Sponsoring Student Mobility for Development and Authoritarian Stability: Kazakhstan's Bolashak Programme." *Globalizations* 15, 2:215–231. https://doi.org/10.1080/14747731.2017.1403780.

SRI International. 2005. "Outcome Assessment of the Visiting Fulbright Scholar Program." Washington, DC: U.S. Department of State Bureau of Educational and Cultural Affairs.

TechWomen. 2018. "Overview." TechWomen. https://www.techwomen.org/program/overview.

Trent, Deborah L. 2016. "Cultural Diplomacy Partnerships: Cracking the Credibility Nut with Inclusive Participation." In *Nontraditional U.S. Public Diplomacy: Past, Present, and Future*, ed. Deborah L. Trent. Washington, DC: Public Diplomacy Council. https://www.uscpublicdiplomacy.org/sites/uscpublicdiplomacy.org/files/useruploads/u39301/Nontraditional%20U.S.%20Public%20Diplomacy_PDC%20Copyright.pdf.

United Kingdom Foreign and Commonwealth Office. 2015. "About Chevening." United Kingdom Foreign and Commonwealth Office. https://www.chevening.org/about-chevening.

U.S. Department of Education. 2012. "Succeeding Globally Through International Education and Engagement: U.S. Department of Education International Strategy 2012–2016." Washington, DC: U.S. Department of Education. https://www2.ed.gov/about/inits/ed/internationaled/international-strategy-2012-16.pdf.

U.S. Department of State. 2016. "Bolashak International Scholarship." Washington, DC: U.S. Department of State EducationUSA. https://educationusa.state.gov/scholarships/bolashak-international-scholarship-0.

U.S. Department of State. 2018a. "Benjamin A. Gilman International Scholarship Program." Washington, DC: U.S. Department of State. https://exchanges.state.gov/us/program/benjamin-gilman-international-scholarship-program.

U.S. Department of State. 2018b. "Hubert H. Humphrey Fellowship Program." Washington, DC: U.S. Department of State. https://www.humphreyfellowship.org/.

U.S. Department of State. 2018c. "International Military Education and Training Account Summary." Washington, DC: U.S. Department of State. https://www.dsca.mil/programs/international-military-education-training-imet.

Wang, Jay, and Erik Nisbet. 2018. "Reimagining the Exchange Experience: The Local Impact of Cultural Exchanges." In *The Soft Power 30: A Global Ranking of Soft Power 2018*, ed. Jonathan McClory. Los Angeles, CA: University of Southern California (USC) Center for

Public Diplomacy. https://softpower30.com/wp-content/uploads/2018/07/The-Soft-Power-30-Report-2018.pdf.

Wilson, Iain. 2017. "Exchanges and Peacemaking: Counterfactuals and Unexplored Possibilities." In *International Education Exchanges and Intercultural Understanding: Promoting Peace and Global Relations*, ed. Julie Mathews-Aydinli. Cham, Switzerland: Springer International Publishing.

Yang, Rui. 2018. "China's Soft Power Projection through Higher Education: A Preliminary Assessment." In *The Rise of China-U.S. International Cooperation in Higher Education: Views from the Field*, eds. Christopher J. Johnstone and Li Li Ji. Leiden, The Netherlands: Brill Sense.

Yun, Seong-Hun. 2015. "Does Student Exchange Bring Symmetrical Benefits to Both Countries? An Exploration Case for China and Korea." *International Journal of Communication* 9, 1:710–731.

Chapter 10

Related Fields

International education is a broad field that engages professionals to work in a wide range of specialties and sectors. Drawing its knowledge from a breadth of scholarly fields, international education is highly interdisciplinary. This chapter introduces eight professional fields that are related to international education in part because of their shared goals. These goals include supporting student development, ensuring success and sustainability in educational organizations, fostering intercultural and global competence in others, and contributing to a more peaceful world. Familiarity with the scholarship of intersecting professional fields can expand the knowledge and skills of international educators, enabling them to strengthen the impact of their work.

Some of the related fields have day-to-day work that is similar to international education. Common tasks include advising students, organizing programming, facilitating intercultural training, managing educational organizations, and assessing educational outcomes. Many international education practitioners develop expertise in related fields and may move back and forth between fields over the course of their career. The related fields included in this chapter are (in alphabetical order):

- Comparative and international education;
- Global mobility;
- Higher education administration;
- Intercultural training;
- International development and education;
- Language program administration;
- Peacebuilding; and
- Student services.

International education does not function in isolation, but in a broader global context. Professionals in international education can increase the effectiveness of their work by building collegial relationships with professionals across related fields. Additionally, international educators can benefit from studying the trends and research of these fields. To further that aim, each section of this chapter introduces one related field, providing a necessarily brief overview of key topics and themes, a description of the field's intersections with international education, considerations for practitioners, and resources for further exploration.

Comparative and International Education

Comparative and international education is a social science research field focused on examining educational systems around the world. The field seeks to describe educational systems and learning communities within their societal contexts. It studies education at all levels, including early childhood, primary, secondary, higher education, vocational, and adult education programs. The analysis helps to explain how societies shape education and how education shapes societies (Wolhuter 2015; Bartram 2017).

The field dates back to at least the early nineteenth century when French scholars argued that research on foreign educational systems could help to strengthen the French educational system (Crossley and Watson 2010). The field boomed in the 1960s and 1970s and continues to see growth today as globalization has heightened interest in cross-cultural issues, accelerated the internationalization of teacher education, and increased recognition of the importance of global perspectives in education (Crossley 2012; Crossley and Watson 2010).

Comparative and international education as a scholarly field has strong connections with international education as a professional field. Epstein (2016) argues that comparative education focuses on using research and analysis to develop understanding. He argues that international education then uses the understanding generated by comparative education to effectively administer education programs. If thought of in this way, the two fields are complementary, or even integral, to each other. For example, internationalization and the development of global competence is one subject of study in comparative and international education research projects. The findings of this research can help inform international education practitioners working on curriculum development.

Another example of the connection relates to academic mobility. When receiving international students and scholars from another country or sending students abroad to participate in another educational system, it is extremely helpful for international education practitioners to understand the diversity of educational systems around the world. Knowing that teaching norms, grading, testing, teacher training, and more vary from system to system helps practitioners to prepare and support the individuals who are adapting to new educational systems. Comparative research can inform international education practitioners as they develop strategies for internationalization, create curriculum for developing students' global competence, and support individuals in transitions to new cultures. In turn, the needs of international education practitioners can inform comparative and international education research agendas.

Comparison as a Methodology

While acknowledging that what is successful in one educational system cannot simply be transferred unchanged to another country or culture, one of the foundational beliefs of the comparative and international education field is that learning about education in one society or context can prompt reflection on and insight into the educational system of another. Put into other words, educators can learn about one educational system through the mechanism of exploring others and comparing and contrasting. The comparative research approach is common in many disciplines. Using observation and interpretation as its approach, a breadth of information is collected. Still, there is ongoing debate on the relevance of the information in other contexts (Teichler 2014).

Comparisons can be made between different countries' educational systems and structures, time periods, particular demographic groups, values, policies, curricula, teaching approaches, and more. Some of the benefits of the comparative study of education include (Manzon 2011):

- Developing understanding of education in different communities and countries;
- Increased understanding of own educational system;
- Testing of educational designs, reforms, and innovations;
- Identification of global trends in education;
- Decreasing ethnocentrism and cultural bias, leading to increased international understanding and peace; and
- Developing tools for technical assistance in less developed countries.

The methodology of comparison, whatever the specific focus, helps to deepen understanding of what might be considered as good practices in education. That knowledge can be applied, thoughtfully, both at home and elsewhere.

Key Topics

Comparative and international education research can cover any education-related topic. Studies may be broad or narrow in scope. Comparison, as a methodology, may happen explicitly in studies that compare some aspect of education in two or more countries or contexts. Alternatively, the comparison may be implicit. In this case, a study examines one educational context with the implied understanding that it is being compared with the author's or reader's home educational context.

Equity of Access and Achievement

Some of the research in comparative and international education relates to issues of equity of access and achievement in education. These studies typically look at particular demographic groups and whether they are accessing education at rates similar to other demographic groups, as well as whether they are graduating or achieving the same outcomes at the same rates as other groups. The research attempts to identify causes of and solutions for any inequities found. The research may focus on gender, socioeconomic groups, religious minorities, linguistic minorities, students with disabilities, rural students, and many other groups (Kubow and Fossum 2003; Engsig and Johnstone 2015; Jackson 2014; Blum 2009). International development policy goals related to gender equity in education and the enrollment of all school-aged children have propelled this line of research within comparative and international education.

Alternative Education

There is no strict definition of alternative education; rather it is a collection of perspectives that challenge assumptions about how education and schools should function. Within comparative and international education, scholarship about alternative education may question whether schools are more focused on discipline than learning, or whether programs of study are being adapted to individual students' needs and interests (Wiseman 2017). The field has grown over the last 40 years, with increasing interest focused on restructuring education, curriculum, and teaching.

Farrell (2008) asks why it is assumed that:

- Schools should house hundreds of children together in a building called a "school" for some consecutive hours each day;
- Individuals aged 6 to 16 should be required to attend school;
- Students should be divided into groups by age and study with that group;
- A single "certified" teacher should be paired with each group of students;
- Each classroom full of students should be studying the same thing at the same time;
- A curriculum should be prescribed by an educational authority;
- Course materials (books, etc.) are mass produced;
- The teacher has most of the knowledge and must "pass" it to the students;
- Students should be able to "report back" what they have learned;

- There are formal recognitions for passing particular grades or levels; and

- Financial support for schools comes from the state or national government, rather than the local community.

Instead of these assumptions, Farrell (2008) observes that many alternative education programs have common characteristics: child-centered pedagogy, active learning, multigrade learning where older children help younger children, each child progressing at his or her own pace, teachers and students developing the learning materials, community involvement, extensive peer mentoring for teachers, and more focus on learning than teaching.

Alternative education initiatives may grow from single schools into global systems. Well-known systems include Montessori schools, Waldorf schools, Round Square schools, and Escuela Nuevas (Wiseman 2017). Research in alternative education might examine schools without walls, schools within a school, multicultural schools, continuation schools, fundamental (back-to-basics) schools, and magnet schools (Wiseman 2017).

Individual studies and articles often use both qualitative and quantitative research to explore these approaches to education, and theorists pose questions to challenge assumptions about what is normal in education. For example, Majidi and Restoule (2008) recommend that indigenous ways of knowing be incorporated into classrooms through the use of music, art, storytelling, talking circles, rituals, meditation, etc. They suggest teaching about indigenous beliefs, such as the medicine wheel or the Seven Sacred Teachings (Majidi and Restoule 2008).

Educational Structures and Policies

The study of educational structures might examine particular funding models, policies, centralization of decisionmaking, curricular choices, class sizes, facilities, teacher training practices, quality assurance mechanisms, etc., to determine their impacts on student learning, progression to higher education, professional outcomes, and more (Bray, Adamson, and Mason 2014). These choices happen within specific international policy environments, and comparative and international education research can gauge the impacts of the policies and, through the findings, can influence the policies themselves. Yang (2014) emphasizes that the context of the policy is as important to understand as the policy itself because that gives insight into whether or not a policy that works in one part of the world might work in another.

Considerations for Practitioners

Comparative and international education is a knowledge base typically developed in master's- and doctoral-level graduate programs. Many graduates go on to academic careers working as professors and researchers in colleges and universities. Others pursue careers in government, research, industry, nonprofits, consulting organizations, and foundations (Stanford University 2016).

As in all fields, comparative and international education professionals must be thoughtful and conscientious about their work. They must ensure that they bring a critical perspective to their work to avoid reproducing inequitable global power structures or assuming that developed countries have better systems in place than developing countries (Crossley and Watson 2010). As both producers and readers of research, comparative and international education professionals need to be careful to consider intercultural context in describing the culture-specific limitations of their research in order to avoid the assumption that educational policies and innovations can be flawlessly transported and installed in another culture (Crossley 2012).

Comparative education researchers must ensure that in their choice of collaborators, they partner with individuals who will bring perspectives different from their own, in order to strengthen the work. It is essential to encourage debate about methods, approaches, and interpretations (Crossley and Watson 2010). Comparison prompts reflection that is intended to both increase international understanding and help identify promising practices. Professionals working in the field of comparative and international education must be intentional in their work and recognize the limitations of their research, so that they can help consumers of the research identify whether the findings might be applicable to other contexts.

Resources

READINGS:

- Bartram, Brendan, ed. 2017. *International and Comparative Education: Contemporary Issues and Debates*. London, United Kingdom: Routledge.

- Bray, Mark, Bob Adamson, and Mark Mason. 2014. *Comparative Education Research: Approaches and Methods, Second Edition*. Hong Kong, China: Comparative Education Research Centre.

JOURNALS:

- *Comparative Education*

- *Comparative Education Review*

- *Compare: A Journal of Comparative and International Education*

- *International Higher Education*

- *International Journal of Comparative Education and Development*

- *Research in Comparative and International Education*

ORGANIZATIONS:

- Center for International Higher Education (CIHE) https://www.bc.edu/content/bc-web/schools/lynch-school/sites/cihe.html

- Comparative and International Education Society (CIES) www.cies.us

Global Mobility

As the world becomes increasingly globalized and interconnected, greater numbers of individuals are working outside of their home country. It is becoming increasingly common for (academic, work, research, business, etc.) teams to be multinational, collaborating in person with colleagues of diverse cultural backgrounds. Global mobility professionals support individuals and companies in managing the inevitable logistical and cross-cultural challenges that arise before and after individuals move abroad for work. Other terms that may be used to describe this sector include "expatriate management" and "international relocation services."

The global mobility field is related to international education because both areas support individuals and groups in their transitions to new countries and cultures. Professionals in each field must have a deep understanding of the acculturation process and be able to guide and support people through what may sometimes be a difficult and stressful adjustment process. Professionals must recognize the logistical, physical, linguistic, academic, professional, social, and cultural differences between cultures and organizations and be able to offer information and services to the individuals they serve to manage those changes. Knowledge sets, such as expertise in immigration and visa regulations, as well as skills in advising, coaching, and intercultural training are useful and transferable between the two fields. Professionals in each field can learn from each other about the types of services that can provide effective support during cultural transitions.

The Roles of Global Mobility Professionals

Global mobility is often considered a specialization within the human resources field. Human resources management not only deals with personnel matters such as selection, training, employee performance review, and compensation, it also seeks to ensure that these personnel actions are aligned with the overall strategy of the organization (Tayeb 2004). Professionals typically make their way into the field by working in human resources and gradually gaining experience in global mobility, or by applying directly to a job posting for a global mobility specialist. They may work in the human resources or training divisions of large multinational corporations or for specialist consulting/business services organizations that contract out to other companies to provide this support.

Similar to the role of international educators, the role of the global mobility professional is to help employees develop the knowledge, attitudes, and skills they need to succeed in a new cultural environment (Safdar and Berno 2016). To address knowledge, professionals supply information about the culture, economy, geography, religion, history, and more to the employees going abroad. To address attitudes, intercultural trainings are developed to increase empathy, humility, and tolerance for ambiguity, while decreasing ethnocentrism (see chapter 2). Skills can be further developed through role-plays, simulations, and field experience. The global mobility professional might provide this training personally, may make arrangements for the employees to be given training, or may recommend resources for the employees to pursue on their own. There will likely be some combination of these approaches. In addition to these aspects of preparation, language study is often an essential component of the preparation that global mobility professionals would help to arrange. Support is also typically provided for logistical matters including housing, the shipping of personal goods, school enrollment for children, visas, and taxes. Global mobility support may continue during the time overseas and be provided again to support the logistical and cultural transition back home.

The Global Workforce Context

The global workforce has significantly evolved over the past few decades, which has impacted the role of global mobility professionals. In their review of 50 years of studies related to global workforce mobility, Caligiuri and Bonache (2016) identify some of the changes: From the 1960s through the 1980s, the majority of expatriates sent by their companies to work in other countries were senior-level married men, sent from headquarters to run a subsidiary branch in order to ensure that business abroad was conducted in the way it was done at home. Those men were usually accompanied by a nonworking spouse. The men and their wives and families received generous salaries, benefits, and housing in compensation for the "hardship" of working in another country.

However, Caligiuri and Bonache (2016) explain that, today, 43 percent of expatriates are coming from nonheadquarters locations, 59 percent of the men are married, 19 percent of the expatriates are women, and 82 percent of the expatriates are under the age of 50. There is now much greater diversity of gender, more dual-career couples, and more nontraditional families. While expatriates were once sent abroad to fill specific management needs, they are now just as likely to be sent abroad with the primary goal of developing their global competence to prepare them for future management responsibilities (Caligiuri and Bonache 2016).

With advances in technology, communication, and travel, global mobility is becoming much more common (Safdar and Berno 2016; Caligiuri and Bonache 2016). Yet, the challenges of adapting to living and working in another culture remain intense, placing a greater emphasis on the preparation and support provided to expatriates by global mobility professionals. Companies spend as much as one-and-a-half to four times as much on an expatriate as they would on a local employee, so the costs are high if the employee underperforms (Safdar and Berno 2016). Expatriate employees will need to have some basic knowledge of the host culture and confidence in that knowledge. They will also have to have the skills for appropriate and effective behaviors in the workplace and daily life. While the demographics of expatriates have changed over the decades, natural human response to the acculturation process has not; support is needed to promote a successful experience that results in the employees' professional development as well as effective work for the company (Caligiuri and Bonache 2016).

Key Topics

Caligiuri and Bonache (2016) identify five strategic areas where companies need to adjust their support services for expatriates to better suit the changing contexts of global work and the demographics of globally mobile workers:

1. Assess early career potential for global roles. One unchanging aspect of global mobility research over the decades is that there are certain motivations and career traits that are more likely to lead to a successful overseas experience. Human resources personnel should assess employees for these traits and motivations much earlier in their careers. Individuals with these predispositions can then start intercultural and language training earlier in their career.

2. Integrate with talent management planning. Talent management refers to identifying and preparing workers for advancement in order to meet the predicted future needs of an organization. Given that organizations are increasingly working internationally, global mobility professionals need to work more closely with talent management teams to ensure that their company is intentionally developing both cross-cultural and technical skills in professionals who may later be called upon to work internationally.

3. Offer a wider range of benefits to globally mobile employees. Recognizing that the demographics of expatriate employees are much more diverse than in the past, and their needs more varied, organizations should consider offering support such as eldercare, benefits for nonmarried partners, etc.

4. Manage international contractors. Organizations need to recognize that the workforce is changing and diversify their global mobility support services for a wider range of employees. Organizations should consider developing services for contractors and individuals on short-term assignments overseas, for example.

5. Measure intercultural competence. Rather than assuming that employees who have lived abroad have developed cross-cultural skills, organizations need to measure those competencies. Assessments can identify areas of strength and areas for improvement in order to guide the employees' development.

These five areas are among those being discussed in the global mobility sector. Each is a response to a change in the global workforce context and the broadening of the profiles of expatriate employees who move overseas for the long term. Organizations will also need to prepare for the increasing frequency of multinational teams that work remotely and the employees who have short-term assignments overseas (Safdar and Berno 2016; PricewaterhouseCoopers 2010). The team leaders and employees in these groups will still need language and cross-cultural training, as well as the knowledge and skills to work together, but their needs will be different from those of employees who move abroad and are immersed in a single culture that is new to them.

Considerations for Practitioners

As practitioners approach their work in the global mobility field, they must be conscious of the fact that much of the research and many of the practices of the field were developed in an era when most expatriates were Western married men (Safdar and Berno 2016; Caligiuri and Bonache 2016). Now there is a much greater diversity of nationalities, genders, ages, relationship statuses, etc. Many of the expatriate workers are not going from headquarters to a branch location, but from a branch to headquarters or a branch to another branch (Vance and Paik 2006). Further, many more multinational corporations are now headquartered in Asia or other non-Western parts of the word (Vance and Paik 2006). Global mobility professionals need to recognize and adapt to this diversity.

As in international education, an urgent undertaking for global mobility professionals is providing support for the family members who are also relocating. In both fields, it is inevitable that all of the accompanying family members will experience some degree of stress as part of the acculturation process. Global mobility professionals must recognize that this dynamic may increase the stress for the employee (Vedder and Motto-Stefanidi 2016; Foote 2013). The family members' experiences should be structured so that they feel comfortable, but also so that they have experiences in work, school, or housing beyond an expatriate enclave. This not only improves the learning experience for the family, it also supports the professional development of the employee.

In the global mobility field, the goal of current expatriate assignments is often focused on developing the cross-cultural knowledge and skills of the overseas employee. Therefore, it is ideal if his or her home life outside of work also offers opportunities for exposure to the local culture. This will not happen if accompanying family members are not also supported in interacting and integrating with local people (Caligiuri and Bonache 2016). For this reason, global mobility services must include structures for family members to be integrated into the community. Working with a wide spectrum of topics and situations ranging from cross-cultural to logistical, global mobility professionals are responsible for effectively supporting employees, and their families, before, during, and after their overseas assignment.

Resources

READINGS:

- Caligiuri, Paula, and Jaime Bonache. 2016. "Evolving and Enduring Challenges in Global Mobility." *Journal of World Business* 51, 1:127–141. https://doi.org/10.1016/j.jwb.2015.10.001.

- Safdar, Saba, and Tracy Berno. 2016. "Sojourners." In *Acculturation Psychology, Second Edition*, eds. David L. Sam and John W. Berry. New York, NY: Cambridge University Press.

JOURNALS AND PUBLICATIONS:

- *Human Resource Management International Digest*
- *The International Journal of Human Resource Management*
- *Journal of Global Mobility*
- *Mobility Magazine*

Higher Education Administration

Higher education administration, also sometimes referred to as "higher education leadership," is focused on leading and managing colleges and universities. As with international education, it is both a scholarly field of study and a profession. The study of higher education administration tends to focus on the application of theory to practice. Common areas of research include institutional types and missions, educational and professional outcomes for students, institutional cultures, decisionmaking processes, diversity and inclusion issues, and power and politics within organizations (Powers and Schloss 2017).

Another area of study examines the forces, internal and external, that influence institutions. External forces include economic shifts and changing demographics and political landscapes, many of which were described in chapter 1. Internal influences include the values, structures, history, and goals of each institution. These shape what is done, who is doing it, and the processes that guide the work (Tierney 2011). The present-day choices made by institutions about how to respond to external forces with internal processes will determine the viability and success of the institution for many years into the future, making this an area of great interest to scholars of higher education (Kienle and Loyd 2005).

Given the growing emphasis on global learning, higher education administration and international education are closely linked fields. One connection is that many international education positions are within higher education organizations. At numerous colleges and universities around the world, internationalization has become an institutional priority because of the need to remain competitive and to prepare undergraduate and graduate students for engaging in the global workforce.

Another linkage is that many international educators earn graduate degrees in this field and use the scholarship of the field to help guide their practice as educators and administrators. Graduate degrees in higher education administration are plentiful around the world. There are more than 200 graduate programs in the United States focused on higher education administration and leadership (Association for the Study of Higher Education 2018). Graduates of these programs may initially take on lower- and mid-level management positions in colleges and universities, or may find careers in government agencies, think tanks, and related areas. Over time, individuals may move up to senior administrative positions (Freeman and Kochan 2012).

Higher education administration and student services (discussed later in the chapter) are also related fields. The primary difference is that higher education administration emphasizes organizational behavior and decisionmaking, while student services emphasizes student development theory. Individuals in both fields study organizational behavior and student development; it is just a difference in the degree of focus.

Institution Types

One of the things that makes the study and practice of higher education both fascinating and confounding is the range of institutional missions and the many diverse constituencies they serve. Even when institutions are of the same general type, there can be great difference. Higher education institutions can have similar missions and values and yet perform differently due to the leadership styles and the way their own identities are communicated to others within and outside of the institutions themselves. There are more than 4,800 higher education institutions in the United States (Henderson and Powers 2017). The number of institutions is divided fairly evenly between public institutions, private nonprofit institutions, and private for-profit institutions. Despite the roughly equal division of institutions in these groups, student enrollments, as shown in table 1, heavily favor public institutions (Henderson and Powers 2017).

TABLE 1 U.S. Higher Education Institution Types

	Percentage of All Institutions	Number of Students Enrolled (approx.)
Public Institutions	35%	14.6 million
Private, Nonprofit	35%	4.0 million
Private, For-Profit	30%	1.5 million
All Institutions	100%	20.1 million

Source: Henderson and Powers (2017).

The Carnegie Classifications divides U.S. higher education institutions into categories. First published in 1973 (Hendrickson et al. 2013; Indiana University Center for Postsecondary Research 2018), the system uses data submitted to the U.S. government to answer the questions: What is taught, to whom, and in what setting? The Carnegie Basic Classification presented in table 2 divides institutions into categories based on number, level, and focus of degree offerings.

TABLE 2 Carnegie Basic Classifications of U.S. Higher Education Institutions

Classification	Subclassifications	Degrees Awarded Annually
Doctoral Universities	• R1: Doctoral universities with very high research activity • R2: Doctoral universities with high research activity • D/PU: Doctoral/professional universities	Institutions that awarded at least 20 research/scholarship doctoral degrees or at least 30 professional practice doctoral degrees in at least two programs.
Master's Colleges and Universities	• M1: Master's colleges and universities – larger programs • M2: Master's colleges and universities – medium programs • M3: Master's colleges and universities – smaller programs	Generally, institutions that awarded at least 50 master's degrees and fewer than 20 doctoral degrees.
Baccalaureate Colleges	• Arts and sciences focus • Diverse fields	Generally, institutions in which baccalaureate or higher degrees represent at least 50 percent of all degrees awarded, and fewer than 50 master's degrees or 20 doctoral degrees are awarded.
Baccalaureate/ Associate's Colleges	• Mixed baccalaureate/associate's colleges • Associate's dominant	Institutions in which 50 percent or higher degrees awarded are at the associate's level. May include four-year colleges in the case of colleges with at least one baccalaureate degree program.
Associate's Colleges	• High transfer – high traditional • High transfer – mixed traditional/nontraditional • High transfer – high nontraditional • Mixed transfer/career and technical – high traditional • Mixed transfer/career and technical – mixed traditional/nontraditional • Mixed transfer/career and technical – high nontraditional • High transfer/career and technical – high traditional • High transfer/career and technical – mixed traditional/nontraditional • High transfer/career and technical – high nontraditional	Institutions in which an associate's degree is the highest degree level. Subcategories are based on the combination of two factors: disciplinary focus (transfer, career and technical, or mixed) and dominant student type (traditional, nontraditional, or mixed).

(continued on next page)

Table 2. Carnegie Basic Classifications of U.S. Higher Education Institutions (continued)

Classification	Subclassifications	Degrees Awarded Annually
Special Focus Institutions	Two-Year - Arts and design - Health professions - Technical professions - Other fields Four-Year - Arts, music, and design schools - Business and management schools - Engineering schools - Faith-related institutions - Law schools - Medical schools and centers - Other health professions schools - Other technology-related schools - Other special focus institutions	Institutions where most degrees are in a single field or in a set of related fields.
Tribal Colleges		Colleges and universities that are members of the American Indian Higher Education Consortium.

Source: Indiana University Center for Postsecondary Research (2018).

U.S. higher education institutions have a wide range of missions. Some, such as community colleges, are intended to serve the local community with open access admissions policies, adult education programs, and ongoing training and development for local professionals. In contrast, the mission of doctoral institutions emphasizes scientific research and the production of knowledge in all fields. Yet, both types of institutions also provide undergraduate education. The Carnegie Classifications provides a very important function by allowing researchers and others to compare institutions with similar missions. In addition to the basic classification system, Carnegie Classifications also has classification systems to divide institutions by the type of undergraduate instructional program, graduate instructional program, enrollment profile, undergraduate profile, size and setting, and community engagement (Indiana University Center for Postsecondary Research 2018).

Key Topics

Higher education administrators focus on the internal decisions and processes that will help them to fulfill their institutional mission, in light of external forces to which they must respond. A survey of more than 1,500 U.S. college and university presidents (American Council on Education 2017) identified areas of greatest concern in higher education administration, including budget and financial management, enrollment management, and diversity and equity issues. This section introduces key topics in the field of higher education administration.

Organizational Structures

Higher education institutions have characteristics that make them different from most for-profit and nonprofit organizations (Hendrickson et al. 2013):

- Goal ambiguity. Colleges and universities serve a wide range of constituents, including students, community members, industries, governments, and the ideological pursuit of knowledge. This often leaves institutions without a clear, focused mission.

- Highly professionalized staff. Professionalized staff have expectations of workplace autonomy and the right to be evaluated by peers. They may feel torn between loyalty to their field and to their institution.

- Unclear decisionmaking processes. Many institutions do not have a clear set of procedures explaining which office or individual has the right to make which decisions.

One way in which these characteristics merge and become complicated is through shared governance. A fundamental principle of U.S. higher education is that faculty have the right to oversee the curriculum of the institution, while administrators oversee the operations of the organization (Hendrickson et al. 2013). However, in practice, this can become a point of tension between faculty and administrators as the administrators want to make decisions about the viability of programs or to launch of new programs for financial reasons. At the same time, faculty members want to be involved in decisions that have a direct impact on curriculum and learning, such as admissions requirements, modes of teaching (e.g., online), student support services provided, etc. Tensions arise when groups have different expectations of the role of faculty, staff, students, and administration in making decisions in these areas.

Organizational Cultures

In the field of higher education administration, much attention is given to organizational values and culture. It is important to understand both the dominant values of the campus community as a whole, as well as the individual values of campus leaders, in order to understand how and why particular decisions are made and to strategize to bring about change (Tierney 2011). The organizational cultures are evidenced in the specific language, norms, institutional ideologies, shared stories, and attitudes that are prominent in organizations (Tierney 2011).

Bergquist and Pawlak (2008) describe six dominant cultures in U.S. higher education:

- Collegial. This culture focuses on faculty research and autonomy, the dissemination of knowledge, and the role of faculty in guiding the institution's directions.

- **Managerial.** This culture focuses on efficiency and measurable outcomes, with oversight through a top-down, hierarchical leadership structure.

- **Developmental.** This culture focuses on the learner and learner-centered education, alongside the professional development of faculty and staff.

- **Advocacy.** This culture focuses on social justice, confrontation, and bargaining, with a goal of establishing equitable policies and procedures.

- **Virtual.** This culture focuses on access to knowledge and information and the use of technology to engage students in learning.

- **Tangible.** This culture focuses on traditions and community ties, particularly alumni, and values the beauty of the campus grounds, state of the art facilities, and high reputation of the institution.

While each of these cultures exists on every campus, and most individuals value most or all of these areas, Bergquist and Pawlak (2008) argue that certain cultures tend to dominate particular organizations. Which cultures, or combinations of cultures, dominate, and in which spheres of the campus they dominate, affect the decisions that are made on campus. Much of the disagreement and struggle over politics and power in institutions may be attributed to differences in these cultures.

Budget and Finance

As government funding for public higher education has decreased in recent years, much of the cost of attending higher education has shifted to students in the form of increased tuition fees (Altbach, Gumport, and Berdahl 2011). Increased tuition fees have resulted in increased student loans, and many fear that a nationwide economic crisis will result from the inability of graduates and nongraduates to repay the loans. For institutions, there is added pressure to increase domestic and international enrollments to ensure that there is enough operating revenue for the institution. Yet, as shifting demographics and political and economic changes occur, enrollments may decrease for reasons beyond the control of the institutions. At the time of publication, international student enrollments were decreasing, affecting overall enrollment numbers, especially for graduate programs (Institute of International Education 2018; Okahana and Zhou 2018). Managing the finances of an institution is, thus, one of the key priorities of higher education administrators.

Retention and Success

Because educational institutions are increasingly expected to be accountable for their outcomes and evidence-based in their work, as discussed in chapter 1, there has been a strong focus on student retention and success. Both higher education administrators in general and international educators specifically are being asked to show evidence that the programs they run contribute positively to student retention and success.

Student retention is typically measured in terms of the percentage of students who continue their studies from year to year. Success is usually defined as students' attainment of their educational goal, such as a degree. When success is measured in terms of graduation rates, the metric typically utilized is the percentage of students who have completed their degree program within 150 percent of the normal length of time for the degree. The National Center for Education Statistics (NCES) (2018), a U.S. government agency, reports:

- 95 percent of all first-time, full-time undergraduates at institutions offering four-year degrees continued to the second year.

- 62 percent of all first-time, full-time undergraduates at institutions offering two-year degrees continued to the second year.

- 60 percent of all first-time, full-time bachelor's degree-seeking students completed their degrees within 6 years.

- 26 percent of first-time, full-time bachelor's degree-seeking students at private, for-profit schools completed their degrees within 6 years.

These data show that institutions are failing to support millions of students in achieving their goals. They also demonstrate that there is a disparity between institution types. Additional data collected and analyzed by NCES show differences by gender, ethnicity, state, and other categories. It is important for higher education administrators to use such data to identify barriers to student retention and success and then make improvements.

Considerations for Practitioners

Retention and success are critical issues in higher education administration. Far too few students are achieving their educational goals; this trend is all the more worrying when the data are sorted by demographic group and by institution type. The results of this disaggregation clearly demonstrate that there are inequitable student outcomes in U.S. higher education.

Inequities exist within the administration as well. Though it is improving, there are still disproportionately few women and people of color leading higher education institutions (American Council on Education 2017). Knowledgeable and informed higher education administrators have the chance to bring about change to organizations, helping them to better achieve their missions, serve students, and contribute to society. These improvements can work toward minimizing inequities between privileged and disadvantaged groups.

Resources

READINGS:

- Altbach, Philip G., Patricia J. Gumport, and Robert O. Berdahl. 2011. *American Higher Education in the Twenty-First Century: Social, Political, and Economic Challenges*. Baltimore, MD: Johns Hopkins University Press.

- Powers, Kristina, and Patrick J. Schloss. 2017. *Organization and Administration in Higher Education, Second Edition*. New York, NY: Routledge.

JOURNALS:

- *American Educational Research Journal*
- *ASHE Higher Education Report*
- *Community College Review*
- *Educational Evaluation and Policy Analysis*
- *Educational Policy*
- *Educational Researcher*
- *Higher Education*
- *Higher Education Quarterly*
- *Innovative Higher Education*
- *The Journal of Higher Education*
- *Journal of Higher Education Policy and Management*
- *Research in Higher Education*
- *Review of Educational Research*
- *The Review of Higher Education*
- *Studies in Higher Education*

ORGANIZATIONS:

- American Association of Community Colleges (AACC) www.aacc.nche.edu/
- American Association of State Colleges and Universities (AASCU) www.aascu.org

- American Council on Education (ACE) www.acenet.edu
- Association for the Study of Higher Education (ASHE) www.ashe.ws/
- Association of American Colleges & Universities (AAC&U) www.aacu.org/
- Association of American Universities (AAU) www.aau.edu/
- Association of Public and Land-grant Universities (APLU) www.aplu.org/
- Council for the Advancement of Standards in Higher Education (CAS) www.cas.edu/

OTHER:

- Carnegie Classifications carnegieclassifications.iu.edu/
- *Chronicle of Higher Education* www.chronicle.com/
- College Navigator nces.ed.gov/collegenavigator/
- Higher Education Research Centers: www.higher-ed.org/research_centers.htm
- *Inside Higher Ed* www.insidehighered.com/
- National Center for Education Statistics nces.ed.gov/

Intercultural Training

Intercultural training draws on research about intercultural communication, intercultural competence, global competence, acculturation, conflict resolution, and other topics. Using this theoretical and practical knowledge, intercultural trainers design and facilitate trainings and educational programs for corporate employees, nonprofit organization personnel, government employees, students, and community groups. Some intercultural trainers work full time for one organization, while others work as freelancers, contracting with multiple organizations. They may specialize in particular areas (Meares 2015; The Intercultural Communication Institute 2018); for example, some may focus on providing support to individuals (and their families) as they prepare to move abroad for work. Some professionals are corporate trainers. They may work in the human resources division for a large multinational corporation, work for a cross-cultural training organization, or work as a self-employed independent contractor. Others have training-related positions within government agencies, higher education, or international education organizations.

The fields of intercultural training and international education are connected. As discussed in previous chapters of this volume, an explicit goal of many international education programs is developing the intercultural competence of students. In fact, NAFSA: Association of International Educators's *NAFSA International Education Professional Competencies* framework describes intercultural communication and training as a cross-cutting competency relevant to all sectors of the field. Included among the knowledge and skills that international education professionals should have (NAFSA 2015) are:

- Knowledge of own identity and culture;
- Knowledge of other cultural norms;
- Ability to communicate with intercultural sensitivity; and
- Ability to identify and articulate cultural similarities and differences.

While these and other skills are required to work effectively and appropriately with individuals from diverse cultural backgrounds, international educators are also frequently responsible for helping others develop these abilities.

NAFSA's (2015) *Competencies* describes ways to develop the intercultural competence of others:

- Champion diversity, equity, and inclusion;
- Use intercultural encounters as education opportunities;
- Ensure staff has adequate training and experience in intercultural communication;
- Lead others in appreciating multiple perspectives; and
- Provide intercultural training for constituencies.

Many international educators, as an aspect of their work, develop and facilitate trainings and educational programs specifically designed to strengthen the intercultural competence of students. These professionals may also conduct trainings for staff, faculty, and community members. Some individuals facilitate trainings as consultants outside of their organization; others may build on this additional work to transition to full-time careers as intercultural trainers. Similarly, many intercultural trainers have extensive international and intercultural experience and may be well qualified to take on international education positions. In this way, professionals may move back and forth between these two related fields.

Intercultural Training Contexts

As with international educators, intercultural trainers help learners to shift their perspectives by increasing their awareness of the role of culture in their experiences. The intercultural trainer is a person who "uses reflective tools to assist others in their intercultural development, while… [they] make immediate decisions about the most appropriate and effective next steps to take in a learning environment" (Kappler Mikk and Bjarndottir 2017, 141). The trainers help learners to recognize that they are viewing an experience through their own cultural lens and that there are other valid interpretations to consider (Kappler Mikk and Bjarndottir 2017).

Key Topics

Intercultural training is an interdisciplinary field that synthesizes ideas from education, communication, psychology, sociology, and many other arenas. Some of the foundational topics in the intercultural training field are introduced here.

Acculturation Theory

Intercultural trainers, and international educators, must be familiar with theories of acculturation. "Acculturation is the process whereby you adapt to a new culture by adopting its values, attitudes, and practices" (Neuliep 2017, 403). It is characterized by the gradual letting go of some long-held beliefs and habits that emerged from the culture(s) in which a person is raised, and the gradual adoption of some new beliefs and habits from the culture in which a person is immersed (Kim 2001). Acculturation may manifest in tangible ways, such as changes in speech or behavior, or intangible ways, such as shifts in values and opinions. This transition may prompt physiological or psychological stress for some individuals (Neuliep 2017). In fact, acculturation theory suggests that some level of stress is necessary for growth—though too much stress is detrimental (Kim 2001). The study of acculturation examines theories and models of acculturation; the role of identity development and change; the role of personality; the ways in which particular groups such as immigrants, refugees, travelers, and students experience acculturation; and the settings of acculturation, including schools, the workplace, and social service programs (Sam and Berry 2016).

Intersectionality of Identity

Individuals simultaneously hold multiple identities, including nationality, race, ethnicity, socioeconomic class, gender, sexuality, age, religion, profession, and many others. The most important concept of intersectionality is that individuals are not characterized by just one identity, but rather that the combination of identities influences both their sense of self and how they are treated by others. At the same time, the theory of intersectionality also emphasizes that the identities are constantly changing, with different identities holding greater salience at different points in time, in different contexts, and at different phases in a person's life (Wijeyesinghe 2012; Dervin and Tournebise 2013; Collins 2015). Intercultural trainers must recognize the ways in which learners' identities affect their intercultural interactions.

Assessment of Intercultural Competence

In order to develop the intercultural competence of others, intercultural trainers must be able to assess individuals' current intercultural competence. One way to do so is to develop familiarity with a paradigm, such as the Developmental Model of Intercultural Sensitivity (introduced in chapter 2), that includes guidance on how to recognize an individual's learning stage. Another option is to use a tool such as the Intercultural Development Inventory (IDI), Cross-Cultural Adaptability Inventory (CCAI), or others (see list in chapter 2). Many of these tools require certification in order to be able to administer and interpret the assessment. Trainers must be familiar with a wide range of theories and tools in order to use the combination that will be most effective for a group of learners and their particular training goals.

Training Design and Facilitation Skills

For program design, intercultural trainers must be aware of theories related to teaching and learning. They also need to know how to conduct needs assessments in advance of trainings to guide the development of the program; they use this information about participant and organizational goals and expectations to make choices about training content and activities (Deardorff and Arasaratnam-Smith 2017; Kappler Mikk and Bjarndottir 2017). Trainers must develop facilitation skills, including the ability to set expectations, motivate learners, shape group dynamics, recognize learning opportunities, deepen engagement, respond to emotional reactions, and address conflict (Roberts 2015).

Considerations for Practitioners

One of the challenges for intercultural trainers is that they bring their own perspectives and biases to the work. Trainers must be aware of how their own values shape what they are teaching and, thus, validate, invalidate, or influence other people's values (Byram, Nichols, and Stevens 2001). To mitigate the risk that the trainer's cultural viewpoint will invalidate learners' perspectives, the trainer must work to constantly observe and reflect on his or her own beliefs and judgments; this is a lifelong process of self-reflection, self-critique, and self-development (Deardorff and Arasaratnam-Smith 2017). The trainer must ensure that he or she is conscientious about recognizing and validating perspectives from all learners, particularly those whose perspectives are most different from the trainer, and those learners who are the most disadvantaged within society (Miike 2007).

Resources
READINGS:

- Kappler Mikk, Barbara, and Inge Ellen Steglitz, eds. 2017. *Learning Across Cultures: Locally and Globally, Third Edition*. Washington, DC: NAFSA: Association of International Educators and Stylus Publishing.

- Meares, Mary. 2015. *Intercultural Career Planning*. Portland, OR: The Intercultural Communication Institute. https://intercultural.org/intercultural-bibliographies/.

- Sam, David L., and John W. Berry. 2016. *Acculturation Psychology, Second Edition*. New York, NY: Cambridge University Press.

JOURNALS:

- *Cross-Cultural Research*
- *Intercultural Education*
- *International Journal of Intercultural Relations*
- *Journal of Intercultural Communication Research*
- *Journal of International and Intercultural Communication*

ORGANIZATIONS:

- The Intercultural Communication Institute (ICI) intercultural.org/
- Society for Intercultural Education, Training and Research (SIETAR) www.sietarusa.org/

OTHER:

- NAFSA Core Education Program Workshop: Intercultural Communication in Practice www.nafsa.org/Professional_Resources/Learning_and_Training/Workshops/Intercultural_Communication_in_Practice/
- NAFSA Intercultural Communication and Training Resources network.nafsa.org/nafsa-resources
- NAFSA Resources for Intercultural Practitioners www.nafsa.org/Professional_Resources/Browse_by_Interest/Internationalizing_Higher_Education/Network_Resources/Teaching,_Learning,_and_Scholarship/Resources_for_Intercultural_Practitioners/
- SIETAR *Living Code of Ethical Behavior* www.sietarusa.org/resources/Documents/EoEArticles/SIETAR2013_LivingCode.pdf

International Development and Education

International development, as a field, aims to help less wealthy countries and communities to develop economically. Alongside economic development is a focus on social welfare, including health care, human rights, good governance, and human security. The scholarship of the field examines the effectiveness of development approaches and initiatives in order to guide practice. Because of its focus on expanding the capabilities of people, education is at the forefront of development initiatives (Thouez 2015).

The fields of international development and international education share several elements. The efforts of both fields aim to address global issues and connect people within international networks to bring about positive change in the world (Mueller and Overmann 2014). To achieve this, they both focus on moving people, information, and, sometimes, supplies across national borders. Some higher education institutions include international development work among the internationalization activities in which they engage. Additionally, some of the largest international education nonprofit organizations also work in the international development field, creating further connections and opportunities for collaboration between the two fields.

International Development

International development has its origins in the colonial era when Europeans began to build systems of global labor to support their economic growth. At that time, the focus was on economic development. The field gradually shifted to include an emphasis on social good, reinforced by the 1948 United Nations's Declaration of Universal Human Rights. From this era onward, development began to be perceived as a joint obligation of governments, markets, and citizens (McMichael 2017). By the late 1990s, there was broad consensus that development progress should be measured not only by economic growth, but also by human capacity (Thouez 2015).

The term "sustainable development" is often used in place of the term "international development" to emphasize that economic development needs to happen in ways that will continue to be viable into the future. This means both the protection of the Earth's natural resources and the use of economic models that do not create economic dependence on donors (Kadatska 2016). In short, sustainable approaches to international development must meet the needs of the present, without compromising the future (Kates, Parris, and Leiserowitz 2005).

Today, educational initiatives remain a priority. International development work in education or in other sectors is often carried out by nongovernmental organizations (NGOs). The work of these organizations may be partially or fully funded by governments through competitive grants, but the employees are not government employees. NGOs may also receive funding from donors, charities, and foundations (Kadatska 2016). International development work is also carried out by intergovernmental organizations such as the Organisation for Economic Co-operation and Development (OECD), United Nations International Children's Emergency Fund (UNICEF), United Nations Educational, Scientific and Cultural Organization (UNESCO), and the World Bank. Other organizations that are active in international development include transnational corporations, philanthropic foundations, international consultants, and transnational civil society coalitions (Verger, Altinyelken, and Novelli 2018).

Sustainable Development Goals

In 2015, members of the United Nations came together to draft the 2030 Agenda for Sustainable Development. This document identifies 17 Sustainable Development Goals (SDGs) that the international community will strive to achieve by 2030. These goals are (United Nations 2018):

1. End poverty in all its forms everywhere.
2. End hunger, achieve food security and improved nutrition and promote sustainable agriculture.
3. Ensure healthy lives and promote well-being for all at all ages.
4. Ensure inclusive and equitable quality education and promote lifelong learning opportunities for all.
5. Achieve gender equality and empower all women and girls.
6. Ensure availability and sustainable management of water and sanitation for all.
7. Ensure access to affordable, reliable, sustainable and modern energy for all.
8. Promote sustained, inclusive and sustainable economic growth, full and productive employment and decent work for all.
9. Build resilient infrastructure, promote inclusive and sustainable industrialization and foster innovation.
10. Reduce inequality within and among countries.
11. Make cities and human settlements inclusive, safe, resilient and sustainable.
12. Ensure sustainable consumption and production patterns.
13. Take urgent action to combat climate change and its impacts.

14. Conserve and sustainably use the oceans, seas and marine resources for sustainable development.

15. Protect, restore and promote sustainable use of terrestrial ecosystems, sustainably manage forests, combat desertification, and halt and reverse land degradation and halt biodiversity loss.

16. Promote peaceful and inclusive societies for sustainable development, provide access to justice for all and build effective, accountable and inclusive institutions at all levels.

17. Strengthen the means of implementation and revitalize the global partnership for sustainable development.

These goals provide a foundation for many of the international development policies, including the funding priorities. The United Nations produces reports by country and region, measuring key data points for each of the 17 SDGs in order to track achievements, or lack of achievement, over time (United Nations 2018).

Development and Education

Education is widely believed to be integral to international development. Increased educational achievement is not only one of the SDGs, it is also considered to be a method of achieving other SDGs. Education is understood to be essential to the development of individuals, communities, and nations (McGrath 2018). Education, at home and abroad, can contribute to development by providing individuals with the knowledge and skills to understand the complex intersections of economics, societies, and the natural environment; education can help to build peace or recover from conflict; and education can raise awareness of social injustice (McGrath 2018; Leicht, Heiss, and Byun 2018).

Sustainable Development Goal 4 calls on countries to "ensure inclusive and equitable quality education and promote lifelong learning opportunities for all" (United Nations 2018). This goal has a series of specific objectives, referred to as "targets," to be achieved by 2030. They are summarized here (United Nations 2018):

- 4.1 Ensure free, equitable, quality primary and secondary education for all girls and boys.

- 4.2 Ensure quality early childhood development, care, and preprimary education for all girls and boys.

- 4.3 Ensure equal access for women and men to affordable, quality vocational education and higher education.

- 4.4 Substantially increase the number of youth and adults with the skills for decent jobs and entrepreneurship.

- 4.5 Eliminate gender disparities in education; ensure access to education for everyone including people with disabilities, indigenous people, and children in vulnerable situations.

- 4.6 Ensure that all youth and a substantial proportion of men and women achieve literacy and numeracy.

- 4.7 Ensure that all learners have the knowledge and skills to promote sustainable development, human rights, gender equality, peace and non-violence, global citizenship, and appreciation of cultural diversity.

- 4.A Build and upgrade education facilities that are safe and inclusive.

- 4.B Substantially expand the number of scholarships available to developing countries for higher education enrollment in developed and other developing countries.

- 4.C Substantially increase the supply of qualified teachers.

As is apparent among the SDG targets, education contributes to development at every level, from early childhood through to higher education and programs for adult learning. The targets emphasize overcoming the inequities in access to education associated with poverty and gender, the importance of education for employability and economic development, the positive impacts of learning on individuals and societies, and the importance of an internationalized education (Thouez 2015). Leicht, Heiss, and Byun (2018), in a UNESCO publication, mirror some of these topics as they identify priorities for education and development: advancing policy, transforming learning and training environments, building educator capacity, empowering and mobilizing youth, and accelerating sustainable solutions.

Specializations

Within the broad field of international development and education, many professionals and scholars specialize in a particular facet of the field (McCowan and Unterhalter 2015; Rieckmann 2018). Some specialize in girls' education and gender equity in schooling; others focus on education in emergencies, including education in conflict and postconflict zones as well as education in refugee camps. Early childhood development can be an area of focus, as can adult learning, such as literacy programs and training. Others study capacity building in higher education or the impact of international education scholarships on development. Still others focus on how educational development impacts economies or promotes environmental sustainability.

The field of international development and education is broad, bringing together many academic disciplines and professions. Types of jobs include but are not limited to (University of Oxford The Careers Service 2018):

- Practitioners who manage and implement projects in the field;

- Policy/advisory professionals who conduct research and evaluation and make policy recommendations;

- Advocacy/outreach professionals who campaign, lobby, fundraise, and run media campaigns to influence the public as well as policymakers; and

- Professionals who provide professional support and services in areas such as human resources, accounting, information technology, etc., to assist the work of development organizations.

Employers include governmental organizations, intergovernmental organizations, NGOs, academic institutions, research organizations, and consultancies.

Considerations for Practitioners

The concerns that practitioners must be cognizant of in relation to the field of international development and education are similar to those for the international development field as a whole. Three considerations are presented here.

One chief ethical concern in international development is the question of who establishes development priorities and policies. Is it the citizens and governments of the societies being developed, or is it external forces? Because many development projects receive external funding from foreign governments, intergovernmental agencies, and private donors, the receiving communities must comply with the donor's policies and priorities for projects if they wish to receive the money. In this way, it has been observed that wealthier countries that have the money to give have tended to dominate the establishment of priorities, rather than the local communities that would be most aware of their needs (McGrath 2018; McMichael 2017). To counter some of these challenges, del Castillo (2017) recommends that aid be funneled through national budgets and that national governments be given primary control of how the funds are used, in order to ensure that national needs are met. Some critics also argue that the field needs to commit more strongly to using evidence-based practice, rather than simply using development approaches that fit the dominant narrative (McGrath 2018).

A second concern for practitioners relates to the life cycles of international development projects. Because the projects are primarily grant funded, the projects often have a defined end date. The grant-funded nature of international development work affects the employment of practitioners. Practitioners may find that their career has a pattern of moving from project to project in a series of short-term contracts (Heathershaw 2016). While long-term employment is available in some settings, development practitioners should be aware that many initiatives are limited in duration.

A final concern for practitioners is also related to the time-limited duration of grant-funded projects. The nature of grant funding raises questions of sustainability and dependency. Projects need to have a pathway to becoming sustainable when the grant funding ends, otherwise any gains from the projects will be lost. If a plan for sustainability is not built into a project, the receiving community may come to rely on the services provided and then remain dependent on continued donor support, rather than developing the capacity to meet its own needs (Kadatska 2016). Helping individuals, communities, and countries develop capacity is the fundamental goal of development, therefore, long-term sustainability plans need to be part of all international development initiatives.

Resources

READINGS:

- Leicht, Alexander, Julia Heiss, and Won Jung Byun. 2018. *Issues and Trends in Education for Sustainable Development.* Paris, France: United Nations Educational, Scientific and Cultural Organization. https://unesdoc.unesco.org/ark:/48223/pf0000261445.

- McGrath, Simon. 2018. *Education and Development.* London, United Kingdom: Routledge.

- McMichael, Philip. 2017. *Development and Social Change: A Global Perspective, Sixth Edition.* Thousand Oaks, CA: Sage Publications.

JOURNALS:

- *International Journal of Educational Development*

- *Journal of Education for Sustainable Development*

CAREER EXPLORATION RESOURCES:

- Mueller, Sherry Lee, and Mark Overmann. 2014. *Working World: Careers in International Education, Exchange, and Development, Second Edition.* Washington, DC: Georgetown University Press.

- University of Oxford The Careers Service. 2018. "International Development." Oxford, United Kingdom: University of Oxford The Careers Service. https://www.careers.ox.ac.uk/international-development/.

OTHER:

- UNESCO Global Education Monitoring Report en.unesco.org/gem-report
- United Nations's Sustainable Development Goals sustainabledevelopment.un.org/
- World Bank Education Resources www.worldbank.org/en/topic/education

Language Program Administration

Language program administration brings together the administrative skills of the international educator with the teaching knowledge of language educators. It is grounded in the research on language learning and complemented by scholarship on international education and management. Many of the tasks of international education managers and language program administrators are the same: student recruitment, admissions, marketing, curriculum design, budgeting and financial oversight, staff management, student services, assessment of learning, and program assessment. Thus, international education and language program administration are closely associated fields of both research and practice.

While language programs can focus on any language, the largest segment of the field is English language programs. This is in direct response to the global demand for English language education for non-native speakers. English is spoken by approximately a quarter of the world's population, and there is more demand for English language instruction than there are qualified teachers (British Council 2013). Leaders in business, politics, science, and education agree that current global proficiency in English is not strong enough to meet the needs of a world that is more connected than ever (American Academy of Arts and Sciences 2016). This has led to the proliferation of English language programs, each of which needs program administrators. As national education policies around the world progressively emphasize English language learning, and the increasingly mobile and connected workforce relies on English as the primary language of communication, this is a growing sector of the global economy (British Council 2013; Brecht 2015).

Language Program Contexts

Contexts in which language program administrators work include intensive English programs (IEPs), language immersion programs, public and private schools, adult schools, and community programs. Language program administrators may engage in many modalities of instruction, such as traditional classroom-based programs, experiential programs, dual-language immersion programs, online education, part-time programs, summer programs, language camps, and language immersion study abroad (Brecht 2015). Exact numbers of programs and learners are unavailable, but there are some indicators of the scope of the field. EnglishUSA's website lists more than 400 IEPs among its U.S. member list (EnglishUSA n.d.). And Go Overseas's website profiles more than 1,400 listings for language schools around the world (Go Overseas n.d.). Programs may target many types of learners including youths, international students, immigrants, and community members who do not speak the local language (Long and Doughty 2011).

Historically, language program administrators were language teachers who were appointed or coaxed into taking over administrative responsibility for a program. They often had to learn the skills for this new role through trial and error or by talking to colleagues in similar situations (Panferov 2012). Today, however, as the number of language programs expands, demand for skilled language program administrators continues to grow and the field is becoming more professionalized (Panferov 2012).

A survey of language program administrators found that 60 percent have degrees in teaching English to speakers of other languages (TESOL) or applied linguistics, while only 9 percent of respondents held the second most common degree, educational administration (Panferov 2012). Yet, both of these skill sets are essential to the field. In recent years, there has been a trend toward individuals intentionally training for careers as language program administrators. Language program administration courses and certifications are being added to TESOL and teaching foreign language (TFL) graduate programs (Bailey and Llamas 2012). This training covers content from the fields of applied linguistics, assessment, business management, curriculum development, educational leadership, entrepreneurial education, human resources, immigration law, intercultural communication, language planning, language education pedagogy, marketing, and organizational management (Panferov 2012).

The Roles of Language Program Administrators

Language program administrators have a broad range of responsibilities, including oversight of the curriculum, student placement and testing, establishment of program goals and work plans, supervision of faculty and staff, budgeting and financial oversight, and program quality assurance. Some language program administrators also oversee student services, immigration issues, facilities, housing, health insurance, marketing, recruitment, and admissions (Panferov 2012; Bailey and Llamas 2012). Additional responsibilities may include developing policies, managing technology, fundraising, building partnerships, and representing the program to outside audiences (Panferov 2012; Bailey and Llamas 2012).

The types of responsibilities a language program administrator has vary by context. Leading a program in a K–12 school, for example, tends to focus on curriculum and teaching;

there is no need for recruitment and the school system handles the human resources, accounting, facilities, and technology responsibilities. In a large IEP, there may be specialized staff to take on marketing, recruitment, admissions, accounting, etc. On the other hand, in a small IEP or community program, the language program administrator may take on many roles at once (Bailey and Llamas 2012). Some of the primary responsibilities of language program administrators are discussed in this section.

Marketing and Recruitment

As with international educators, marketing and recruitment is a primary responsibility of many language program administrators. Recruitment methods may involve direct communication with prospective students, such as through educational fairs or tours, in-person contact with potential participants, brochures, posters, print advertisements, online advertisements, videos, commercials, and email campaigns. Other methods may be indirect, such as word-of-mouth communication, use of agents, or a partnership with a university to serve as a bridge program for international students who need to develop their English language skills prior to university matriculation (Panferov 2008).

Student Services

For language programs that serve international students, the student services needed may be similar to those described in chapter 7, "International Student and Scholar Services." Student services will likely include prearrival information, orientation, intercultural programs, academic advising, career advising, personal advising, events, and field trips. International students enrolled in IEPs and bridge programs may need support in adjusting to U.S. teaching styles and classroom norms. Knowledge of the acculturation process, including the role of language and identity, can be helpful to language program administrators as they seek to support student success both in and out of the classroom (Panferov 2012). For language programs aimed at residents, such as immigrants who are learning the local language, student support may emphasize connections to community services and resources. Programs may provide information on health care, childcare, libraries, employment services, tutoring, counseling, citizenship exams, and other areas (Rodríguez et al. 2009).

Curriculum and Assessment of Learning

The language program administrator is responsible for ensuring the quality of education that students receive. This requires making choices about curriculum design and classroom materials, informed by knowledge of language acquisition processes (Rodríguez et al. 2009). The administrator leads this effort, in collaboration with teachers (Mercado 2012; Soppelsa 2012). While the teachers assess individual student learning through tests, projects, and observations, the administrator is responsible for ensuring that the appropriate tools are being used to measure growth in student language proficiency (Brown 2001; Mercado 2012). Common standards and exams used to evaluate language proficiency include (Mercado 2012):

- American Council on the Teaching of Foreign Languages (ACTFL);
- Common European Framework of Reference for Languages (CEFR);
- Test of English as a Foreign Language (TOEFL);
- TESOL Pre K–12 Standards;
- U.S. Department of Education State Standards for English for Speakers of Other Languages (ESOL);
- University of Cambridge ESOL Examinations;
- University of Michigan Examination for the Certificate of Competency in English (ECCE); and
- University of Michigan Examination for the Certificate of Proficiency in English (ECPE).

The language program administrator is responsible for analyzing the collated data on student language learning in order to determine the effectiveness of the program's teachers, teaching methods, and curriculum.

Teacher and Staff Supervision

Language program administrators are tasked with recruiting, screening, interviewing, and hiring new employees (Geddes and Marks 2012). The administrator must be familiar with the organization's human resources processes as well as relevant labor laws that ensure the ethical treatment of applicants and employees. Once employees are hired, the administrator must supervise the staff, a process that comprises orientation, training, coaching, and evaluation (Geddes and Marks 2012). The administrator must also create professional development plans for the employees, which may involve helping to identify areas for improvement, courses to take, and conferences to attend (Soppelsa 2012).

In order to be able to observe and coach language teachers, administrators need to have extensive knowledge of good practices in language teaching and learning (Rodríguez et al. 2009). For most language program administrators, this comes from their years of experience as language teachers. However, they should also seek out formal training in teacher supervision and stay up to date on the latest research and practices in the field (Mercado 2012; Panferov 2012).

Operations Management

Much of the language program administrator's time is spent on operations management, including managing budgets, record-keeping, facilities, and technology. A survey of language program administrators, most of whom had taken on the role after years of language teaching, revealed that most administrators wished they had learned more about managing budgets, personnel, and university partnerships prior to taking on the position (Panferov 2012). Administering the organization's finances necessitates finding revenue sources such as recruiting sources or garnering government or philanthropic support (Rodríguez et al. 2009). Additionally, administrators need to monitor a system of billing and payments, track expenditures, and maintain financial records, ensuring that spending remains within budget. Budgets must be adjusted when enrollments or other income fluctuates.

Considerations for Practitioners

Like international educators, language program administrators consider issues of social justice and equity in their work. They are concerned about who has access to education and the disparities in opportunities between those who are privileged and those who are not. Believing in the power of foreign language learning to help bridge cultures, some professionals have raised concerns that the study of foreign languages in the United States is declining. Some are concerned about the growing dominance of English as a world language.

Another consideration within the field of language teaching is that some professionals argue that there is hiring discrimination against non-native English speakers and individuals of some ethnic backgrounds (Kamhi-Stein 2016). Others raise concerns that the positioning of many language programs outside of formal educational systems, and the absence of international accreditation bodies, results in limited oversight of the sector, which may mean that program quality is not assured (Baker 2018).

Resources

READINGS:

- Christison, MaryAnn, and Fredricka L. Stollers, eds. 2012. *A Handbook for Language Program Administrators*. Palm Springs, CA: Alta Book Center.

ORGANIZATIONS:

- American Council on the Teaching of Foreign Languages (ACTFL) www.actfl.org/
- EnglishUSA www.englishusa.org/
- IATEFL Leadership and Management Special Interest Group lamsig.iatefl.org/

- NAFSA International Enrollment Management Knowledge Community www.nafsa.org/IEM
- TESOL Program Administration Interest Section www.tesol.org/connect/communities-of-practice

Peacebuilding

Peacebuilding and the related field of conflict resolution focus on repairing and strengthening relationships between individuals, groups, communities, and countries. Where there is conflict, the field aims to foster understanding. Where resolutions are desired, the goal is to find agreement between all sides whereby the stakeholders get most of their needs met, without the use of force or pressure to reach an accord. Inclusivity in peacebuilding requires global and intercultural competence, so that opportunities for stakeholders to hold and share diverse perspectives are not blocked (Donais and McCandless 2017). Scholarship on peacebuilding examines the contexts, approaches, methods, and outcomes of peacebuilding and conflict resolution efforts, both in the short term and over time.

The peacebuilding field is interconnected with international education in many ways. One connection is that both strive to facilitate peace and understanding. In fact, the work of international education organizations in helping students develop global competence fosters a necessary prerequisite for peacebuilding. It helps students strengthen their ability to understand how their own identities shape their perspectives, which is a precursor to establishing meaningful relationships across cultures (NAFSA n.d.).

Due to the shared aims of nurturing intercultural communication and understanding, many international education and peacebuilding organizations, especially those in the citizen diplomacy sector, work on both international education exchange and peacebuilding initiatives. Thomas P. O'Neill, chair of the International Conflict Research Institute at Ulster University, identified five ways in which international educators and higher education institutions can promote peacebuilding (West 2018):

1. Bring people together in spaces for dialogue;
2. Conduct evidence-based research to influence policy;
3. Provide a forum for local communities and marginalized populations;
4. Educate students on peacebuilding; and
5. Create more opportunities for access to higher education to change society.

The Context of Peacebuilding

Rothman (2017) describes conflict not as something inherently negative to be avoided, but rather an opportunity for learning for all involved, including the professionals engaged in the work of peacebuilding. He suggests that "conflict resolution" would be better referred to as "conflict engagement," with the goal that all stakeholders learn more about themselves, the other side(s), and the world through the process (Rothman 2017). According to Rothman (2017), success in the process would help them deal with future potential conflicts more constructively; on the other hand, failure is a norm in the work and not inherently negative. Failure is not something to be embarrassed about or to deny; instead, it is an opportunity for deep learning. Learning how to "name, frame, engage and learn" from both success and failure is necessary for the field and the world to flourish, from his perspective (Rothman 2017, 2).

While Rothman's thoughts are inspirational and grounding, the context and subject matter of peacebuilding and conflict resolution can often be grim. The work may sometimes involve facilitating cross-cultural communication or mediation of a minor dispute, but the skill sets of peacebuilders are also put to use in situations of trauma, war, and humanitarian crises. The field depends on collaboration between governments, civil society organizations, individual citizens, and peacebuilding professionals. Organizations that may be involved in peacebuilding include religious organizations, human rights networks, peace groups, development organizations, women's groups, educational institutions, international education organizations, trade unions, professional associations, and the media (van Leeuwen 2009).

Career Specializations

There are a variety of ways for professionals to engage in peacebuilding. The Kroc Institute for International Peace Studies (2010) has identified 11 overlapping career specializations within the peacebuilding field, listed in table 3.

TABLE 3. Peacebuilding Career Specializations

Development	Working toward economic development, gender equality, housing/urban development, small business development, international development, sustainable development, democratic participation
Dialogue/Conflict Resolution	Using mediation or conflict resolution strategies to foster dialogue
Education	Contributing to educational programs for adult education, peace education, service-learning, vocational education, etc., or on educational policy
Governmental and Multilateral Efforts	Working in areas such as civil-military relations, disarmament, diplomacy, policy analysis, postconflict resolution
Humanitarian Action	Providing social services, humanitarian aid, emergency response services, public health, etc.

(continued on next page)

Table 3. Peacebuilding Career Specializations (continued)

Law: Advocacy and Solidarity	Working in an area of law such as human rights law, domestic violence protection, immigration law, labor law, children's rights, etc.
Nonviolent Social Change	Organizing and mobilizing social movements using active nonviolence
Restorative Justice	Addressing harms against groups such as indigenous peoples, prisoners, etc.
Transitional Justice	Seeking justice through the International Criminal Court and national and local legal system.
Transnational and Global Threats	Working on issues such as corruption, genocide, human trafficking, nuclear proliferation, poverty, terrorism, war
Trauma Healing	Supporting efforts such as child soldier reintegration, collective community healing, refugee resettlement, trauma therapy, and victim support

Source: Kroc Institute for International Peace Studies (2010).

The Process of Peacebuilding

Peacebuilding is a process, not a goal. Peacebuilding is more than the cessation of war or conflict, it needs to develop positive and sustained peace characterized by socioeconomic, structural, political, and cultural stability (Ozerdem and Lee 2015). It requires having something positive for people and societies to move toward. For sustainable conflict resolution in war-torn areas, there must be economic and social gains felt by the citizenry (del Castillo 2017).

Reaching an agreement to end hostilities typically goes through a five-step process: pre-talks, peace negotiation, peace agreement, endorsement, and implementation (Ozerdem and Lee 2015). Historically, following this negotiated settlement, several other phases typically occur. First is the deployment of international military forces to maintain security, usually under United Nations auspices. Then comes humanitarian aid, reconstruction of the infrastructure, and social services. Some of the social and psychological aspects of reconstruction are challenging to undertake, such as repatriating refugees and reintegrating former combatants into society. As part of the negotiated agreement, ideological transitions often follow as steps are taken to transition the political system to a democracy and the economy to a market-based capitalist system (Ozerdem and Lee 2015).

While the phases described have been common patterns, there are serious concerns about the effectiveness of these approaches. del Castillo (2017) points out that the majority of countries that followed this pattern, usually under the auspices of United Nations peacekeeping operations, relapsed into violent conflict within the first decade. Even those areas that did not return to armed conflict have not typically prospered economically. Ozerdem and Lee (2015) remark on an additional criticism of the process, pointing out that peacebuilding is highly politicized and deals with complex, sensitive power dynamics. They argue that even if this progression of conflict resolution stages was somewhat effective in the past, it has not been possible to implement the stages in recent conflicts in which nonstate actors with fervent anti-Western views are key players.

Considerations for Practitioners

While engaging in peacebuilding work, practitioners must guard against bias. Unfortunately, it is easy for international observers to uncritically adopt particular understandings of what a conflict is about, especially when those understandings are in line with their experiences and their ideologies (van Leeuwen 2009). Another unproductive outlook that is all too common is that ethnic and religious conflict are inevitable. The advantage of holding this belief is that it removes the burden of responsibility to do much about the conflict. Yet, the belief is plainly untrue. It is a fact that there are many multicultural, multireligious, and diverse societies not divided by war. To counter this false belief, it is essential to look more deeply at the underlying political, economic, and social causes and contexts of conflicts (Nascimento 2017). Practitioners working in peacebuilding need to be willing to examine whether the very work they are doing is in any way contributing to sustaining the inequities that underlie conflicts (Nascimento 2017). Civil society organizations often consider themselves to be nonpartisan and, thus, apolitical, ignoring their own biases and the historical links between civil society and formal political structures (van Leeuwen 2009).

Critics argue that the United Nations, World Bank, and International Monetary Fund are ill-equipped to support the sustained development initiatives needed to grow a prosperous peacetime economy (Nascimento 2017; del Castillo 2017). Beyond ending the armed conflict and delivering humanitarian aid, in order to create a context for peace to flourish, they would also have to be able to tackle corruption, organized crime, drug trafficking, and terrorism; accommodate and support refugees; and strengthen health care (del Castillo 2017). International development needs to be economically and environmentally sustainable so that there is not a dependency on international aid (del Castillo 2017). For peacebuilding in postconflict areas to be successful in the long run, aid funding should be used in ways that offer job training, engage the private sector to create employment opportunities, bring improved services to all parts of the nation, and protect the natural environment.

Resources

READINGS:

- del Castillo, Graciana. 2017. *Obstacles to Peacebuilding*. London, United Kingdom: Routledge.

- Nascimento, Daniela. 2017. *International Conflict Resolution and Peacebuilding Strategies: The Complexities of War and Peace in the Sudans*. London, United Kingdom: Routledge.

- Ozerdem, Alpaslan, and SungYong Lee. 2015. *International Peacebuilding: An Introduction*. London, United Kingdom: Routledge.

- Rothman, Jay. 2017. *Re-Envisioning Conflict Resolution: Vision, Action, and Evaluation in Creative Conflict Engagement*. London, United Kingdom: Routledge.

Student Services

Student services, also referred to as "student affairs," is a broad, interdisciplinary field focused on supporting students in their academic, personal, and professional lives. It integrates perspectives from counseling, psychology, sociology, history, law, and organizational development, among others (Magolda and Magolda 2011). In a college or university setting, student services departments comprise one of the major divisions of the university. The offices might include academic advising, career advising, civic engagement, counseling services, financial aid, Greek life, multicultural center, orientation programs, religious services, residential life, student activities, student conduct, tutoring center, veterans' center, women's center, writing center, and many others.

Student services departments focus on developing programming and offering individual advising to support student development and promote academic success (Schuh, Jones, and Torres 2017). Student services and international education are closely aligned for several reasons: (a) many international educators have earned degrees in student services and approach their work informed by these perspectives; (b) international educators frequently collaborate with colleagues in student services offices; and (c) the nature of the work they do is similar. This work might include the marketing of programs and services, program design, program coordination, facilitation of reflection, individual advising, program assessment, etc.

Student Development Theory

Student development theories (see chapter 4, table 3) steer the work of student services professionals. They use these theories to structure programs for students (Jones and Stewart 2016). Student development theories can be grouped into categories including psychosocial (focused on personal traits, emotions, and interpersonal interactions), cognitive-structural (focused on patterns of thinking), and typological (focused on categorizing students into types). Each theory brings its own assumptions about learning and student development, so the theories that a professional chooses to use as a lens to analyze situations will affect the outcomes of the professional's work (King and Howard–Hamilton 2000).

Many recent student development theories focus on identity development and, particularly, the intersectionality of identity development (Jones, Abes, and Baxter Magolda 2013). In other words, there is an explicit recognition that student development theories can oversimplify understanding of individual students' identities. To counter this risk, there is conscious effort being made to recognize the complexity of the many overlapping elements of students' identities.

Key Topics

Student services professionals focus on a wide range of issues. NASPA: Student Affairs Administrators in Higher Education is a professional organization in this sector. In addition to offering resources by specialty (e.g., veterans' services, wellness, etc.), the association also identifies broad topics of current interest and provides resources for practitioners. Topics that NASPA (2019) has identified as focus areas include:

- Alcohol and drug abuse prevention;
- Assessment and evaluation;
- Civic learning and democratic engagement;
- Equity and diversity;
- Gender issues;
- Globalism;
- Law and policy;
- Mental health;
- Technology; and
- Violence prevention.

A NASPA survey of chief student services officers at U.S. colleges and universities found that the top areas of concern for them are mental health, diminishing resources, the ever-changing student demographics, and the need for improvement in graduation rates (Wesaw and Sponsler 2014). Student services professionals also find that they are regularly dealing with crisis management issues including responding to specific instances of student mental health concerns, alcohol abuse, illicit drug use, suicide prevention, sexual assault, violence, and firearms (Wesaw and Sponsler 2014).

ACPA: College Student Educators International has identified several key policy issues of importance to the student services field. The association crafted position statements on each of the following: access to health services on campus; affirmative action; affordability and accessibility; budgeting allocations and tax regulations in higher education; campus safety; Deferred Action for Childhood Arrivals; development of student leaders and the student development profession; disabilities and higher education; freedom of religion; freedom of speech; funding and finance; guns on campus; Higher Education Act reauthorization; immigrant and international students; mental health; opioid/drug addiction on campus;

physical activity; the proposal to merge the departments of education and labor; sexual and gender identity; social justice; sustainability; Title IX and sexual harassment and assault on campus; the Trump administration's travel ban decision; and the Violence Against Women Act (ACPA n.d.). As this list demonstrates, the work of student services is closely linked with the political and social issues that challenge society, and it overlaps in some areas with the work of international education. Student services professionals and international educators both strive to prioritize student development despite the challenges.

Professionals in student services are typically committed to the idea that the work they do is integral to the institution's mission to support student learning (McClellan and Stringer 2016). They appreciate the real and observable differences they can make in the lives of students, as well as the nature of the work as they engage in advising, programming, event planning, program coordination, management, and more. Typically, student services professionals value and are motivated by a concern for the welfare of others, a commitment to ensuring that all people have the same rights and privileges, a support for individuals' rights to make their own choices, a belief in the inherent worth of every individual, a faith in truth and justice, and a conviction in the power and importance of community (Reason and Broido 2017).

Considerations for Practitioners

Student services professionals typically have graduate degrees in counseling, student services, higher education, or related fields. Graduate students in this field often pursue an internship or professional practicum in order to gain real-world experience to complement their coursework. Senior-level positions may require a doctoral degree, which would typically involve both coursework and a demonstration of the ability to conduct research (Wesaw and Sponsler 2014). Through graduate education, on-the-job-learning, and training from professional associations, student services professionals can develop skills in leadership, staff management, teaching, advising, conflict resolution, team building, community development, partnership building, budgeting, legal issues, program planning and implementation, and technology (Schuh, Jones, and Harper 2011; McClellan and Stringer 2016). With the increase in online education, there is also a need for student services personnel to not only understand technology, but rethink what student services might look like and how they can be delivered remotely (McClellan and Stringer 2016).

One challenge for student services professionals is that there can sometimes be a schism between the student services division and the academic affairs division, which is comprised mostly of faculty. While there are many individuals who seek to collaborate across the divide, others will dispute who has the right and the expertise to make decisions for the institution, particularly as it relates to student learning. Individuals working in student services may encounter a wide range of perceptions from others regarding the levels and areas of expertise that student services professionals possess and how much their contributions to institutional strategy and curriculum are actually valued (Hogan 2016). Building bridges and relationships across the institution, thus, becomes an even more important priority for student services practitioners.

McClellan and Stringer (2016) suggest that student services practitioners need to respond to current trends in education, including pressures for efficiency, continued inequality of access and attainment, and threats to academic freedom and tenure. McClellan and Stringer (2016) also argue that professionals need to be able to respond to allegations that financial challenges affecting the institution are the result of massive growth in the number of campus staff and administrators, including student services personnel. Student services professionals must be able to provide rationales and evidence for the work they do, as well as build collaborative relationships across campus. This work can be guided by standards set by professional associations in the field. ACPA's (2006) *Statement of Ethical Principles and Standards* addresses expectations for professional competence, values and behaviors that support student learning, responsibility of the individual to the institution, and responsibility to society. As a broad field, student services must constantly be responding to contemporary societal issues.

Resources

READINGS:

- ACPA: College Student Educators International. 2006. *Statement of Ethical Principles and Standards.* Washington, DC: ACPA: College Student Educators International. http://www.myacpa.org/ethics.

- Holzweiss, Peggy C., and Kelli Peck Parrott. 2017. *Careers in Student Affairs: A Holistic Guide to Professional Development in Higher Education.* Washington DC: NASPA: Student Affairs Administrators in Higher Education.

- McClellan, George S., and Jeremy Stringer. 2016. *The Handbook of Student Affairs Administration, Fourth Edition.* San Francisco, CA: Jossey-Bass.

- Schuh, John H., Susan R. Jones, and Vasti Torres. 2017. *Student Services: A Handbook for the Profession, Sixth Edition.* San Francisco, CA: Jossey-Bass.

ASSOCIATIONS:

- ACPA: College Student Educators International www.myacpa.org/

- NASPA: Student Affairs Administrators in Higher Education www.naspa.org/

Conclusion

As an interdisciplinary field, international education draws on the scholarship of a broad range of related areas of research to inform practice. International educators may find it advantageous to develop expertise not only in international education but also in some of the related fields presented in this chapter. At the same time, professionals in intersecting fields can also benefit from studying international education. Throughout the course of their careers, professionals may move back and forth between these fields and international education or, more likely, they may integrate their understanding of two or more of these fields into the work they do. Beyond developing individual expertise, it is also advisable for international educators to develop professional relationships across these fields, to be able to call on colleagues for advice and to partner as collaborators. As a group, the eight related fields in this chapter complement and contribute to the goals of international education: supporting student development, fostering intercultural and global competence, effectively managing education organizations, contributing to positive social change, and promoting peace.

References

ACPA: College Student Educators International. n.d. "ACPA Position Statements." Washington, DC: ACPA: College Student Educators International. http://www.myacpa.org/positions.

ACPA: College Student Educators International. 2006. *Statement of Ethical Principles and Standards.* Washington, DC: ACPA: College Student Educators International. http://www.myacpa.org/ethics.

Altbach, Philip G., Patricia J. Gumport, and Robert O. Berdahl. 2011. *American Higher Education in the Twenty-First Century: Social, Political, and Economic Challenges.* Baltimore, MD: Johns Hopkins University Press.

American Academy of Arts and Sciences. 2016. *The State of Languages in the U.S.: A Statistical Report.* Cambridge, MA: American Academy of Arts and Sciences. https://www.amacad.org/multimedia/pdfs/publications/researchpapersmonographs/State-of-Languages-in-US.pdf.

American Council on Education. 2017. *American College President Study.* Washington, DC: American Council on Education. https://www.acenet.edu/news-room/Pages/American-College-President-Study.aspx.

Association for the Study of Higher Education. 2018. "Higher Education Program Directory." Las Vegas, NV: Association for the Study of Higher Education. https://www.ashe.ws/ashe_heprogram.

Bailey, Kathleen M., and Cara N. Llamas. 2012. "Language Program Administrators' Knowledge and Skills." In *A Handbook for Language Program Administrators, Second Edition*, eds. MaryAnn Christison and Fredricka L. Stoller. Palm Springs, CA: Alta Book Center.

Baker, Clare. 2018. "EFL and Quality Assurance. Does It Matter?" *British Accreditation Council* (blog). March 28, 2018. http://www.the-bac.org/2018/03/28/efl-quality-assurance-matter/.

Bartram, Brendan, ed. 2017. *International and Comparative Education: Contemporary Issues and Debates*. London, United Kingdom: Routledge. Cambridge University Press.

Bergquist, William H., and Kenneth Pawlak. 2008. *Engaging the Six Cultures of the Academy: Revised and Expanded Edition of The Four Cultures of the Academy*. San Francisco, CA: John Wiley & Sons.

Blum, Nicole. 2009. "Small NGO Schools in India: Implications for Access and Innovation." *Compare: A Journal of Comparative and International Education* 39, 2:235–248. https://doi.org/10.1080/03057920902750491.

Bray, Mark, Bob Adamson, and Mark Mason. 2014. *Comparative Education Research: Approaches and Methods, Second Edition*. Hong Kong, China: Comparative Education Research Centre.

Brecht, Richard D. 2015. "America's Languages: Challenges and Promise." Cambridge, MA: American Councils for International Education. https://www.amacad.org/multimedia/pdfs/AmericasLanguagesChallengesandPromise.pdf.

British Council. 2013. *The English Effect*. London, United Kingdom: British Council. https://www.britishcouncil.org/sites/default/files/english-effect-report-v2.pdf.

Brown, James Dean. 2001. *Using Surveys in Language Programs*. Cambridge, United Kingdom: Cambridge University Press.

Byram, Michael, Adam Nichols, and David Stevens. 2001. *Developing Intercultural Competence in Practice: Developing Intercultural Competence in Practice*. Bristol, United Kingdom: Channel View Publications.

Caligiuri, Paula, and Jaime Bonache. 2016. "Evolving and Enduring Challenges in Global Mobility." *Journal of World Business* 51, 1:127–141. https://doi.org/10.1016/j.jwb.2015.10.001.

Collins, Patricia Hill. 2015. "Intersectionality's Definitional Dilemmas." *Annual Review of Sociology* 41, 1:1–20. https://doi.org/10.1146/annurev-soc-073014-112142.

Crossley, Michael. 2012. "Comparative Education and Research Capacity Building: Reflections on International Transfer and the Significance of Context." *Journal of International and Comparative Education* 1, 1:4–12.

Crossley, Michael, and Keith Watson. 2010. "Comparative and International Education Policy Transfer, Context Sensitivity and Professional Development." In *Disciplines of Education Their Role in the Future of Education Research* eds. John Furlong and Martin Lawn. London, United Kingdom: Routledge.

Deardorff, Darla K., and Lily A. Arasaratnam-Smith, eds. 2017. *Intercultural Competence in Higher Education: International Approaches, Assessment and Application*. London, United Kingdom: Routledge.

del Castillo, Graciana. 2017. *Obstacles to Peacebuilding*. London, United Kingdom: Routledge.

Dervin, Fred, and Céline Tournebise. 2013. "Turbulence in Intercultural Communication Education (ICE): Does It Affect Higher Education?" *Intercultural Education* 24, 6:532–543. https://doi.org/10.1080/14675986.2013.866935.

Donais, Timothy, and Erin McCandless. 2017. "International Peace Building and the Emerging Inclusivity Norm." *Third World Quarterly* 38, 2:291–310. https://doi.org/10.1080/01436597.2016.1191344.

EnglishUSA. n.d. "Program Directory." Atlanta, GA: EnglishUSA. Accessed December 13, 2018. https://www.englishusa.org/search/.

Engsig, Thomas T., and Christopher J. Johnstone. 2015. "Is There Something Rotten in the State of Denmark? The Paradoxical Policies of Inclusive Education – Lessons from Denmark." *International Journal of Inclusive Education* 19, 5:469–486. https://doi.org/10.1080/13603116.2014.940068.

Epstein, Erwin H. 2016. "Why Comparative and International Education? Reflections on the Conflation of Names." In *Teaching Comparative Education: Trends and Issues Informing Practice*, eds. Patricia K. Kubow and Allison H. Blosser. Oxford, United Kingdom: Symposium Books.

Farrell, Joseph P. 2008. "Teaching and Learning to Teach; Successful Radical Alternatives from the Developing World." In *Comparative and International Education: Issues for Teachers*, eds. Karen Mundy, Kathy Bickmore, Ruth Hayhoe, Meggan Madden, and Katherine Madjidi. New York, NY: Teachers College Press.

Foote, Ken. 2013. "Supporting and Mentoring International Faculty: Issues and Strategies." In *International Students and Scholars in the United States: Coming from Abroad*, eds. Heike C. Alberts and Helen D. Hazen. New York, NY: Palgrave Macmillan.

Freeman, Sydney, Jr., and Frances K. Kochan. 2012. "Academic Pathways to University Leadership: Presidents' Descriptions of Their Doctoral Education." *International Journal of Doctoral Studies* 7:93–124.

Geddes, Joann M., and Doris R. Marks. 2012. "Personnel Matters." In *A Handbook for Language Program Administrators, Second Edition*, eds. MaryAnn Christison and Fredricka L. Stoller. Palm Springs, CA: Alta Book Center.

Go Overseas. n.d. "Language Schools." Go Overseas. Accessed December 13, 2018. https://www.gooverseas.com/language-schools.

Heathershaw, John. 2016. "Who Are the 'International Community'? Development Professionals and Liminal Subjectivity." *Journal of Intervention and Statebuilding* 10, 1:77–96. https://doi.org/10.1080/17502977.2015.1137395.

Henderson, Angela E., and Kristina Powers. 2017. "Understanding the Range of Postsecondary Institutions and Programs." In *Organization and Administration in Higher Education, Second Edition*, eds. Kristina Powers and Patrick J. Schloss. New York, NY: Routledge.

Hendrickson, Robert M., Jason E. Lane, James T. Harris, and Richard H. Dorman. 2013. *Academic Leadership and Governance of Higher Education: A Guide for Trustees, Leaders, and Aspiring Leaders of Two- and Four-Year Institutions*. Sterling, VA: Stylus Publishing.

Hogan, T. Lynn. 2016. *Student Affairs for Academic Administrators*. Sterling, VA: Stylus Publishing.

Indiana University Center for Postsecondary Research. 2018. "The Carnegie Classification of Institutions of Higher Education, 2018 Edition." Bloomington, IN: Indiana University Center for Postsecondary Research. http://carnegieclassifications.iu.edu/.

Institute of International Education. 2018. *Open Door Report on International Education Exchange*. Institute of International Education. http://www.iie.org/opendoors.

The Intercultural Communication Institute. 2018. *Directory of Selected Resources*. Portland, OR: The Intercultural Communication Institute.

Jackson, Liz. 2014. "Comparing Race, Class and Gender." In *Comparative Education Research: Approaches and Methods, Second Edition*, eds. Mark Bray, Bob Adamson, and Mark Mason. Hong Kong, China: Comparative Education Research Centre.

Jones, Susan R., Elisa S. Abes, and Marcia B. Baxter Magolda. 2013. *Identity Development of College Students: Advancing Frameworks for Multiple Dimensions of Identity*. San Francisco, CA: John Wiley & Sons.

Jones, Susan R., and Dafina-Lazarus Stewart. 2016. "Evolution of Student Development Theory." *New Directions for Student Services* 2016, 154:17–28. https://doi.org/10.1002/ss.20172.

Kadatska, Polina. 2016. "'Mind the Gap': The Standardization of Master-Level Education Competencies among Humanitarian and International Development Professionals." Doctoral dissertation, University of Missouri-Saint Louis.

Kamhi-Stein, Lía D. 2016. "The Non-Native English Speaker Teachers in TESOL Movement." *ELT Journal* 70, 2:180–189. https://doi.org/10.1093/elt/ccv076.

Kappler Mikk, Barbara, and Inge Ellen Steglitz, eds. 2017. *Learning Across Cultures: Locally and Globally, Third Edition*. Washington, DC: NAFSA: Association of International Educators and Stylus Publishing.

Kates, Robert W., Thomas M. Parris, and Anthony A. Leiserowitz. 2005. "What Is Sustainable Development? Goals, Indicators, Values, and Practice." *Environment: Science and Policy for Sustainable Development* 47, 3:8–21.

Kienle, Alyson W., and Nicole L. Loyd. 2005. "Globalization and the Emergence of Supranational Organizations: Implications for Graduate Programs in Higher Education Administration." *College Student Journal* 39, 3:580–587.

Kim, Young Yun. 2001. *Becoming Intercultural*. Thousand Oaks, CA: Sage Publications.

King, Patricia M., and Mary F. Howard–Hamilton. 2000. "Using Student Development Theory to Inform Institutional Research." *New Directions for Institutional Research* 2000, 108:19–36. https://doi.org/10.1002/ir.10802.

Kroc Institute for International Peace Studies. 2010. "Strategic Peacebuilding Pathways (Wheel)." Notre Dame, IN: Kroc Institute for International Peace Studies. https://kroc.nd.edu/alumni/strategic-peacebuilding-pathways/.

Kubow, Patricia K., and Paul R. Fossum. 2003. *Comparative Education: Exploring Issues in International Context*. Upper Saddle River, NJ: Pearson Education.

Leicht, Alexander, Julia Heiss, and Won Jung Byun. 2018. *Issues and Trends in Education for Sustainable Development*. Paris, France: United Nations Educational, Scientific and Cultural Organization. https://unesdoc.unesco.org/ark:/48223/pf0000261445.

Long, Michael H., and Catherine J. Doughty, eds. 2011. *The Handbook of Language Teaching*. United Kingdom: Blackwell Publishing Ltd.

Magolda, Peter M., and Marcia B. Baxter Magolda. 2011. *Contested Issues in Student Affairs: Diverse Perspectives and Respectful Dialogue*. Sterling, VA: Stylus Publishing.

Majidi, Katherine, and Jean-Paul Restoule. 2008. "Comparative Indigenous Ways of Knowing." In *Comparative and International Education: Issues for Teachers*, eds. Karen Mundy, Kathy Bickmore, Ruth Hayhoe, Meggan Madden, and Katherine Majidi. New York, NY: Teachers College Press.

Manzon, Maria. 2011. "Mapping the Intellectual Discourse on 'Comparative Education.'" In *Comparative Education*, by Maria Manzon. Dordrecht, The Netherlands: Springer Netherlands.

McClellan, George S., and Jeremy Stringer. 2016. *The Handbook of Student Affairs Administration, Fourth Edition*. San Francisco, CA: Jossey-Bass.

McCowan, Tristan, and Elaine Unterhalter, eds. 2015. *Education and International Development: An Introduction*. London, United Kingdom: Bloomsbury Academic.

McGrath, Simon. 2018. *Education and Development*. London, United Kingdom: Routledge.

McMichael, Philip. 2017. *Development and Social Change: A Global Perspective, Fifth Edition*. Thousand Oaks, CA: Sage Publications.

Meares, Mary. 2015. *Intercultural Career Planning*. Portland, OR: The Intercultural Communication Institute.

Mercado, Leonardo A. 2012. "Guarantor of Quality Assurance." In *A Handbook for Language Program Administrators, Second Edition*, eds. MaryAnn Christison and Fredricka L. Stoller. Palm Springs, CA: Alta Book Center.

Miike, Yoshitaka. 2007. "An Asiacentric Reflection on Eurocentric Bias in Communication Theory." *Communication Monographs* 74, 2:272–278. https://doi.org/10.1080/03637750701390093.

Mueller, Sherry Lee, and Mark Overmann. 2014. *Working World: Careers in International Education, Exchange, and Development, Second Edition*. Washington, DC: Georgetown University Press.

NAFSA: Association of International Educators. n.d. "International Education for Peacebuilding: Youth Diplomats for Peace." Washington, DC: NAFSA: Association of

International Educators. Accessed January 3, 2019. https://www.nafsa.org/About_Us/About_International_Education/International_Education_for_Peacebuilding__Youth_Diplomats_for_Peace/.

NAFSA: Association of International Educators. 2015. *NAFSA International Education Professional Competencies*. Washington, DC: NAFSA: Association of International Educators.

Nascimento, Daniela. 2017. *International Conflict Resolution and Peacebuilding Strategies: The Complexities of War and Peace in the Sudans*. London, United Kingdom: Routledge.

NASPA: Student Affairs Administrators in Higher Education. 2019. "NASPA Focus Areas." Washington, DC: NASPA: Student Affairs Administrators in Higher Education. https://www.naspa.org/focus-areas.

National Center for Education Statistics (NCES). 2018. "Undergraduate Retention and Graduation Rates." Washington, DC: National Center for Education Statistics. https://nces.ed.gov/programs/coe/indicator_ctr.asp.

Neuliep, James W. 2017. *Intercultural Communication: A Contextual Approach*. Thousand Oaks, CA: Sage Publications.

Okahana, Hironao, and Enyu Zhou. 2018. *Graduate Enrollment and Degrees: 2007 to 2017*. Washington, DC: Council of Graduate Schools. https://cgsnet.org/first-time-enrollment-holds-steady-application-counts-slightly-decline-us-graduate-schools.

Ozerdem, Alpaslan, and SungYong Lee. 2015. *International Peacebuilding: An Introduction*. London, United Kingdom: Routledge.

Panferov, Suzanne K. 2008. "Promoting Intensive ESL Programs: Taking Charge of a Market." In *Leadership in English Language Teaching and Learning*, eds. Christine Coombe, Mary Lou McCloskey, Lauren Stephenson, and Neil J. Anderson. Ann Arbor, MI: University of Michigan Press.

Panferov, Suzanne K. 2012. "Transitioning from Teacher to Language Program Administrator." In *A Handbook for Language Program Administrators, Second Edition*, eds. MaryAnn Christison and Fredricka L. Stoller. Palm Springs, CA: Alta Book Center.

Powers, Kristina, and Patrick J. Schloss, eds. 2017. *Organization and Administration in Higher Education, Second Edition*. New York, NY: Routledge.

PricewaterhouseCoopers. 2010. *Talent Mobility 2020: The Next Generation of International Assignments*. PricewaterhouseCoopers. https://www.pwc.com/gx/en/managing-tomorrows-people/future-of-work/pdf/talent-mobility-2020.pdf.

Reason, Robert D., and Ellen M. Broido. 2017. "Philosophies and Values." In *Student Services: A Handbook for the Profession, Sixth Edition*, eds. John H. Schuh, Susan R. Jones, and Vasti Torres. San Francisco, CA: Jossey-Bass.

Rieckmann, Marco. 2018. "Key Themes in Education for Sustainable Development." In *Issues and Trends in Education for Sustainable Development*, eds. Alexander Leicht, Julia Heiss, and Won Jung Byun. Paris, France: United Nations Educational, Scientific and Cultural Organization. https://unesdoc.unesco.org/ark:/48223/pf0000261445.

Roberts, Jay W. 2015. *Experiential Education in the College Context: What It Is, How It Works, and Why It Matters*. New York, NY: Routledge.

Rodríguez, Amber Gallup, Miriam Burt, Joy Kreeft Peyton, and Michelle Ueland. 2009. "Managing Programs for Adults Learning English." *CAELA Network Brief* September:1–11.

Rothman, Jay. 2017. *Re-Envisioning Conflict Resolution: Vision, Action, and Evaluation in Creative Conflict Engagement*. London, United Kingdom: Routledge.

Safdar, Saba, and Tracy Berno. 2016. "Sojourners." In *Acculturation Psychology, Second Edition*, eds. David L. Sam and John W. Berry. New York, NY: Cambridge University Press.

Sam, David L., and John W. Berry. 2016. *Acculturation Psychology, Second Edition*. New York, NY: Cambridge University Press.

Schuh, John H., Susan R. Jones, and Shaun R. Harper. 2011. *Student Services: A Handbook for the Profession, Fifth Edition*. San Francisco, CA: Jossey-Bass.

Schuh, John H., Susan R. Jones, and Vasti Torres. 2017. *Student Services: A Handbook for the Profession, Sixth Edition*. San Francisco, CA: Jossey-Bass.

Soppelsa, Elizabeth F. 2012. "Empowerment of Faculty." In *A Handbook for Language Program Administrators, Second Edition*, eds. MaryAnn Christison and Fredricka L. Stoller. Palm Springs, CA: Alta Book Center.

Stanford University. 2016. "Careers in ICE." Stanford, CA: Stanford Graduate School of Education. January 22, 2016. https://ed.stanford.edu/ice/students/careers.

Tayeb, Monir. 2004. *International Human Resource Management: A Multinational Company Perspective*. Oxford, United Kingdom: Oxford University Press.

Teichler, Ulrich. 2014. "Opportunities and Problems of Comparative Higher Education Research: The Daily Life of Research." *Higher Education* 67, 4:393–408. https://doi.org/10.1007/s10734-013-9682-0.

Thouez, Colleen. 2015. "Education in the New Development Agenda." *IIE Networker* Fall 2015:29–31.

Tierney, William G. 2011. *The Impact of Culture on Organizational Decision-Making: Theory and Practice in Higher Education*. Sterling, VA: Stylus Publishing.

United Nations. 2018. *The Sustainable Development Goals Report*. New York, NY: United Nations. https://unstats.un.org/sdgs/files/report/2018/TheSustainableDevelopmentGoalsReport2018-EN.pdf.

University of Oxford The Careers Service. 2018. "International Development." Oxford, United Kingdom: University of Oxford The Careers Service. https://www.careers.ox.ac.uk/international-development/.

Vance, Charles M., and Yongsun Paik. 2006. *Managing a Global Workforce: Challenges and Opportunities in International Human Resource Management*. Armonk, NY: M.E. Sharpe, Inc.

van Leeuwen, Mathijs. 2009. *Partners in Peace: Discourses and Practices of Civil-Society Peacebuilding*. Farnham, United Kingdom: Taylor & Francis Group.

Vedder, Paul, and Frosso Motto-Stefanidi. 2016. "Children, Families, and Schools." In *Acculturation Psychology, Second Edition*, eds. David L. Sam and John W. Berry. New York, NY: Cambridge University Press.

Verger, Antoni, Hulya K. Altinyelken, and Mario Novelli. 2018. *Global Education Policy and International Development: New Agendas, Issues and Policies*. London, United Kingdom: Bloomsbury Publishing.

Wesaw, Alexis J., and Brian A. Sponsler. 2014. *Chief Student Affairs Officer: Responsibilities, Opinions and Professional Pathways of Leaders in Student Affairs*. Washington, DC: NASPA Research and Policy Institute.

West, Charlotte. 2018. *Evolving Roles and Responsibilities of International Education in Peacebuilding*. Washington, DC: NAFSA: Association of International Educators. https://www.nafsa.org/_/File/_/evolving_roles_peacebuilding.pdf.

Wijeyesinghe, Charmaine L. 2012. "The Intersectional Model of Multiracial Identity." In *New Perspectives on Racial Identity Development, Second Edition*, eds. Charmaine L. Wijeyesinghe and Bailey W. Jackson. New York, NY: New York University Press.

Wiseman, Paul. 2017. "Alternative Education." In *International and Comparative Education: Contemporary Issues and Debates*, ed. Brendan Bartram. London, United Kingdom: Routledge.

Wolhuter, Charl C. 2015. "The Case for Including Comparative and International Educations in Teacher Education Programmes." *Science and Technology* 2, 2:20–40.

Yang, Rui. 2014. "Comparing Policies." In *Comparative Education Research: Approaches and Methods, Second Edition*, eds. Mark Bray, Bob Adamson, and Mark Mason. Hong Kong, China: Comparative Education Research Centre.

Glossary

Abstract conceptualization	The stage in Kolb's (1984) Experiential Learning Cycle in which students theorize on possible meanings and explanations for the patterns they observed during the concrete experience.
Academic advising	A type of advising that focuses on course selection and ensuring that the student is on track to meet graduation requirements, as well as conversations related to the skills and habits needed for academic success.
Academic capitalism	Academic institutions engaging in practices driven primarily by market forces.
Academic mobility	The movement of students and scholars across national borders for purposes related to academic study, teaching, and research.
Acculturation	The process of questioning and letting go of some aspects of one's own culture and gradually adopting elements of another culture.
Active experimentation	The stage in Kolb's (1984) Experiential Learning Cycle in which students test their new understanding for accuracy.
Adult learning	A theory about the education of adults that emphasizes that adults should know why content is being taught; adults should be involved in directing their learning; learning should connect to the adult's prior experience; and learning should be applicable to the adult's current goals and needs (Merriam and Bierema 2014).
Advising	Support provided to individuals, most often in one-on-one, face-to-face meetings.

Advising as coaching model	An advising model, built on theories of business executive coaching, that offers a six-step ADVISE model for the advising conversation (McClellan and Moser 2011).
Advising as teaching and learning model	An advising model that emphasizes thinking of the adviser as a teacher and the advisee as a learner, whereby advisers work to cultivate specific knowledge, skills, and attitudes in the advisee.
Advocacy culture	A culture in U.S. higher education that focuses on social justice, confrontation, and bargaining, with a goal of establishing equitable policies and procedures (Bergquist and Pawlak 2008).
Alien physician	A category of the U.S. exchange visitor visa (J-1) program by which foreign medical graduates undertake graduate medical education or training at an accredited school of medicine or scientific institution, or pursue professional activities involving observation, consultation, teaching, or research.
Alternate responsible officers (AROs)	Professionals designated by approved U.S. institutions and organizations to access the records in SEVIS of exchange visitors hosted on J visas. There may be one or more AROs per institution or organization, supporting a responsible officer (RO).
Alternative break	"Opportunities for small groups of students to travel to a different city, state, or country to participate in a service-learning project during their academic break" (Niehaus and Kurotsuchi Inkelas 2015, 134).
Alternative education	A collection of perspectives that challenge assumptions about how education and schools should function.
Anti-push factors	Barriers that make it difficult for students to leave their home country for travel, even if that is their goal.
Appreciative advising	A type of advising that intentionally focuses on positive dialogue about the advisee's strengths, dreams, and goals.
Au pair	A category of the U.S. exchange visitor visa (J-1) program by which young adults experience U.S. culture while living with a host family for up to 12 months, providing child care and taking courses at an accredited U.S. postsecondary institution.
Backward design	A program design process that starts with the outcomes assessment and moves toward the design.

Bilateral exchange program	An education abroad program in which students from two universities "trade places" and take courses at the other school.
Borderless education	Initiatives that move people and/or programs across national borders; also known as "cross-border education" and "transnational education."
Brain drain	The movement of students, recent graduates, and academics away from less developed countries to more developed countries.
Branch campus	A campus set up by a university in another location, including in another country, as a site offering full degrees.
Bridge program	A program that provides a "bridge" from intensive language study to full-time academic study before students begin a university degree.
Camp counselor	A category of the U.S. exchange visitor visa (J-1) program by which postsecondary students, youth workers, teachers, and others with specialized skills oversee American youths at U.S. camps.
Career advising	A type of advising that focuses on students' career goals and plans for future degrees. Scholars such as visiting professors and postdoctoral researchers may also seek career advising as they are considering their next career opportunity.
Certificate of eligibility	An immigration document issued to international students listing the start and end dates of their program. For students with F and M visas, the document is called an I-20; for exchange visitors with a J visa, it is called a DS-2019.
Citizen diplomacy	The Center for Citizen Diplomacy (2017) defines citizen diplomacy as "the concept that every global citizen has the right, even the responsibility, to engage across cultural differences and create shared understanding through person-to-person interactions."
Citizen diplomacy exchange program	A program in which students from two countries visit each other's country, typically based on agreements between governments.
Citizen diplomacy program	A program that emphasizes individual engagement with the goal of promoting mutual understanding, awareness of shared values, and the exchange of knowledge.

Citizen diplomats	Individuals who participate in one-on-one interactions to engage across cultural differences and create shared understanding; they may be teachers, students, professionals, retirees, athletes, artists, humanitarians, or others.
Civic engagement	"Acting upon a heightened sense of responsibility to one's communities through both political and non-political means" (Jacoby 2015, 4).
College and university student	A category of the U.S. exchange visitor visa (J-1) program by which students study in a degree or nondegree program at a U.S. college or university.
Collegial culture	A culture in U.S. higher education that focuses on faculty research and autonomy, the dissemination of knowledge, and the role of faculty in guiding the institution's directions (Bergquist and Pawlak 2008).
Commodification of education	The treatment of education as a commodity rather than a public service.
Communicative competence	The ability to communicate effectively and appropriately using linguistic and social/intercultural skills.
Comparative and international education	A social science research field that focuses on examining educational systems around the world.
Concrete experience	The stage in Kolb's (1984) Experiential Learning Cycle in which students actively participate in an activity.
Conditional admission	An agreement between a U.S. institution and an intensive English program (IEP) by which student admission is offered by both partners at the same time; if students complete a specified course level in the IEP program, they will then be able to begin degree studies.
Consortium program	An education abroad program in which multiple institutions collaborate to offer the program.
Content-based instruction (CBI)	A method of foreign language teaching that teaches school subjects using a foreign language as the medium of instruction, rather than having a stand-alone foreign language course.
Credential evaluation	The process of determining equivalency between courses or degrees from two countries.

Glossary

Credit mobility	A type of academic mobility whereby students study abroad for a short period of time and then transfer the academic credit back to their home institution.
Critical inquiry	Within the context of education, the incorporation of intentional reflection on the historical, political, economic, and social structures that create power and inequity and impact one's own assumptions and biases.
Critical race theory	A theory that examines the interactions between race, racism, and power (Delgado and Stefancic 2017).
Cross-border education	Initiatives that move people and/or programs across national borders; also known as "borderless education" and "transnational education."
Cultural diplomacy programs	Citizen diplomacy programs that focus on sharing cultural expressions such as art, music, dance, language, etc.
Curricular Practical Training (CPT)	A form of off-campus work authorization for F-1 students governed by U.S. international student regulations.
Curriculum enrichment	The addition of an international project to enrich a unit of study, performed by individual teachers.
Curriculum integration	The restructuring of department- or school-wide curricula to center around global themes, to involve other colleagues and disciplines, and to foster collaboration with schools in the United States and abroad, performed by teams of teachers and the administration.
Customized program	An education abroad program designed and operated by a provider specifically for one institution or group, enrolling only that group of students in the program.
Deficit thinking	A negative way of thinking about people that assumes that they are lacking in some way and need bolstering. Those with deficit thinking may assume that international students are lacking in terms of language skills or U.S. cultural knowledge.
Degree mobility	A type of academic mobility whereby students study outside their home country for an entire degree program.
Designated school officials (DSOs)	Professionals designated by certified U.S. institutions to access the records in SEVIS of international students hosted on F and M visas. There may be one or more DSOs per institution, supporting a principal designated school official (PDSO).

Developmental advising	A broad category of advising that emphasizes helping the advisee develop knowledge and skills to increase his or her self-sufficiency and academic and professional success.
Developmental culture	A culture in U.S. higher education that focuses on the learner and learner-centered education, alongside the professional development of faculty and staff (Bergquist and Pawlak 2008).
DIY program	Borrowed from the home improvement term that means "do it yourself," an education abroad program for which university faculty and staff arrange the logistics rather than contracting with a provider.
Double degree	Degrees awarded to a student from each of two partner institutions.
Duration of status	A concept in U.S. immigration regulations that means that an international student can legally remain in the United States as long as the student is abiding by the regulations governing his or her status.
Education abroad	Educational programs that move people across national borders, including study abroad, work abroad, intern abroad, volunteer abroad, research abroad, and international service-learning.
Educational agents	Representatives of educational agencies, "defined as an organization, company, or association that recruits and places non-resident U.S. students into accredited colleges, universities, and other educational institutions on a commercial 'fee for service' basis" (Bridge Education Group 2016, 10).
Educational travel	Travel for primarily recreational purposes, with an educational component, such as a lecture series, often organized around a theme.
Embedded program	An education abroad program that is part of a regular on-campus course.
Emerging adulthood	A developmental period that focuses on young adults aged 18 to 25 that is characterized by frequent change and exploration in the areas of housing, love, education, work, and worldview (Arnett 2000).
Ethnocentrism	A view of the world through one's own cultural lens.
Ethnorelativism	The ability to interpret the world through multiple cultural lenses and largely free of judgment.

Exchange program	An education abroad program in which students from two or more universities "trade places" and take courses at other institutions.
Experiential education	Both an educational philosophy and an educational method in which a real-life experience serves as the foundation for structured reflection, resulting in student learning.
Experiential learning	A learning model, based on Kolb's (1984) Experiential Learning Cycle, that involves four stages: concrete experience, reflective observation, abstract conceptualization, and active experimentation.
Faculty-led program	An education abroad program in which a faculty member from the home institution travels abroad with a group of students and teaches one or more courses in her or his area of expertise.
Faith-based program	An education abroad program rooted in the values of a religious faith; may be organized by religious colleges/universities, religious institutions, or nonprofit organizations.
Feminist theory	Feminist theories look at the intersections between gender, race, socioeconomic class, and other identities, and how these intersectional identities are reflected in power and control in interpersonal interactions and in society.
Field study program	An education abroad program offering hands-on experience to students in a particular discipline.
Formal education	Education through the national systems of schooling, including higher education.
Formative assessment	An evaluation conducted partway through the learning process to see what progress the student has made and to allow time for modification of the learning process.
Freshman/First-Year program	An education abroad program offered to first-year university students.
Full-time enrollment	International students are required by U.S. regulations to be primarily engaged in their studies, with specific minimum courseloads based on visa category and immigration status.
Gap year	A year between high school and university or between higher education and professional life sometimes used to pursue an education abroad opportunity.

Gender identity development	Theories that historically explored the development of women's sense of identity; more recent theories of gender identity development also examine male and nonbinary gender identities.
Global competence	"The capacity to examine local, global and intercultural issues; to understand and appreciate the perspectives and world views of others; to engage in open, appropriate, and effective interactions with people from different cultures; and to act for collective well-being and sustainable development" (Asia Society and OECD 2018, 5).
Global health programs	A subset of international service-learning and/or intern abroad programs that enable students to gain hands-on experience related to health fields.
Global mobility	A field in which professionals support individuals and companies in the inevitable logistical and cross-cultural challenges that arise before and after individuals move abroad for work; also referred to as "expatriate management" and "international relocation services."
Global nomads	Children who grow up in one or more countries abroad due to their parents' work and often do not feel truly at home in either their passport country or the country in which they are living; also known as "third culture kids."
Government visitor	A category of the U.S. exchange visitor visa (J-1) program by which international visitors develop and strengthen professional and personal relationships with their counterparts in U.S. federal, state, and local government agencies.
Hard power	The use of military or economic power to pressure foreign governments to act in ways desired by the nation wielding the power.
Higher education administration	A scholarly field of study and a profession that focuses on leading and managing colleges and universities; also referred to as "higher education leadership."
Immersion	A term used to describe an education abroad program that requires extensive student engagement with the host culture and people.
Immigration advising	A type of advising that focuses on immigration regulations and compliance; one of the primary responsibilities of international student and scholar advisers.
Independent study	A component of an education abroad program in which students work on an individual research project to complement their other studies.

Informal learning	Learning that is unplanned.
Intensive English program (IEP)	A program that helps students to develop English language skills; this may include academic English skills needed to enroll in U.S. higher education institutions.
Intercultural training	An interdisciplinary field that synthesizes ideas from education, communication, psychology, sociology, and many other arenas to provide intercultural training to a wide range of populations.
Intern	A category of the U.S. exchange visitor visa (J-1) program by which college and university students and recent graduates gain exposure to U.S. culture and business practices in their chosen professional field.
Intern abroad	A program in which participants engage in an internship abroad; individual programs may or may not qualify as experiential education.
International cooperative education	"Paid work programs that are usually integrated into a university-level degree, in which terms of study and degree major-related work are alternated. They tend to be in the technical, business, and healthcare fields" (Nolting et al. 2013, pp. 1–2).
International development	A field that aims to help less wealthy countries and communities to develop economically, with a focus on social welfare.
International education	The profession of designing, managing, and facilitating programs that help people learn to appropriately, effectively, and ethically engage in interactions with culturally diverse people.
International enrollment management	A subset of enrollment management initiatives aligning institutional marketing, recruitment, admissions, enrollment, and student support services that focus on the recruitment and enrollment of international students.
Internationalization	While many definitions exist, the most commonly cited is: "The process of integrating an international, intercultural, or global dimension into the purpose, functions or delivery of post-secondary education" (Knight 2004, 11).
International schools	Historically, these schools have had three main characteristics: (a) they offer a curriculum other than the one of the host country; (b) they enroll a large percentage of students who are not host country nationals; and (c) teachers and administrators are mostly expatriates. However, more and more public schools, under the auspices of the national or local governments, are becoming international schools that serve local populations.

International service-learning	A program in which participants engage in service-learning while abroad.
International student and scholar services (ISSS)	The services and resources that higher education institutions provide to international students and scholars to support them in achieving academic and professional success.
International visitor	A category of the U.S. exchange visitor visa (J-1) program by which participants are in exchange programs sponsored and funded by the U.S. Department of State.
Internship abroad program	An education abroad program that includes an internship component.
Intersectionality of identity	The recognition that each individual belongs to multiple cultures and groups concurrently and, thus, identifies with not just one identity but with multiple identities simultaneously. Individuals' various identities and group memberships hold more or less salience in their sense of self at a particular point in time, depending on the context.
Intrusive advising	An advising model that emphasizes the role of the adviser in initiating advising sessions; also known as "proactive advising."
Island program	An education abroad program in which students from the home country are together for coursework and/or housing abroad; often used with a derogatory meaning in the field because this type of program, by its design, limits interactions with local people.
Joint degree	A degree awarded to a student jointly by two or more partner institutions.
Language immersion program	An education abroad program that aims to immerse students not only in the culture, but also in the local language.
Language program administration	A field that brings together the administrative skills of the international educator with the teaching knowledge of language educators to develop and run language learning programs.
Managerial culture	A culture in U.S. higher education that focuses on efficiency and measurable outcomes, with oversight through a top-down, hierarchical leadership structure (Bergquist and Pawlak 2008).

Massification of education	The shift toward education serving the masses, with an emphasis on creating educational opportunities for people of all socioeconomic, ethnic, and religious backgrounds, as well as ensuring gender equality.
Multilateral exchange program	An education abroad program in which students from more than two universities "trade places" and take courses at other institutions.
Multistop program	An education abroad program in which students spend significant time in two or more locations.
Neoliberalism	Political philosophy that values the idea of free market capitalism; purports that free, unfettered competition—without government subsidy or policy interference—results in the best outcomes for consumers and for the economy.
Nonformal education	Educational programs with structured curricula that happen outside of the formal school system, such as extracurricular programs.
Nongovernmental organizations (NGOs)	Organizations whose employees do not work for a government, though the organization may be partially or fully funded by governments through competitive grants.
Ongoing orientation	Orientation programming throughout the first weeks or months of education abroad programs.
On-site orientation	Orientation programming given to students in-country at the beginning of education abroad programs.
Optional Practical Training (OPT)	A form of off-campus work authorization for F-1 students governed by U.S. international student regulations.
Outcomes	"Changes that occur in learners and in programs (could be short-, medium-, and long-term outcomes), usually focused on changes in skills, knowledge, attitudes, and behavior" (Deardorff 2015, 57).
Outputs	"Deliverable targets measured most often through numbers" (Deardorff 2015, 57).
Pathway program	A program that provides a foundation year or a year of concurrent enrollment in which students are enrolled in both language courses and academic courses after matriculation into the university.

Peacebuilding	A field that focuses on repairing and strengthening relationships between individuals, groups, communities, and countries; closely related to the field of conflict resolution.
Peer mentoring	A model by which students or scholars, with training and mentorship from advisers, conduct some advising sessions for their peers.
Personal advising	A type of advising that focuses on personal issues that students and scholars are finding challenging, such as adjustments to the culture, homesickness, roommate problems, difficult relations with an instructor or peers, etc.
Predeparture orientation	Orientation programming given to students prior to education abroad programs.
Prescriptive advising	A broad category of advising in which communication is primarily unidirectional, with the adviser telling the advisee what to do, and the advisee doing what he or she was told to do.
Principal designated school officials (PDSOs)	Professionals designated by certified U.S. institutions to access the records in SEVIS of international students hosted on F and M visas. There may be only one per institution, though the PDSO may be supported by one or more designated school officials (DSOs).
Proactive advising	An advising model that emphasizes the role of the adviser in initiating advising sessions; also known as "intrusive advising."
Professional training	Citizen diplomacy programs designed for professionals; may be structured as exchange programs, or groups of professionals from similar fields may travel together to explore their profession in another cultural context.
Professor/research scholar	A category of the U.S. exchange visitor visa (J-1) program by which individuals engage in work focused on the exchange of ideas and research that strengthens connections between research and academic institutions.
Programming	Initiatives that provide support for groups of students and scholars.
Program provider	A nonprofit or for-profit organization that specializes in running education abroad programs.
Public diplomacy	Most commonly defined as "international political communication aimed at creating mutually beneficial relations with the public abroad in order to support the communicator's objectives" (Ociepka 2018, 290).

Pull factors	The reasons why international students are attracted to studying in host countries.
Push factors	The reasons why international students find their home country's educational opportunities insufficient.
Racial identity development	There are many models of racial identity development, including those for African Americans, Asian Americans, Latinx Americans, Native Americans, and white Americans. Common themes include the findings that there are many possible healthy identities, that identities may shift over time, and that identities may shift based on the specific situation a person is in (Evans et al. 2009). Biracial identity development is also increasingly being explored (Renn 2008).
Reciprocity	A key principle in the success of service-learning programs, meaning that "service-learning educators relate to the community in the spirit of partnership, viewing the institution and the community in terms of both assets and needs" (Jacoby 2018, 71). Both partners give and gain fairly equally.
Recruitment channels	The approaches by which multiple qualified students can be recruited.
Reentry orientation	Orientation programming given to students prior to and/or after their return home from education abroad programs.
Reflection	A term commonly used to describe the process of intentionally guiding students through the three stages of Kolb's (1984) Experiential Learning Cycle following the concrete experience.
Reflective observation	The stage in Kolb's (1984) Experiential Learning Cycle where students take note (in writing, in their minds, or in some other format) of what happened during the concrete experience.
Research abroad	A program in which participants engage in research activities abroad; individual programs may or may not qualify as experiential education.
Responsible officers (ROs)	Professionals designated by approved U.S. institutions and organizations to access the records in SEVIS of exchange visitors hosted on J visas. There may be only one per institution or organization, though the RO may be supported by one or more alternate responsible officers (AROs).
Retention	The goal of ensuring that students remain enrolled in an institution and make progress toward completing their degree.

Scholarship programs	Citizen diplomacy programs that aim to offer international education to students who would otherwise be unable to access the opportunities.
School restructuring	The acts of changing policies and practices of staffing, instruction, and outreach, all of which are performed by principals and administrators, the school board, the entire teaching staff, and the community.
Secondary school student	A category of the U.S. exchange visitor visa (J-1) program by which secondary school students study at an accredited public or private high school and live with an American host family or at a boarding school.
Self-authorship	The ability to define one's own identity, beliefs, and social relations (Magolda 2001).
Service-learning	"A form of experiential education in which students engage in activities that address human and community needs, together with structured opportunities for reflection designed to achieve desired learning outcomes" (Jacoby 2015, pp. 1–2).
Service-learning program	An education abroad program that brings together the act of community service with the learning of an intentionally designed curriculum.
Seven vectors	Chickering's seven vectors describe seven areas of personal development that are common among university-aged students. These include developing competence, managing emotions, moving through autonomy toward interdependence, developing mature interpersonal relationships, establishing identity, developing purpose, and developing integrity (Evans et al. 2009).
Shared governance	A fundamental principle of U.S. higher education by which faculty have the right to oversee the curriculum of the institution while administrators oversee the operations of the organization.
Short-term scholar	A category of the U.S. exchange visitor visa (J-1) program by which professors, scholars, and other accomplished individuals are on a short-term visit (6 months or less) to teach, research, consult, train, or demonstrate special skills at U.S. research and academic institutions, museums, and libraries.
Soft power	Efforts to influence foreign governments through the development of positive relations, cultivated by initiatives that highlight the attractiveness of a country's culture, values, and political ideals.

Specialist	A category of the U.S. exchange visitor visa (J-1) program by which experts in a field of specialized knowledge observe U.S. organizations and practices and share their knowledge with U.S. colleagues.
Sponsored student	A sponsored student is "an individual who receives funding for the purpose of education, training, or professional development from a sponsor" (Schmiegel 2017, 138).
Sports diplomacy programs	Citizen diplomacy programs that focus on groups and individuals traveling internationally to promote exchange through a common interest in sports.
Stages of psychosocial development	Erik Erikson's model that describes eight stages of life based on approximate age; in each stage, he identifies a core tension, or area of personal growth (Evans et al. 2009).
Stationary program	An education abroad program based in a single location for its duration.
Student affairs	A broad, interdisciplinary field that focuses on supporting students in their academic, personal, and professional lives; also known as "student services."
Student and Exchange Visitor Information System (SEVIS)	U.S. Department of Homeland Security database used to collect and monitor information on international students and exchange visitors on F, M, and J visas.
Student engagement and student success	Research on student engagement and student success emphasizes that students will be most successful if they are held to high standards, introduced to the resources available for support, and engaged with cocurricular programs (Kuh 2011; National Survey of Student Engagement 2018).
Student involvement	A student development theory that states that the more physical time and emotional and mental energy that students put into being involved in their education, the greater their learning (Astin 1999).
Student retention	A metric of student success, typically measured in terms of the percentage of students who continue their studies from year to year.
Student services	A broad, interdisciplinary field that focuses on supporting students in their academic, personal, and professional lives; also known as "student affairs."
Student success	The degree to which students achieve their educational goals; sometimes measured in terms of graduation rates.

Study abroad	Education abroad programs in which students take academic courses for credit.
Study tour	A short multistop education abroad program that focuses on a particular theme.
Summative assessment	An evaluation that takes place at the end of, or after, a course or program and usually makes a judgment about whether the student has learned enough to satisfactorily complete the module, course, or program.
Summer work travel program	A category of the U.S. exchange visitor visa (J-1) program by which college and university students from foreign universities work in seasonal or temporary jobs and explore the United States during their summer vacation.
Sustainable development	An alternative term for "international development," used to emphasize that economic development needs to happen in ways that will continue to be viable into the future.
Tangible culture	A culture in U.S. higher education that focuses on traditions and community ties, particularly alumni, and values the beauty of the campus grounds, state of the art facilities, and high reputation of the institution (Bergquist and Pawlak 2008).
Teach abroad	A program in which participants teach abroad; individual programs may or may not qualify as experiential education.
Teacher	A category of the U.S. exchange visitor visa (J-1) program by which educators teach full time at a U.S. accredited kindergarten, primary, or secondary school.
Third culture kids	Children who grow up in one or more countries abroad due to their parents' work and often do not feel truly at home in either their passport country or the country in which they are living; also known as "global nomads."
Trainee	A category of the U.S. exchange visitor visa (J-1) program by which professionals with a degree, professional certificate, or relevant work experience gain exposure to U.S. culture and business practices through a guided work-based program.
Transactional conversations	Conversations that focus on the exchange of information.
Transition theory	A theory that any life transition, whether anticipated or not, can cause stress and challenge (Schlossberg 1995).

Transnational education	Initiatives that move people and/or programs across national borders; also known as "borderless education" and "cross-border education."
U.S. exchange visitor visa (J-1)	A U.S. visa type, created under the Mutual Educational and Cultural Exchange Act, granting temporary (nonimmigrant) status to "exchange visitors" of many categories for the purpose of cross-cultural exchange.
Virtual culture	A culture in U.S. higher education that focuses on access to knowledge and information and the use of technology to engage students in learning (Bergquist and Pawlak 2008).
Volunteer abroad	A program in which participants engage in volunteer activities abroad; individual programs may or may not qualify as experiential education.
WIVA	An acronym for "work, intern, and volunteer abroad"; sometimes meant to encompass all types of related international experiential education programs.
WIVRA	An acronym for "work, intern, volunteer, and research abroad."
Work abroad	A program in which participants engage in professional activities abroad; individual programs may or may not qualify as experiential education.

References

Arnett, Jeffrey Jensen. 2000. "Emerging Adulthood: A Theory of Development from the Late Teens Through the Twenties." *American Psychologist* 55, 5:469–480.

Asia Society and OECD. 2018. *Teaching for Global Competence in a Rapidly Changing World*. Asia Society and OECD. https://asiasociety.org/sites/default/files/inline-files/teaching-for-global-competence-in-a-rapidly-changing-world-edu.pdf.

Astin, Alexander W. 1999. "Student Involvement: A Developmental Theory for Higher Education." *Journal of College Student Development* 40, 5:518–529.

Bergquist, William H., and Kenneth Pawlak. 2008. *Engaging the Six Cultures of the Academy: Revised and Expanded Edition of The Four Cultures of the Academy*. San Francisco, CA: John Wiley & Sons.

Bridge Education Group. 2016. *Pace of Adoption of International Student Recruitment Agencies by U.S. Institutions*. Denver, CO: Bridge Education Group, Inc. https://www.bridge.edu/assets/bridge-edu.pdf.

The Center for Citizen Diplomacy. 2017. "About Us." Washington, DC: The Center for Citizen Diplomacy. https://www.centerforcitizendiplomacy.org/about-us/.

Deardorff, Darla K. 2015. *Demystifying Outcomes for Assessment for International Educators: A Practical Approach*. Sterling, VA: Stylus Publishing.

Delgado, Richard, and Jean Stefancic. 2017. *Critical Race Theory: An Introduction, Third Edition*. New York, NY: New York University Press.

Evans, Nancy J., Deanna S. Forney, Florence M. Guido, Lori D. Patton, and Kristen A. Renn. 2009. *Student Development in College: Theory, Research, and Practice, Second Edition*. San Francisco, CA: Jossey-Bass.

Jacoby, Barbara. 2015. *Service-Learning Essentials: Questions, Answers, and Lessons Learned*. San Francisco, CA: Jossey-Bass.

Jacoby, Barbara. 2018. "Integrating Service-Learning into Student Affairs Pedagogy." In *Learning Everywhere on Campus: Teaching Strategies for Student Affairs Professionals*, eds. Jane Fried and Ruth Harper. New York, NY: Routledge.

Knight, Jane. 2004. "Internationalization Remodeled: Definition, Approaches, and Rationales." *Journal of Studies in International Education* 8, 1:5–31.

Kolb, David A. 1984. *Experiential Learning: Experience as the Source of Learning and Development*. Upper Saddle River, NJ: Prentice Hall.

Kuh, George D. 2011. "Student Success." In *Student Services: A Handbook for the Profession*, eds. John H. Schuh, Susan R. Jones, and Shaun R. Harper. San Francisco, CA: Jossey-Bass.

Magolda, Marcia B. Baxter. 2001. *Making Their Own Way: Narratives for Transforming Higher Education to Promote Self-Development*. Sterling, VA: Stylus Publishing.

McClellan, Jeffrey, and Clint Moser. 2011. "Advising as Coaching." Manhattan, KS: NACADA Clearinghouse. http://www.nacada.ksu.edu/Resources/Clearinghouse/View-Articles/Advising-as-coaching.aspx.

Merriam, Sharan B., and Laura L. Bierema. 2014. *Adult Learning: Linking Theory and Practice*. San Francisco, CA: Jossey-Bass.

National Survey of Student Engagement. 2018. "High-Impact Practices." Bloomington, IN: Indiana University Center for Postsecondary Research. http://nsse.indiana.edu/html/high_impact_practices.cfm.

Niehaus, Elizabeth, and Karen Kurotsuchi Inkelas. 2015. "Exploring the Role of Alternative Break Programs in Students' Career Development." *Journal of Student Affairs Research and Practice* 52, 2:134–148. https://doi.org/10.1080/19496591.2015.1020247.

Nolting, William, Debbie Donohue, Cheryl Matherly, and Martin Tillman, eds. 2013. *Internships, Service Learning, and Volunteering Abroad: Successful Models and Best Practices*. Washington, DC: NAFSA: Association of International Educators.

Ociepka, Beata. 2018. "Public Diplomacy as Political Communication: Lessons from Case Studies." *European Journal of Communication* 33, 3:290–303. https://doi.org/10.1177/0267323118763909.

Renn, Kristen A. 2008. "Research on Biracial and Multiracial Identity Development: Overview and Synthesis." *New Directions for Student Services* 2008, 123:13–21. https://doi.org/10.1002/ss.282.

Schlossberg, Nancy K. 1995. *Counseling Adults in Transition: Linking Practice With Theory*. New York, NY: Springer Publishing Company.

Schmiegel, Gabriele. 2017. "It Takes a Village: Recruiting, Enrolling, and Supporting Sponsored Students at Your Institution." In *NAFSA's Guide to International Student Recruitment, Third Edition*, ed. Jessica Black Sandberg. Washington, DC: NAFSA: Association of International Educators.

Appendix

NAFSA: Association of International Educators Resources

NAFSA: Association of International Educators, the publisher of this book, is the world's largest nonprofit professional association dedicated to supporting international education professionals. With more than 10,000 members worldwide, NAFSA works to advance the policies and practices of the field. A key facet of NAFSA's work is providing international educators with opportunities and resources for professional development and training. Some of those opportunities are discussed below.

ANNUAL CONFERENCE

The NAFSA Annual Conference & Expo brings together approximately 10,000 international educators from around the world for a weeklong conference each May. Together, the attendees represent more than 3,500 organizations from over 100 countries. The annual conference offers more than 100 sessions presented by practitioners on a wide range of beginning and advanced topics affecting the field. The keynote speakers are often Nobel Peace Prize recipients, renowned authors, and civil rights leaders.

In the Expo Hall, exhibitors fill a space roughly the size of an American football field, sharing updates about their organizations and the latest tools offered or utilized. Networking receptions, poster fairs, colloquia, open meetings, and daylong workshops are just some of the additional events that provide annual conference participants with opportunities for professional development and networking. For more information on the conference, visit www.nafsa.org/ac.

REGIONAL CONFERENCES

NAFSA's U.S. membership base is categorized into 11 geographic regions, each of which offers professional development conferences in the fall every year. Additionally, many state and local NAFSA groups organize conferences during the year. Each event includes presentations by practitioners, workshops, networking events, and time to engage with the exhibitors. For the full list of regions, visit www.nafsa.org/regions.

NETWORKING GROUPS

The NAFSA regions provide members with networking events, e-newsletters, listservs, an online discussion forum, and other ways to connect locally and regionally. Additionally, NAFSA has five Knowledge Communities (KCs) that deliver more targeted programming and resources based on different sectors of the field. The NAFSA Knowledge Communities are Education Abroad; International Education Leadership; International Enrollment Management; International Student and Scholar Services; and Teaching, Learning, and Scholarship. Each KC has listservs for real-time discussions, networking events at the annual conference, and volunteer leadership positions for those interested in further advancing the field. For more information on the KCs, visit www.nafsa.org/kc.

NAFSA has additional Member Interest Groups (MIGs) geared toward professionals who work in community colleges, historically black colleges and universities, one-person offices, and other workplace settings. Other MIGs focus on regions of the world, including Africa, the Middle East, and Latin America. Additional groups are based on shared professional and personal interests, such as the Christian special interest group, rainbow special interest group, returned Peace Corps volunteers group, and women and leadership group, to name a few. For the full list of networking groups, visit www.nafsa.org/migs.

THE ACADEMY FOR INTERNATIONAL EDUCATION

The Academy for International Education is an intensive yearlong training program offers professional mentorship and training for participants that includes a three-day training event, participation in annual and regional NAFSA conferences, and workshop participation. Key components of the program are supported learning from an experienced coach and professional networks with a cohort of peers. For more information on the Academy, visit www.nafsa.org/academy.

WORKSHOPS AND E-LEARNING COURSES

Core Education Program (CEP) Workshops are offered in person at the annual and regional conferences, and e-Learning courses are available online throughout the year. Some of topics covered include advising on immigration regulations, international student recruitment, education abroad advising, crisis management, campus and community programming, credential evaluation, intercultural communication, and much more. For more information on CEP Workshops and e-Learning courses, visit www.nafsa.org/workshops and www.nafsa.org/elearning, respectively.

RESOURCES AND PUBLICATIONS

NAFSA members receive the weekly e-newsletter, *NAFSA.news*, and the flagship *International Educator* magazine. Additionally, NAFSA publishes an extensive collection of books, reports, and articles. Numerous international education resources are available on NAFSA's website (www.nafsa.org) and Network. NAFSA, the online community forum (network.nafsa.org).

Index

Abimbola, Seye, 312
abstract conceptualization, 148, 175, 381
academic advising, 231–232, 381
academic benefits
 of foreign language proficiency, 45
 as global competence education rationale, 35–36
academic capitalism, 13–15, 381
academic expectations, in U.S., 225–226
academic mobility, 18, 65–68, 381
 ACE on, 68
 comparative and international education and, 330–331
 data on, 66–68
 internationalization and, 65–68
 Project Atlas tracking of, 66, 67
 push, pull, and anti-push factors and, 66
 UNESCO on, 66
academic norms, in U.S.
 academic expectations and, 225–226
 classroom behaviors and expectations, 226–227
Academic Ranking of World Universities (ARWU), 22, 23
academic research, nonuniversity sources sponsorship of, 14
academic success support, 241–242
Academy for International Education, 402
accreditation, 20–21, 43, 46, 88, 208, 256, 283
acculturation, 229–230, 360, 381
acculturation theory, 349
ACPA: College Student Educators International, 368
ACPA *Statement of Ethical Principles and Standards*, 370
active experimentation, 148–149, 175, 381
activism, in global competence education, 48–49

activities. *see also* learning activities
 internationalization, 60–61
 for structuring reflection, 175–176
ad hoc IEM model, 191
adjunct instruction, 12
administration, of citizen diplomacy program, 314–316
admissions, 122–123
 applications for, 205–206
 conditional, 199–200, 384
 credential evaluation in, 207–208
 financial aid and, 208
 IEM, 205–210
 language proficiency and, 206–207
adult learning, 114, 153, 358, 381
advising, 24, 119, 381
 as coaching model, 237, 382
 ISSS, 231–239
 by professionals, 123–124
 as teaching and learning model, 237–238, 382
advising approaches, 234
 advising structures, 238
 appreciative advising, 236–237, 382
 career advising, 232, 383
 developmental advising, 236, 386
 immigration advising, 233, 388
 intrusive advising, 236, 390
 logistics advising, 231
 McClellan and Moser on, 235, 237
 peer advising, 238
 personal advising, 127–128, 232–233, 392
 prescriptive advising, 235–236, 392
 proactive advising, 236, 392
 referrals, 238–239
advocacy
 in education abroad, 102–104
 of professionals, 120, 168
advocacy culture, 344, 382

Africa, internationalization in, 81–82, 85
Agenda for Sustainable Development, 2030, 33, 353–354
agent debate, 198–199
Agnew, Melanie, 42, 49–50, 114–115
Aktas, Fatih, 50–51
alien physician, 302, 382
Alliance Française, 307
Altbach, Philip G., 20, 21, 22, 23
alternate responsible officers (AROs), 209–210, 382
alternative break, 153, 382
alternative education, 332–333, 382
Althen, Gary, 235, 246
alumni engagement, 198
American Association of Collegiate Registrars and Admissions Officers (AACRAO), 207
American Council on Education (ACE)
 on academic mobility, 68
 on faculty guidelines, 71
 on internationalization, 60, 61
 Internationalization Laboratory, 72
 Internationalization Through Technology Awards Program, 62
 Internationalizing the Tenure Code: Policies to Promote a Globally Focused Faculty, 71
 Mapping Internationalization on U.S. Campuses survey, 188, 201
 on study abroad, 272–273
American Council on the Teaching of Foreign Languages (ACTFL), 35, 361
 Proficiency Scale and Guidelines, 45
American Councils for International Education (American Councils), 314
 on internationalization planning seven-step process, 72–73
American International Recruitment Council (AIRC), 199

American Music Abroad, 304, 308
AMIDEAST, 314
Andrews, Cathryn, 204
Annual Conference & Expo, NAFSA, 401
anti-push factors, 66, 382
applications, for admissions, 205–206
appreciative advising, 236–237, 382
Aquila School in Dubai, 271
Arasaratnam-Smith, Lily A., 50
Araújo e Sá, Helena, 279
Asia-Pacific, internationalization in, 82, 85
Asia-Pacific Association for International Education (APAIE), 134
Asia Society
 Educating for Global Competence model and, 39–41, 266
 on extracurricular programs, 274–275
 Graduation Performance System, 277
 ISSN of, 264–265
 survey, 31
assessments. *see also* global competence assessments
 of citizen diplomacy, 316–318
 formative, 44, 47, 387
 The Forum on Education Abroad guidelines for, 45
 of intercultural competence, 350
 in internationalization planning, 79–80
 international schools and development of, 277
 learning, language program administrators role in, 360–361
 program, 43–44, 169–170
 summative, 44–45, 47, 396
Asset-Based Community Development approach, 177
associate's colleges, 341
Association Internationale des Etudiants en Sciences Economiques et Commerciales (AISEC), 150
Association of American Colleges & Universities (AAC&U), 31
 on global competence academic competence, 35–36
 VALUE Rubrics, 45
Association of American Voices, 308
Association of International Credential Evaluators (AICE), 207
Association of International Education Administrators (AIEA), 134–135
au pair, 302, 382
Australia
 IB system in, 260–261
 international students in, 18
 language education in, 268
 recruitment channels, 190

baccalaureate/associate's colleges, 341
baccalaureate colleges, 341

backward design, 111, 113, 382
Barker, Michelle, 32, 41, 112–113
Barrett, Angeline M., 65
Barrett, Pamela K., 211–212
Bastos, Mónica, 279
Beatty, Matthew R., 193
Beliefs, Events, and Values Inventory (BEVI), 45
Benjamin A. Gilman International Scholarship Program, U.S., 304, 309, 312–313
Bennett, Milton J., 36–37, 49, 350
Bergquist, William H., 343–344
bilateral exchange programs, 106, 383
Blair, Scott G., 47, 49
Boix Mansilla, Veronica, 40, 267, 278, 288
Bolashak International Scholarship Program, 310
Bologna Process, 82, 83
Bonache, Jaime, 336, 337
borderless education, 18, 383
Boren Fellowships, 87
brain drain, 17, 81, 85, 86, 89, 383
branch campuses, 16, 19, 69–70, 84, 383
 cross-border education and, 19
 Cross-Border Education Research Team on, 19, 69
 programs administered in English at, 20
Brazilian Science Without Borders Program, 304, 306
Brendel, Nina, 284
bridge programs, 200, 360, 383
British Council, 186, 307
budget and finance, in higher education administration, 344
BUNAC, 151, 158
Bureau of Educational and Cultural Affairs
 Association of American Voices and, 307
 on citizen diplomacy program administration, 314
 exchange programs, 305
 Notice of Funding Opportunity publications, 314–315
 Office of U.S. Study Abroad in, 87
 on sports diplomacy programs, 308
Byram, Michael, 38
Byun, Won Jung, 355

Caligiuri, Paula, 336, 337
Campbell, Anne C., 312, 319
camp counselor, 302, 383
campus community readiness and involvement, 246–247
Canada, IB system in, 261
career advising, 232, 383
career impact, of citizen diplomacy program, 312–313
Career-Related Programme, in IB system, 261
career specializations, for peacebuilding, 364–365

career support, of ISSS, 242
Carnegie Basic Classifications, of U.S. higher education institutions
 associate's colleges, 341–342
 baccalaureate/associate's colleges, 341
 baccalaureate colleges, 341
 doctoral universities, 341
 master's colleges and universities, 351
 special focus institutions, 342
 tribal colleges, 342
del Castillo, Graciana, 356, 365
Center on Public Diplomacy (CPD), of University of Southern California, 307
Central Intelligence Agency (CIA), U.S., 301
central recruitment office IEM model, 191
certificate of eligibility, 209, 210, 383
Chang, Li, 196
characteristics
 of education abroad program models, 109–110
 of international schools, 258
Chevening Scholarships and Fellowships, 310
China
 international students in, 18
 scholarships in, 304
Chinese Bridge Summer Camp for American High School Students, 310
Choudaha, Rahul, 195–196
Chronicle of Higher Education, 64
citizen diplomacy, 5, 299, 383
 assessment of, 316–318
 considerations for practitioners on, 318–319
 history of U.S., 300–303
 public diplomacy and, 300, 392
 sector size of, 303–305
citizen diplomacy exchange program, 305, 308–311, 383
citizen diplomacy international government programs
 Bolashak International Scholarship Program, 310
 Chevening Scholarships and Fellowships, 310
 Chinese Bridge Summer Camp for American High School Students, 310
 Confucius Institutes, 304, 307, 310
 Erasmus+, 310
 German Chancellor Fellowship, 310
 JET, 158, 311
 Libyan-North American Scholarship Program, 311
citizen diplomacy nongovernmental programs
 Open Society Foundation Scholarship Programs, 311
 Rotary Youth Exchange, 311
 Schwarzman Scholars Program, 311
 Sister Cities International, 264, 311

citizen diplomacy program administration
　Bureau of Educational and Cultural Affairs on, 314
　implementation for, 315–316
　IVLP and, 314
　proposals in, 314–315
　selection process for, 315
citizen diplomacy programs
　administration of, 314–316
　career impact of, 312–313
　country values impact from, 313
　cultural diplomacy programs, 307–308, 385
　examples of, 308–311
　exchange programs, 304, 308–311, 383
　impact of, 311–313
　merit-based selection process for, 317
　positive regard impact from, 313
　postprogram support for, 319
　professional training, 306–307, 392
　reinforced inequities in, 318–319
　research on, 312
　scholarship programs, 305–306
　sports diplomacy programs, 308, 395
citizen diplomacy U.S. government programs, 306
　FLEX Program, 309
　Fulbright Program, 30, 150, 158, 304, 305, 309
　Gilman International Scholarship Program, 304, 309, 312–313
　Global Sports Mentoring Program, 309
　Hubert H. Humphrey Fellowship, 309
　IMET Program, 309
　IVLP, 86, 304, 307, 310, 314
　Kennedy-Lugar YES Program, 302, 310
　Open World Leadership Center Programs, 310
　TechWomen, 310
citizen diplomats, 299, 384
citizenship and governance, as global competence education rationale, 35
civic engagement, 153, 384
classroom behaviors and expectations, in U.S., 226–227
Clinton, Hillary, 310
coaching model, advising as, 237, 382
code of ethics, 133, 189, 192
Code of Ethics and Professional Practices, of National Association for College Admission Counseling, 192
Code of Ethics for Education Abroad, of The Forum on Education Abroad, 133
Code of Federal Regulations, U.S., 233, 239
collaboration with diverse others, in learning activities, 116
Collaborative Online International Learning (COIL) center, of SUNY, 62
college and university student, 302, 384

College of Staten Island High School for International Studies (CSIHSIS), 264, 270
collegial culture, 343, 384
Colloquium on Internationalizing Teacher Education, of NAFSA, 278–279
Comenius Programme, 82
commercialization of education, 87, 89
commodification of education, 87, 384
　Altbach on, 21
　GATS treaty and, 15–16, 17
　neoliberalism in global politics and finance, 15
Common European Framework of Reference for Language (CEFR), 361
communicative competence, 37–38, 384
community colleges, recruitment from, 203
comparative and international education, 330–335, 384
　academic mobility and, 330–331
　alternative education, 332–333, 382
　benefits of, 331
　comparison as methodology, 331
　considerations for practitioners on, 333
　educational structures and policies, 333
　Epstein on, 330
　equity of access and achievement in, 332
　history of, 330
　key topics for, 331–333
　resources for, 334–335
comparisons, as methodology, 331
competencies, of professionals, 120
competitiveness
　as global competence education rationale, 32–33
　Suarez-Orozco and Qin-Hilliard on, 33
Concordia Language Villages, 276
concrete experience, 148, 175, 384
conditional admission, 199–200, 384
Confucius Institutes, 264, 304, 307, 310
Connor-Linton, Jeffrey, 117, 118
considerations for practitioners
　on citizen diplomacy, 318–319
　on comparative and international education, 333–334
　on development and education, 356–357
　on global mobility, 338–339
　on intercultural training, 350
　on international schools, 284–286
　on ISSS, 246–249
　on language program administration, 362
　on student services, 369–370
Consortium for Overseas Student Teaching (COST), 283
consortium program, 109, 384
consumption abroad, 16
content-based instruction (CBI), 269, 384
content dissemination phase, in digital marketing, 205

cooperative education (co-ops), 152, 153, 164
Core Education Program (CEP) Workshops, 403
Council of Chief State School Officers, Educating for Global Competence model of, 39–41, 266
Council of International Schools, *Guiding Principles for Higher Education* of, 192
Council on International Educational Exchange (CIEE), 134, 151
Council on Standards for International Education Travel (CSIET), 273–274
crafting, in internationalization planning, 74–76
CRDF Global, 314
credential evaluation, 207–208, 384
credit awarding, in experiential education, 168–169
credit mobility, 67, 385
crisis management, by professionals, 131–132
Crisis Management for Education Abroad, of NAFSA, 134
critical inquiry, 34, 385
critical race theory, 124, 385
critical reflection, 176–177
cross-border education, 385
　branch campuses and, 19
　English language programs and, 20
　growth in, 18–19
　online or distance learning in, 19
　partnering institutions and, 19
　programs and, 18–19
Cross-Border Education Research Team, on branch campuses, 19, 69
cross-border supply, 16
Cross-Cultural Adaptability Inventory (CCAI), 45, 350
cross-cultural education efforts, 1–2
Crossley, Michael, 65
Cultural Bridges Act, of 2002, 301–302
cultural diplomacy programs, 307–308, 385
cultural relativism
　DMIS model and, 49
　in global competence education, 48–49
　Lucas and Blair on, 49
Cultural Vistas, 150, 314
culture
　advocacy, 344, 382
　collegial, 343, 384
　developmental, 344, 386
　managerial, 344, 390
　organization, in higher education administration, 343–344
　tangible, 344, 396
　virtual, 344, 397
Curricular Practical Training (CPT), 234, 385

curriculum
  enrichment, 267, 385
  of IB system, 261–262
  integration, 267, 385
  internationalization of, 61–62, 266–267, 276
  learning assessment role, of language program administrators and, 360–361
Cushman, Jenifer, 35
customer relationship management (CRM) technologies, 186
customized program, 105–106, 109, 385
cyclical process, of assessments, 47

data
  on academic mobility, 66–68
  collection, by professionals, 129
  from ISC, 256–257
  on study abroad, 273–274
Davis, Vicki A., 271–272
Deardorff, Darla K.
  Process Model of Intercultural Competence of, 38–39
  on student learning assessments, 43
Declaration of Universal Human Rights, UN, 352
Deferred Action for Childhood Arrivals, 368
deficit thinking, 247, 385
degree mobility, 67, 385
Department of Education, U.S.
  international strategy of, 302
  State Standards for ESOL, 361
  2012 international strategy of, 30
Department of Homeland Security, U.S., 209, 210, 233
DePaul, Stephen C., 103
designated school officials (DSOs), 209–210, 385
developmental advising, 236, 386
developmental culture, 344, 386
Developmental Model of Intercultural Sensitivity (DMIS), of Bennett, 36–37, 350
  on cultural relativism, 49
  stages and learning goals of, 37
development and education, 354
  considerations for practitioners on, 356–357
  resources on, 357–358
  specializations in, 355–356
Dewey, John, 147–148, 174, 261
DeWinter, Urbain J., 123
digital marketing, 204–205
  implementation phase in, 205
Di Maria, David L., 191
Diploma Programme, in IB system, 260–262, 264, 277

direct enrollment, as education abroad program model, 104–105, 106, 107
distance learning, in cross-border education, 19
diversity, IEM and, 212–213
Diversity Abroad, 133
DIY program, 109, 386
doctoral universities, 341
Doherty, Catherine, 286
double degrees, 67, 69, 202–203, 386
duration of status (D/S), 234, 386

Educating for Global Competence model, 39–41, 266
Educating for Global Competence: Preparing Our Youth to Engage the World (Boix Mansilla and Jackson), 39, 266
education abroad, 5, 386
  advocates, 103–104
  finances and logistics in, 103
  management software for, 122–123
  professional organizations and standards, 133–135
  professionals roles and responsibilities, 118–132
  program providers, 105–106, 122, 129, 130, 131, 147, 152, 156–158, 162–163
  race and ethnicity in, 101–102
  study abroad outcomes, 117–118
  U.S. study abroad, 99–101
education abroad adviser, 119, 121, 122, 123, 126, 128, 156, 157, 170
Education Abroad KC, 134, 402
Education Abroad KC Network, 134
education abroad program design process, 111–116
  evidence of learning identification, 112–113
  learning activities selection and teaching methodologies, 113–116
  learning outcomes determination, 111–112
  resources secured in, 116
education abroad program models
  characteristics of, 109–110
  direct enrollment, 104–105
  exchange programs, 106–107
  faculty-led programs, 107–108, 121, 130, 387
  providers for, 105–106, 130, 147
educational agents, 189, 386
educational travel, 153, 386
Education for All framework, of UNESCO, 10
education service sector, in GATS, 15–16, 17
Eisenhower, Dwight D., 301
e-Learning courses, 403

embedded program, 109, 386
emerging adulthood, 124, 386
employment, international student immigration regulations and, 234
English as a second language (ESL), 192, 234, 265
English for Speakers of Other Languages (ESOL)
  examinations, of University of Cambridge, 361
  U.S. Department of Education State Standards for, 361
English language programs, 20, 187, 358
English Program in Korea (EPIK), 158
English Teaching Assistant (ETA), of Fulbright Program, 158, 309
equity of access and achievement, 332
Erasmus+, 310
Erasmus Programme, 82–83
Escuela Nuevas, 333
ethical and social responsibility, for global competence, 42
ethical practice standards, for international education, 3
ethnocentrism, 36, 331, 336, 386
ethnorelativism, 36, 39, 386
Europe, internationalization in, 82–83, 85
Europe 2020 Strategy, 82–83
European Association for International Education (EAIE), 134
Examination for the Certificate of Competency in English (ECCE), of University of Michigan, 261
Examination for the Certificate of Proficiency in English (ECPE), of University of Michigan, 361
exchange programs, 387
  bilateral, 106, 383
  Bureau of Educational and Cultural Affairs and, 305
  citizen diplomacy, 304, 308–311, 383
  as education abroad program model, 106–107
  multilateral, 107, 391
exchange visitor J-1 visa category, 187, 209–210, 234, 302–303, 397
expatriates, 336–338
experiential education, 147–150, 153–161, 163–169, 387. *see also* international experiential education
  facilitation of, 170–178
  history of international, 150–151
  participation benefits, 151–152
  programs, stakeholder and, 162
experiential education theory
  Dewey on, 147–148
  Kolb's Experiential Learning Cycle, 123, 148–150, 160, 175
experiential learning, 110, 387

Experiential Learning Cycle, of Kolb, 123, 160
   abstract conceptualization stage of, 148, 381
   active experimentation stage of, 148–149, 381
   concrete experience stage of, 148, 384
   in practice, 149–150
   reflective observation stage of, 148, 175, 393
extracurricular programs
   Asia Society on, 274–275
   Concordia Language Villages, 276
   Global Glimpse, 276
   Global Kids, 276
   Global Young Leaders Conference, 276
   Global Youth Village, 276
   John Hopkins Center for Talented Youth, 276
   Model United Nations, 276
   OneWorld Now!, 276
   Smink on, 275
   WE, 276

F-1 student visa category, 187, 209–210, 234
facilitation, of experiential education, 170
   activities for structuring reflection, 175–176
   critical reflection, 176–177
   discomfort and emotion, 173–174
   follow-up and outcomes, 177–178
   reflection importance, 175
   Roberts on facilitation skills, 171–173
Facilitator's Guide (Punteney and Winn), 6
faculty
   development, internationalization and, 70–72
   engagement, in internationalization planning, 77–78
   faculty-led programs, 103, 105–106, 121, 387
   as education abroad program model, 107–108
   funding for, 130
faith-based program, 153, 387
Farrell, Joseph P., 333
feminist theory, 124, 387
FHI360 nonprofit organization, 308, 314
field study program, 110, 387
finances and logistics, in education abroad, 103
financial aid, 208
Flattening Classrooms, Engaging Minds (Lindsay and Davis), 271–272
Fon, Titanji Peter, 65
for-credit programs, 160
foreign language proficiency, academic benefits of, 45
formal education, 113, 387
formative assessment, 44, 47, 387

Form DS-2019 Certificate of Eligibility, for J-1 nonimmigrants, 209–210
Form I-20 Certificate of Eligibility, for F-1 and M-1 nonimmigrants, 209–210
The Forum on Education Abroad
   assessment guidelines of, 45
   Code of Ethics for Education Abroad, 133
   on education abroad professionals, 132
   Leading Short-Term Education Abroad Programs, 133
   QUIP of, 134
   Standards of Good Practice for Education Abroad, 133
   2012 State of the Field Survey of, 31
France, international students in, 18
Freshman/first-year program, 110, 387
friendship programs, 243–244
Fulbright Distinguished Awards in Teaching Semester Research Program, 307
Fulbright-Hays Act, of 1961, 30, 301
   J-1 visa creation by, 302–303
Fulbright Program, 30, 86, 150, 304, 305, 309
   ETA Programs, 158
Fulbright Teachers for Global Classrooms Program, 307
full-time enrollment, 234, 387
funding
   for faculty-led programs, 130
   financing and, by professionals, 129–130, 169
   higher education insufficient public, 11–13
   as management role and responsibility, 169
   private, in higher education, 12
   U.S. government research, 63
Future Leaders Exchange (FLEX) Program, 309
future trends, for international schools, 286–288

gap year, 153, 387
gender identity development, 124, 388
General Agreement on Trade in Services (GATS) treaty, of WTO
   education service sector in, 15–16, 17
   neoliberalism and, 15–16
Georgetown Consortium Project, 117–118
German Chancellor Fellowship, 310
Ghandi, Miloni, 193
Gillespie, Joan, 118
Gilman International Scholarship Program, 304, 309, 312–313
global careers, 118
Global Citizen Program, in Sweden, 270–271
global citizenship
   Aktas on university programs for, 50–51
   Green on, 29
   Oxfam on, 35
Global Citizenship Education model, of UNESCO, 266

Global Citizenship Education: Topics and Learning Objectives, of UNESCO, 266
global competence, 5, 23, 29, 44–52, 266, 388
   attitudes for, 41–42
   core concepts of, 41–43
   defined, 1
   effective and appropriate responses from, 42
   ethical and social responsibility and, 42
   intersectionality of identity and, 42
   knowledge, skills, and attitudes development for, 41
   as lifelong learning process, 42–43
   Lilley, Barker, and Harris, N., on, 32, 41, 112–113
   OECD definition of, 31–32, 112
   Oxfam definition of, 32
   relevance of, 41
   self-awareness and, 42
   for teachers, 278–279
   terminology and definitions of, 31–32
   in U.S., 30–31
global competence assessments
   AAC&U VALUE Rubrics tool, 45
   ACTFL Proficiency Scale and Guidelines tool, 45
   BEVI, 45
   CCAI tool, 45
   cyclical process of, 47
   evaluation of tools for, 46
   focus of, 47
   GPI, ICS, and IDI tools, 45
   iterative process of, 46–47
   methods triangulation, 47
   organization specific, 46
   PISA, 48
   principles of, 46–47
   process of, 44–46
   self-reporting limits, 47
   of student learning and programs, 43–44
   tools for, 45
global competence education considerations
   assessment challenges, 50
   of cultural relativism and activism, 48–49
   need for more substantive efforts, 50–51
   of UNESCO Global Citizenship Education, 266
   Western bias, 49–50
global competence education rationales
   academic benefits, 35–36
   citizenship and governance, 35
   competitiveness, 32–33
   global problems solutions, 33
   multiculturalism, 34–35
global competence models
   DMIS, 36–37, 49, 350
   Educating for Global Competence model, 39–41
   Intercultural Communicative Competence model, 37–38

global finance, neoliberalism and, 15
Global Gateway for Teachers Program, 283
Global Glimpse, 276
global health programs, 161, 388
Global Kids, 276
Global Learning VALUE Rubric, 36, 45
Globally Competent Learning Continuum, 279
global mobility, 335–339, 388
    Caligiuri and Bonache on, 336, 337
    considerations for practitioners on, 338–339
    global workforce context, 336–337
    professionals, roles of, 335–336
    resources for, 339
global nomads, 260, 388
Global Partnership Schools program, in UK, 259, 270
Global Perspectives Inventory (GPI), 45
global politics, neoliberalism in, 15
global problems solutions, as global competence education rationale, 33
global rankings
    by ARWU, *THE*, and QS, 22, 23
    competition for, 21–23
    national policies interest in, 21
    research universities and, 22–23
Global Sports Mentoring Program, 309
Global Ties U.S., 307, 314
Global Young Leaders Conference, 276
Global Youth Village, 276
GLOSSARI Project, 117
GoAbroad.com, 154
Goethe Institute, 307
Go Overseas, 359
GoOverseas.com, 154
Goren, Heela, 42, 50
government motivations, for IB system, 262
government visitor, 303, 388
Grabe, William, 269
graduate programs, for international education, 2, 4
Graduate School USA, 314
Graduation Performance System, of Asia Society, 277
Grand Tour, 100–101
Green, Madeleine F., 29
gross domestic product (GDP), English language programs and, 20
growth
    of international schools, 256–257
    of knowledge economy, 9–10
Grusky, Sara, 160, 173–174
The Guide to Successful Short-Term Programs Abroad, of NAFSA, 134
Guiding Principles for Higher Education, of Council of International Schools, 192

Hallgarten, Joe, 256
The Handbook of International Student Advising (Young and Althen), 235
hard power, 299, 388
Harris, Anita, 29
Harris, Neil, 32, 41, 112–113
Hayden, Mary, 258
Heiss, Julia, 355
higher education
    insufficient public funding of, 11–13
    internationalization of, 60
    private funding of, 12
    students as revenue source for, 12
    system, U.S. establishment of, 11
Higher Education Act, of 1992, 130
higher education administration, 339–347, 388
    Bergquist and Pawlak on, 343–344
    budget and finance in, 344
    Carnegie Basic Classifications of U.S. higher education institutions, 341–342
    graduate degrees in, 340
    inequities in, 345
    key topics for, 342–345
    organizational cultures in, 343–344
    organizational structures in, 343
    resources for, 346–347
    retention and success in, 344–345
    U.S. institution types, 340–342
high-impact practices, 151–152
high schools, recruitment from, 203–204
history
    of comparative and international education, 330
    of IB system, 259–260
    of international experiential education, 150–151
    of international schools, 255–256
    of study abroad, 100–101
A History of U.S. Study Abroad: Beginnings to 1965 (Hoffa), 100–101
Hobert, Carl, 286–287
Hoffa, William, 100–101, 103
homestays, 127, 272
housing, professionals and, 127
Hubert H. Humphrey Fellowship, 309
Hudzik, John K., 59, 75–76
Humphrey Fellowships, 86

ICEF, 199
IES Abroad, 134, 151
immersion, 109, 388
immigration advising, 233, 388
implementation
    in citizen diplomacy program administration, 315–316
    in internationalization planning, 77–79
    phase, in digital marketing, 205

independent study, 110, 388
informal learning, 113, 275, 389
Institute for Study Abroad (IFSA Butler), 134
Institute of International Education (IIE), 134–135, 303–304, 314
    Open Doors publication of, 99–100, 155
institutional policies, internationalization planning and, 79
institutional position, in ISSS, 248–249
institutional reasons, for IB system, 263
intensive English program (IEP), 186, 199, 358, 360, 389
interactions with diverse others, in learning activities, 115
Intercultural Communicative Competence model, of Byram, 38
intercultural competence, 5
    assessment of, 350
    definition of, 32
Intercultural Conflict Style Inventory (ICS), 45
Intercultural Development Inventory (IDI), 45, 350
Intercultural Knowledge and Competence VALUE Rubric, 36, 45
intercultural skills, for students, 41
intercultural training, 347–351, 389
    on acculturation theory, 349
    considerations for practitioners on, 350
    contexts, 348–349
    on intercultural competence assessment, 350
    on intersectionality of identity, 349
    key topics, 349–350
    resources for, 350–351
    training design and facilitation skills, 350
intern, 110, 389
intern abroad, 156–157, 389
International Association for the Exchange of Students for Technical Experience (IASTE), 150–151
International Association of Universities (IAU)
    on internationalization, 60, 80–89
    on student learning outcomes, 44
    2013 survey, 33, 60
International Baccalaureate (IB) system
    Career-Related Programme in, 261
    curriculum of, 261–262
    Diploma Programme in, 260–262, 264, 277
    expansion of, 260–261
    government motivations for, 262
    history of, 259–260
    institutional reasons for, 263
    Middle Years Programme in, 261, 263
    parent and student demand for, 263–264
    political ideologies for, 263
    Primary Years Programme in, 260, 261

rationales for public education adoption of, 262–264
reinforced inequities in, 286
in U.S., 260–261
international cooperative education, 153, 389
international development, 389
education and, 352–358
international education, 389
cross-border education and programs for, 18–19
defined, 1
ethical practice standards for, 3
GATS service modes, 16
graduate programs for, 2, 4
job marketplace, 4–5
professionals, 3–4
profession of, 2–5
quality assurance demand in, 20–21
International Education Leadership KC, 402
International Educator magazine, 403
International English Language Testing System (IELTS), 198, 206
international enrollment management (IEM), 5, 185, 214, 389
admissions, 205–210
competencies, 192
considerations for, 211–212
diversity and, 212–213
international students in U.S. and, 186–189
KC, 402
marketing and brand management, 204–205
national enrollment management policies, 190–191
recruitment methods and channels, 195–204
responsibility for, 191–192
retention, 211
risks in, 211–212
strategic planning, 192–195
international experiential education, 171–178
adult learning and, 153
alternative break in, 153, 382
civic engagement, 153
co-ops, 153
definitions and terminology, 152–154
educational travel, 153
faith-based programs, 153
gap year, 153, 387
management roles and responsibilities, 167–170
partnerships, 161–167
program types, 155–161
related terms, 153
sector size, 154–155
WIVA, 153

internationalization, 3, 5, 16, 23, 389
academic mobility and, 65–68
ACE on, 60, 61
activities, 60–61
considerations for, 87–89
of curriculum, 61–62, 266–267, 276
faculty development and, 70–72
of higher education, 60
Hudzik on, 59
IAU on, 60
international school strategies, 265–277
Knight on, 59
of language education, 62–63, 267–268
Meda and Monnapula-Mapesela on, 59
myths about, 88
national policies support of, 17
of research, 63–65
of research partnerships, 64–65
as revenue generator, 17
strategic partnerships and, 19–20, 67–70, 383
strategic planning process of, 2
of teacher education programs, 282–283
of U.S. international schools, 264–265
internationalization at home (IaH), 18, 60
internationalization initiatives, 20
Internationalization Laboratory, of ACE, 72
internationalization planning, 17
assessment in, 79–80
crafting in, 74–76
faculty engagement in, 77–78
getting started with, 73–74
Hudzik on, 75–76
implementation in, 77–79
institutional policies and, 79
revision in, 80
seven-step process for, 72–80
stakeholders collaboration in, 76–77
structure in, 78
SWOT analysis in, 74
internationalization regional differences, 80, 85
Africa, 81–82, 85
Asia-Pacific, 82, 85
Europe, 82–83, 85
Latin America and Caribbean, 83–84, 85
Middle East, 84–86
North America, 85, 86–87
Internationalization Through Technology Awards Program, of ACE, 62
Internationalizing the Tenure Code: Policies to Promote a Globally Focused Faculty, of ACE, 71
International Military Education and Training (IMET) Program, 309
International Monetary Fund, 366
International Partnership for Service-Learning, 151

international partnerships, for international schools, 269–271
International School Consultancy (ISC), data from, 256–257
International School Manila, 270
International School of Geneva, 255–256
international schools, 5, 24, 389
Asia Society ISSN services for, 264–265
characteristics of, 258
considerations for practitioners on, 284–286
definitions and types of, 257–259
future trends for, 286–288
growth of, 256–257
Hallgarten, Tabberer, and McCarthy on, 256
Hayden and Thompson categorization of, 258
history of, 255–256
IB system, 259–264
internationalization in U.S., 264–265
internationalization strategies, 265–277
in public education, 259
reinforced inequities, 286
Skelton on categorization of, 258
teacher training and development, 278–284
UWC as, 257
values deficit in, 286
Western emphasis in, 284–285
WPCP, CSIHSIS, and JSIS as, 264
international schools, internationalization strategies for, 265–268
of extracurricular programming, 274–277
of global outcomes and assessment development, 277
of partnerships development, 269–271
of student mobility opportunities, 272–274
international service-learning, 159–161, 166, 390
international student and scholar services (ISSS), 5, 223–224, 390
acculturation process in, 229–230
advising in, 231–239
benefits of hosting in, 224
campus community readiness and involvement in, 246–247
considerations for practitioners on, 246–249
institutional position in, 248–249
KC, 402
professional philosophy of, 247–248
professional skills and specialties of, 245–246
supportive programming of, 239–245
support services of, 230–231
U.S. adjustments in, 225–229

international student immigration regulations
  D/S of, 234
  employment and, 234
  F-1 visas, 233, 234
  full-time enrollment and, 234, 387
  J-1 visas, 233, 234
  M-1 visas, 233, 234
  NAFSA: Association of International Educators on, 233–234
international students, 66
  in Australia, China, France, and UK, 18
  in U.S., 18, 23, 186–189
International Studies Schools Network (ISSN), of Asia Society, 264–265
international travel, 197–198
international visitor, 303, 390
International Visitor Leadership Program (IVLP), 86, 304, 307, 310, 314
interns, 303
internship abroad program, 390
Internships, Service Learning, and Volunteering Abroad: Successful Models and Best Practices (Nolting, Donohue, Matherly, and Tillman), 150–151
intersectionality of identity, 42, 124, 349, 390
intrusive advising, 236, 390
island program, 109, 390
Italian Cultural Institute, 307
iterative process
  of assessments, 46–47
  of program design, 111
Iverson, Ben, 213

J-1 exchange visitor visa category, 209–210, 239, 234, 244, 302, 304, 397
Jackson, Anthony, 267, 288
Jacoby, Barbara, 160, 167, 176
  on reflection structuring, 175–176
Japan Exchange and Teaching Program (JET), 158, 311
job marketplace, in international education, 4–5
John Hopkins Center for Talented Youth, 276
Johnson, Mathew, 173
John Stanford International School (JSIS), 264
joint degrees, 69, 70, 202–203, 390

Kahn, Hilary E., 42, 49–50, 114–115
Kennedy, John F., 301
Kennedy-Lugar Youth Exchange and Study (YES) Program, 302, 310
key topics
  for comparative and international education, 331–333
  for higher education administration, 342–345
  for intercultural training, 349–350
  for student services, 368–369

Kim, Young Yun, 229
King, Patricia M., 124
Knight, Jane, 16, 59, 88, 224
Knowledge Communities (KCs), NAFSA, 402
  Education Abroad, 134, 402
  International Education Leadership, 402
  International Enrollment Management, 402
  International Student and Scholar Services, 402
  Teaching, Learning, and Scholarship, 402
knowledge economy
  growth of, 9–10
  research universities role in, 9–10
  Stewart on, 32–33
  technology support of, 9
  university enrollment and, 11
Kolb, David, 123, 148–150
Kono, Yoko, 196

language education
  approaches to, 268–269
  CBI approach, 269, 384
  internationalization of, 62–63, 267–268
  in UK and U.S., 268
language immersion program, 110, 358, 390
language of instruction, 105, 285
language proficiency, admissions and, 20, 199, 200, 206–207
language program administration, 358–363, 390
  considerations for practitioners on, 362
  language program contexts, 358–359
  resources for, 362–363
language program administrators
  curriculum and learning assessment role, 360–361
  marketing and recruitment role, 360
  operations management role, 362
  responsibilities, 359
  student services role, 360
  teacher and staff supervision role, 361
Latin America and Caribbean, internationalization in, 83–84, 85
Leading Short-Term Education Abroad Programs, of The Forum on Education Abroad, 133
learning, evidence of, 112
learning activities
  collaboration with diverse others in, 116
  examination of difference in, 114–115
  interactions with diverse others in, 115
  range of possible, 114
  self-reflection in, 114
  student motivations for, 113–114
Lee, Sung Yong, 365
Leicht, Alexander, 355
lesbian, gay, bisexual, transgender, and queer (LGBTQ) students, 104

Lessels, Richard, 100–101
Libyan-North American Scholarship Program, 311
lifelong learning process, of global competence, 42–43
Lilley, Kathleen, 32, 41, 112–113
Lindsay, Julie, 271–272
Lisbon Strategy, 82–83
Liu Yandong, 310
local partnerships, 270
logistical support, 239, 241
logistics advising, 231
Lough, Benjamin J., 154
Lucas, James M., 47
  on cultural relativism, 49

M-1 vocational student visa category, 209–210, 234, 244
Majidi, Katherine, 333
Malveaux, Gregory F., 131
management roles and responsibilities, in experiential education, 167, 170
  advocacy as, 168
  credit awarding as, 168–169
  funding as, 169
  on-campus partnerships as, 169
management software, for education abroad, 122–123
managerial culture, 344, 390
Mapping Internationalization on U.S. Campuses survey, of American Council on Education, 188, 201
marketing and brand management, in IEM, 204–205
marketing and recruitment, by professionals, 122
marketing and recruitment role, of language program administrators, 360
massification of education, 10, 391
  benefits of, 11
  higher education demand from, 11–12
master's colleges and universities, 341
McBride, Amanda Moore, 165
McCarthy, Kenny, 256
McClellan, George, 370
McClellan, Jeffrey, 235, 237
McClure, Kevin R., 102
McFarland, Miko, 158, 168
Meda, Lawrence, 59
Member Interest Groups (MIGs), 402
Meridian International Center, 314
merit-based selection process, 317
Mezirow, Jack, 123
Middle East
  branch campuses in, 69
  internationalization in, 84–86
Middle Years Programme, in IB system, 261, 263

Mississippi Consortium for International Development, 314
Mlyn, Eric, 165
Model United Nations, 276
Modern Language Association of America, 62
Mohajeri Norris, Emily, 118
Monnapula-Mapesela, Mabokang, 59
Montessori schools, 333
Moser, Clint, 235, 237
multiculturalism
  as global competence education rationale, 34–35
  Leeman on, 34
multilateral exchange program, 107, 391
multistop program, 110, 391
Mutual Education and Cultural Exchange Act. *see* Fulbright-Hays Act, of 1961
myCAP tool, of NAFSA, 282–283
myths, about internationalization, 88

NAFSA: Association of International Educators, 4, 120, 192
  Annual Conference & Expo, 401
  assessment guidelines of, 46
  Colloquium on Internationalizing Teacher Education, 278–279
  on international student immigration regulations, 233–234
  KCs of, 402
  myCAP tool of, 282–283
  Network, 134, 403
  networking groups of, 402
  regional conferences of, 402
  SECUSSA Sourcebook: A Guide for Advisers of U.S. Students Planning an Overseas Experience, 151
NAFSA Career Print Tool, 4, 246
NAFSA International Education Professional Competencies, 4–5, 120, 192, 246, 348
NAFSA.news e-newsletter, 403
NAFSA's Guide to Education Abroad for Advisers and Administrators, 134
NAFSA's *Statement of Ethical Principles*, 192
NASPA: Student Affairs Administration in Higher Education, 368
National Assessment of Educational Progress, 31
National Association for College Admission Counseling (NACAC), 198–199
  Code of Ethics and Professional Practices, 192
National Center for Education Statistics (NCES), on retention, 345
National Defense Education Act, of 1958, Title VI of, 30
National Education Association (NEA), 32
  on foreign language learning benefits, 35

national enrollment management policies, 190–191
National Geographic survey, 31
National Institutes of Health, 63
national policies
  global rankings interest from, 21
  internationalization supported by, 17
National Science Foundation, 63, 158
National Survey of Student Engagement (NSSE), 151–152
neoliberalism, 391
  GATS and, 15–16
  in global politics and finance, 15
Network, NAFSA, 134, 403
networking groups, NAFSA, 402
nonformal education, 113, 391
nongovernmental organizations (NGOs), 264, 311, 352–353, 391
nonimmigrant visa types
  F-1, 209, 210, 233, 234, 273–374, 302–303
  J-1, 209, 210, 239, 244, 302, 304, 397
  M-1, 209, 210, 233, 234, 244
nonuniversity sources, for academic research, 14
North America, internationalization in, 85, 86–87
Notice of Funding Opportunity publication, of Bureau of Educational and Cultural Affairs, 314–315

Office of U.S. Study Abroad, 87
Olympic Committee, U.S., 308
on-campus partnerships, 169
O'Neill, Thomas P., 363
OneWorld Now!, 276
ongoing orientation, 125–126, 240, 391
online learning, in cross-border education, 19
on-site orientation, 125, 391
Open Doors publication, of IIE, 99–100, 155
  on race and ethnicity, 101
Open Society Foundation Scholarship Programs, 311
Open World Leadership Center Programs, 310
operations management role, of language program administrators, 362
Optional Practical Training (OPT), 189, 208, 234, 391
Organisation for Economic Co-operation and Development (OECD), 13, 353
  global competence definition by, 31–32, 112
  IB support by, 263
  on SDGs, 33
organizational cultures, in higher education administration, 343–344
organizational structures, in higher education administration, 343

organization specific assessments, 46
orientation, by professionals, 125–126
orientation programs, 125–127, 239–240
outcomes, 79, 391
  of experiential education programs, 177–178
  international schools and global, 277
  Stewart on global education, 33
  student learning, 44
  study abroad, 117–118
  universities proof of, 20
outputs, 79, 391
Oxfam
  on global citizenship, 35
  global competence definition by, 32
Ozerdem, Alpaslan, 365
Ozturgut, Osman, 196

Paige, R. Michael, 117, 118
parent and student demand, for IB system, 263–264
Parker, Walter C., 287
partner and stakeholder relationships, 120–121
partnering institutions, cross-border education and, 19
partnerships
  in international experiential education, 161–167
  on-campus, in experiential education, 169
  research, 64–65
  service-based, 165–167
  strategic, 19–20, 67–70, 383
  work-based, 162–165
partnerships, for international schools, 269
  international, 270–271
  local, 270
pathway programs, 200–201, 391
Pawlak, Kenneth, 343–344
peacebuilding, 363–367, 392
  career specializations, 364–365
  context of, 363–366
  O'Neill on, 363
  process of, 365–366
  resources for, 366–367
  Rothman on, 364
Peace Corps, U.S., 151, 301
peer advising, 238
peer mentoring, 238, 243–244, 392
People-to-People Program, of Eisenhower, 301
personal advising, 232–233, 392
  by professionals, 127–128
physical and logistical challenges, in U.S., 228–229
political ideologies, for IB system, 263
positions, for professionals, 119–120
postprogram support, for citizen diplomacy program, 319

predeparture orientation, 125, 132, 392
prescriptive advising, 235–236, 392
presence of natural persons, 16
Primary Years Programme, in IB system, 260, 261
principal designated school officials (PDSOs), 209–210, 392
print and digital materials, 198
private funding, of higher education, 12
proactive advising, 236, 392
Process Model of Intercultural Competence, of Deardorff, 38–39
profession, of international education, 2–5
professional organizations, 135. *see also*
  NAFSA: Association of International Educators
  Diversity Abroad, 133
  The Forum on Education Abroad, 31, 45, 132, 133–134
professional philosophy, in ISSS, 247–248
professionals, international education, 4
  admissions and, 122–123
  advising by, 123–124
  advocacy of, 120
  benefits for, 3
  competencies, 120
  data collection by, 129
  The Forum on Education Abroad on, 132
  funding and financing by, 129–130
  group dynamics and personal advising, 127–128
  housing and, 127
  marketing and recruitment by, 122
  orientation by, 125–126
  partner and stakeholder relationships, 120–121
  positions for, 119–120
  program development by, 121–122
  reentry and, 128, 393
  risk prevention and crisis management, 131–132
  roles and responsibilities of, 118–132
  specializations within, 132
Professionals in International Education (PIE) News website, 62–63
professional training, 306, 392
  CPD program, 307
  Fulbright Distinguished Awards in Teaching Semester Research Program, 307
  Fulbright Teachers for Global Classrooms Program, 307
  IVLP, 307
professor/research scholar, 303, 392
Proficiency Scale and Guidelines, of ACTFL, 45
program assessments, 43–44, 169–170
program development, by professionals, 121–122
Programme for International Student Assessment (PISA), 48

programming, 5, 114, 134, 190, 214, 230–231, 392, 402
program providers, 309, 310, 392
  education abroad, 105–106, 122, 129, 147, 152, 156–158, 162–163
Project Atlas, academic mobility tracked by, 66, 67
proposals, in citizen diplomacy program administration, 314–315
public diplomacy, 300, 392
public education, international schools and, 259
public funding, higher education insufficient, 11–13
pull factors, 66, 204, 393
Punteney, Katherine, 6, 49
push factors, 66, 204, 393

Qin-Hilliard, Desiree B., 33
QS World University Rankings, 22, 23
quality assurance, international education demand for, 20–21
Quality Improvement Program (QUIP), 134

race and ethnicity
  in education abroad, 101–102
  Open Doors on, 101
racial identity development, 124, 393
reciprocity, 161, 177, 393
recruitment channels, 393
  in Australia, 190
  bridge programs, 200
  from community colleges, 203
  conditional admission, 199–200, 384
  from high schools, 203–204
  joint and double degrees, 202–203
  pathway programs, 200–201
  sponsored student programs, 201–202
recruitment committee IEM model, 191
recruitment fairs, 196–197
recruitment methods
  agent debate, 198–199
  alumni engagement, 198
  international travel, 197–198
  Ozturgut on, 196
  print and digital materials, 198
  recruitment fairs, 196–197
recruitment specialist IEM model, 191
reentry orientation, 128, 393
reflection, 393
  activities for structuring, 175–176
  critical, 176–177
reflective observation, 148, 175, 393
regional conferences, NAFSA, 402
reinforced inequities
  in citizen diplomacy program, 318–319
  in higher education administration, 345
  in IB system, 286

research
  academic, nonuniversity sources for, 14
  on citizen diplomacy programs, 312
  internationalization of, 63–65
  U.S. government funding of, 63
research abroad, 158–159, 393
research partnerships, 63, 64–65
research universities
  global rankings and, 22–23
  knowledge economy and role of, 9–10
residence halls, 127, 204, 228
  ISSS support in, 242–243
resources
  for comparative and international education, 334–335
  for development and education, 357–358
  for global mobility, 339
  for higher education administration, 346–347
  for intercultural training, 350–351
  for language program administration, 362–363
  for peacebuilding, 366–367
  secured, in education abroad program design process, 116
  securing of needed, 116
  for student services, 370
responsible officers (ROs), 209–210, 393
Restoule, Jean-Paul, 333
retention, 211, 393
  NCES on, 345
  success and, in higher education administration, 344–345
revenues, internationalization as generator of, 17
revision, in internationalization planning, 80
Rhoades, Gary, 13–14
risk prevention
  liability and, 131–132
  Malveaux on, 131
  predeparture orientation and, 132
  by professionals, 131–132
Roberts, Jay W., 149, 153, 174
  on facilitation skills, 171–173
  on reflection structuring, 175–176
roles and responsibilities, of professionals, 118–132
Rotary Youth Exchange, 311
Rothman, Jay, 364
Round Square schools, 333
Rumbley, Laura E., 123

Sanford, Nevitt, 148, 174
Schlossberg, Nancy, 123, 125
scholarship programs, 305–306, 394
scholarship sponsors, 306
School of Leadership and Education Sciences (SOLES), 282
school restructuring, 267, 394

Schwarzman Scholars Program, 311
science, technology, engineering, and
    mathematics (STEM) fields, 103, 189
secondary school student, 303, 394
sector size
    of citizen diplomacy, 303–305
    of international experiential education,
        154–155
*SECUSSA Sourcebook: A Guide for Advisers
    of U.S. Students Planning an Overseas
    Experience*, of NAFSA, 151
selection process
    for citizen diplomacy program
        administration, 315
    merit-based, 317
self-authorship, 124, 394
self-awareness, global competence and, 42
self-reflection, in learning activities, 114
self-reporting limits, in assessments, 47
service-based partnerships, 165–167
    challenges of, 166
    effectiveness of, 166–167
    Mlyn and McBride on, 165
service-learning, 51, 110, 151, 159–160, 394
Seven Sacred Teachings, 333
seven-step process, for internationalization
    planning, 72–80
seven vectors, 125, 394
shared governance, 343, 394
short-term scholar, 209, 303, 394
Singapore, Tanglin Trust School in, 255–256
Sister Cities International program, 264, 311
Skelton, Martin, 258
Slaughter, Sheila, 13–14
Smink, Jeffrey D., 275
social and cultural norms, in U.S., 227–228
soft power, 299–300, 394
special focus institutions, 342
specialist, 303, 395
specializations
    in development and education, 355–356
    within professionals, 132
sponsored students, 201–202, 395
sports diplomacy programs, 308, 395
spouse and family programs, 244–245
stages of psychosocial development, 125,
    395
stakeholder
    experiential education programs and, 162
    internationalization planning collaboration
        by, 76–77
    professional relationships with, 120–121
*Standards of Good Practice for Education
    Abroad*, of The Forum on Education
    Abroad, 133
State of the Field Survey 2012, of The
    Forum on Education Abroad, 31
State University of New York (SUNY),
    COIL Center of, 62

stationary program, 110, 395
Stewart, Vivien
    on global education outcomes, 33
    on knowledge economy, 32–33
Strange, C. Carney, 124
strategic partnerships
    branch campuses, 19–20, 67–70, 383
    double and joint degrees, 67
    internationalization and, 68–70
strategic planning process
    of IEM, 192–195
    of internationalization, 2
Strengths, Weaknesses, Opportunities,
    Threats (SWOT) analysis, 74
Stringer, Jeremy, 370
Stroller, Fredericka L., 269
structure, in internationalization planning,
    78
student affairs, 118, 236, 238, 367, 395
Student and Exchange Visitor Information
    System (SEVIS), 209–210, 395
student development theories, 367–368
    critical race theory, 124, 385
    emerging adulthood theory, 124, 386
    feminist theory, 124, 387
    gender identity theory, 124, 388
    intersectionality of identity theory, 42,
        124, 349, 390
    Kolb's Experiential Learning Cycle, 123,
        148–150, 160, 175, 381, 384, 393
    racial identity development theory, 124,
        393
    self-authorship theory, 124, 394
    seven vectors, 125, 394
    stages of psychosocial development, 125,
        395
    student engagement and student success
        theory, 125, 395
    transformational learning theory, 123
    transition theory, 123, 125, 396
student engagement and student success,
    125, 395
student F-1 visa category, 209–210, 234,
    273–274, 302–303
student involvement, 125, 395
student learning
    assessments, 43–44
    outcomes, 44
student retention, 211, 344–345, 393, 395
students. *see also* international students
    college and university, 302, 384
    expectations, in work-based programs,
        163–164
    as higher education revenue source, 12
    intercultural skills for, 41
    learning activities motivations by, 113–114
    LGBTQ, 104
    mobility opportunities for, 272–274

student services, 367–370, 395
    considerations for practitioners on,
        369–370
    key topics and, 368–369
    McClellan and Stringer on, 370
    resources for, 370
    student development theory, 367–368
student services role, of language program
    administrators, 360
student success, 125, 360, 395
study abroad, 396
    ACE on interest in, 272–273
    data on, 273–274
    history of, 100–101
    outcomes, 117–118
    programs, 23
    race and ethnicity percentage in, 102
    of student teachers, 283–284
    U.S., 99–101
Study California initiative, 190–191
study tour, 106, 110, 396
Suarez-Orozco, Marcelo, 33
summative assessment, 44–45, 47, 396
summer work travel program, 303, 396
supportive programming, in ISSS, 239–240
    academic success support, 241–242
    campus and community engagement
        programs, 245
    career support, 242
    friendship and peer mentor programs,
        243–244
    logistical support, 241
    residence life support, 242–243
    spouse and family programs, 244–245
support services, in ISSS, 230–231
sustainable development, 352, 396
Sustainable Development Goals (SDGs), UN,
    10, 33, 344–345, 353–354
Sweden, Global Citizen Program of, 270–271

Tabberer, Ralph, 256
tangible culture, 344, 396
Tanglin Trust School, in Singapore, 255–256
teach abroad, 158, 396
teacher, 303, 396
    globally competent, 278–279
    training and development, 278–284
teacher and staff supervision role, of language
    program administrators, 361
teacher education programs, 279
    classroom materials biases for, 280–281
    COST, 283
    internationalization of, 282–283
    SOLES and, 282
    student teachers study abroad, 283–284
    West on, 281–282
Teaching, Learning, and Scholarship KC, 402
teaching and learning model, advising as,
    237–238, 382

Teaching Assistant Program in France (TAPIF), 158
Teaching English as a foreign language (TEFL) courses, 154
teaching English to speakers of other languages (TESOL), 359
teaching foreign language (TFL), 359
technology
  for classrooms connections, 271–272
  CRM, 186
  international school partnerships and, 271
  knowledge economy support from, 9
TechWomen, 310
TESOL Pre K–12 Standards, 361
Test of English as a Foreign Language (TOEFL), 194, 206, 361
third culture kids, 3, 396
Thompson, Jeff, 258
Times Higher Education (*THE*), 22
Title VI, of National Defense Education Act, of 1958, 30
trainee, 303, 396
training design and facilitation skills, 350
Tran, Ly Thi, 230
transactional conversations, 231, 396
transformational learning theory, of Mezirow, 123
transition theory, 123, 125, 396
transnational education, 18, 397
travel ban decision, of Trump, 369
tribal colleges, 342
Trump, Donald, 369
two-step migration policy, 190

United Kingdom (UK)
  Global Partnership Schools program in, 259
  IB system in, 260–261
  international partnerships in, 270
  international students in, 18
  language education in, 268
United Nations (UN)
  Declaration of Universal Human Rights, 156, 352
  SDGs of, 10, 33, 344–345, 353–354
United Nations Educational, Scientific and Cultural Organization (UNESCO), 353
  on academic mobility, 66
  Education for All framework, 10

  Global Citizenship Education model of, 266
  on scholarship programs, 306
United Nations International Children's Emergency Fund (UNICEF), 353
United States (U.S.). *see also* citizen diplomacy U.S. government programs; *specific departments*
  academic norms in, 225–227
  Carnegie Basic Classifications, of higher education institutions in, 341–342
  citizen diplomacy history in, 300–303
  classroom behaviors and expectations in, 226–227
  Code of Federal Regulations, 239
  global competence in, 30–31
  higher education institution types, 340–342
  higher education system establishment in, 11
  IB system in, 260
  international students in, 18, 23, 186–189
  language education in, 268
  physical and logistical challenges in, 228–229
  research government funding, 63
  social and cultural norms in, 227–228
  study abroad and, 99–101
United States adjustments, in ISSS
  academic norms, 225–227
  physical and logistical challenges, 228–229
  social and cultural norms, 227–228
United States Information Agency, 301
United World Colleges (UWC), 257
universities
  Aktas on global citizenship programs at, 50–51
  doctoral, 341
  enrollment, knowledge economy and, 11
  knowledge economy and research, 9–10
  master's colleges and, 341
  outcome proof at, 20
  program quality evaluation by, 170
  research, 9–10, 22–23
  students at, 302, 384
University of Cambridge ESOL Examinations, 361
University of Michigan, ECCE and ECPE of, 361

University of Southern California CPD, 307
Uraneck, Madeline, 267, 280

values
  citizen diplomacy programs impact on, 313
  deficit, in international schools, 286
Vande Berg, Michael, 117, 118
Vietnam War, 301
Violence Against Women Act, 369
virtual culture, 344, 397
vocational student M-1 visa category, 209–210, 234, 244
volunteer abroad, 154, 159, 397
Voyage to Italy (Lessels), 100–101
Vu, Thao Thi Phuong, 230
Vygotsky, Lev, 174

Wächter, Bernd, 67
Waldorf schools, 333
Walter Payton College Preparatory (WPCP) High School, as international school, 264
Waxman, Ben, 204
WE, 276
website, NAFSA, 403
West, Charlotte, 281–282
Western bias, in global competence education, 49–50
Western emphasis, in international schools, 284–285
Winn, Jayna, 6
work, intern, and volunteer abroad (WIVA), 153, 397
work, intern, volunteer, and research abroad (WIVRA), 153, 397
work abroad, 157–158, 397
work-based partnerships, 162–165
work permits, 157–158
Workshop on Intercultural Skills Enhancement (WISE), 134
World Bank, 263, 353, 366
World Learning, 314
World Trade Organization (WTO), GATS treaty of, 15–16, 17

Yang, Rui, 300, 333
Yemini, Miri, 42, 50, 59
Young, Nancy E., 235, 246